THE LABOUR PARTY'S POLI
A HISTORY

Also by Geoffrey Foote

A CHRONOLOGY OF BRITISH POLITICS, 1945–1987

The Labour Party's Political Thought: A History

Geoffrey Foote

Third Edition

First published 1997 by
MACMILLAN PRESS LTD
Houndmills, Basingstoke, Hampshire RG21 6XS
and London
Companies and representatives
throughout the world

ISBN 0–333–66944–4 hardcover
ISBN 0–333–66945–2 paperback

A catalogue record for this book is available
from the British Library.

This book is printed on paper suitable for recycling and
made from fully managed and sustained forest sources.

10	9	8	7	6	5	4	3	2	1
06	05	04	03	02	01	00	99	98	97

Printed and bound in Great Britain by
Antony Rowe Ltd, Chippenham, Wiltshire

Published in the United States of America by
ST. MARTIN'S PRESS, INC.,
Scholarly and Reference Division
175 Fifth Avenue, New York, N.Y. 10010

ISBN 0–312–16528–5 (cloth)
ISBN 0–312–16529–3 (paperback)

For Laurie and Adam, my parents, and for Rowena

Contents

Preface

An American poet called Delmore Schwartz once said that every point of view, like every experience, is limited and ignorant. He was an unhappy man, by all accounts, but it is a good starting point for any intellectual historian. The fact that there is something human behind the most abstract viewpoint should be the main motive for anyone interested in political ideas. The process by which ideas are developed and related to one another is a relationship between people as well as a reflection of historical circumstance.

It is this process of ideas in the Labour Party that I have hoped to make accessible in one volume for people interested in socialism in Britain today. I have tried to avoid an approach which either over- or under-estimates the importance of ideas in the formation of policy and attitudes. I have also tried to take into account the historical context, though in the final analysis the book is a history of political ideas, their connections and their differentiations. Ideas have their own time-scale, and any history must be sensitive to it. Even so, the author is only too aware of what he has been forced to leave out from the many books read and indexed during the years of preparation for this account, and takes responsibility for any mistakes made.

The fact that this is a third edition testifies to the fact that not too many people were offended by any omissions of thinkers they may consider important, and has given me the opportunity to update the text at various points, especially in the final chapter. My hope remains that this book will prove of use and value to socialists and the labour movement at a time of great uncertainty, as well as to students of British politics. I am aware that the interpretation is contentious at various points – inevitably so, given the nature of the subject matter – but I believe that to be a strength. Without the free debate which thrives on contention and on people saying unpopular and unfashionable things, intellectual life becomes hollow indeed.

I remain grateful to many individuals, both academic and non-academic, for their help and support during and after the writing of this book. I am thankful for the help given in the various libraries used, especially the librarians at the Marx Memorial Library, the British Library, the British Library of Political and Economic Science, the University of Teesside and the Thomas Cooper Library of the University of South Carolina. My colleagues of the History

Section in the School of Human Studies, at the University of Teesside, gave me some financial help to prepare this new edition, and I am grateful to the History Department of the University of South Carolina for their help in the final stage of preparation of this edition and for their hospitality. The typing of the original script by Hilary Tomris, Patsy Gallagher and my sister, Jennifer, has been supplemented by the work of my wife, Rowena, to whom I am indebted. My sons, Laurie and Adam, have made the time more human, and my parents gave me help at a critical point in the first writing of this book.

GEOFFREY FOOTE

Part I

Labourism and the Labour Party

1 Introduction

At a special conference in April 1995, the Labour Party decided to change Clause IV of its constitution, adopted in 1918 and committing the party to the common ownership of the means of production, distribution and exchange, based on the democratic control of industry. In its place, a clause was adopted committing the party to a sense of community and to a dynamic market economy, the sort of economy which since its foundation Labour had regarded with at least a profound mistrust. The adoption of the new clause occurs as relations with the trade union movement, from which it had emerged and from which it has always received the greatest share of its finance, have been weakened to the point where the abolition of the union block vote at conference is discussed. It does appear that the Labour Party is being transformed beyond recognition, in danger of cutting all links with its socialist and labourist past.

In such a situation it becomes particularly important to understand the past, especially in terms of the diversity and limitations of its political thought. Once accepted views that Labour is a non-ideological party, intent merely on gaining parliamentary power irrespective of principle, must be at least modified once the history of the party is taken into account. Indeed, the fundamental changes taking place in today's Labour Party, disturbing or exciting as they must appear to party members, are illuminated and given much more depth when placed in their historical and ideological context.

However, histories of the Labour Party have tended to ignore the political thought underlying its development. A mass of information is available on the political history of the Labour Party in the past ninety years; its achievements and failures in office and opposition; its policies and organisation; and biographies of its leaders and important figures. Anthologies of documents, speeches, manifesto commitments and policy statements have been assiduously collected, but a *history* of the Labour Party's political thought – its conceptual connections and development – has been missing for too many years.[1] Its absence is both surprising and deplorable, given the importance of Labour as a programmatic party and the contribution of thinkers like Tawney, Cole and Crosland to British political thought in this century.

IDEAS AND POLITICAL POWER

The problems and difficulties of tracing such a history can be easily under-estimated. The development of Labour's thought is not a simple sequence of one set of ideas replacing another, but any tracing of the conceptual connections which make up the web of Labour's thought needs to relate ideas to power, and then to create a model in which ideas are understood as abstractions within history.[2] The relationship between power and political thought is a complex one, and cannot be reduced to the simplicities of one determining the other. On the one hand, Labour is a party seeking political power, rather than a party attempting to put a pre-conceived philosophy into practice. On the other hand, it does not merely seek power for its own sake, but has ideas which inspire its policies to a certain extent. The general theories held about society and the state lead to definite prescriptions and attitudes for the Labour Party as much as for parties which are more inflexible and dogmatic in their ideas. John Maynard Keynes was well aware of this when he wrote that

> the ideas of economists and political philosophers, both when they are right and when they are wrong, are more powerful than is commonly understood. Indeed, the world is ruled by little else. Practical men, who believe themselves to be quite exempt from any intellectual influences, are usually the slave of some defunct economist.[3]

As an example, Labour's view of the State as an essentially neutral administration to be contested at election times has led to its attempt to maximise votes by appealing to the middle classes as well as the working class, and to an acceptance of the demands of loyalty and national unity at times of emergency.

The political thought of any party seeking power in a parliamentary democracy cannot be looked at in a vacuum. It is subject to social, economic and political circumstances outside any rational control. As a result, any history of Labour's political thought must show to the best of its ability how it has been shaped and formed by the history of the British working class and the Labour Party's own political experience. An individual philosopher's thought may evolve by obeying certain rules and canons of logic and internal consistency, but we are not dealing with an individual thinker, or a philosophical school here. Labour is a living political organism, always seeking new ways to adapt and develop older ideas, if only to gain and maintain political power.

As a result, the major difficulty in the way of tracing a history of Labour's political thought is the absence of any agreed ideological boundaries within which we can point to a specifically Labour ideology. This is in marked contrast to Marxism which, for all its diversities, can be referred back to one thinker's fairly rigorous social and economic analysis. The Labour Party is a particularly *British* institution, stressing specific policies to meet specific problems and only occasionally feeling the need to take its theorists seriously. Labour's leaders have never attempted to square their experience and practice in government with any worked-out theory, in sharp contrast to the constant attempts by the old Russian Communist leaders to justify their political practice with Marxist and Leninist theory.

It becomes a difficult and controversial task to trace a pattern of development in Labour's political thought in the light of this. The Labour Party is, as it constantly asserts, a 'broad church'. It has contained many minority strands in its history – Christian pacifists like Alfred Salter and George Lansbury, neo-Stalinists like D.N. Pritt and Konni Zilliacus, and various Trotskyist groups like the Militant Tendency. However, none of them is remotely near the mainstream of Labour thinking and it has been necessary for that reason to ignore them. Lansbury was actually leader of the party in the early 1930s, but this had nothing to do with his pacifist beliefs. An attempt to document every minority in the Labour Party would confuse rather than clarify the essential elements which set Labour apart from its rivals on both Right and Left in terms of ideology.

The existence of such minority groupings, and the apparently indistinct boundaries of Labour's political thought, have misled too many commentators in the past. As an example, H. M. Drucker regards the Socialist doctrine of the Labour Party as insignificant compared with the ethos of loyalty to leaders and rigid adherence to the rulebook held by its dominant social group.[4] Labour's ideology is narrowed down to the doctrine of the mandate, as expressed in the election manifesto. In this interpretation, the specific commitments of the manifesto replace any general and divisive ideology.

The party manifesto is certainly used to rally all the main factions of the party, and is usually put in a sufficiently vague form of wording to satisfy Left and Right. However, it is a misunderstanding to say that the manifesto *replaces* ideology. The policy proposals, and the assumptions that underlie them, reflect the political thought of the dominant faction in the Labour Party at any one time – whether Morrisonian nationalisation in the 1940s, Gaitskellite revisionism in the 1950s, Wilsonian technocracy in the 1960s, the Bennite Left in the 1970s, or 'New Labour' today. It is vaguely written so that all sections of the party can rally round the dominant group at election times, but its vagueness does *not* indicate an absence of ideology.

It is therefore necessary to single out the fundamental similarity of ideas which has united the disparate groups of radicals, trades unionists, Christian Socialists and Marxists in one political party since 1900. The diverse factions which have constituted the Labour Party since its birth have somehow been able to find a common factor to keep them together for all the fury and frustration of their debates, and this unifying force cannot be simply reduced to one of mere tactical alliances. Their debates have been carried on within specific ideological limits, so that they could all be described as related to 'labourism', distinct from the Liberal Party on their Right and from various types of revolutionary on their Left. Once this 'labourism' can be singled out and described, then it will be possible to document the changes which have developed and modified the fundamental tenets of the Labour Party's political thought.

LABOUR AND THE UNIONS

To disentangle the fundamental ideas of 'labourism' from the medley of political ideas proposed and fought over within the confines of the Labour Party, it is necessary to withdraw from the realm of ideas to look at the party's basic power structure. The relationship of the Labour Party to its trade union base provides the key to understanding the limits within which political debate has been held, and within which political theory has evolved. If it can be discovered that this relationship has been expressed ideologically – that is, as an elaborated and coherent set of ideas – then the 'labourist' boundaries of political thought within the Labour Party can be delineated.

The paradoxical relationship that Labour has with the trade unions has been most recently pointed out by Leo Panitch[5] (although Communist leaders like Lenin and Trotsky noted it years earlier). The Labour Party was basically established by the trade unions as their political extension. As such, it was an expression of trade union politics – that is, the protection of workers' living standards by political action. Labour remains, even under Tony Blair, financially and politically dependent on the unions, and yet is often forced to attack them when in office. This paradox emerged in its clearest form during the Wilson government of 1964–70, when a series of attempts to curb workers' living standards culminated in the White Paper *In Place of Strife*, which sought to establish legal restrictions on union activities. The government was forced to back down in the face of open union and backbench revolt. On the one hand, its position as a 'national' party in office led the Labour government to attack the unions; on the other hand, its dependence on the unions meant that it was unable to push the White Paper onto the statute book.

Labour's reliance on the unions has *ultimately* proved more important than its commitment to 'national' policies time and again. The Labour Party was founded in 1900 to pursue the interests of the unions in the parliamentary sphere, and it cannot escape this obligation without threatening its power base. Whenever the party has tried to pursue 'national' interests at the expense of the organised labour movement, as in the 1920s and 1960s, it has been rudely brought back into line – the General Council of the Trades Union Congress (TUC) was the real leadership of the party in the 1930s, and Wilson had enough political acumen to realize that a 'social contract' with the unions was necessary in the 1970s, whether he liked it or not. Tony Blair's ability to escape this paradox in the 1990s is ultimately dependent on his ability to free the party from its 'labourist' base in the unions.

This social and political relationship between the Labour Party and the trades unions is therefore crucial. It is what makes the Labour Party a *labour* party. It is also what makes it so difficult to pinpoint 'labourism' – trade union politics – as an elaborated ideology. Trade union aspirations within a capitalist society have been generally restricted to protecting and enhancing their members' living standards. Higher wages, shorter hours and better working conditions do not lend themselves to a general philosophy of society. The clearest hint of such a 'labourist' ideology can be found in the aims adopted at the 1900 foundation conference of the Labour Representation Committee (LRC), as the Labour Party was originally called. The purpose of the new party was to work for

a distinct Labour group in Parliament, who shall have their own whips, and agree upon their policy, which must embrace a readiness to cooperate with any party which for the time being may be engaged in promoting legislation in the direct interest of labour, and be equally ready to associate themselves with any party in opposing measures having an opposite tendency.[6]

It can hardly be summed up as an ideology, but it reveals a set of assumptions which were to prove the bedrock onto which other political theories were to be grafted. To understand the fundamental ideological boundaries of the Labour Party's thought, it is necessary to look behind the socialist face worn by the party for much of its history to see this labourism, free of the clutter of any political doctrine other than pure and simple trade union politics.

The labourist assumptions on which the Labour Party had been founded had, in fact, been expressed very clearly in ideological terms long before 1900. Indeed, to understand labourism as an ideology rather than a cultural process, it is necessary to look back much earlier than the conservative, mid-Victorian trades unions normally described as labourist to the very origins of the organised labour movement in the early nineteenth century. It was in 1825, the year after the Combination Laws repressing unions had been repealed, that labourism was presented as a theory disentangled from extraneous doctrines like Paineite radicalism, utilitarianism, or Owenite socialism.

LABOURISM

Thomas Hodgskin (1787–1869) was the first to present trade union politics as a consistent theory in his *Labour Defended Against the Claims of Capital* (1825). Now largely forgotten,[7] Hodgskin was a former naval officer, dismissed for insubordination, whose interest in working-class education led him to become a dominant figure in the free labour movement at its birth. His pamphlet, seen as the manifesto of the emerging trade union movement, channelled the arguments of the most advanced school of political economy into the defence of that movement. In doing so, Hodgskin presented labourism as a political theory with a clarity and lucidity which marked him out from other labour theorists. As an elaborated ideology, it was to be buried by the defeat of Chartism and the onset of a general period of prosperity in the middle of the century, but as a set of assumptions governing the political operation of trades unionists it was to survive into the very different conditions of 1900 and beyond.

The first characteristic of the labourism elaborated by Hodgskin was to be a particular interpretation of the labour theory of value, then the dominant school of economic thought. This theory, holding that the value of all commodities was determined by the amount of labour expended on them, had been used by David Ricardo to attack the landowners as a parasitic class, battening onto the industrious classes. Hodgskin gave it a further twist by turning it against the capitalists. If labour created all wealth, he argued that labour received back only a part of its wealth. The surplus produce was being pocketed by the capitalists who were cheating the labourers of their rightful share, and a combination of workers in trade unions was necessary in order to fight for their rightful wages.

As an economic theory, it could not serve as a model of economic expansion, or of understanding how to cope with unemployment or under-investment. Marx sharpened the theory to give it a revolutionary dimension, but this was of little use to trades unionists seeking to ameliorate their members' living conditions. Nevertheless, as the basic economic philosophy expounded by Hodgskin, the theory has become a fundamental assumption in trade union attitudes, and indirectly in the policies of the Labour Left. The belief that somehow labour is prevented from getting its fair share of the national income provides a strong rationale for union organisers whose job it has been to bargain over the purchase and sale of their members' labour power. Other economic theories – the marginal utility arguments of the Fabians, the demand expansionism of the neo-Keynesians – were to serve as the Labour Party's practical approach to overcoming the harsh cycle of boom and slump characterising capitalism, but the fundamental assumption that labour was denied its just share of the nation's wealth is ultimately derived from the arguments put forward by Hodgskin at the birth of the modern labour movement.

This leads to a second characteristic of labourism, which was the call to redistribute the wealth of the nation to those who create it. Hodgskin believed wealth to be badly distributed in favour of the capitalist. The employers had too much, while labour had too little, and the purpose of union activity was to cure this maldistribution by fighting for higher wages. Hodgskin argued that

> because those who have been masters, planners, contrivers, etc.... have in general also been capitalists and have also had a command over the labour of those who have worked with their

hands, their labour has been paid as much too high as common labour has been underpaid.[8]

In reducing the profits of the idle capitalists by increasing the wages of their members, unions have a major role to play in curing the maldistribution of wealth. This belief in redistribution was to prove a crucial point in labourism, where the trade union movement could shape the particular form British Socialism was to take. The major difference was that, in the very different conditions of the twentieth century, the Labour Party was to see Parliament as a more important instrument of redistribution than the unions, whereas Hodgskin ignored Parliament altogether.

A third characteristic of labourism revealed in Hodgskin's thought was its attitude to the capitalists. While Hodgskin was in favour of redistribution of wealth, he did not question the social system by which wealth was produced. He was vigorously opposed to capitalists, but never to capital as a social and economic system. This point was noted by Marx, who held it to be a common characteristic of English Socialists.[9] Hodgskin constantly made a distinction between capitalists, who were bad, and employers, who were good. This was due to his identification of capitalism with usury and interest. As a result, he could argue that

> the wages of the master, employer or contriver have been blended with the profit of the capitalist.... Masters are labourers as much as their journeymen. In this character, their interests are precisely the same as their men.[10]

As capitalists they idly reap profits at the expense of their workers, but as employers their labour deserves a reward as much as their employees. This mixture of hostility to capitalists and indifference to capital was to recur constantly in the Labour Party, where socialist language often sounded more militant than it actually was.

Hodgskin's ideas on this point were to be far reaching because they expressed the paradox of the trade union movement. Unless they were prepared to launch a profound social upheaval, the unions had to work both with and against the employers. Hodgskin's combination of hostility to capitalists and acceptance of a social system of bargaining between unions and employers expressed in theoretical terms the practical work of the trade union movement as it was to develop in Britain. His distinction between capitalists and employers was a fundamental characteristic of trade union politics, whose essential business was to be that of bargaining and negotiation over the system whereby labour power was bought and sold, not the abolition of that system.

The fourth characteristic of labourism flows from Hodgskin's hostility to capitalists. His version of the labour theory of value, geared as it was to the defence of the trades unions in their struggle against the capitalists, stressed the independence and self-reliance of workers as a class. Hodgskin's opposition to state intervention in trade union affairs has often been mistaken for a form of anarchism, but he never called for the abolition of the state. He argued only that its corrupt nature, whereby the capitalists used it against the unions, should be purged. If the state continued to support the capitalists, then the workers might turn their attention from 'combining for higher wages to amending the state'.[11] In the context of the times, with most workers denied the vote, Hodgskin's hint of independent political action had the air of a revolutionary threat. However, with the later expansion of the suffrage to the working class, his rejection of the existing parties and his stress on the self-reliance of labour was to be echoed by trades unionists who sought to defend their interests in Parliament. Hodgskin's own political views were not totally synonymous with labourism later in the century – his belief that parliamentary action could not remedy social problems was alien to the labourist tradition – but his belief in labour's self-reliance was eventually to become an important characteristic of labourism as it turned to the parliamentary sphere.

The fifth and final characteristic of labourism was implicit in Hodgskin's theory. His call for a redistribution of wealth was always seen in a national context. In *Labour Defended*, Hodgskin protested that the Irish 'are imported here in crowds and beat down the wages of our labour',[12] giving a nationalist expression to the trade union demand for the protection of living standards from the threat of cheap labour. As the system whereby labour power was bought and sold, whether dearly or cheaply, was not called into question, it was inevitable that labourism should demand that the workers of its own nation should be defended against the workers of other nations. Such a demand does not necessarily lead to racism or chauvinism, which have often been attacked by labour and union leaders. However, the liberal internationalism which was to be so strong in the Labour Party was always based on adherence and loyal obedience to the nation state. Any threat to that loyalty, as posed in their very different ways by revolutionary Leninism and by the European integrationism, could find no real home in a labourist party.

These characteristics of labourism – the theory that labour receives little of the wealth that it creates, redistributionism, hostility to capitalists and maintenance of capital, workers' self-reliance, and loyalty to the nation state – survived to become a set of political assumptions in the labour movement. Hodgskin was long forgotten, but his political theory of trade unionism is of relevance because it was an expression of collective bargaining in a society where trade unions were independent organisations, not creatures of the State. These assumptions were flexible enough to accommodate a large number of political ideas, while distinct enough eventually to exclude the Liberal Party on the Right and various types of revolutionary on the Left.

THE LIMITS OF LABOURISM

The trade union politics expressed so clearly by Hodgskin and surviving as the political assumptions of trade union practice constitute the fundamental labourist tenets of the Labour Party. They are flexible and loose enough to be capable of absorbing and modifying ideologies as diverse as militant syndicalism and Christian communitarianism. Within its limits, different policies are fought for by different groups, and different political discourses compete and evolve.

Whichever particular ideology is dominant at whichever particular time is a result of a complex of factors ranging from the broad social and economic factors to the sordid mechanics of power politics (it was said at one union conference that the brothers were so confused that they were stabbing one another in the front – until recently, Labour politicians have rarely needed the excuse of confusion for such activity). If a group holding any of Labour's diverse ideologies fails to adapt it to the dominant trade union section of the party, it either cuts itself off from the mainstream of Labour thinking (like the Independent Labour Party (ILP) on the Left in 1932 or, perhaps temporarily, the Social Democratic Party (SDP) on the Right in 1981), or it is soon brought back into line (like the Wilson technocrats). If the ideological faction was to have any success, it must adapt itself in some way to the labourism of the trade unions. The limits of Blair's reforms of today are thus set unless the labourist base can somehow be broken.

It follows that this 'labourist' ideology has limits, and excludes ideologies incompatible with it. As it involves a bargain over the sale of workers' labour-power, aiming to achieve a better position of wage-earners against their employers, labourism tends to be more compatible with gradual and piecemeal solutions to problems than it is with radical and fundamental solutions. The Socialist ideology which Labour had accepted in 1918 has generally been interpreted in a gradualist manner.

However, labourism does exclude political solutions which involve the overthrow of the state. Marxism was only acceptable to labourist leaders if it was shorn of any commitment to a workers' dictatorship – if its radical economic analysis was abstracted from its revolutionary political conclusions. Marxists who have refused to do this have been expelled, as happened to the Communists in the 1920s, or to the Trotskyists in the 1960s or since the 1980s.

Moreover, while liberal internationalism is strong in the Labour Party, the anti-British nationalism of many Marxists is unacceptable. The political structure accepted by labourism in which to conduct its social and economic struggle is the structure of the nation state. At times of national emergency when the country is under external threat, Labour rallies to the national flag. Pacifist dissent has been tolerated, but Lenin's policy of revolutionary defeatism has proved unacceptable. In the late 1940s, the neutralist Keep Left group was (grudgingly) permitted to fight for its ideas, but perceived 'fellow-travellers' such as Dennis Pritt and Konni Zilliacus were expelled. Public association of the British Communist Party with the Soviet Union doomed its persistent attempts to affiliate to the Labour Party, despite its renunciation of proletarian dictatorship in 1951.

If labourism is distinct from revolutionary and anti-nationalist ideologies on its Left, it is also distinct from the Liberal Party on its Right. This is due to its stress on self-reliance and independence against the employers. In the late nineteenth and early twentieth centuries, many unions did support the Liberals, sending a small collection of 'Lib–Lab' members to Westminster. The militant social liberalism of the Lloyd George variety could have adapted itself to the labourism of the trade unions, and for a while looked as though it would do so, but historical circumstance prevented the Liberals from ever agreeing to become a labourist party, and the growth of the corporate society of organized employers and unions favoured the formation of a new labour party. Many Liberals (such as J.A. Hobson) found a home in the Labour Party as the main radical alternative in British politics, but had to pay the price of conforming in some way to labourism if they were to have any effect. The attempt by New Labour to break from the labourist base of the unions is a symptom of the profound crisis shaking the labour movement, and its outcome will determine how far Labour remains a labourist party.

The ideological limits of labourism, flexible as they are, have thus marked the Labour Party off from its rivals on Right and Left. Within these limits, the party is ideologically amorphous – a 'broad church' incorporating diverse ideas.

THE DEVELOPMENT OF LABOUR'S THOUGHT

Labourism, or trade union politics 'pure and simple', was more an assumption than an elaborated ideology when the Labour Party was formed in 1900. To pass beyond its vague assumptions to a clearly expressed theory it has proved necessary to turn to the birth of the modern trade union movement in the early nineteenth century. It was at this time, with no established tradition of successful negotiation behind them, that working class theorists found it necessary to express clearly and unambiguously the political theory of trades unionism. The ideas of Thomas Hodgskin have been chosen as the sharpest and most popular expression of this theory. His analysis, buried with the defeat of Chartism, expressed both the flexibility and the limits of the ideology which was to lie at the heart of the Labour Party.

This labourism has assumed a dynamic due to its ability to absorb or reject a series of challenges to its assumptions. The strengths and weaknesses of these challenges have determined the development of Labour's political thought. The emergence of an ethical, peculiarly British, Socialism in the late nineteenth and early twentieth centuries owes much to the weakness of the Marxist challenge to labourism. Marx's critique of capitalism was considerably diluted in its British form. The resulting theoretical weaknesses of British Marxism allowed its challenge to be contained by the Fabians and blunted by the Ethical Socialists of the ILP. Certain notions of the Marxists and the Fabians had to be excluded, but in their different ways they gave a sharp focus to the blend of British Socialism which eventually triumphed over 'pure and simple' trade union politics to be enshrined in Labour's 1918 Constitution.

In a similar way, the evolution of this British Socialism into its corporate form was partly due to the weakness of the syndicalist challenge to labourism. The syndicalist theories were easily accommodated into the Labour Party's mainstream, unlike the challenge of revolutionary Leninism after 1917. Shorn of its anarchist and revolutionary conclusions, Syndicalism served as the foundation of the Guild Socialism expounded by G.D.H. Cole, one of Labour's greatest political theorists. In this form it was adopted by the ILP and by left-wing trade union leaders. It also became the foundation on which Corporate Socialism, with its stress on nationalisation and union participation in the welfare state, was able to evolve. The other foundation was supplied by the challenge of the Liberal economist, J.M. Keynes, with his prescriptions of state intervention in a mixed economy. The blend of Corporate Socialism that emerged was accepted by both the Left and Right of the Labour Party in its heyday of the 1940s, when it refashioned British society under Attlee, Morrison and Bevan.

Having fulfilled its main role, Corporate Socialism came increasingly to seem inadequate as an ideology for Labour. It has come under two successive challenges, from the revisionists on the Right and from the Bennites on the Left. Each challenge was conditioned by the evolution of the British economy and society after the traumas of the war and immediate post-war period. The prosperity of the 1950s and 1960s seemed to the revisionists to call for a fundamental redefinition of British Socialism. Some even called for a break with labourism altogether, although this was generally dismissed as political suicide. The revisionist challenge culminated in the technocratic, meritocratic ideology of the Wilson era, but revisionism broke on the resistance of the unions at a time of increasing economic recession. As an ideology more suited to prosperity and full employment, revisionism seemed out of date and irrelevant to Labour in the new conditions of stagflation in the 1970s. The result of this crisis of the Right was the evolution of a new ideology of social democracy, and the secession of several leading Labour politicians to form the SDP in 1981.

The disappointments of the Wilson era led to a new awakening of ideas on the Left. The seeds of this lie in the 1950s with the emergence of the New Left, disillusioned with Stalinism and dissatisfied with the ideological sterility of the Bevanite Left in the Labour Party. Burgeoning in the Campaign for Nuclear Disarmament (CND), Vietnam Solidarity and the Women's Movement, the New Left became very hostile to the Labour Party, which it saw as hopelessly lost to the British Establishment. Nevertheless, despite this hostility, the Bennite Left had strong ideological roots in the protest movement, and by the early 1980s the Labour Left had channelled much of it into the confines of labourism. Their political unpopularity within the country, manifested in the 1980s, may have led to the marginalisation of the Bennites, but the revolt against corporatism has become an accepted part of Labour thinking, as seen by the new stress on communitarian and republican thinking. At the same time, the labourist core of the party has been thrown into doubt by the decline of the traditional working class and a significant weakening of the confidence and bargaining strength of the trade union movement.

A clearer understanding of the *history* of the Labour Party's political thought as a process of development has now emerged. Labourism – its flexibility and limits – is the key to the variety of political ideas adopted by Labour in the last ninety years. The ability of new ideologies to fit into the labourist framework determines their chance of political success in the party.

The over-simplicity of reducing every new development to labourism must be avoided, of course. However, contemporary arguments which read off the present crisis of Labour into its past[13] appear to fall into the opposite simplicity. In denying 'labourism' as a useful model for understanding the Labour Party, they deny structure and pattern altogether in favour of circumstance and conjuncture. Such an approach certainly has the advantage of recognising the flux of history, but in its view of the Party as an empty shell which can be filled by currently contending political forces and aspirations, it overestimates the flexibility of the Party as an organisation. It ignores the *limits* of the Party's ideology – of the factors which separate the Party from both Right and Left – and consequently ignores the *unity* of the Party. Above all, it underestimates the extent to which the Labour Party is dependent on the trade union movement for its finances and its motivation. Many members would prefer to weaken, or even abolish, the links between Labour and the unions, but the controversies over full employment, the minimum wage, and the Social Chapter of the Maastricht treaty demonstrate even today the fundamental continuity in the Party despite the evident diversity of ideas and the often unexpected unfolding of events over the past century.

Part II

The Formation of British Socialism

Introduction to Part II

The Labour Party was created in 1900 as a federation of a number of trades unions with various socialist groups – the Marxists of the Social Democratic Federation (SDF), the gradualists of the Fabian Society, and the Ethical Socialists of the Independent Labour Party (ILP). Unlike many of the working-class parties then emerging in Europe, the new party had no precise and worked-out ideology to guide its actions. However, an ideology of sorts was emerging as a result of the ferment of socialist ideas which had been taking place since 1880. The ideology, acknowledged finally in the party's 1918 constitution, was a distinctive brand of British socialism which has fed the party's basic ideals and ethics to the present day.

In his foreword to a 1948 book entitled *Socialism: The British Way*, Herbert Morrison wrote, 'I like the title of this book. The British Socialists, and our Labour Government, have a distinctive approach to the problems of democracy, of economics, of Socialism.'[1] British Socialism had an ethic and a political outlook of its own, stamped with peculiarly British characteristics and separate from the socialist parties elsewhere in Europe. In other countries, a dogmatic form of Marxism prevailed, as in Germany; or socialist parties were divorced from the trade union movement, marked by fractious dissent and revolutionary tendencies, as in France, Italy or Russia. The debates which consumed European Socialism appeared in Britain too, but on the margins of working-class politics. The main form of socialism in Britain was intimately woven into the labourism of the trade union movement, and connected in countless ways to the social, political and intellectual environment in which that movement grew.

To understand the nature of the new ideology of British Socialism, it is necessary to separate its different strands. The ideas of Labour Marxism, Fabianism and Ethical Socialism held by the constituent organisations and individuals supporting the Labour Party had been formed in the last two decades of the nineteenth century and were still evolving in the early years of the new party. Keir Hardie, the first Labour leader, was to bring the strands together and to seal the conjunction with a labourism which would attract the unions. The new ideology, developed in different directions by prominent Labour politicians such as Ramsay MacDonald and H.N. Brailsford, was to be severely tested by war and slump after 1914, but in its heyday it served to keep divergent political groups in a party still unsure as to whether it had a future.

2 Marxists, Fabians and Ethical Socialists: The Traditions of British Socialism

It was in the turmoil of the 1880s that the different and conflicting approaches which were to make up the ideas of British Socialism were formed and fought over. At a time of a major crisis of profitability in world capitalism, with riots by the unemployed and strikes by unskilled workers, the educated and critical sections of the middle and working classes began to seriously challenge the traditional assumptions of *laissez-faire* liberalism. In their different ways, they began to call for the regulation of an economy which was no longer satisfying the aspirations and needs of the population.

THE LABOUR MARXISTS

The Marxism of the Social Democratic Federation (SDF) appealed to many young workers who sought an explanation of the poverty and unemployment around them. Major party and union leaders of the future – Tom Mann, George Lansbury, Ramsay MacDonald and Herbert Morrison among them – served their political apprenticeships in its ranks,[1] and its interpretation of Karl Marx was to play a major role in the Labour Party's politics.

The political and economic ideas elaborated by Marx were, however, fundamentally opposed to the labourism of the British trade union movement. In his central work, *Capital*, written while in exile in Britain, Marx had sharpened the labour theory of value into a revolutionary understanding of the dynamics of capitalist society. He attempted to demonstrate that capitalism was trapped in a fatal mechanism in which it would eventually fall into increasingly severe crises, transforming the many capitalist firms into a few monopolies and trusts. This crisis was not the result of the greed of the usurers, as Hodgskin believed, but was inherent in the system whereby labour power was bought and sold.

The very fact that the working class, which created all value, was divorced from the means of production and had a surplus value extorted from it, led not merely to class conflict but to the drive to accumulate capital. If any capitalist failed to accumulate, another would take his place:

> Accumulate, accumulate! That is Moses and the prophets!... Accumulation for accumulation's sake, production for production's sake; by this formula classical economy expressed the historical mission of the bourgeoisie, and did not for a single instant deceive itself over the birth-throes of wealth.[2]

As capital accumulated, the amount of surplus value would become smaller and smaller against the total capital needed for production, and crisis would set in as the rate of profit fell.[3] There were many factors which could delay this event – such as increasing the exploitation of the working class, colonial acquisition or export of capital – but *eventually* the rate of profit would fall, and crisis ensue. The class war inherent in capitalism would then turn into the overthrow of the system by the working class.

Marx and Labourism

Marx's revolutionary analysis of capitalism was incompatible with the labourism of the British trade union movement in number of ways. He never regarded unions as ends in themselves, as Hodgskin did. To Marx, they were centres of resistance to capitalist rule which could only be partially effective. Where the unions negotiated over the sale of their members' labour-power, Marx called for the abolition of wage labour altogether. The destruction of the employing class, not simply better wages and working conditions, was the conclusion of Marx's theory of value, and it flew in the face of the labourism of the union leaders of that time.

It also flew in the face of the ideas of redistribution of wealth so popular among English socialists, then and since. Marx derided those French and English radicals like Proudhon and Hodgskin who did not connect the glaring inequalities of wealth and poverty to the system of wage labour which underlay them. The consequences of such a partial understanding would be to turn socialism into a question of ameliorating the effects of capitalism rather than digging out the root cause of inequality. They were attacking the symptoms rather than the disease.

This was directly connected to Marx's attack on the labourist belief that it was capitalists, not capital as a social system, who were the enemy. Marx criticised Hodgskin for such a view,[4] and asserted that the behaviour of the capitalists was determined by the harsh rhythms of capital accumulation. Where Hodgskin (and labourists since) saw the employer as just another worker who happened to control the purse-strings of wage labour, Marx saw the employer as a representative of a class which had to be destroyed. Where Hodgskin's labourism saw greed, Marx saw wage labour as the disease to be cured.

However, the greatest challenge to labourism lay in Marx's attack on loyalty to the nation state. His call for a proletarian dictatorship seemed a foreign expression of tyranny to the majority of British workers, especially after they gained the vote. Labourism could easily have accepted that the state was controlled by the employers and needed to be captured by a workers' party during elections, but this was not Marx's prescription. In *The Civil War in France* (1871) Marx specifically asserted that the state was to be smashed and replaced by a totally different state machine to protect the workers' interests. This view of the state as an instrument of class violence, to be destroyed by violence, was inimical to the labourist tradition. Labour disputes could be occasionally violent, but to admit that violence was inherent in all sections of society, underlying power relationships from the factory to the state, would lead to intolerable conclusions for the majority of trade union leaders. When Marx called on English workers to side with the Irish Fenians against their own state,[5] a call for virtual treason against that state, he placed himself outside the pale of the labourist tradition.

On one point Marx did agree with labourism, and that was the issue of class independence and self-reliance. Marx constantly argued that the liberation of the working class was the task of the working class itself, acting in its own interests and thereby in the interests of humanity as a whole. As a result, he argued that 'the working class cannot act as a class, except by constituting itself into a political party, distinct from, and opposed to, all old parties formed by the propertied classes'.[6] His belief in an independent working class party, acting in its own interests against the interests of the employers, generally fell on deaf ears until the formation of the SDF in 1881.

Labour Marxism

However, the Marxism of the SDF was dominated by the autocratic rule of H. M. Hyndman, an amateur cricketer who became a Marxist after reading *Capital* in French during an American cruise. Hyndman's Marxist terminology concealed a crude national chauvinism and a belief that socialism could be achieved by the existing state. Marx found him personally and politically abhorrent, while Engels eventually derided the SDF as 'purely a sect. It has ossified Marxism into a dogma and, by rejecting *every* labour movement which is not orthodox Marxism... it renders itself incapable of ever becoming anything else but a sect.'[7]

Hyndman's sectarian rejection of trade unions[8] as simply reactionary doomed him from playing any major part in the labour movement, and the SDF was to withdraw from the Labour Party, only a year after its creation, in pique at their failure to force an acceptance of class war on the new party. However, his state socialism was to play a major part among those Labour Marxists who rejected the SDF and sought to win the Labour Party to a policy of class warfare and to a view of socialism as synonymous with simple nationalisation of industry.

Many of the individuals who were forced out of the SDF because of their opposition to Hyndman – people like William Morris, Eleanor Marx, John Burns and Tom Mann, a list of individuals whose loss was enough to guarantee failure for the parent group – took an active part in the militant labour movement then emerging in Britain. They sought to build a more genuine Marxist party with roots in the British working class, and many were to see the Labour Party as the organisation which had to be won over to Marxism. Their political ideas were generally ill-formulated, but they looked for guidance to Marx's collaborator and friend, Friedrich Engels.

Engels (1821–95) inherited Marx's belief in an independent working class party in Britain, opposed to both Conservatives and Liberals. In contrast to the SDF, he believed that such a party must be based on the unions if it were to have any chance of success, and argued that the erosion of the privileges of the old 'aristocracy of labour' which had dominated the unions was creating the possibility of a party of the entire working class. Even before the growth of New Unionism among the unskilled, Engels considered it 'an immediate question of forming an English Labour Party with an independent class programme'.[9]

In doing so, Engels modified, if he did not push aside, Marx's revolutionary view of the state. In an Introduction to Marx's *Class Struggles in France*, Engels called for socialist parties to place their emphasis on the gradual and patient work of winning the working class to the socialist standard by means of electoral struggle. He continued to maintain the right of revolution if Parliament tried to prevent socialists from attaining their goal by constitutional means, but he argued that the rise of universal suffrage, together with the developments in military technology which made the barricade and the insurrection outmoded forms of struggle, called for a major change in political tactics.

Marx had not been dogmatic in his political views and had admitted that in the special conditions of Britain a peaceful transition to socialism was possible. He saw as a possibility that a working class majority in Parliament could transform traditional political institutions into expressions of working class rule, but he was much more cautious than Engels in his attitude to the bourgeois state. His hope that violence could be avoided in a country like Britain was always tentative and he never modified his views on the need for a different *type* of state institution from bourgeois parliaments. However, Engels was able to throw his considerable authority behind a constitutionalist socialist movement and, in doing so, helped the Labour Marxists to dilute considerably Marx's revolutionary view of the state. The far Left of labourism was to accept Marx's theory of class war and to warn of possible contempt for the institution by the ruling class, but the need raised by Marx for a new type of state was forgotten. This had the indirect effect of removing a major barrier preventing Marxism from becoming assimilated to labourism.

The role of the Labour Marxists in the beginnings of the Labour Party was to serve as a channel for ideas formulated by Marx and Engels rather than as a directly innovatory force. With the exception of William Morris, their theoretical contribution was a poor affair, partly because of their reaction to the abstract propaganda of the SDF. Moreover, Morris himself cannot be said to have made any real contribution to *Labour* Marxism – his contempt for Parliament and his denunciations of the capitalist state machine remove him from consideration as a Labour theorist – and his main influence was to be felt through the Ethical Socialists.

Tom Mann (1856–1941) was the most famous of the SDF dissidents. He was born the son of a colliery clerk and was working in the mines at the age of ten. He eventually became an apprentice in the engineering trade. As a member of the Amalgamated Society of Engineers (ASE) he remained committed to the union movement throughout his life, a commitment which eventually led him out of the SDF and into the leadership of the 1889 Dockers' Strike. He became a symbol of the New Unionism, disregarding old craft distinctions in its emphasis on class unity.

Mann based himself on the trade unions, attacking the old union leaders for their class collaboration, and calling on the union rank and file to stress their own interests against those of the employers. Once their independence was recognised by workers through their trade union struggles, then political organisation would follow. It was a view which was to lead him into the ILP, where he stressed the need for both political and industrial mobilisation:

> as a collectivist and a member of the ILP, I know for a certainty that the greatest hindrance to the democratic movement of the present time is the lack of effective industrial organization, backed up by equally effective political organization, for purposes of industrial change.[10]

His recognition of the importance of the industrial organisation of his class was eventually to blossom into syndicalism.

The Labour Marxists were instrumental in making Marxism a force in the British labour movement and in the Labour Party. Although it was never to be acceptable to more than a small section of the labour movement, that section was to be influential beyond its numbers. Indeed, while the original Labour Marxists were to move on to greener pastures – Mann and Champion emigrated to Australia, while John Burns left labour politics altogether to become a Liberal cabinet minister – their stress on class war lives on in the Labour Party today.

Marxism has served as a constant point of reference, fascinating and repelling Labour theorists. The strength and coherence of Marx's analysis has forced them continually to relate themselves to, or distinguish themselves from, him in a way they never needed to do with Robert Owen or John Ruskin. The criticisms of labourism inherent in his theories were to make Marxism an uncomfortable ideology in the Labour Party, however, exposing the party constantly to attack from its political opponents on the Right and just as constantly serving as a critical force from within.

THE FABIANS

The social foundations on which British politics rested proved too solid to be shaken by the Marxist challenge. Marx's prophecy that sections of the middle class and the intelligentsia would break away from bourgeois domination may have proved to be correct on the Continent, but in Britain their pragmatic and reformist traditions proved impervious to revolutionary politics, partly because of the dogmatic manner in which they were presented by the SDF. However, a number of intellectuals in the Fabian Society did feel the need to formulate a British version of the socialist ideas beginning to make headway in Europe.

The Fabian Society, formed in 1884 by a group of disillusioned mystics and bohemians, soon attracted a serious following. George Bernard Shaw (1856–1950), an Irish playwright then struggling against poverty and English class snobbery, attempted to convert them to Marxism. However, a series of discussions at the home of Mrs Charlotte Wilson led to Shaw's Marxist views being criticised and rejected in favour of the more orthodox economic viewpoint of W. S. Jevons, who emphasised the needs of the consumer in the market-place rather than the relations of production in the factory. Shaw admitted defeat eventually, writing:

> My last word for the present is – Read Jevons and the rest for your economics; and read Marx for the history of their working in the past, and the conditions of their application in the present.[11]

In rejecting Marx the Fabians were mainly influenced by Sidney Webb (1859–1947), a regular contributor to Mrs Wilson's economic tea parties. Born into a lower middle class family, Webb became a junior clerk at the age of fifteen. His high results in Civil Service examinations led him to the top Administrative Grade within eight years and to a study of law at London University. Webb joined the Fabians in May 1885 and rapidly stamped his intellectual dominance on its politics. Fascinated by the prevailing doctrines of Positivism, with its belief in a gradual evolution of a harmonious and well-ordered society guided by an educated elite, Webb's Civil Service background reinforced his collectivist belief that individuals must subordinate themselves to the common good. In a letter, he wrote that his theory of life was 'to feel at every moment that I am acting as a member of a committee.... I aspire never to act alone or for myself'. His intellectual grasp of sociology and economics set him apart in the eyes of the young Fabians.

However, his dominance was never exercised in the same way as Hyndman's control over the SDF. Both Webb and Shaw were matched by other individual Fabians. Graham Wallas (1858–1932) brought his intellectual abilities to bear on questions of morality and political theory, though he was never happy with the anti-liberal elitism of most of his colleagues. Annie Besant (1847–1933), a free-thinking radical, was probably the most prominent woman in British politics when she joined the Fabians. Sidney Olivier (1859–1943), another Civil Servant, believed that the virtues of socialism lay in its moral superiority over 'the evils of the Capitalist system which, if moralized, I am not sure is not economically superior.' Hubert Bland (1856–1914), an ex-Tory journalist, was much more sympathetic to the ideas of the Labour Marxists than the other Fabians.

It was such a varied and individualistic collection of writers and journalists as these that put the Fabian Society on the map with their *Fabian Essays in Socialism* in 1889. In stark contrast to the didactic Marxism of the SDF, Shaw claimed in his Preface that 'there are at present no authoritative teachers of Socialism. The essayists make no claim to be more than communicative learners.' They sought to make socialism perfectly compatible with the traditions of British liberalism and tolerance.

Such differences should not, however, disguise the fact that the Fabians were united by a certain conception of politics, economics and society. Moreover, a definite informal leadership emerged as a constant factor in the society's writings and discussions. It was the agreement among a few leading Fabians which set the distinctive seal on Fabian thinking, despite the disagreements over the importance of the Labour Party and the nature of imperialism. After Olivier left for British Honduras in 1890 and as Wallas became increasingly disillusioned with Fabian socialism, the dominant figures were Shaw, Webb and his wife Beatrice.

Beatrice Potter (1858–1943) was the daughter of a pottery manufacturer who, after the failure of a passionate romance with Joseph Chamberlain, had sought solace in studies of poverty and labour in London. Her work led her to become a socialist and she eventually married Webb in August 1892. It was initially a rather sad marriage. Sydney was not the most handsome of men and repelled Beatrice at first before she finally agreed to 'an act of renunciation of self and not of indulgence of self'[12] – but it soon turned into a remarkably

successful intellectual partnership. After 1892, the informal Fabian
leadership of Shaw and the Webbs had taken definite shape.

Fabian Economics

In their economic thinking, the Fabians found themselves initially in
an impasse after rejecting Marx's labour theory of value. If Jevons
was correct in concentrating on market price and the consumer, then
any notion of surplus value was invalid. This had important implications for socialist politics, which rested on protest against social
privilege in the midst of poverty. If Marx was incorrect in his argument that the worker was exploited by the employer, as the Fabians
believed him to be, then a new notion of how one class enjoyed the
surplus produced by another was produced. The Fabians attempted
to construct such a notion in their analysis of rent. They believed that
the wages of the workers were determined by the demand for their
different skills. Any wages above a basic subsistence level were seen
by the Fabians as a form of rent for ability – just as economic rent
was a reward for the advantages of a particular site and rent of
opportunity (or profits) a reward for speculation. However, in capitalist society a large proportion of the workers' rent was directed into
the pockets of the private owners and preserved for the children of
the capitalists. In this way, skilled workers were robbed of the full
fruit of their skills through the sale of their abilities to the capitalists.

Thus, the Fabians believed that they had discovered the real nature
of the class war. It lay not between workers and employers but
between the idle rich and the industrious masses. 'The material interests of the small nation pledged to exact rent from its monopolies,
and the great nation, thereby driven to receive only the remnant of
the product, are permanently opposed.' They drew a distinction
which was very similar to that drawn by Hodgskin between the
leisured classes and the talented leaders of society – tradesmen, managers, supervisors, writers – who worked hard for their living. These
latter are in fact workers who 'render inestimable services to the
community and receive rewards relative to the scarcity of their abilities',[13] among which Webb pointed explicitly to profits and salaries.

The Fabian notion of rent was intrinsic to their politics. Where
Marx attacked the capitalists as a class of employers, the Fabians
attacked them as a class of parasites. It was not the hard-working
employers but the 'leisured class' which aroused their anger. As a
result, the evils of society could be overcome by taxation of the

capitalists' unearned income rather than by the expropriation of the capitalists. The economic thinking of the Fabians was a necessary premise for their political thinking.

Fabian Politics

In contrast to the revolutionary politics of Marx and the wild insurrectionism of the SDF, the Fabians sought to show that socialism was perfectly compatible with British political institutions and modes of behaviour. They were strict constitutionalists who looked on Parliament and the Civil Service as an adequate means of achieving socialism, especially after their limited constitutional demands for the extension of the franchise, payment of MPs and reform of the House of Lords had been granted.

Where Marx had called for the existing state machinery to be replaced with a very different type of state, the Fabians identified socialism with the extension of the existing British State – with its monarch, parliament, courts and military. As Shaw pointed out, 'The Socialism advocated by the Fabian Society is State Socialism exclusively.' While Fabians might accept that the state was at the moment controlled by the leisured classes, it could be captured by the industrious classes through their socialist representatives by means of elections. This was the reason for the rejection of violence and unconstitutional action as being totally inappropriate for the British political scene. In Fabian eyes the state was *fundamentally* neutral, despite the class nature of some of its actions. It could be used to hinder progress or it could be used to further the evolution of humanity towards its collectivist goal. There was nothing inherent in the state which dictated its class nature. The problem was merely one of which class was in control of the state's function and, therefore, of which class controlled the House of Commons. The state machine of army, police and law courts 'will continue to be used against the people by the classes until it is used by the people against the classes with equal ability and equal resolution.'[14]

A socialist majority at Westminster was therefore the goal of the Fabians. This could be done by persuasion, local exercises in municipal socialism and working towards a parliamentary majority. As Sidney Webb argued in 1923:

For the Labour Party, it must be plain. Socialism is rooted in political democracy; which necessarily compels us to recognize that every step towards our goal is dependent on gaining the assent and support of at least a numerical majority of the whole people.[15]

The future arguments by the Labour Right that Labour must appeal to middle-class interests as well as those of the working class if it wished to obtain parliamentary power can be found in Fabian political thought.

This faith in parliamentary democracy as the best means of moving towards socialism was reinforced by the Fabian belief that they were acting in accordance with the gradual and irreversible evolution of history – 'the inevitability of gradualism,' as Sidney Webb told the 1923 Labour Party Conference. The rapid progress of collectivism, as seen by the spread of municipal socialism and increasing state regulation of factories, was a result of social laws by which humanity was being led into a realm of reason and order. Nobody could stop this progress, or accelerate it beyond its natural pace, and the task of socialists was to point to the inevitability of the development so that it could take place in a totally rational manner. This faith in the inevitability of progress was an optimistic belief which ignored the demands of capital accumulation, and it has come into much disrepute after the horrors of the twentieth century, but its importance for Labour could be seen in the assumption until recently that the welfare gains of Labour governments were irreversible.

The Fabian acceptance of parliamentary representative democracy did rule out, however, any alternative view of democracy as direct participation by the producers. The participation of the working class was ruled out by the Fabian leadership as impractical:

> the utmost function that can be allotted to a mass meeting in the machinery of democracy is the ratification or rejection of a policy already prepared for it, and the publication of decisions to those concerned.[16]

Direct democracy would merely ensure that orators would be elected, rather than responsible representatives; even the referendum and initiative were ruled out as inefficient, impeding the decisions of the expert.

In Fabian eyes, the civil servant was to be the real governor of a socialist Britain, with representative democracy acting as a mere check on the administrators. To Webb:

a body of expert representatives is the only form capable of coping with expert administrators. The only way to choose expert representatives is popular election, but that is just the worst way to obtain expert administrators.[17]

Officials should be chosen by a select committee from a short list drawn up after competitive examinations. The class background and interests of these administrators, and the possibility that they might attempt to hamper a socialist government, were ignored by Webb as irrelevant.

The elitism which came so naturally to the Fabian leaders went hand-in-hand with a commitment to a socialist Empire. This became clear in a series of articles entitled 'What is Socialism?' in the *New Statesman* in 1913. At home, guided by an elite army of expert administrators, the British people were to be guided towards adulthood; abroad, the British elite would govern the non-adult races in a co-operative empire free of the selfish competitive spirit of private owners. Such an empire could prove the basis of international co-operation – 'In the Socialist view, the guardianship of the non-Adult races of the world must be undertaken as a corporate duty by the Eight Great Powers, either jointly or separately.'[18]

At home, the Fabian leaders supported the campaign for national efficiency launched by Unionists and Liberal Imperialists after the Boer War had revealed the poor physical conditions of working class recruits. They dabbled in eugenics, with Shaw proposing in his play *Man and Superman* (1903) that national suicide could be averted only by scientific breeding. In a Minority Poor Law Report in 1909, the Webbs called for labour training camps, or 'human sorting houses,' in which paupers were to be given a course of rigorous physical training to prevent national waste. The more recalcitrant and rebellious would be packed off to semi-penal detention colonies.

Abroad, they were led by their political adherence to the nation state to support the government in the Boer War of 1899–1902, when Britain annexed two small Afrikaans republics which happened to corner much of the world's gold supply. This policy alienated many in the Society, like Ramsay MacDonald and Graham Wallas, who held to a liberal internationalist approach, but the leaders justified their support in *Fabianism and the Empire*, edited by Shaw in 1900. They argued that, as the world was going to be partitioned by the Great Powers anyway, Britain must ensure that it would not be relegated to the status of an unimportant and uninfluential island.

However, the Fabian leaders insisted that Britain should be a *beneficial* world power, underpinning its imperialism with socialism. 'The British Empire, wisely governed, is invincible. The British Empire, handled as we handled Ireland and the American colonies ... will fall to pieces without the firing of a foreign shot.' Such wise policies would include self-government and democracy within the Empire for the white Dominions, and benevolent bureaucracy for the lower breeds who were unfit for parliamentary democracy – 'the democratic institutions that mean freedom in Australasia and Canada would mean slavery in India and Soudan'. In this way, the early Fabian leaders linked their demand for benevolent socialism at home with their support for imperialism abroad.

Fabianism and Labour

The early Fabians made little attempt to adapt their socialism to the labourist assumptions of the trade union leaders, if only because of their contempt for the working class. Where other middle class socialists often took a romanticised view of the labour movement, Beatrice Webb was horrified at the immorality and mental dullness of the lower orders. At the turn of the century she noted, 'To us, public affairs seem gloomy; the middle classes are materialistic, and the working class stupid and in large sections sottish, with no interest except in racing odds.'[19]

The Fabian leaders were constantly exasperated by the narrow-minded prejudice of the class which suffered most from the existing system, and looked instead to enlightened members of the two main parties, rejecting the idea of an independent workers' party. Some Fabians, such as Hubert Bland, were more sympathetic to a workers' party than others, but the general attitude of the Fabian leadership was to permeate the Liberal and Conservative parties, municipally and nationally.

Their conception of permeation was reinforced by their extremely narrow conception of trade unionism as a limited *economic* instrument. In *Industrial Democracy* (1897), the Webbs defined the fundamental object of trade unions as 'the deliberate regulation of the conditions of employment in such a way as to ward off from the manual working producers the evil effects of industrial competition.' This was perfectly compatible with capitalist or socialist government, but it ruled out any extra-parliamentary action concerning questions of national politics. Their belief that unions were legitimately concerned with the protection of their trade, not the overall class of workers, led the Webbs to argue that unions could not become political bodies dealing with questions wider than their trade. Their legal needs did force the unions 'to secure a permanent influence in the House of Commons,'[20] but this could be fulfilled by either the Conservatives or the Liberals.

This attitude dictated a general indifference by the Fabians to the new Labour Party from its foundation. They had a member, Edward Pease, on the new party's executive, but continued their interest in permeation. It was only the rejection of their Minority Poor Law Report in 1909 that pushed the early Fabian leaders into the Labour Party, with Beatrice noting privately as late as February 1914 that socialists were 'by their adhesion to the present parliamentary party bolstering up a fraud...[But] to go back on the creation of a Labour Party would be to admit failure.' Only Sidney Webb was enthusiastic for the new party. Wallas moved away from Fabian socialism to concentrate on political psychology in *Human Nature in Politics* (1908). Shaw eventually became disillusioned with Parliament, and was to praise the national efficiency inculcated by Stalin and Mussolini. The Webbs still had a contribution to make to the Labour Party, but in the 1930s they were to appland Stalin's Russia as a fulfilment of their dream of a well-ordered and harmonious society run by a benevolent elite.

Nevertheless, these early Fabians gave to the Labour Party an intellectual framework to fit its labourist structure. They made a major contribution to the emerging ideology of British socialism with their doctrines of gradual progress towards a collectivised economy and the necessity of constitutional action, as well as a new theory of the economic surplus which could counter the Marxists. Not all their views were acceptable to British Socialism – their pro-imperial strain offended the liberal element in most socialists – but they succeeded in giving socialism a distinct British form, distancing it from subverting European trappings. They gave the Labour Party a credibility which was *supplement*, not *replace*, its labourism. To make British Socialism a popular force, however, more than theoretical coherence was needed, and this the Ethical Socialists were to provide.

THE ETHICAL SOCIALISTS[21]

The Fabians appeared too cold-blooded and abstract to fire the imaginations of a class whose collective emotions had been formed by radical Christian and libertarian traditions stretching back to the seventeenth century and beyond. The Ethical Socialists emerged to fill the emotional gap left by the Fabians. They espoused the consequences of the Fabian theory of rent and the commitment to constitutional action, and in some cases they combined this with an acceptance of the Labour Marxists' motions of class war and an independent workers' party. However, in their utopian vision of á New Jerusalem, they contributed a religious fervour to the early Labour Party. The ILP, formed in Bradford in 1893, served as their political centre. It was committed to a socialist objective – the collective ownership of the means of production, distribution and exchange – interpreted in the light of Christian nonconformity rather than Marxism or Fabian elitism. The intellectual abstractions and legal nostrums of socialist theory were regarded, at least initially, as distinctly inferior to the genuine and honest feelings of nobility and dignity offered by a socialist morality. They looked to the cooperative notions of Robert Owen and the medievalist values of John Ruskin for their ideas, and saw in the utopian fantasies of William Morris – particularly *John Ball's Dream* (1887) and *News from Nowhere* (1891) – a vision of a new socialist world. It was a vision of dignity and craftsmanship, in which beauty and a community spirit replaced the grubby and self-seeking search for money which characterised the ugly, dehumanised values of competitive capitalism. This vision inspired Edward Carpenter, and through him the Glasiers and Robert Blatchford, to impart to the Labour Party a highly emotional, near-religious passion.

Carpenter

Edward Carpenter (1844–1929) was born into a wealthy middle-class family but renounced a career in the Church after a major crisis of identity. His poetic dream of an alternative society where social hypocrisy would be replaced by a natural camaraderie led him to the democratic and agrarian values of American radicals like Thoreau and Whitman, and to a farm which an inheritance allowed him to buy. His acceptance of his own homosexuality, combined with an ecstatic feeling of relief at his mother's death, led him to write *Towards Democracy* (1882). This book was Carpenter's central statement about the unhappiness he saw around him, and its gradual replacement by a new age of liberation and natural relationships. It went through several editions, each one more infused than the last with Carpenter's personal vision of socialism.

His attacks were on modern civilisation rather than capitalism as a social and economic system of exploitation. He bitterly pointed to capitalist *ethics* in which money is accumulated and worshipped, and in which all human values were sacrificed for material gain. He saw private property as the institution by which the spiritual beauty and dignity of man was stained by the disease of artificial manners and culture. He portrayed the nightmare of competing and aggressive 'individuals' which destroyed the simplicity of honest and warm human relations.

Carpenter's ethical criticisms applied to the sentiments and values of capitalism rather than its institutions. The close analyses of Marx and the Fabians were irrelevant to his vision. Carpenter's enemy was neither the capitalist class nor the parasitic leisured class but the indifference and artificiality of civilised manners and culture. The fact that these were entangled in a system of private property was almost accidental. Since the problem was one of a sentiment to be replaced by a better sentiment, there was no fundamental need to change formal capitalist institutions. In a speech at a by-election in Chesterfield in 1908, Carpenter acknowledged as such:

> We should be able to say to private owners of industries that if they managed their own concerns in the public interest, with fair consideration for the health and welfare of their employees, the day for taking over those structures might be indefinitely postponed.[22]

It was not capital, but the selfish behaviour of capitalists, which was Carpenter's concern.

Carpenter's influence was felt directly by the propagandists of the early Labour Party, particularly the Glasiers and Blatchford, who gave his vision a more substantial political form.

The Glasiers

John Bruce Glasier (1859–1920) was the illegitimate son of a radical Scots farmer. His stern Calvinist faith was carried into his political activities, and he became a leading member of the ILP, serving as Chairman and allying himself with Keir Hardie and Ramsay MacDonald in establishing it as a major political force.

The apocalyptic strain in his thought was reinforced by his wife, Katharine St. John Conway (1867–1950), the daughter of a well-to-do preacher who became a socialist after seeing bedraggled strikers invading one of the rich Bristol churches in which she worshipped. To Katharine, the ILP was 'a child of the spirit of liberty. Life, love, liberty and labour make liquid music. The Labour Party is in league with life, and works for liberty that man may live.' It was in this spirit that she married Glasier, and it was this spirit which inspired their writings from *The Religion of Socialism* (1890) to *The Meaning of Socialism* (1919).

They saw socialism as a religion free of supernatural beliefs and expressing the highest ideals of human life. In his Chairman's Address to the 1903 Conference, Glasier talked of 'the sacrament of socialism,' which the rich were welcome to receive as much as the poor. A belief in the co-operative commonwealth was the faith that fired the martyrs of the socialist religion; men and women who fought and died 'in the hope of making a heaven for you and me and all mankind upon earth.'[23]

Their vision was anchored, however, by a more down-to-earth view of the state as the agency by which the New Jerusalem was to be achieved and organised. Far from being an instrument of class violence, the state was 'the expression, however imperfect or erroneous, of the communal or national body politic.' It had swept away the rack and the thumbscrew to guarantee political and religious freedom. It was not the state which had forced children to work long hours, but the capitalists – the State, true to its selfless nature, had restricted harsh labour conditions. It was not the state which broke up pacifist protest meetings during the Great War, but vigilante mobs – the state had granted exemption to conscientious objectors. It could be argued that the state praised by Glasier also sent millions to fight in the trenches of Flanders; deported and harassed militant socialists and shop stewards; and detained pacifist and Marxist conscientious objectors in conditions which killed 73 of them and made 31 mad. Glasier did admit that the state had been somewhat tyrannical during the war, but this was due to the prevailing political conditions – 'it would be most unfair . . . to judge the State, or indeed nations, by their comportment during the anarchical condition'. However, the violent reaction of the peacetime state to nationalist resistance in Ireland and India, the increasingly sophisticated weaponry being created and used for the defence of the nation and the plans being forged to suppress major strikes within Britain itself were indications ignored by Glasier of the state's merciless capacity to crush any threat to its supremacy. Glasier's stress on the welfare aspect of State activity had led him to belittle or ignore its violent and coercive ability to protect the existing power structure in any society.

Blatchford

Robert Blatchford (1851–1943) was the most important propagandist of the early labour movement. Born into a working class family in Halifax, he eventually became a popular journalist with the Manchester *Sunday Chronicle*. He set up a socialist journal, *The Clarion*, in 1891, combining radical politics with entertaining populist articles on sport and other working class hobbies, and encouraged social activities through the Glee Clubs and Clarion Cycling Clubs. Above all, he gave Carpenter's evangelical vision a popular form in *Merrie England* (1894), a bluff and no-nonsense appeal to a mythical working man, John Smith, which won an enormous readership.

It was the dehumanising and loveless nature of the city slums which appalled Blatchford. In a didactic and rhetorical style, he drew a picture of destitution and filth where vice and hooliganism flourished. In the midst of enormous riches, the people were plagued by misery, poverty and ill health. Patriotism, to Blatchford the noblest of virtues, had been turned into a mockery and disgrace in a country peopled with caricatures of human beings trapped in a selfish and cruel society.

In its place, Blatchford pointed to a Utopian vision of socialism as the earthly realisation of the New Jerusalem. In his direct style, he argued that this was the only solution to the social evils blighting Britain:

> John Smith, do you know what Socialism is? You have heard it denounced many times, and it is said that you do not believe in it, but do you know what it is? Good or bad, wise or foolish, it is all I have to offer as a remedy.[24]

However, such a practical style was not matched by a similar grasp of practical realities. Blatchford's revulsion from the hideous factory system led him to a Luddite dream of ridding the country of industry. He believed that Britain should turn the clock back to a de-industrialised society where pure air and fine food produced the sturdy breed of English yeomen who had first made the nation great. Britain oould then feed itself, existing in isolation from world trade by the application of scientific agriculture.

At the same time, he put forward the vision of a beautifully planned community free of the filth and squalor of the slums. He foresaw 'wide streets with detached houses, with gardens and fountains and avenues of trees.... I would institute public dining halls, public baths, public wash-houses on the best plans.'[25] These sentiments echoed a real need in the workers' movement, and worked themselves into the ethos of that movement. The concept of town and country planning, together with the creation of new towns, owed much to this ethos.

However, it was an ethos resting on a narrowly insular basis. Blatchford's faith was in the *British* working class, exploited by the unpatriotic monopolists. He described the process of state ownership as nationalisation, not socialisation. He even opposed the manufacture of British goods for sale abroad, holding to a 'little England' ideal of a self-sufficient community free from foreign influences. To Blatchford, 'We want Britain for the British. We want the fruits of labour for those who produce them.'[26] The nation and the working class were identical for him, so that the working class of other nations were always potential enemies. It was an ugly side to labourism, and unfortunately left its legacy in the labour movement.

CONCLUSION

It would be too easy to mock the naïveté of Ethical Socialism. This naïveté was important, because it was to reverberate in the hopes and aspirations of the labour movement. Its conception of a society of healthy and happy families living in a New Jerusalem was to be echoed by Labour politicians throughout the first half of the twentieth century. Its moralistic critique of the corruption and degradation of a competitive society was to be at the heart of British Socialism. It may have verged on self-righteousness but this was perfectly in keeping with the traditions of the chapel and the God-fearing, upright workman who was to be the backbone of the early Labour Party. It may have been unrealistic, but in that lay its appeal. Like religion, it was a cry from the heart – a vision that there was an alternative to the mean and stunted life of an ugly industrialised society, and an affirmation that an unselfish and caring community would one day replace an indifferent and cruel social order.

However, the appealing and attractive qualities of the Ethical Socialist vision should not blind us to the basic fact that it was ingenuous and ultimately consequential. It was incapable of delivering what it promised. Horrified by the ugliness and ruthless brutality of capitalism, the political thought of the Ethical Socialists was utopian in the worst sense of the word. It was basically a withdrawal from the world and, as such, it was impossible to translate into the practical politics of government. It had no answer to the problem of budget deficits, mass unemployment or the conflict between national and class loyalties which would be forced on the labour movement by war. Even in its grander notions of transforming a selfish society, it had no answer to the real world of armies and police, of the scheming political manoeuvres and cynical contempt for human life which has characterised the twentieth century's politics. When those problems were brought out by the sharp tests of war and slump, British Socialism would be found wanting as a result.

3   The Emergence of British Socialism

The debates and discussions around the different options facing the socialist movement in Britain took place against a background of change in capitalism. Capital accumulation was resumed on an extended scale, yet in a very different form than in earlier periods. The real nature of the crisis in Britain – a crisis of gradually declining profitability – was both disguised and offset by a massive export of capital overseas by British finance houses. Capital investment was expanding rapidly, but it was expanding outside Britain. The massive profits reaped by the financial houses increased the divisions between financial and industrial capital with important consequences for British politics, but from the point of view of capital as a whole, accumulation was able to take place on a far wider scale than before.

In Britain itself, despite a decline in real wages through most of the period, the prospect of economic collapse receded after 1890. As a result, the dogmatic Marxism of the SDF became increasingly irrelevant as social revolution appeared less imminent. Class struggle within capitalism over the share of national income was certainly seen as an essential need by an increasing number of workers, and the number organized in trades unions rose from 8 per cent in 1890 to 27 per cent in 1914. However, the moral considerations of the Ethical Socialists were far more appealing than the economistic considerations of the variants of Marxism then on offer, while the bulk of the organised working class remained committed to the Liberal Party. The socialist movement's attempt to relate to the labourism of the trade union movement thus inevitably expressed itself as an ideological relationship to Liberalism.

The debate between different sections of the socialist movement was, in the final analysis, meaningless if socialists could not gain the support of the labour movement. The ILP did not really have this support – all 28 ILP candidates were defeated in the 1895 election, while the trade union movement remained committed to the Liberal Party. After a great deal of ILP manoeuvring, a resolution calling for more labour representatives in Westminster was passed at the 1899 TUC, and a few unions joined the socialist factions to form the Labour Representation Committee (LRC) in February 1900.

However, the bulk of the unions continued to support the Liberals, and only two LRC MPs were returned at the 1900 election, fought amidst a wave of chauvinism after victories in the Boer War. It was the Taff Vale judgement of 1901, threatening the financial status of trades unions, which gave the LRC more of a basis in the labour movement, with unions like the Engineers (ASE) and the Textile Workers affiliating. Even so, a major union like the Mineworkers remained faithful to the Liberals until 1909. Even the LRC victory in the 1906 election, when 29 MPs were returned, was mainly due to an electoral pact worked out with the Liberal Party by the LRC secretary, Ramsay MacDonald, three years earlier.

The new Labour Party's relations with the Liberals were crucial, and not merely in organisational terms. In terms of ideas, the Labour Party became the battleground in which British Socialism had to work out its precise relationship with the labourist assumptions of trades unions that remained essentially Liberal in politics. The Labour Party did not have any sort of socialist programme (one of the reasons for the SDF withdrawal in 1901), and any attempt to force one on the unions would destroy the new grouping. Moreover, the ideological sterility of Gladstonian Liberalism was being replaced in the new century by the more collectivist New Liberalism represented by politicians like Haldane and Lloyd George. Their rejection of the old *laissez-faire* in favour of an active role in welfare and redistribution by the State posed a major ideological problem and political challenge to the British socialists.

The new party had already been distinguished from the Left by the Fabians and Ethical Socialists by their rejection of the revolutionary Marxist theories of value and the state. It was in this period that the leaders of the Labour Party distinguished it ideologically from the Right. This distinction did not lie in an acceptance of the nationalisation of basic industry (at least not until 1918). It lay in developing the contradictions, both logical and political, between labourism and the Liberal Party. It was a fine distinction, and was indeed seen by the ILP Left as a practically negligible distinction in the period between 1906 and the Great War. Nevertheless, the principles separating Labour from the Liberals, delineated in these formative years by Labour leaders like Hardie, were labourist rather than socialist. It was the socialist movement's absorption of labourism which completed the formation of a specific 'ideology' of British Socialism.[1]

KEIR HARDIE

James Keir Hardie (1856–1915) was a particularly apt figure in the evolution of British Socialism. His political views were not formed as a result of disillusionment with his class background, as with Hynd-man and Carpenter, nor as a result of any visit to the poverty-stricken, as with Beatrice Webb or Blatchford. Still less did he bring to bear the analytical subtlety and insights of Marx. Hardie's politics were formed as a result of a lifetime's experience in the trade union movement and in Parliament.

His main influences lay in his poor background, particularly in the democratic traditions of the Scottish working class. Hardie had been born the illegitimate son of a farm servant in Lanarkshire. He was raised in a grim and restrictive poverty, constantly on the brink of destitution; he worked as an errand boy at the age of eight, and down the mines from the age of ten. This experience of misery and recurrent economic worries nourished the Christian egalitarian instincts which remained the lifeblood of his political thinking. He combined temperance reform work with labour activity, helping to form the Ayrshire Miners Union. His trade union background made him particularly representative of the new type of labourism growing in the 1880s, critical as it was of the Gladstonian Liberalism espoused by the Lib–Lab MPs. At the 1887 TUC, he launched a stinging attack on Henry Broadhurst, the General Secretary, for supporting Liberal candidates who were bad employers. Hardie wanted the Liberals to adopt the eight-hour day in their platform, and was incensed at Liberal indifference to the trade union movement. When in 1888 the Liberals rejected his candidacy at the Mid-Lanark by-election, preferring a London barrister, he stood as an independent labour candidate. He came bottom of the poll, but the support given to him by Labour Marxists such as Champion and Mann was indicative of the political direction in which he was now travelling. Under their influence, together with socialists in the Scottish Land and Labour League, Hardie formed the Scottish Labour Party in August, 1888. The crucial organisational break with the Liberal Party had been made.

Socialism and Labourism

Hardie had rejected the Liberals, but he did not accept the tenets of the Labour Marxists. In 'An Indictment of the Class War', written for the ILP paper, the *Labour Leader*, Hardie made clear his opposition to the unemotional and dry nature of Marxism, deriding the *Communist Manifesto* as devoid of feeling. To Hardie, the Marxist notion of class war reduced socialism from the level of a crusade against materialism and selfishness to that of a faction fight. The antagonism which existed between capital and labour would be intensified by Marxism, whereas Hardie wished to remove that antagonism – 'Socialism makes war upon a system, not upon a class.'[2] It was hardly a rigorous critique of Marxism – after all, Marx also called for a war upon the system – but it was not intended to be.

It was the Liberal Party, not Marxism, which presented itself to Hardie as the chief enemy. In an earlier editorial in the *Labour Leader* arguing against an alliance with the Liberals, Hardie declared, 'I take it that the aim of the Labour Party is to wean the workers from their allegiance to Liberalism and Toryism, and to unite them under a standard of their own raising.'[3] Unlike the SDF, Hardie saw the need to look to the workers organised in the trades unions if Labour was to have any chance of political success. They had the numbers, the organisation, the money and, most importantly, they were the only force capable of emancipating themselves. To emancipate the working class from above, as sought by the middle-class Fabians, would be dictatorial and self-defeating. To Hardie, as a democrat, the workers must stand on their own feet without the help of intellectuals or benefactors.

This belief was the basis of Hardie's socialism. It was a labourist basis, in that he appealed to the almost instinctive assumptions of a trade union movement which found itself in a fundamental conflict with capitalist employers. Indeed, this labourism was essential if he was to be successful in creating a trade union political party. If the union leaders could not be won to a socialist party as was clear after the ILP electoral defeat in 1895, then Hardie would give his socialism a secondary place to his labourism. At the LRC foundation conference in 1900, he willingly accepted a power structure in which the unions had an institutionalised predominance over the socialist groups. He willingly acquiesced in the rejection of socialism as an aim of the new party in favour of the defence of trade union principles and organisation by political means.

His conception of socialism was particularly fitted for these concessions to labourism. The traditions of radical Christianity and egalitarian democracy in Hardie's upbringing gave him a sense of socialism as a religious creed rather than as a political or economic system. It was a new conception of society based upon Christian teaching, rejecting the evil selfishness of drunkenness and competition in favour of the selfless co-operation of a people who would care for one another. Hardie wrote that 'Socialism, like every other problem of life, is at bottom a question of ethics or morals. It has mainly to do with the relationships which should exist between a man and his fellows.'[4] As such, it was an extension of the teachings of the Christian fathers, in particular the Sermon on the Mount with its message of hope for the poor and forgotten. Christianity had been a creed of the poor for hundreds of years before being taken over cynically by the rich. Hardie saw the task of socialism as being the recovery of the original Christian teachings, attacking the inequalities of wealth and banishing unhealthy competition. It was 'a handmaiden of religion, and as such entitled to the support of all who pray for the coming of Christ's Kingdom upon earth.'[5]

This Christian ethic was very vague – not many people would wish to replace kindliness with selfish cruelty, at least not explicitly – but in that lay its strength and appeal. In being vague, it was malleable, capable of being applied to the semi-anarchist Utopia of Edward Carpenter or the welfare state socialism of the ILP. Hardie applied it to the native democratic tradition of his class to call for labour to capture the institutions of the State in order to emancipate itself from industrial serfdom. These institutions, which had protected the dominant class in society throughout history, could now be used by the working class as the new dominant force. In protecting its interests, the working class would be forced by necessity to nationalise the property which was owned by a small and undemocratic group – 'The fundamental fact which the working class is now beginning to recognize is that property, or at least its possession, is power. This is an axiom which admits of no contradiction.'[6] Since the possession of property was power, it followed that a real democracy must 'democratise' property. The democracy won by male workers in the political sphere must be extended to the wider industrial sphere.

This socialist element in Hardie's political thought certainly differentiated labour's interest from any possible Liberal conception, and the ILP's adoption of a programme calling for the collective ownership of the means of production, distribution and exchange was a recognition of this. However, as it became clear that the unions were not falling over themselves to endorse a socialist party, the vagueness of Hardie's conception allowed him to postpone the demand for a New Jerusalem to a more politically expedient time. It was not socialism, but labourism which was to be the line separating the new Labour Party from the Liberals on their Right.

As the bulk of the working class supported the Liberal Party, and could not be weaned away by the call for a new socialist society, then Hardie was forced to stress the contradiction existing between labourism and liberalism. He argued that the trade union movement, in its industrial conflict with the employers, was hamstrung by its political support of the employers' party in parliament. He sought to bring out the logic of the independent industrial organisation of the workers by calling for its extension to the political arena. Only by resurrecting this crucial aspect of independence, elaborated by Hodgskin and all but buried as a political theory since the defeat of Chartism, could Hardie succeed in winning the unions to a new party. The other aspects of labourism – its demand for the redistribution of wealth, for example – were not logically incompatible with the Liberal Party. The Liberals had generally ignored social questions, but this did not mean that hard work and argument could not force the Liberals to adopt a radical stand on social inequality. Indeed, the emergence of the New Liberalism around Asquith, Haldane and Lloyd George augured well for any advocate who might argue that labour should work within the Liberal Party. However, the fundamental antagonism which set employers and unions against one another in industry could not be resolved by their political co-operation in the same party. This industrial conflict demanded political expression, and Hardie's political instinct led him to a recognition of this.

Unless the unions realised the need to organise politically as well as industrially, Hardie argued that they would never fulfil their aim of protecting labour. Trades unions could regulate wages and protect living standards, but this could only go so far. The miner, for example, would be paid the minimum wage for the number of days he is given work, as negotiated by his union, but he may only be employed half the week:

> Neither he nor his union had any hand in shaping the circumstances which led to his being fully employed. ...He feels himself to be under the sway of forces which work quite without his ken, and which have the power to make him the victim of their caprice.[7]

The working class may have attained a measure of political democracy, but in industry they were mere serfs, totally at the mercy of their masters, the employers. The unions were of little use against unemployment and hunger, and were powerless against the closely-knit and omnipotent industrial autocracies which were increasingly replacing the small employers. The only answer left was for the unions to organise politically to defend their interests in Parliament. Hardie was confident that the worker 'will use the political freedom which his fathers won for him to win industrial freedom for his children ... the real inward meaning of the rise of the Labour Party'.[8]

As a result, Hardie's main attacks were on labour collaboration with the Liberal Party, the party of their employers. He pointed to the inactivity and careerism of the Lib–Lab MPs as an example of the results of the political subservience of the unions:

> Irksome as it is to endure the apathy of the [Liberal] government, it is tenfold more so to look at the inaction of these men. They are supposed to a special degree to represent labour, and so long as they are silent the Government can, with some show of justification, plead not guilty to the charge of neglect. If men who have been sent to Parliament holding a special brief for labour have nothing to say, why should a Cabinet drawn exclusively from the wealthy classes begin to make a fuss?[9]

Only a genuine, independent labour party could take up the cudgels on behalf of organised labour. Through political independence, the self-respect and manhood of the workers could be developed, forcing the major parties to take labour questions seriously. Without it, the worker would be forced into political submission, scrounging for charity from the high and mighty. As Hardie put it in 1903,

> I aim at a party which, on labour questions, shall lead Liberalism and the nation, and which shall not be content to play the part of a political Lazarus sitting at the gate of a rich man's party humbly begging crumbs from his table.[10]

Once a Labour Party had been established, however, the difference between labourism and liberalism appeared harder to define. With the Liberal government pursuing a policy of social reform after 1906, the precise role of the Labour Party appeared highly problematic. Indeed, its very electoral success had been due to a secret pact worked out with the Liberals by Hardie and MacDonald. It appeared to many on the socialist Left after 1906 that Hardie's stress on labourism had been incorrect, as the difference between the social liberalism of Lloyd George and a non-socialist labourism seemed inconsequential. This left-wing discontent, manifesting itself with Victor Grayson's by-election victory at Colne Valley in 1907 as a 'Labour and Socialist' candidate, was a threat to the ILP leadership's established strategy. In 1908, Ben Tillett attacked the non-socialist labourism of the Labour Party in his pamphlet *Is the Parliamentary Party a Failure?*, where he described the Labour MPs as hypocrites corrupted by a superficial careerism, repaying 'with gross betrayal the class that willingly supports them.'

Hardie agreed with the principles of the ILP Left, but he disagreed with their tactics. The organisational independence of the Labour Party was all-important, and only after its consolidation could the socialist goal be asserted. As he wrote in a rejoinder to the Left in 1909,

> the friction does not lie between old-fashioned Trade Unionists who want to improve the condition of the worker and Socialists who want to change the industrial order. The friction lies between people, all of whom are Socialists, who want Socialism, who put Socialism before anything else.[11]

It was a question of *how* the Labour Party was to be won to socialism, not *whether* it could be.

Hardie may have been secretly chafing at the unimaginative way in which the Labour leaders were going about this task, but he was convinced that it was a gradual process which must not be disrupted by impatience. For Hardie, a socialist movement was useless unless it was connected to the labour movement, based on the trade union and co-operative organisations of the working class. This was the strength of the new party – 'the outstanding value of the Labour Party is that it is what its name implies, an uprising of the working class. overseered and guided by that class, painfully and slowly working out its own emancipation.'[12] Only with the support of the Labour Party could socialists be elected to Westminster, and only through the Labour Party could socialists appeal to workers as part and parcel of their own movement, rather than as outside missionaries. Hardie was only recognising political realities when he wrote, 'It is not so much Socialism, nor the absence of it, which wins elections, as the fact that the candidate is representing a party which the average man who does not indulge over-much in theories, understands and approves.'[13]

There was no fundamental change to his labourist version of socialism, merely a different response to a different situation. His main aim was to instil a sense of political independence into the ranks of the labour movement. Only socialism could do this properly, but his labourist interpretation made sure that the dividing line between Labour and the Liberals was not the question of collective ownership, but that of trade union independence. This was Hardie's fundamental contribution to the Labour Party's political thought.

Its political consequences were never really thought through by Hardie. His opposition to dogmatic thinking was also an aversion to theory as such, which he saw as abstract and divisive compared with the living emotions of the democratic sentiment of socialism. This sentiment was all that workers needed – 'Abstract theories with them count for very little.... Socialism supplies the vision and a united working class satisfies the senses as a practical method of attaining its realization.'[14] He had an intuitive grasp of the needs and understanding of his class, and he sought to embody its traditions and its hopes through his actions, as when he was driven to Parliament in 1892 in a two-horse carriage, dressed in a tweed jacket and cloth cap. He was aware of the importance of symbols, much to the chagrin of other Labour MPs who were annoyed by his showmanship. He knew how to win an audience by his clear and simple style of speaking, expressing the hopes of a new society in the style of the Sunday School. In one speech, typical of many in its description of his socialism, Hardie assured his listeners that

> the ugliness and squalor which now meets you at every turn in some of the most beautiful valleys in the world would disappear, the rivers would run pure and clear as they did of yore ... and in the winter the log would glow on the fire the while that the youths and maidens made glad the heart with mirth and song, and there would be beauty and joy everywhere.[15]

It may be churlish to ask how this state of affairs was to be brought about – after all, such sentiments were a major motivating factor in the lives of thousands of socialists – but, given subsequent events, perhaps more people should have raised objections. Hardie was lulling himself and his audience into a state of vague elevation while concealing unresolved political problems in his conception which would have profound consequences for the movement he sought to serve. He was aware of the economic and social problems of poverty, unemployment, ignorance and bad health, yet he had no real policies to overcome these problems beyond the vague panacea of co-operation and state regulation. He saw capitalism as the cause of all suffering in industrial societies, but the real nature of this capitalism was never explored. Capitalism was often just another word for self-ishness, and socialism another word for democratic Christianity, so that the speed and urgency of replacing capitalism was determined by the education of people in basic goodness. Where capitalism was identified as an economic system of private ownership, the nature of its workings and the manner of its possible replacement were never analysed seriously. The potential resistance to change by the capitalist class was never measured, and plans to counter this resistance were never seriously countenanced. Instead, Hardie's socialism remained labourist and radical democratic, rather than collectivist. The limitations of this approach can be seen in his reactions to women's suffrage and imperialism.

Feminism and Imperialism

Unlike other Labour leaders, such as MacDonald and Snowden, who were opposed to all forms of extra-parliamentary activity, Hardie fully supported the struggle of the Suffragettes for the vote. He did so as a result of his democratic conviction that all of humanity, men *and* women, were equal. It was a sentiment with deep roots in the British radical tradition, but it also ran against a deep prejudice in the labour movement. Bruce Glasier was only too representative in his rejection of women's suffrage, so that Hardie was forced to take up the demand of socialist feminists for equality of work and regard. In 1909, he called attention to the opposition to women's equality in the socialist movement, arguing that 'our work will be handicapped and our movement lopsided until women take their place with men as comrades and political equals in our great world-wide agitation for industrial and economic freedom.'[16]

In this, he was taking up the call of an increasing number of women in the ILP who were attempting to link the feminist demand for the vote with the socialist demand for the emancipation of labour. Isabella Ford, an ILP feminist from Leeds, was much more aware of the oppression of working-class women than were many of the middle class Suffragette leaders, yet she was involved in a constant fight against male prejudice in the ILP and Labour Party. In her pamphlet *Women and Socialism* (1904), she attacked both the Labour party and the Suffragette movement for failing to recognise the economic basis of women's oppression in their total dependence on men for a living. The ruling parties were hostile to state protection of women by maternity benefits and other social measures, which could only be won by the pressure of the labour movement. She called for both Labour and the suffrage movement to recognise that working-class women are particularly oppressed through low wages and miserable working conditions. These were examples of

> moral evils which are eating at the heart of the nation, pressing the most heavily, as do all such evils, on the lives of the very poorest and most helpless women, and long experience has shown that they will never be remedied till women have full political power, and can themselves deal with them [17]

She argued that only the vote would give women the political protection which the trades union movement was incapable of providing.

Hardie echoed such sentiments in his writings and speeches, attempting to show the labourist nature of women's oppression – 'the sex problem is, at bottom, the Labour problem'.[18] Women were economically dependent on men in all classes, with the daughters of the middle class groomed for a 'successful' marriage. However, working-class women were particularly oppressed at home and work, and Hardie called on the trade union movement and the Labour Party to recognise that without equality between the sexes, social progress was impossible. This call was couched in terms of his romantic view of socialism, however, rather than in any thorough analysis of whether women were *necessarily* oppressed by capitalism (in contrast to Marxists such as Dora Montefiore and Lily Gair Wilkinson). To Hardie, women's emancipation in a socialist society seemed to mean that women would mate with men for other than economic reasons:

> the strong, good-looking male attracts the best of the females, and thus the best qualities get transmitted to offspring and are by them passed on to succeeding generations until they become permanently incorporated.[19]

Apart from Hardie's own contribution to the current debate on eugenics, his conception of women's emancipation was as vague as that of labour emancipation. There was no reason, given the understanding of Ford and Hardie, why women could not throw off their chains within the confines of capitalist society. Indeed, their demands for the vote and state welfare have all to a greater or lesser extent been obtained from governments of all parties. The freedom of women to choose good-looking males is too controversial a subject to be touched upon here, but in Hardie's analysis the economic subjection of working-class women was due more to the selfishness of individual capitalists than to capital as a system. It was to be overcome by trade union action and state regulation rather than by the ending of a particular society.

The difficulty of extending labourism beyond the nation-state meant that Hardie's opposition to imperialism had its roots in the democratic traditions of nineteenth-century liberalism, with its opposition to the oppression of small nations. Unlike the Fabians, Hardie belonged to the vociferous anti-war movement during the Boer War of 1899–1902. He denounced it as a war fought for the benefit of capitalists, grinding down the poor and independent Afrikaner, but in this he did not differ from the main Liberal opposition to the war. The Liberals also argued that the selfish gains of a few capitalists was no justification for the subjugation of a small nation. Thus, Hardie could mourn Queen Victoria's death as an example of the war's most tragic victim,[20] and warn that the war was harming the interests of the Empire. In one article castigating the war as a capitalist conflict, Hardie wrote that

> there is not a single British interest at stake.... Russia wants to see us out of India, France out of Egypt, Germany out of Africa. With the entire British army locked up, and our last gun with it, it only needs these three powers to agree and the Empire goes to pieces like a house of cards. By ending the war, this becomes at once impossible, the Empire would be saved, and the national honour redeemed.[21]

The fact that class interests and national interests may not coincide was obviously not clear to Hardie because labourism was an insufficient basis for an analysis of imperialism.

This was demonstrated in Hardie's call for the reform rather than the destruction of the British Empire. His visit to India in 1908 convinced him that reforms were desperately needed, as British rule there resembled a military despotism tempered by a civilian bureaucracy. He called for Home Rule, not independence, to prevent the Congress Party from becoming seditious. Only an effective self-government could preserve both the Empire and the liberties of the native peoples. Hardie's essential loyalty to British institutions at home was thus reflected in his loyalty to their extension abroad. This was why he could argue for reform of the imperial institutions as essential 'if India is to be pacified and kept loyal to the British Raj'.[22] He was not opposed to imperialism as such, merely to its militarist and undemocratic form.

Hardie's democratic radicalism and his evident sympathy for the sufferings of his class gave him a special place in the affections of the Labour Party. He made no original contribution to the party's political thought – echoing an eclectic mixture of Ethical Socialism, Labour Marxism and Fabianism – and was almost deliberately obscure and contradictory in his statements. As a politician, he had to demonstrate a necessary flexibility in order to build the Labour Party, although in his belief in the necessity to build that party he never wavered. As a political thinker Hardie did have a significance, but it did not lie in his conception of socialism. In his resurrection of labourism as a political idea, he helped to form the contours of the Labour Party's political thought, separating it from the Liberals on the Right.

PHILIP SNOWDEN AND RAMSAY MacDONALD

Hardie marked out the contours of British Socialism, separating it from the Liberal Party by his demands for Labour's political independence, from a political position on the Left of the new party. His past experience of suffering and trade union struggle gave him a conception of class struggle which was similar in substance to that of Labour Marxists like Tom Mann. However, the flexibility of the new party's political thinking was shown by two other Labour leaders of the time, Philip Snowden and Ramsay MacDonald, who paradoxically occupied a position on the Right of the new party while claiming to be Socialists. Each made his specific contribution to Labour Party thinking in this formative Edwardian era and each was to follow through the logic of his conceptions when faced with the reality of government office in a later decade.

Snowden

Philip Snowden (1864–1937) was born in Yorkshire's West Riding, the son of a poor weaver. He was steeped from an early age in Liberal politics and Methodist religion, and worked in a local tax office at the lowest Civil Service grade until an illness paralysed his legs. His interest in temperance and the evangelical nature of his religion quickly won him to the Ethical Socialism then being preached in the West Riding by Blatchford's *Clarion*, and he joined the ILP in the mid-1890s. His evangelical and blood-curdling speeches, in which the present system was seen as a moral hell and socialism as the earthly paradise, went down well with his audience, and Snowden's pamphlet *The Christ That Is To Be* (1903) established him as a popular figure. After his election as a Labour MP in 1906, Snowden was chosen as the party's spokesman on finance, and his gaunt, crippled figure seemed to symbolise the puritanical inflexibility of his socialism. He was described as the new Robespierre, the symbol of an incorruptible refusal to compromise the capitalist face of Mammon.

In fact, Snowden's political conceptions were much less intractably hostile to capitalism than appeared on the surface. The economic policies with which he became associated were very close in some important respects to the Gladstonian doctrines of the most orthodox Liberal, and the differences separating Labour from the Liberals were paradoxically blurred by someone who regarded himself as belonging to the socialist wing of the new party. This should not be misunderstood, however. When he became Chancellor of the Exchequer in the Labour Governments of the 1920s, the economic orthodoxy of Snowden's thinking was wickedly encapsulated in Churchill's biting prose:

> We must imagine with what joy Mr Snowden was welcomed at the Treasury by the permanent officials.... Here was the High Priest entering the sanctuary. The Treasury mind and the Snowden mind embraced each other with the fervour of two long-separated lizards.[23]

The image is misleading in one respect, in that Snowden's economic orthodoxy did lay claim to a socialist basis. He was particularly firm in his belief that capitalism was an immoral system based on privilege and injustice, and that political economy was merely a justification for such a system. In *The Christ That Is To Be*, he wrote, 'We care not a rap about your political economy. It is enough for us to know that the many who toil hard and long are in poverty, and the few never work at all.'[24] The paradox cannot be explained away merely by political expediency, or a sense of awe at the Treasury mandarins. Other ministers have been tough enough to overcome the resistance of their civil servants, and Snowden was not one to waver when faced with hostility to his views.

It was the very nature of his socialist outlook which lent itself to the orthodox economics of the Treasury. Snowden conceived his socialism in moral rather than economic terms. He was profoundly opposed to the individualist basis of Liberal economics, as presented by nineteenth century free traders like Richard Cobden and John Bright. He did not see politics and economics as separate from religion and ethics; indeed a healthy religious life was impossible under a corrupt political or a selfish economic system. Individualist competition was particularly immoral – 'it is not in harmony with the essential conditions of a healthy social life. Unhealthy industrial and social conditions spring from the want of harmony and co-operation between things which are essentially and vitally connected.'[25] Such a system had bred the idle rich, a leisured and parasitic class which took no part in creating the wealth which it enjoyed. The anarchic system of competition on which that class fed had placed the community at the hands of cartels and combines, and the unearned rent of this class of usurers was merely the other side of a coin which contained overcrowding, slums, drunkenness and pauperism.

However, Snowden believed that a moral economic system of co-operation was growing within the old society. Production had grown so interdependent that there would no longer be an individual operation for individual use in factory and commercial life, but a social operation for the use of all. This growing co-operative system was making nonsense of the structure of distribution in capitalist society, exposing for all to see the antagonism between the industrious classes and the usurers who lived off unearned rent. Snowden made it clear that it was the usurer, not the private employer, who was the parasitic enemy. Like the Fabians (and Hodgskin) he distinguished between the earned and the unearned elements in the capitalist's income. While the capitalist was wrong to take unearned income in his role as a usurer, he was an essential aspect of production in his role as a manager – 'Many landlords and many capitalists act as the directors of agriculture or commerce, and in so far as this work is useful, the remuneration they take is not rent or profit, but salary.'[26]

It was a highly muted form of opposition to capitalism which was proposed by Snowden. The transfer of ownership from the rentier class to the State was a purely nominal change in his conception, leaving the basic structure and organisation of production intact. Indeed, Snowden was explicit in leaving a role for capitalists who happened to have technical knowledge and managerial ability. Such efficient capitalists would be allowed to continue their firms as long as they recognised and maintained decent living standards for their employees. Snowden's acceptance of a mixed rather than a socialised economy was evident from his argument that

> it would be unwise on the part of the community to deprive private enterprise of the opportunity of proving its superiority over nationalization. But private enterprise could not be permitted to exist unless it conformed to the standard of wages, hours, and conditions prevailing under public employment.[27]

It was not the capitalist nature of production, but its results of low wages and exploitative working conditions which was criticised by Snowden. Along with the Fabians, he accepted the system of production as natural and eternal.

It was the system of distribution which was at fault, and Snowden sought to correct this through a policy of taxation of unearned wealth. He rejected the Gladstonian idea of taxation as an evil burden on the individual to be reduced to a bare minimum. On the contrary, taxation had a special usefulness in helping to secure some of the wealth accrued by the monopolist in order to use it for the community. The decadent gains of such usurers could be disgorged from them by the State through a strict fiscal policy, redistributing the wealth from the parasites to the industrious classes. Such a redistribution would revitalise the economy, overcoming the deficient demand of the workforce and leading to more production through the increased consumption of the people.

Such political and economic thinking had little in common with the orthodox Gladstonian political economy of which Snowden has so often been accused, owing much more to the Fabian outlook than any concept of *laissez-faire*. Snowden's conception of socialism led him to oppose strikes as an example of the immoral competitive spirit. Since the system of distribution was governed by competition, then obviously there was an inevitable conflict between capital and labour over the share of industry's product. However, this industrial strife was an example of the worst kind of conflict – civil war – in which there were no victors, only the vanquished. This was fatal to industrial progress, keeping alive a sectional outlook which blinded the employer and the worker to their common interests in industrial progress. In pamphlets such as *The Living Wage* (1912)

and *Socialism and Syndicalism* (1913), Snowden opposed the current
strike movement as an expression of a competitive spirit alien to
socialism.

It was a belief which continued to be held by Snowden in the post-
war period, dictating his policies as Chancellor. He called for the
labour movement to be more far-sighted in its methods, making
the existing system more efficient and productive, and devising
plans by which the worker could get a just reward for his work.
He argued for Wages Boards and Industrial Courts to establish a
rational and regular system of wage regulation (as was consistent
with his acceptance of the existing system of production), and as
Chancellor claimed in his 1924 Budget speech that his mildly
expansionary measures were 'vindictive against no class and no
interest'.[28] His policies, far from springing from the economic orthodoxy of the Treasury, sprang from his own view of socialism as the
co-operative aspect of the present society. In Snowden's view
the gradual redistribution of wealth, regulated by the popular support
for a socialist government, would extend the spirit of co-operation.
This spirit

> will permeate everybody from the most responsible manager to the
> humblest worker, and each will feel that in doing his best he is not
> only contributing to the common good, but is promoting his own
> personal interests.[29]

In this way, Snowden's conception of socialism converged with the
orthodox Liberal belief in the collaboration of capital and labour in
the national interest. His socialism was far less connected to labourism than that of Keir Hardie.

The lack of a parliamentary majority in the 1920s, forcing Labour
to rely on the Liberals, was to prevent Snowden from carrying out his
belief in even a mild redistribution of wealth. The monetarist orthodoxy of his economic policies, with their devastating consequences
for working-class living standards, should not lead to any misunderstanding about his political and economic thought. It was a
right-wing interpretation of British Socialism, not at all akin to
Gladstonian Liberalism. He merely lacked any immediate programme
to counter the effects of capitalist slump, forcing him to carry out the
policies dictated by the logic of an economic system in crisis. Socialism was postponed until the capitalist crisis had sorted itself out. As
he told the Commons in February 1931,

I have been in active political life for forty years, and my only object has been to improve the lot of the toiling millions. That is still my aim and object, and, if I ask for some temporary suspensions, some temporary sacrifices, it is because that is necessary to make future progress possible.[30]

The failure of his policies was a failure of British socialism as much as one of orthodox political economy.

MacDonald

It was Ramsay MacDonald who amplified the right-wing interpretation of British Socialism in Labour's political thinking, as Snowden had done in his economic approach. MacDonald was a leading member of the ILP, and then the Labour Party, because of his socialist ideas rather than any sympathy with trade unionism. Where Hardie's socialism had a strong ground in the labourism of the trade union movement, MacDonald attempted to link his socialism to the more advanced strands of Liberal thinking at the turn of the century. His charismatic personality and administrative ability pushed him to the foremost place in British politics, and he became the country's first Labour Prime Minister. However, his agreement to form a coalition with the Conservatives and Liberals in 1931 led to his expulsion from Labour's ranks, and he was to become a pariah for the party he helped to create, a prime example of class collaboration and treachery. The reasons for his success, and his ultimate infidelity, can be traced to the political conception of socialism which MacDonald brought to bear on the problems of the day.

James Ramsay MacDonald (1866–1937) was, like Hardie, an illegitimate child, born to a Scottish fisherwoman in Lossiemouth. Driven by the type of burning ambition often felt by intelligent people whose youth had been spent in poverty, he moved to Bristol at the age of 19, where he had a brief flirtation with the SDF. Repelled by their dogmatic Marxism, he became a private secretary to a Liberal MP, joining the Fabians shortly afterwards. He was ambivalent on the Fabian notion of 'permeating' the Liberal Party, but after being rejected by the local Liberals of Southampton as their parliamentary candidate he became convinced that the Liberals were dissociating themselves from the advancing socialist and labour movements. He joined the ILP in July 1894, declaring that the decision of the Southampton Liberal Council was but part of a national policy which is compelling what was once the advanced wing of Liberalism to sever itself from an old alliance and form itself into an independent Labour party.[31]

His marriage to the wealthy Margaret Gladstone enabled him to work as a journalist while maintaining a comfortable financial position, and he threw all his energies into the ILP, moving onto its National Council in 1896.

When the LRC was set up in 1900, MacDonald took the crucial post of secretary. In this position, he established himself as the leading administrator of the organisation, consuming his great energy in the wearing work of building a new party. The Liberal predilections, which had never left him, and the political realities of the new party's weakness, led him to make a secret electoral pact with the Liberal Chief Whip, Herbert Gladstone, in 1903. This pact, known only to Hardie and himself, created the conditions for the return of 29 Labour MPs in 1906. Only five of the new MPs were returned against Liberal opposition, and MacDonald himself entered the Commons in tandem with a Liberal at Leicester. He rapidly became associated with the moderate image presented by Labour which came under increasing attack from the ILP Left, an image intensified after he became chairman of the parliamentary party in 1911. With MacDonald as leader, Labour seemed barely distinguishable from the Liberals, and soon began to lose electoral popularity. Nevertheless, MacDonald's opposition to the Great War in 1914, leading to his resignation as parliamentary chairman and subjection to a campaign of personal slurs, gave him an image as a man of the Left. It was an image only too wide of the mark.

Unlike Hardie, whose stress on the independence of Labour made him aware of the Liberals as a party of employers, MacDonald had a much closer intellectual and political relationship with the Liberals. Indeed, shortly after joining the ILP, he worked with Liberal collectivists such as Herbert Samuel and J.A. Hobson in the Rainbow Circle. He went much further than most of his ILP colleagues in associating Socialism with Liberalism, and in advocating friendship with the Liberals who would bring respectability and intellect to a party sorely lacking in both qualities. It was a far cry from Hardie's simple faith in the working class.

The clarity with which MacDonald expressed his theory of society gives us an insight into his political conceptions. He had much more respect for theory than Hardie, and often bewailed the philistinism of the British labour movement. The replacement of reason by blind party loyalty in Parliament, and the failure of government to recognise social problems, were an expression of the British distrust of theory. In books such as *Socialism and Society* (1905), *Socialism* (1907) and *Socialism and Government* (1909) he attempted to express the relationship between Socialism and Liberalism in terms of a scientific analysis.

Evolution and Society

Marx had, of course, seen his own analysis as 'scientific,' counterposing it to the Utopians who merely wished to bring about socialism. However, MacDonald lumped Marx together with the Utopians as trapped in a pre-Darwinian conception of society. He saw Marx as critical and destructive in his dialectical method, whereas the new biological views stressed an evolutionary and constructive approach to society which could be applied much more accurately than the revolutionary method. The class war had not destroyed capital, but had created constructive trades unions; the working classes had not become pauperised, but had become citizens with a stake in society. Marx had taken the superficial clash of social forces at its face value, whereas MacDonald pointed to the underlying progress being achieved *within* society.

Only biology could explain this, as it studied changes in physical organisms. The organic form was not merely a physical shape, as in plants or animals, but could be seen in social terms. Society, too, had an organic form, in which the different relations between the organs were co-ordinated to make a living whole which was greater than its constituent parts. These social organs were 'connected by a living tissue of law, of habit and custom, of economic inter-dependence, of public opinion, of political unity',[32] to create a general stability. These laws and customs were evidence of a keen *social* self-consciousness, standing above the thought of the individuals and classes which were the organs constituting the social whole. To MacDonald,

society belongs to the biological type of existence because it is no mere collection of separate individuals ... but a unified and organized system of relationships, in which certain people and classes perform certain functions and others perform other functions.[33]

However, the competitive nature of capitalist society totally disrupted the organic nature of the community. Instead of the different organs – capital, land, labour, for example – co-operating in the interests of the whole, they preyed on one another to the detriment of the whole. The wealth of the nation was controlled by private interests, with the result that two civilisations were growing side by side – 'the civilization of the idle or uselessly employed rich, and the civilization of the industrious poor'.[34] The physical and moral conditions of the poor degenerated under the impact of periodic unemployment and chronic insecurity, while the capitalists suffered as the intense competition and threat of business failure led them to spend their lives in business rather than leisure. Conflict, rather than co-operation, between the different organs, or social functions, became the norm.

MacDonald counterposed the organic community of socialism to the present state of affairs, a community where the different functions would be co-ordinated and regulated in the interests of the whole. In such a community, true social individuality would flourish as each person would be happily integrated in the advanced whole and would work for that whole. Just as in biology the individual cell has both a function *and* an individual existence through the totality, so in society the different classes and people would have a social function *and* an individual part to play in the whole. In the gradual process of social evolution by which the new organic phase was developing, conflicts between different functions like capital and labour did occur. However, 'the predominant or vital fact is not that conflict, but rather the steady subordination of all functional and sectional interests to the living needs of the whole community'.[35] The conflicts and contests would gradually die out as the *cause* of the conflicts – the selfish and sectional nature of the different functions – were removed by the co-ordination of the State.

It was the establishment of political democracy which provided the foundations of the new phase of social evolution, according to MacDonald. With the extension of the franchise and the increasing power of the House of Commons, the State could no longer be taken as an authority external to the community, imposing its laws on unwilling subjects. It had become a part of the community, expressing the will of the social organism and demanding the obedience of its constituent parts.

The democratic State is an organization of the people, democratic government is self-government, democratic law is an expression of the will of the people who have to obey the law – not perhaps the will of every individual, but the communal will voicing the need of all classes in their relation to the community.[36]

As such, the State was an instrument capable of responding to the public will in the form of Parliament. It was an extension of the biological analogy – 'Parliament is a laboratory; its legislative experiments must be undertaken in precisely the same scientific frame of mind as those of the chemist or the physicist.'[37]

Labour and Liberalism

His conception of society as an organism composed of different social classes performing different functions gave MacDonald a very different outlook on the labour movement and on labourism from that held by Keir Hardie. To MacDonald, labour constituted merely one element in the social whole. It was a functional part which was important only in terms of the whole community, headed by the State. Therefore capital was as important as labour, and the consumer was as much a part of the community as the producer. In capitalism, labour had to look out for itself, so that its strikes were not to be condemned outside the context of a society in which each function and group preyed on the other. A socialistic party, to MacDonald, must therefore base itself and its appeals to the *community*, rather than to the working class as a class. Its practical policy must be based,

> not on functions [like labour], but on the complete civic unity to which functions are only contributory, and upon the citizen, of whom the worker is only a differentiated and specialised aspect.... The community idea must be the dominant note; the thought must be of the co-operation of citizens, not of workmen nor of consumers.[38]

It was a conception which made MacDonald more akin to the New Liberals than to labourists like Hardie. The working class suffered materially at the hands of the capitalists, but material suffering was not all. The capitalists also suffered, developing a selfish and unsentimental attitude to life. MacDonald's socialism was more to do with a sense of social community rather than class unity – 'Socialism marks the growth of society, not the growth of a class. The consciousness

which it seeks to quicken is not one of economic class solidarity, but
one of... growth towards organic wholeness.'[39]

It was a conception which led him to reject the partisan labour
theory of value, held to by Hodgskin and Marx in their different
ways. For MacDonald, the quashing of the dogmas of this working
class theory would not hurt socialism at all. Of course, the worker's
service in capitalism carried an inadequate payment – 'poverty rather
than property is the reward of labour today.'[40] The labourer's whole
life was spent in servitude to capitalists, who absorbed and used up
his energies before casting him on the scrapheap of retirement. However, this was due to the competitive nature of a de-regulated society,
rather than to the class exploitation held by labour theorists of value.
It would be ended by bringing capital and labour together in a moral
partnership. It was perfectly logical for MacDonald to argue that
'capital creates values too.... Therefore, labour's quarrel with capitalism is not in the sphere of production, but in that of distribution.'[41]
Capital and labour were antagonists in the distribution of wealth,
but in the production of wealth they were necessary partners. In
MacDonald's conception of socialism, their partnership would be
affirmed as their different functions were co-ordinated.

MacDonald's belief that 'there must be co-operation and not conflict between labour and capital'[42] led to his hostility to all manifestations of class conflict. Unlike Snowden, MacDonald did not reject
strikes out of hand; he held them to be a rational action of the trade
unions in their defence of living standards. However, unlike Hardie,
MacDonald was unsympathetic to strikes. They expressed an instinctive, rather than a rational aspect of the labour movement, encoura-
ging resentment towards good employers as well as bad. Labour had
to look to Parliament, not to its own resources, if it was to achieve its
aims. He argued that the trade union conflict should be turned into a
movement towards organic regulation and co-ordination – 'the field
upon which it [the trade union conflict] has to be fought out is the
State, not the workshop; the weapon is to be the ballot box and the
Act of Parliament, not collective bargaining'.[43]

MacDonald saw the Labour Party in socialist terms, then, but it
was a socialism which was much more loosely connected with the
labour movement than that held by Hardie and other Labour politicians. Labour representation was the awakening of the submerged
elements of society, but its intention was to raise the worker to be a
full citizen, just as MacDonald himself had fought his way out of
poverty to become a respected member of the community. In an

important article in the *New Liberal Review* in September 1903, he expressed his distinctive attitude to his party:

> If the new Labour movement were simply an attempt of Trade Unionists to use their political power for purely sectional ends... it would be a menace to all the qualities that mark public life with distinction and honour. ...Trade Unionism in politics must identify itself with something higher and wider than Trade Union industrial demands. It must set those demands into a system of national well-being; the wage earner must become the citizen; the Union must become the guardian of economic justice.[44]

Labour politics was a national, not a class, question. That Labour's interests should ever clash with the interests of the nation was incomprehensible to MacDonald.

His understanding of Labour's needs led MacDonald to a much more conciliatory attitude to the Liberal Party than that of Hardie and the ILP Left. He believed that the Liberals had exhausted their role in the scheme of social evolution, with the battle for universal suffrage and political democracy being virtually won. They had disrupted the organic relationships of feudal society without replacing them with new organic relationships. Their life was now coming to an end, just as life came to an end in the vegetable and animal kingdoms. However, 'like the cell which is about to divide and create a new organism', new ideas were growing in the Liberal Party, more akin to socialism than to Gladstonian Liberalism. A new epoch was being born in the remnants of the old – 'Socialism, the stage which follows Liberalism, retains everything that was of permanent value that was in Liberalism, by virtue of its being the hereditary heir of Liberalism.'[45] Thus, vital principles of Liberalism such as free trade and national self-determination were taken up much more resolutely by the Labour Party, while the Liberal Party faltered.

MacDonald's conception of socialism was *internally* coherent. His evolutionary method, based on current conceptions of biology, was logically as sound as the revolutionary method of Marx, and it had a far greater rigour than the loose formulations of Keir Hardie. However, its ability to fit the *external* reality of British politics was far more questionable. In one sense, it had a clear grasp of the solidity of British political and social institutions. MacDonald's belief that Socialists should work within these institutions rather than against them had far more of a political future than the hostility demonstrated by the

SDF and other left-wing parties of the time. These institutions – Parliament, the trades unions, the family – commanded the support and obedience of all social classes in the country, and to go against them would isolate the socialist movement in a sectarian impotence.

However, in another sense, the support given to these institutions ran into political dilemmas which were to prove fatal to MacDonald's aspirations. He saw no contradiction between the national interest and the interests of the working class, a notion which logically led to the view that the labour movement should bear the burdens of national crisis as well as share in the wealth of national prosperity. Such a view ran counter to the labourism of the trade union movement, which had set up a party to *protect* its interests, even if those interests were, in MacDonald's terms, merely sectional. As his own view of socialism was not a class but a *national* conception, he was led into constant attempts to collaborate with other parties representing other sections of the national organism. In the debate on the Address in 1929, when he headed a minority Labour government, he asked the opposing parties to join Labour to 'consider ourselves more as a Council of State and less as arrayed regiments facing each other in battle'.[46] When he left the Labour government in 1931, he was genuinely hurt when other Labour politicians responded to his view of the national interest in a hostile and 'sectional' manner. As his biographer has noted, 'later Labour suggestions that he was glad to break with the party and no longer cared what it thought of him do not fit the facts'.[47]

MacDonald's fatal error was to hold to a classless view of the community in a class-divided society. The Labour Party represented one class in that society (although it continually appealed to the middle classes to join it), and MacDonald was unable to accept the consequences of this. His socialism had much more in common with the New Liberalism of the time than it had with the labourism of leaders such as Keir Hardie and Arthur Henderson. It was the absence of labourism in MacDonald's political thinking which blurred the distinctions between Labour and the Liberals, and which led to the eventual decision to break with the party which he had nurtured and led to social respectability.

THE TEST OF WAR

The export of capital, which characterised British capitalism in these years, tied Britain more closely into the world economy, and thereby into the division of the world between a few imperialist nations which had taken place by the turn of the century. The agrarian economies of Africa, Asia and Latin America were subordinated economically to the major industrial powers. On the basis of this economic division of the world between the major capitalist powers, a system of political and military alliances developed from which Britain initially held aloof before naval and colonial rivalry with Germany forced her into the *entente* with France. The capitalist world was being impelled into a major war by a dynamic which seemed to evade the conscious control of its politicians. War, and imperialism, were becoming major questions confronting the British labour movement, forcing it to clarify its conceptions of class and national loyalties.

Upon the outbreak of war in Europe in August, 1914, the Second International collapsed under the pressure of calls for national unity. The most evident symptom of this collapse was the support given by the German Social Democrats, the strongest party of the International, to the Kaiser's demand for war credits. Throughout Europe, the Socialist and Labour parties were each rushing to sanction the actions of their own national governments, leaving numerous pacifist and revolutionary minorities dazed by the ruin of their illusions in workers' internationalism.

The war intensified the divisions between the trade unionist and socialist wings of the Labour Party. The parliamentary party and the unions, together with the Fabians, generally supported the government, while the bulk of the ILP opposed the war. However, despite the strains on the Labour alliance, the Labour Party avoided the deep divisions which split the European socialist movement apart. Indeed, Labour's survival as a united party through the tribulations of war was eloquent testimony to the essential unity of British Socialism as an ideology covering Left and Right.

This unity of British Socialism was not initially clear. The war divided the Labour Party between those who were more interested in national defence and those who were more interested in national change. On the Right, parliamentary and union leaders of the labour movement went on to the recruiting platform, urging workers to serve the national and imperial interest, whether in the charnel-house of the Western Front or in the streets of Dublin. At home, these Labour and union leaders agreed to the suspension of trade union rights, including strike action, for the duration of the war.

On the Left, the ILP took a diametrically opposite approach, issuing a Manifesto on International Socialism a week after the war's outbreak, declaring its faith in international solidarity with German socialists. The Labour Marxists in the ILP, like James Maxton, refused to fight for capitalism; Ethical Socialists and Christian pacifists, like Alfred Salter, rejected violence as immoral; while ILP leaders like Ramsay MacDonald and Philip Snowden saw the war as an example of militarism and secret diplomacy.

However, the differences between Right and Left proved ultimately less important than their compatibility. Keir Hardie, who had led mass anti-war rallies in the days leading up to the outbreak of war, was a broken man when he realised the depth of pro-war sentiment in the British labour movement and in the International. He refused to support the war, but he refused to oppose it, too. His sympathies remained with the *British* working class, even if this meant subordinating the interests of the international socialist movement. In an article in the *Merthyr Pioneer*, in August 1914, he wrote,

> A nation at war must be united, especially when its existence is at stake. With the boom of the enemy's guns within earshot, the lads who have gone forth to fight their country's battles must not be disheartened by any discordant notes at home.[48]

Hardie's sentiments indicate the factors unifying Left and Right in the British labour movement, even though they were not in harmony with the ILP's opposition to the war.

The lynchpin of British Socialism, and of labourism, was the acceptance of a national framework within which the labour movement would operate. Both Left and Right in the Labour Party held steadfast to the belief that the British State, parliamentary and representative, could be used to change British society. The class nature of that society was admitted by all, as was the need to change the balance of class power towards the working class. The class tensions in British society were to be resolved by peaceful and gradual change which would respect British institutions while emptying them of their class nature. However, national change went hand-in-hand with national defence. The fact that changing a class society and defending a capitalist nation-state may be contradictory did not really occur to the founders of British Socialism.

As a result, British Socialism did not disintegrate. The tensions between the Labour majority and the ILP never reached breaking point because both sides were too wary of the dangers of a split. From the point of view of the Left, the ILP felt that its chances of winning support for the anti-war movement could only lie in the Labour Party as the political representative of the working class, and it was very careful in its propaganda and activities as a result. It concentrated its campaigns on issues of civil liberties through the No-Conscription Fellowship, and the defence of trade union rights and conditions in wartime.

In maintaining the Labour alliance, the ILP was prevented from breaking with British Socialism. Its criticisms of the war remained within an ethical and a radical-democratic form. Clifford Allen, a later Chairman of the ILP, spoke at the 1915 Conference in the nostalgic terms of Ethical Socialism:

> We as Socialists are concerned with the sanctity of human life. When we are concerned about improved wages and better facilities for education, it is not merely the material things with which we are concerned, but the spiritual things. Our object is to make life expensive and valuable; war makes it cheap and of no account. As Socialists we must apply to foreign and international affairs the same philosophy as guides us in our social legislation.[49]

On the Right, the pro-war majority still recognised the need for labour to organise, politically and industrially, independently of the employers; they merely saw the co-operation of Labour in the war effort, including participation in the coalition government, as a temporary suspension of independence. It was rather like the tactics of a trade union, which had to recognise both co-operation and conflict with the employer in collective bargaining. This was put succinctly by G. J. Wardle, the chairman of the 1917 Labour Party conference;

> Labour has fought where instinct and reason taught it fighting was essential; it has bargained where it saw a reasonable chance of success; it has entered into partnership where political sagacity and national safety seemed alike to call for that method. It still remains a separate party. Partnerships can be dissolved, arguments can be revived, fighting can be resumed, each in its proper place and each at its proper time.[50]

Indeed, the Labour Party emerged from the war finally agreed on the platform of British Socialism for which Hardie and the ILP had been working for over twenty years. This platform included the foreign policy demands for a democratic peace and a League of

Nations for which the oppositionist Union of Democratic Control (UDC) had been arguing since the outbreak of war, demands which had found a theoretical ground in a major contribution to an understanding of imperialism in the anti-war writings of H.N. Brailsford.

Brailsford

H. N. Brailsford (1873–1958) had been born into a middle-class family of Yorkshire Methodists. After a university education at Glasgow, his youthful rebellion against the Methodism and Liberalism of his parents had led him to the ILP, which he joined in 1907. Influenced by the anti-imperialist writings of J.A. Hobson, he wrote articles on foreign and imperial affairs for various journals. His *War of Steel and Gold* (1914) became a textbook for many on the Left, influencing MacDonald, Snowden (and President Wilson) in their attempts to formulate a new foreign policy.

Brailsford argued that the insecurities and strategic shuffling for power and influence in pre-war Europe were merely symptoms of a much deeper economic malaise. The growing crisis was not really over the vanity of the Kaiser or national feelings of inferiority, but the growing power of financial capitalists. The panics and fears

> are the psychological irrelevancies of the process. The tangible realities at stake are measurable, and they turn out to be nothing but certain opportunities for expansion valued by the restless finance of one power or another.[51]

The magnates of high finance, pursuing their selfish goals of profit through usury, were the real reason why workers were being mobilised to fight one another. Diplomacy was no longer in the hands of the old ruling order, but had become the means whereby these magnates fought over the share-out of the world. Brailsford drew a picture of

> the vast aggregations of modern capital in oil trusts, steel trusts and money trusts.... Wherever rival combinations of capital competing, as British and American oil companies compete in Central America, the reaction will be felt in the relations of their governments. The struggle for the balance of power is in effect a struggle to map out these exclusive areas of financial penetration.[52]

It was a picture very similar to the one drawn by Lenin in his *Imperialism* (1916). Like Lenin, Brailsford pointed to the economic nature of the war, specifically the new power of finance capital. Moreover Brailsford, like Lenin, pointed to the cause of the new imperialism in the export of capital as a means of escaping a crisis of falling profitability and overproduction of capital. Brailsford argued that 'the fundamental fact is the rapid accumulation of surplus capital. It grows in the hands of trust magnates, bankers and ground landlords more rapidly than the demand for it at home.'[53] The resulting slump had been avoided by the export of that capital, but the dangers of war had been intensified by the resulting imperialism.

However, unlike Lenin, Brailsford did not call for the defeat of his own imperialist government. Instead, he joined the UDC, arguing that only an end to secret diplomacy and a democratic control of foreign policy could avoid such wars. To Brailsford, the problem of men who have reached a humane vision of international relations is to bring out some organic changes in the machinery which governs the action of the Powers abroad. A system of free trade, and a European League to carry on foreign policy openly and pacifically, were Brailsford's prescriptions for an international outlook suitable to British Socialism. His arguments became the basis of a foreign policy agreed to by Left and Right, as demonstrated in their adoption in a joint Labour–TUC statement of war aims in December 1917, drafted by MacDonald. This statement was almost indistinguishable from the programme which the UDC had been preaching since the beginning of the war. It was a foreign policy well suited to the ethical aspects of British Socialism.

The divergence of political conclusions between Brailsford and Lenin indicates the reason why Right and Left in the Labour Party maintained their precarious unity. It is a signal of the profound differences separating the Left of British Socialism from revolutionary Marxism in economic analysis.

For Brailsford, imperialism was a militarist *policy* carried on for the benefit of armaments manufacturers and other capitalists. There was nothing inevitable about it, and it could be cured by the existing State – this underlined 'the importance of securing first of all that diplomacy shall control finance, and secondly that public opinion shall control diplomacy'.[54] For Lenin, however, imperialism was not a policy carried on by individual capitalists, to be overcome by a different policy of regulating these capitalists. It was a particular phase of capital accumulation, whereby the crisis of profitability temporarily resolved by the export of capital reasserted itself in a struggle over the world's resources and territory. This struggle was inevitable because it was due to capital rather than merely capitalists.

Where Lenin saw war as the only means whereby capital's tensions could ultimately express themselves, Brailsford took up the cry of Hobson that crisis and war could only be avoided by the redistribution of wealth:

> Had a little more of the profits of a trade 'boom' gone to labour, and a little less to capital, it is manifest that labour would have had more money to spend, and the new surplus capital...might have been employed in meeting this new demand.[55]

The belief that capitalists, rather than capital, were to blame for the fighting, entailing as it did the call for the redistribution of wealth and a new morality in foreign policy, helped to cement the new consensus which emerged between Right and Left at the end of the war.

The war had transformed British society, forcing the State to organise on the lines of a wartime collectivism which delighted the Fabians. The disintegration of the Liberal Party into the supporters of Asquith and Lloyd George, together with the entry of Labour ministers into a coalition government, had pushed the Labour Party into the forefront of British politics. Its status as a small pre-war pressure group had been transformed by the end of the war into the dizzy position of a potential government. To meet its changed role, the Labour Party adopted a new constitution in February 1918, by which it became a much more centralised party with individual membership through constituency parties. A socialist goal was adopted as the aim of the party (the famous 'Clause IV'), while the unions were given even greater power over the National Executive Committee.

Together with *Labour and the New Social Order*, the 1918 constitution linked labourism with British Socialism as complementary and interdependent sets of ideas. It was fitting that it should be mainly the work of the Fabian leader, Sidney Webb, leading one later critic to describe the proposals as 'a Fabian blueprint for a more advanced, more regulated form of capitalism'.[56] It expressed the advance of wartime collectivism, which was lauded by the Fabians as a major step towards state socialism. Labour's calls in 1918 for a capital levy on the idle rich, an extended role for public ownership, and a democratic peace without annexations appealed to the Left as much as to the Right.

In 1918, the ideas of British Socialism – emerging over three decades in the forms of Labour Marxism, Fabianism and Ethical Socialism – finally cohered into an integral whole. They were a *supplement* to, not a replacement of, the labourism of the trade union movement, whose dominance was now assured in its control of the conference and the NEC.

4 R. H. Tawney and the Philosophy of British Socialism

With the adoption of a new constitution in 1918, the Labour Party had an official ideology as well as a new organisational structure. The ideology may have been extremely vague – a commitment to common ownership was intended to be all things to all people – but in the final analysis the old ILP strategy had proved successful. The Labour Party was now committed to socialism.

The formation of British Socialism had been a long process, beginning before the Labour Party had even been born. The Labour Marxists had asserted the need of the trade union movement to break politically from the class enemy; the Fabians had provided an intellectual answer to the revolutionary nature of Marx's thinking, asserting the possibility of peaceful transformation; and the Ethical Socialists had provided a communitarian morality as a guiding light for the new faith. British Socialism had finally emerged in the first decades of the new century, hammered into shape by Hardie, Snowden and MacDonald, its contours bounded by the labourist assumptions of a trade union movement which was the new party's financial lifeblood.

It was to be R. H. Tawney who was to provide a *philosophy* for British Socialism, providing its various strands with a rational and coherent vision of society. His contribution was universally acknowledged, but has been subject to such wide interpretations that both Shirley Williams and Tony Benn could claim him as their intellectual ancestor. The difficulty of categorising him politically was underlined by his own political shifts; from an endorsement of a radical Guild Socialism in 1921 through his authorship of the gradualist *Labour and the Nation* in 1928, his savage attacks on gradualism in the 1930s to his endorsement of revisionism in the 1950s.[1] His major contribution to political thought is recognised, but the nature of this contribution appears to be ambiguous.[2]

However, Tawney's importance lies in his ability to propose a malleable yet coherent socialist philosophy which transcends any particular political situation. In this sense, his mature political thought never *really* changed. His attack on gradualism in the 1930s was always radically distinct from the near-Marxism of Laski and Cripps[3] – a mere change of tactics to bring his socialist philosophy of fellowship into practice much more effectively – and could be dropped as easily as his earlier advocacy of Guild Socialism and gradualism. As Tawney himself wrote, in relation to the British labour movement, 'the essence of a movement is not to be understood merely by an analysis of its constitution and programme...[but] of what, for lack of a better phrase, I will call its social philosophy'.[4] It was to be the elaboration of this philosophy for which British Socialism was to owe Tawney such a debt.

TAWNEY

R. H. Tawney (1880–1962) was born into an upper middle-class family in imperial India, and was educated at Rugby and Oxford. Influenced by the social Christianity of William Booth, he went to Toynbee Hall after his graduation in 1903, and worked there among the poor of East London. His sense of outrage at the poverty and homelessness around him led him to join the Fabians and the ILP. He became particularly identified with the Workers Educational Association (WEA), committing himself to teaching those who had long been rejected and forgotten by the British educational system. He sought to give the WEA a more political tinge, and came to see education as being the essential element in bringing about a socialist society.

On the outbreak of war in 1914, Tawney enlisted in the army, consciously rejecting both pacifism and jingoism. He fought because he identified Prussia with tyranny, and Britain – even a socially blighted and divided Britain – with democracy. His experience of the full horrors of the battle of the Somme, in which he was wounded, was to be brilliantly described in his essay, 'The Attack',[5] but did not shake his national commitment. He was one of those who wrote an appeal to strikers at home not to damage the national cause as symbolised by the fighting soldier in the trenches, and constantly stressed the need for all classes to subordinate their old prejudices in the interests of the war effort.

After the war, Tawney was one of Labour's representatives on the Sankey Commission of 1919, where he made an unheeded call for nationalisation as the solution to the troubles of the coal industry. Thereafter, despite a deep interest in the agrarian situation in China

and his continued commitment to the cause of workingclass education, Tawney's main work was academic. As an economic historian,
he wrote the much-praised *Religion and the Rise of Capitalism* (1926),
where he bemoaned the division between commerce and social morality brought about by the Reformation, leading as it did to the
subordination of Christian teaching to the pursuit of material wealth.
To Tawney, 'compromise is as impossible between the Church of
Christ and the idolatry of wealth, which is the practical religion
of capitalist societies, as it was between the Church and State idolatry
of the Roman Empire'.[6]

It was a moral philosophy which he had painfully evolved just
before the Great War. It was in his diaries[7] that he expressed his
horror at the vulgar materialism and insensitivity towards humanity
which characterised capitalist society. He rejected the crude belief that
the abolition of poverty would make men any happier, and focused
on moral justice rather than any mere amount of wealth as the aim of
socialism. To Tawney, socialism was the social expression of a Christian morality. He wrote that

> in order to believe in human equality it is necessary to believe in
> God. It is only when one contemplates the infinitely great that
> human differences appear so infinitely small as to be negligeable
> [*sic*].... What is wrong with the modern world is that having ceased
> to believe in the greatness of God, and therefore the infinite small-
> ness (or greatness – the same thing!) of *man*, it has to invent or
> emphasize distinctions between men.[8]

Tawney was not unaware of the terrors of the material world and the
deprivation caused by the absence of wealth – far from it – but he was
convinced that such terrors were made by men who had forgotten God.

It was this moral philosophy which received full expression in his
widely acclaimed book, *The Acquisitive Society* (1920). Tawney was
particularly influenced by Guild Socialism at this point, but that was
merely a convenient form in which the substance of his moral philosophy could be expressed. He saw poverty as a symptom and consequence of the much more profound disorder in our social values.

Tawney traced this disorder to the formation of capitalism, when
individual rights were abstracted from any reference to the function
played in society by the individual. This emphasis on rights, divorced
from any social purpose, was aided by the decline of organised
religion. The ritual of the Church was retained,

but what was familiar, and human, and lovable – what was Christian in Christianity had largely disappeared. God had been thrust into the frigid altitudes of infinite space. There was a limited monarchy in Heaven, as well as upon earth.[9]

The very keystone of society had vanished, with the consequence that the eighteenth century Enlightenment brought about a new set of material privileges, hidden behind their abstract categories of property and individual rights. A conflict between individual rights and social functions was created, which was becoming open for all to see as private and public interests began to clash.

In capitalism, argued Tawney, the primary motive and criterion of industry was not the service of the community, but individual gain and self-interest. 'Such societies may be called Acquisitive Societies because their whole tendency and interest and preoccupation is to promote the acquisition of wealth.'[10] They invite people to use their skill and energy without any regard to fundamental principles or morality. To the strong, they give unrestrained freedom to use others as mere instruments of self-advancement; to the weak, they give the hope that one day they may be as ruthless and powerful as the strong. Moral principles and love of humanity dissolve into expedient attempts at material gain.

> Under the impulse of such ideas men do not become religious or wise or artistic; for religion and wisdom and art imply the acceptance of limitations. But they become powerful and rich. They inherit the earth and change the face of nature, if they do not possess their own souls.[11]

This powerful criticism of capitalist morality becomes the philosophical basis of Tawney's acceptance of Fabian economics. The divorce of gains from service, or rewards from functions, leads to a class division between usurers who contribute nothing and the industrious who contribute all. The usurers have persuaded people that they are to be admired and applauded, as though they were the source of wealth; the labourers are regarded with contempt because their function is seen as unimportant. Wealth is the basis of esteem, and work of contempt. In this way, social life is turned from an organic community into an arena of social antagonisms.

Tawney calls instead for a 'functional' society, based on the performance of duties rather than the maintenance of rights. In giving social purpose precedence over individual gain, society must above all re-arrange its values to preach a social Christianity of duties and obligations to society, rather than a stress on rights against society. Such a society would be based on union and co-operation, not division and mutual antagonism. Dignity and esteem would be given to labour, whose purpose would be to provide the material foundations for the good life, while usury would be abolished.

This view differentiated Tawney's approach from the Labour Marxists. It was not private property which was wrong, but the functionless property of the usurer. Thus, he called on socialists to discriminate between the different kinds of property and employer. He argued that

> functionless property is the greatest enemy of legitimate property itself. It is the parasite which kills the organism that produced it.... When property for acquisition or power and property for service or for use jostle each other freely in the market ... the latter tends normally to be absorbed by the former, because it has less resisting power.[12]

To Tawney, property could be morally healthy, but only when it was used for the community rather than for the privileged class of idlers and parasites.

This emphasis on dignity and Christian values, central to Tawney's thought before he became a Guild Socialist, remained after his Guild ideas had fallen away. A social Christianity was the core of his social philosophy, in whatever political guise it presented itself. It enabled him to expand the horizons of British Socialist thought in his seminal work, *Equality* (1931).

This was a ferocious attack on the caste system in British society. The upper classes continually denounced class struggles as damaging to national unity and prosperity, yet they conducted them all the time. They saw it as quite natural that their children could enjoy a serious education, and that employers could control the lives of thousands of families by their right to dismiss workers without appeal. The enormous inequalities in society – of incomes, security, culture and health – were seen as just and inevitable, not as grotesque and barbarous.

However, Tawney did not believe that equality would come about simply through a redistribution of material wealth. He saw equality in very different terms from those normally seen by the labour movement. He pointed out that equality did not merely mean similarity of character or intelligence – a view regarded by Tawney as obviously untenable – but also an equality of esteem and dignity based on a common humanity. He saw a spiritual question at stake in this second, crucial definition of equality:

> men are men, social institutions – property rights, and the organization of industry, and the system of public health and education – should be planned... to emphasize and strengthen, not the class differences which divide, but the common humanity which unites them.[13]

Equality was not the same as identity because differences in education, health and background should not mean superiority or inferiority of consideration by society.

While natural endowments differ considerably, therefore, society must eliminate inequalities which have their source in its own organisation rather than in individual differences. A society which values equality would give a high degree of significance to such natural individual talents and qualities as would exist, but it would give a low degree of significance to economic and social differences between different groups. Only a socialist society could have any sense of civilisation, because only such a society could be based on dignity. 'Where the treasure is, there will the heart be also and, if men are to respect each other for what they are, they must cease to respect each other for what they own.'[14]

When capitalism sought to strip individuals of any human dignity they possessed, Tawney saw the working class as an embodiment of solidarity and social justice. He was not so romantic as to ignore the narrow concerns of material wealth which naturally preoccupied the labour movement, but he believed that questions of poverty and unemployment had to be underpinned by moral faith in a society which cares for people. As a result, Tawney stressed the inequality of power in industry itself. Power was not only political power, nor could politics be seen in isolation from the economy. In industrial societies, economic power was particularly important because of the concentration of ownership and rights in one class. Tawney called for that power to be made more equal by breaking down the rigid divisions between labour and management. The employer must recognise that the wage-earner is as much entitled as the property-owner to claim equitable consideration for his established expectations...and that workmen have precisely the same right to be satisfied that organization is efficient, and management up to date, as management has that workmen are earning their wages.[15]

However, it was the inequality of education and health which particularly concerned Tawney. In the sphere of social services, if nowhere else, it should be possible to ignore the vulgarities of social inequality existing in all other areas of our society. To educate and care for people, we must regard them as human beings, not as employers or workers, masters or servants, rich or poor.

Yet it was in this sphere that inequality was at its most criminally evident. Ill-health, incapacity and high infant mortality rates were concentrated in working-class areas, while education suffered from the hereditary curse of the privileged public school system. Children were taught their class background from an early age, both at home and at school, in the shape of overcrowded classes, lack of facilities, restricted housing space and impoverished medical care. An obsolete social tradition pampered a few children and deprived the rest. Indeed, to Tawney, the grotesque and vicious system of educational privilege and segregation 'does more than any other single cause, except capitalism itself, to perpetuate the division of the nation into classes of which one is almost unintelligible to the other'.[16]

The remedy, he argued, lay in greater collective action to end the social divisions in health and education. A state hospital service, greater care for the expectant mother, increased hospital facilities and the free medical treatment of children were among a series of social reforms proposed by Tawney as immediate measures to improve the health of the nation. In terms of educational reform, he called for open-air nursery schools, a proper staffing and equipment for primary schools, a more nutritious system of school meals, and more state control of the public schools to ensure that they were more socially representative.

Tawney's social ideas fed his conception of the political relationship between liberty and equality. He admitted that if liberty was to be defined as individual freedom from restraint, then it was incompatible with equality, but argued that such a restricted definition would limit freedom to only a few people, while condemning the majority to unfreedom. To Tawney, liberty was the freedom to act positively for the community, as well as to resist its more tyrannical demands. In this sense, freedom for *all* meant the acceptance of certain social rules to prevent the abuse of power.

As economic power had become concentrated in monopolies and oligopolies, the lack of freedom for the many was obvious to all. The working class – the majority of the nation – was forced to work for these firms or starve. As a result of this servitude, with one person's livelihood placed at the mercy of another, any material wealth earned by the worker was at the expense of his freedom. To Tawney,

> society is divided, in its economic and social relations, into classes which are ends and classes which are instruments. Like property, with which in the past it has been closely connected, liberty becomes the privilege of a class, not the possession of a nation.[17]

He always saw freedom in relation to social power, and consequently argued that liberty must be seen in an economic as well as a political sense. In this way, with the freedom of the economically weak taken into account, there would be no incompatibility between liberty and equality.

THE LIMITS OF BRITISH SOCIALISM

Tawney's philosophical elaboration of British Socialism provided a morality which was to remain a constant as an ideal in the Labour Party's political thought. It is difficult for any socialist to disagree with his revulsion at the acquisitive motive which governs our social life, dividing people from one another and stunting their creative initiative. His view of the dignity and respect that must be accorded to the individual (couched though it was in terms of his Christian faith) was ignored by Communists at a catastrophic expense, and cannot fail to strike a chord in the heart of anyone who feels disgust at the anti-humanist obsession with creating material wealth at all costs which lies at the heart of our society.

However, Tawney's moral philosophy failed to advance beyond the fundamental weakness of British Socialism – its lack of any practical proposals to realistically create the social basis of co-operation on which any social advances could be *permanently* based. The economic crisis which destroyed the Labour government in 1931 was to brutally illustrate this, making a mockery as it did of the proposals for social reform written by Tawney for that government. The stable economic prosperity on which such reforms depended was dissipated by the slump in the inter-war market economy, and Tawney had no practical proposals to take the teeth out of that crisis. His calls for love and dignity were mere empty words in the face of the mass unemployment and social misery which engulfed large parts of Britain and Europe in the thirties.

Tawney's Christian approach to sin and the good life allowed him to resist the vulgar Marxist standpoint which related morality to the economy, but his concentration on an acquisitive morality also led him to ignore the economic dynamics of accumulation which determined the revenue against which social reform could be financed. The trade cycle of boom and slump which made a mockery of the hopes expressed in *Labour and the Nation* found only a moral response when a social and economic response was needed as a defence against the wretched conditions to which large numbers of people were reduced. However, such a response depended upon an analysis of the dynamics of a capitalist market economy which the neo-Classical economic theory then prevalent was failing to provide.

Tawney's importance in the realm of political thought, and his contribution to the Labour Party, cannot be overestimated. His call for specific reforms in health and education were important in laying the basis of Labour's plans for a welfare state, while his criticisms of acquisitive morality were an important intellectual and emotional basis for many future politicians who were committed to social reform. However, the reforms in the social services which were eventually to be put into effect by the 1945 Labour government took place within the confines of the acquisitive society condemned by Tawney. The social advances made by the Labour Party were not to be as permanent as many believed, and were eventually to be eroded by the political consequences of a new economic crisis. The absence of any realistic measures to create the social basis of a dignified society were to prove decisive to the hopes of Tawney, and of British Socialism.

Part III

The Formation of Corporate Socialism

Introduction to Part III

The political ideas of British Socialism, accepted by the Labour Party in its 1918 constitution, served as an adequate ethic to unite the overwhelming majority of the organised labour movement. This was particularly important at a time when the example of triumphant Bolshevism in Russia was disrupting European Socialism, dividing it into reformist and revolutionary strands. In Britain, the appeal of the Third International had a very limited impact, failing to detach the ILP or the majority of the shop stewards' movement from their commitment to the Labour Party. Under leaders like Ramsay Mac-Donald and the stolid trade unionist Arthur Henderson, the Labour Party emerged from the Great War as a mass party with a large degree of working-class support. In the 1920s it became the official opposition, forming two minority governments under MacDonald.

However, as the new opportunities forced Labour to see itself as a party of government, it was to become increasingly clear that the ethic of British Socialism was totally unsuited to the demands of a complex economy beset by slump and heavy unemployment. The practical tasks of changing society in accordance with their socialist ethic proved too much for Labour, which was overwhelmed by the world economic crisis in 1931. By the 1930s it had become obvious to the Labour leadership that British Socialism had to be supplemented by a more relevant political theory if it were to reshape society in the interests of the labour movement.

The relationship between ideas and government becomes particularly important to grasp at this point. Capitalism as an efficient method of production, even in its imperialist phase, was manifestly a failure after the onset of world depression at the beginning of the 1930s. There was a desperate need for a drastic reorganisation if a vicious circle of low productivity and general unemployment was to be broken. In the circumstances, the State stood as the only force capable of intervening to restructure capital and overcome the crisis of profitability which beset it. This was done in very different ways in different countries, but a common factor was the corporate form into which the State moulded society. However unequal they may be in terms of prestige and social power, organised business and organised labour were brought into the discussions and the decisions taken on political and economic issues. In Germany and Italy, corporatism was

82

ruthlessly imposed by Fascism, so that labour's participation in industry and society was a hollow formality; in the United States, labour was encouraged to organise by a Democratic administration which had only loose connections with the unions; but in Britain it was to be the Labour Party, the party of a well-organised and independent trade union movement free of state control, which was to champion the corporate solution to the crisis of capitalism.

The formation of Corporate Socialism, like that of British Social-ism, was an intellectual dynamic related to social and political events between the wars. Its origins lay in two challenges to labourism from the Left and the Right. The revolutionary challenge of Syndicalism was incorporated into labourism by the Guild Socialist ideas of G. D. H. Cole, which then became translated into corporate terms. This stood in sharp contrast to the fate of Syndicalism in Italy, serving as it did there as the ideological source of a fascist corporat-ism. At the same time, the Liberal Party challenged labourism from the Right in its espousal of state intervention and welfare expressed by Beveridge and Keynes. This challenge was incorporated into labourism by Labour Keynesians like Ernest Bevin and Hugh Dalton. The final result, emerging in a series of debates in the 1930s, was a Corporate Socialism which gave a more precise form to the vague ethic of British Socialism. This new form of socialist political thought, eventually accepted by both Left and Right in the Labour Party, was to refashion British society in the 1940s.

5 The Syndicalist Challenge

The mass strike movement which shook Britain in the period immediately preceding the Great War alerted many on the British Left to
the new ideas of Syndicalism which had been recently formulated on
the Continent and in the United States. At a time when the Labour
Party seemed hopelessly compromised by parliamentary politics, and
when the trade union leaders were safely shielded from the concerns
of their members by a comfortable bureaucracy, a new Left began to
look to the direct action and spontaneous democracy of the working
class at the point of production, the factory. In doing so, they
presented the greatest challenge to labourism since Marx.

The social and economic circumstances of Britain at that time
favoured the importation of a foreign ideology like Syndicalism onto
British soil. The export of capital which characterised the economic
nature of British imperialism had averted a crisis of profitability by
the turn of the century, but the low yields on capital invested in
British industry at home and the accompanying stagnant productivity
led to a fall in real wages under the impact of inflation. There was still
an aristocracy of skilled labour, where the skilled worker's earnings
might be three times those of the unskilled worker, but his status and
relative privileges were increasingly threatened by mechanisation and
new technology at the turn of the century. These developments undermined the traditional distinctions between the craft unions of skilled
artisans and the general unions of the unskilled which had been so
marked in the British labour movement up to that time. The new
trends were intensified by the powerful new employers' organisations,
made possible by the emergence of cartels and oligopolies in certain
sectors of British industry. The new, centralised power of the employers meant that the old craft forms of workers' organisations were
becoming obsolete and vulnerable, and seemed to call for unity and
centralisation on the workers' side.

At the same time, the long delays in wage settlements caused by the
increasingly professional negotiations, carried on behind closed
doors, led to a disillusionment with centralised, national bargaining
and a sense of alienation from the union leaders. Many workers
looked to their own localised power as a far more effective deterrent
to the demands of the employer than their own national union.
The comparatively low levels of unemployment throughout the

Edwardian era placed workers in a powerful position to obtain concessions from the employers if they were willing to fight for them, strengthening the militant belief in direct action at the local level. The demands for a more powerful and united workers' movement on the one hand and the distrust of a union bureaucracy on the other, were answered by the Syndicalist calls for industrial unionism and direct democracy.

It was not any theoretical challenge which alarmed the rulers of Britain in the Edwardian era, but the violent forms of industrial action in which Syndicalists played a leading role. A fierce strike in the Cambrian Combine coalfields of South Wales in the autumn of 1910 led to rioting and the use of troops as the state, threatened by what it regarded as potential insurrection, rallied to the side of the employers. A mass strike wave in 1911 swept the country's docks and halted its railway system, leading to a widespread deployment of troops and police against mass picketing and to the deaths of strikers in Liverpool and Llanelli. The intense resentment felt by the strikers against both the state and the employers, together with the breakdown of official union leadership, increased the popularity of Syndicalist militants like Tom Mann. The failure of a national strike of miners in early 1912 and the defeat of the London Transport Workers' strike later that summer was a temporary setback, but by 1914, when a Triple Alliance of rail, coalminers' and dockers' unions was formed, trade union membership had nearly doubled from two and a half million four years earlier to over four million.[1]

However, it was the theoretical challenge posed by Syndicalism which was to be more important in the long run for the Labour Party. As such, it has often presented a problem of interpretation, leading one historian to write that 'despite the "ism" which lends it so theoretical an air, it was originally the name given to a movement rather than a theory'. There was definitely a *theory* of Syndicalism, but it often seemed more like a militant practice of class war than a conception of a new society. Moreover, its inchoate nature meant that Syndicalism could take a variety of political forms. Anarchist theoreticians like Fernand Pelloutier and Arturo Labriola elaborated Anarcho-Syndicalism, and Anarchists even temporarily won control of the French union federation, the CGT;[2] Industrial Unionists like 'Big Bill' Haywood of the American IWW (Industrial Workers of the World) saw industrial action by one big union as perfectly compatible with membership of the moderate Socialist Party of America;[3] and some Syndicalists in France and Italy saw nothing wrong with collaboration with ultra nationalist movements like the Italian nationalists or *Action Française*. Syndicalism was nothing if not versatile.

However, the fact that Syndicalism was capable of adapting itself to a range of political ideas from Anarchism to Fascism should not disguise its nature as a positive view of a new society. The Anarchist, Pelloutier, first put forward the idea that the unions were not merely instruments of class struggle but were also the nuclei of a collectivist, stateless society. In doing so, he pointed to the fundamentally anti-parliamentary nature of Syndicalism, which saw the political world as a hollow form which disguised the real decisions taken in the world of the factory.

Daniel De Leon (1852–1914) had been converted to socialism by the American Utopian Edward Bellamy. Shortly after joining the American Socialist Labour Party (SLP) in 1890, he became its leader, ruling it with a stern and autocratic discipline. His views were based on an uncompromising rejection of reformism in all its manifestations. The non-socialist trade union leaders were denounced as 'labour fakers' and 'the labour lieutenants of capital' while the political leaders of the working class, who sought to emancipate it from above, would inevitably be compromised by the parliamentary machine.

The reformist work of parliamentarian and union leaders must, according to De Leon, be replaced by the direct action of unions based on industry rather than craft. These industrial unions, transcending obsolete craft divisions, would eventually call a general lockout of the capitalists, peacefully taking over their industries and thereby abolishing wage labour. In the new Socialist Republic, the bourgeois institutions of representative democracy would be replaced by proletarian institutions of direct democracy. Instead of geographical constituencies, illogical in that they did not express economic realities, there would be the more meaningful industrial constituencies of a workers' democracy. This did not, however, rule out political action – De Leon believed that a strong and disciplined party was essential as an agency of propaganda (a belief which caused a major schism in the IWW).

The ideas of De Leon were imported directly into Great Britain by the Irish revolutionary, James Connolly, together with some of his Scottish allies on the Left of the British SDF. Connolly (1868–1916) had been born in Edinburgh to Irish parents who had been forced by economic necessities to emigrate. He educated himself while in conditions of extreme poverty and, after a few years in the army, became active in the early 1890s in the Scottish Socialist Federation (then the Scottish variant of the SDF). The impossibility of providing for his wife and children forced him to move between Britain, Ireland and the United States, where he was able to keep in touch with the most advanced socialist ideas. Shortly after establishing the Irish Socialist Republican Party in 1896, Connolly seized on De Leon's pamphlets as an uncompromising attack on reformism. His advocacy of De Leonism among his friends in Scotland, dissatisfied as they were with the SDF's opportunism and Hyndman's anti-semitism, led in 1903 to the establishment of the Socialist Labour Party in Britain. The SLP was to be the main exponent of De Leon's ideas and Connolly wrote a series of articles for their paper, *The Socialist*, in which he expounded the theory of Industrial Unionism. In terms of political activity, Connolly was in the USA in 1903–10, working as an organiser for the IWW and the American SLP, and on his return to Ireland was instrumental in organising the Irish Citizens Army, the first Red Army according to Lenin. His execution by the British after the abortive Easter Rising in Dublin in 1916 made him a martyr to the Irish Republican and socialist cause.

Connolly's own interpretation of Industrial Unionism, propagated in Britain by the SLP, was the forerunner of an attempt to create a Syndicalist movement in Britain after 1910. This movement, centred in groups like the Industrial Syndicalist Education League, and expressed in the Labour paper, the *Daily Herald*, was as divided as its European and American counterparts, with both Anarchist and apolitical wings, but it looked to Tom Mann as its principal spokesman. Mann, as may be recalled, had been one of the Labour Marxists in the ILP before he left for Australia in 1901. While he had accepted parliamentary activity, his main interest had been in organising the unskilled into militant unions. This favourably disposed him to the Syndicalist ideas of Industrial Unionism growing in Australia, where an IWW was set up in emulation of the Americans. When Mann returned to Britain in 1910, he brought the fame and experience needed to put Syndicalism on the map of the British Left. Influenced by Connolly, E. J. Allen (who wrote *Revolutionary Unionism* in 1909, denouncing all political activity), and by the French CGT, Mann was instrumental in organising the ISEL (Industrial Syndicalist Education League) in 1910. He took a leading part in the strike wave that followed, sitting on the unofficial committee which ran the 1911 dockers' strike in Liverpool, and was arrested during the 1912 miners' strike for calling on soldiers not to shoot their fellow workers. His tireless advocacy of Industrial Unionism, through mass meetings and through his paper *The Industrial Syndicalist*, made him the foremost exponent of Syndicalism in Britain.

THE NATURE OF SYNDICALISM

Marx's challenge to labourism had been considerably watered down by his British exponents until, diluted of its revolutionary nature, it had become a respected strand on the Left of the Labour Party's thought. In the case of De Leon and the Syndicalists, their British disciples had no need to water down the militancy of the doctrines to suit the conditions of the trade union movement. Indeed, while Syndicalism never won over the majority of British trade unionists, it fitted the realities of an Edwardian Britain in which the violence of industrial strife increased distrust of a respectable labour leadership.

Syndicalism thus presented a real challenge to labourism in Britain. Indeed, in its destructive aspects – its prescriptions for combating the strength of the employing class – it was generally incompatible with labourism as it had developed during the previous century. This was due to its clear demands for the expropriation of capital and the abolition of the system of wage-labour. As the British SLP put it in their manifesto in 1906,

> We call upon the workers to organise themselves, not in trade unions based upon the capitalist principles and trade sectionalism, but in industrial unions recognising the unity and solidarity of the working class and the establishment of socialism as their avowed aim.[4]

As such, the Labour Party was attacked as a political Babel, with no clear aim except the protection of the salaries of those union bureaucrats who supported them.

This uncompromising stance lay behind the rejection by all Syndicalists of the 'Servile State', as the modern state was described by Hilaire Belloc. Their militant opposition to the state socialism of the Labour Party lay in the Syndicalist belief that the mass of the working class must directly and actively participate in its own emancipation. Against this revolutionary conception of direct democracy, Labour's state socialism meant a body of representatives in Parliament who could not be controlled by the workers. Tom Mann pointed out that this political elitism would be extended to the industrial sphere, perpetuating the autocratic despotism of the employer – '*The Industrial Syndicalist* declares that to run industry through Parliament, i.e. by State machinery would be even more mischievous to the working class than the existing method, for it would assuredly mean that the capitalist class would, through Government departments, exercise over natural forces, and over the workers, a domination even more rigid than is the case today.'[5]

It was not so much a protest against private ownership of the means of production as it was a libertarian rejection of industrial autocracy. The Syndicalists inferred that political democracy was a hypocritical sham which concealed the social dictatorship exercised by capital in the industrial life of capitalist countries. Where the Fabians saw the growth of state intervention in the economy as a sign of the capitalists being forced to bow to the necessity of socialism, the Syndicalists argued that state intervention was merely another sign that the capitalists needed the coercive power of the state to support them in the struggle with the workers.

Where British Socialism concentrated on political means to effect social change, Syndicalists argued that the mere right to vote was of no protection to workers unless they developed a strong economic organisation to protect them. It was in the economic struggle over wages and working conditions in which the real decisions would be taken, because it was in the factories that real power lay. To Mann, the Labour Party's reliance on Parliament ignored this basic fact of class society. Parliament was historically a bourgeois institution:

> it was not brought into existence to enable the working class to obtain ownership and mastery over the means of production. Parliament was brought into existence by the ruling class to have more effective means of dominating and subjugating the working class.[6]

As a result, any parliamentary action was subsidiary to the real struggle, industrial in its nature. Until the workers awoke to this fact of their economic oppression, then any political changes would affect only the shadow of reality, not its substance. To Mann and the other Syndicalists

> there is no possibility of achieving economic freedom unless the workers themselves are conscious that what they suffer from, as a class, is economic subjugation. Workers must organize at the point of production.[7]

This faith in the primarily industrial nature of class struggles was closely linked in Syndicalist eyes with an all-out attack upon a major institution of labourism – the trade union bureaucracy. If it was true that the industrial vote, the decision on whether or not to take strike action against the employer, was far more important for the worker than any political vote could be, then the democratic nature of the workers' industrial organisation became fundamental. The tendency of the union leaders to attempt to substitute negotiation for conflict was an indication to the Syndicalists of their class treachery, and was to be explained by the comfortable bureaucratic niche which they had made for themselves in the union. They were seen as the worst sort of parasite, who had risen on the backs of their fellow workers only to turn on the very people who had placed their trust in them. To the Syndicalists, the unions belonged to the rank and file, whose direct involvement in class war purged the tendencies to corruption present in the union leadership. The spontaneous and direct democracy of the unions was therefore essential – as Mann put it, 'The engines of war to fight the workers' battle to overthrow the capitalist class, and to raise the general standard of life while so doing, must be of the workers' own making. The unions are the workers' own.'[8]

This theme was taken up by a group of South Wales miners, organized in an Unofficial Reform Committee of their union, whose *The Miners' Next Step* was published in November 1911. Prominent in this group was Noah Ablett (1883–1935), who had been converted to Marxism at Ruskin College, which he attended after suffering a pit accident. Ablett then organised educational classes in which he taught the new ideas of Industrial Unionism, and successfully fought the moderate leadership of the South Wales miners' union (interestingly, he saw no contradiction between such views and his membership of the ILP). In *The Miners' Next Step*, Ablett and his fellow authors skilfully pointed to the plenary powers over the rank and file which gave the union leaders special privileges among their class. These privileges gave the union leader 'an interest – a vested interest – in stopping progress. They have therefore in some things an antagonism of interests with the rank and file.'[9] Their very jobs as leaders of *trade* unions, representing particular crafts, were challenged when faced with the demands for *industrial* unionism.

Of course, Ablett recognised that leadership had its beneficial qualities, especially efficiency and order, but in the end it implied power, and power held by a leader, no matter how representative, would inevitably lead to corruption. The workers would be as corrupted as the leadership:

> this power of initiative, this sense of responsibility, the self-respect which comes from convinced manhood, is taken from the men and consolidated in the leader. The sum of *their* initiative, *their* responsibility, *their* self-respect, become his.[10]

Against this, the Unofficial Reform Committee proposed a new democratic constitution for their union to place their leaders under the direct control of the rank and file, and to end the sectional character of the workforce in the mining industry.

This attack on the union leadership was not necessarily incompatible with labourism, or even with electoral success in the labour movement (as demonstrated by Ablett's election to the Executive of the South Wales Miners Federation), but many Syndicalists took the anti-bureaucratic stance to the point of breaking with the existing union structure and setting up new revolutionary unions. The SLP put this clearly when, greeting the formation of the American IWW, it called for the emulation of such 'dual unionism' in Britain:

> When we take up the positive work of organizing the workers in the economic field in a clean revolutionary union, those workers upon whom our exposure of and attack on pure-and-simpledom convince, will pass over from their [the established unions'] ranks to ours.[11]

In pursuit of this, the SLP totally isolated themselves from the labour movement (outside a small base in Glasgow), while the ISEL split apart over the question in 1913. Rejecting 'dual unionism' as totally irrelevant to the conditions of the British labour movement, which had struggled over a century to build up the unions, Tom Mann called for the reform, not the destruction of the unions, in order to win them to a policy of class war.

SYNDICALISM AND GOVERNMENT

It is in the context of this general attack on labourism and state socialism that the Syndicalists put forward the constructive aspect of their doctrines. The formation of industrial unions would eventually lead to such intensive class conflict with the capitalists and their state that the working class could then seize control of the factories. They would do this through their industrial unions, the institutions that they had created for their defence. The unions' organisation, thoroughly democratised, would thus be 'the embryo of a working-class republic. Our national unions, local unions and other bodies will be the administrative machinery of an Industrial Commonwealth',[12] as it was put by E. J. Allen in *The Industrial Syndicalist*. In this way, the schema of historical materialism put forward by Marx appeared to approach completion. Just as the bourgeoisie had created the basis of their new society within the confines of the old feudal order, so the proletariat was creating the basis of *their* new society within the confines of the capitalist order. Whereas the bourgeois revolution had taken a political, par-liamentary form, the proletarian revolution would take an economic, industrial form.

The strategy was put at its clearest by James Connolly. The relationship between the formation of industrial unions and the con-stitution of a socialist republic was seen in pure De Leonite terms:

> In the light of this principle of industrial unionism, every fresh shop or factory organised under its banner is a fort wrenched from the control of the capitalist class and manned with soldiers of the revolution to be held by them for the workers. On the day that the political and economic forces of labour finally break with capitalist society and proclaim the Workers' Republic, these shops and factories so manned by industrial unionists will be taken charge of by the workers there employed.... Then and thus the new society will spring into existence ready equipped to perform all the useful functions of its predecessor.[13]

It was a logically impeccable scenario, but the logic disguised its unrealistic nature. The revolutionary response of the working class was seen as an automatic reaction to the development of capitalism in a monopoly form. It was much too mechanical a conception to grasp the nature of social reality. The armed power of the state which would resist what would be an industrial insurrection was almost totally disregarded,[14] while political parties and government were naïvely seen as shallow reflections of the real class struggle.

Nevertheless, it was this conception of Industrial Unionism which underlay the 'functionalist' ideas of the structure of a socialist society put forward by the Syndicalists. Marx had rejected the idea of a detailed blueprint for a new society, but the Syndicalists felt that they had grasped the outline of the future. The geographical constituencies that made up a representative democracy were no longer natural ones. They were a survival from earlier times, when the parish and the local community actually constituted the centre of popular life. In the modern industrial society created by capitalism, democracy should be based upon the factory and the workshop which had become the new focal point of the lives of most people. The unions, based on industry, would democratically control the life of the workshops and would regulate the routine of labour as determined by the needs of industry and society. Such a system would be *more* efficient than the present division between political democracy and industrial despotism. While any capitalist government which took over an industry would be forced to turn to professional experts for advice on technical questions, the industrial government of socialism would have the full expert knowledge born of experience.

This 'functional' view of government was *not* a corporate conception, however. This was because the Syndicalist distrust of union bureaucracy led to their advocacy of direct spontaneous democracy, based on the workshop. Connolly succinctly expressed the difference between the two conceptions of democracy in pointing out that 'Social democracy must proceed from the bottom upward, whereas capitalist political society is organised from above downward.'[15] The rank-and-file union member would elect representatives to the various departments of industry, which would themselves elect representatives to the industrial administration. This administration would take over the tasks allocated by capitalism to a political government. As the life of each workshop would be regulated and governed by the workshop itself, the bureaucratic tendencies of centralised government would be either avoided or placed under strict democratic accountability. In this way, the political state would be replaced by the social republic. Political activity was rejected only by a few 'pure' Syndicalists like E. J. Allen, but it was seen by all Syndicalists as a subsidiary activity of agitation and propaganda for the more important industrial work – 'the workers will be industrially organised on the economic field and, until that organisation is perfected...the Socialist Party will carry on an independent campaign of education and attack upon the political field.'[16]

SYNDICALISM AND LABOURISM

In its destructive aspects – its opposition to state socialism, union bureaucracy and representative democracy – Syndicalism was a direct challenge to the labourist ideology underlying the Labour Party's political thought. It was generally incompatible with British Socialism, and as such had nothing to offer the Labour Party as it sought a doctrine flexible enough to unite its various strands. In its *constructive* aspects, however, Syndicalism was to prove very fruitful for Labour, though its revolutionary trappings would have to be removed first. The Syndicalist proposition that the unions should have a direct role to perform in governing an industrial economy was, of course, intimately connected to their proposition that neither the state nor the capitalist corporations should have any role whatsoever in such government. As such, it was inimical to everything that the Labour Party stood for. However, if such revolutionary encumbrances could be disentangled, then an extension of labourism rather than its destruction could be envisaged.

The possibility of this lay in certain weaknesses inherent in the critique of labourism by the Syndicalists. Indeed, in many important respects, Syndicalism had much in common with the Labour Party and the trade union movement. Its commitment to the independence of the working class from the employers was certainly expressed in much more militant terms than most prominent Labour politicians were prepared to support. At a special national conference of the Mineworkers Federation in January 1911, Noah Ablett pointed to the growing unrest in the minefields and called for militant strike action against the capitalists – 'There is nothing else. There is no other way by which it is possible to beat the employers who are arrogant and insolent in regard to our demands for the minimum wage.'[17] The authors of *The Miners' Next Step* placed as their first policy recommendation for their union that 'the old policy of identity of interest between employers and ourselves be abolished, and a policy of open hostility installed.'[18] However, this militancy was by no means incompatible with labourism. The demand for independence from the employers had been a touchstone of Hodgskin's ideas, and had been made a primary element in the Labour Party's thought by the Labour Marxists and by Keir Hardie. Noah Ablett's Syndicalism did not prevent him from working within the ILP for his ideas, while a group of his Syndicalist followers (including Nye Bevan) were to be active in Labour Party politics.

Apart from this fundamental similarity, the narrow concentration on trade union activity opened up Syndicalism to its eventual absorption into the labourism of the Labour Party. Syndicalism was always marked by a dual nature. While it proclaimed its *eventual* goal as the emancipation of the proletariat through a general strike, it had as its *immediate* task the defence of workers' living standards by militant strike action. Some theorists, particularly in France, attempted to construct a scenario by which strikes over wages would become embroiled in a general revolution, but this had more to do with fantasy than it had with realistic preparations for an industrial insurrection. In practice, such strikes over wages were nothing more than that, ending in either wage-gains or in grim defeats. The Syndicalist doctrine, however revolutionary in rhetoric it might be, essentially emphasised the organisation of mass strikes for higher wages. As such, it was an industrial mirror of the ideas of parliamentary socialists in the Labour Party (and the Second International) who saw a collectivist society as the maximum goal to be achieved in the mythical future while they concentrated on the immediate tasks of social reform through parliamentary action. When Tom Mann called on British workers to emulate the French CGT, he pointed out that 'while working for their revolution, they do not neglect to do all possible to secure general betterment'.[19] Shorn of the revolutionary rhetoric, such ideas were no more than a militant extension of labourism, perfectly acceptable to the Labour Left and to trade unionists like Ernest Bevin, then seeking the amalgamation of unions into powerful corporate bodies to defend workers against the capitalists. The formation of the Transport and General Workers Union (TGWU), the future bulwark of the Labour Party, in 1922, was no more than a labourist application of the Syndicalist principles of Industrial Unionism.

Moreover, the Syndicalists' narrow concentration on the point of production not merely overlooked production outside the factory (the most glaring example being the domestic labour undertaken by women in the family), but also ignored the non-industrial areas of life. The political state was totally underestimated, with the result that Syndicalism was much more ambiguous than at first appeared. Of course, revolutionaries like Connolly and the SLP were absolutely opposed to reformist political action, but this was not a *necessary* tenet of Syndicalism. Many Syndicalists, while regarding political action as definitely secondary to industrial action, remained open to the parliamentary help which political action could give. Tom

Mann oupressed this ambiguity towards politics in *The Industrial Syndicalist*:

> Let the politicians do as much as they can, and the chances are that, once there is an economic fighting force in the country, ready to back them up by action, they will actually be able to do what now would be hopeless for them to attempt to do.[20]

This was less an attack on the Labour Party than it was a reminder that the party represented a powerful force *outside* Parliament. Keir Hardie acknowledged as much when he declared in a speech to the Commons in May 1912 that

> syndicalism is the direct outcome of the apathy and indifference of this House towards working class questions, and I rejoice at the growth of syndicalism. The more syndicalism we have outside, the quicker will be the pace at which this Chamber will move.[21]

The labourist potentialities of Syndicalism were seen in a dramatic manner at the outbreak of the Great War in 1914. The hopes of the revolutionaries throughout Europe that a general strike would greet the declarations of war crumbled in the face of the millions of enthusiastic working-class recruits to the various armies. The diverse tendencies in Syndicalism tended to splinter on the question of national defence. The very nature of Syndicalism, with its narrow concentration on wage struggles, meant that it had no consistent attitude to imperialism or war. It was possible for Syndicalists (such as Gustave Herve in France) to become fiery patriots, while others (like Connolly) saw imperialism as the enemy. It was 'Big' Bill Haywood of the American IWW who summed up the Syndicalist attitude of neutrality when he declared that

> the fight of the IWW is one of the economic field and it is not for me, a man who could not be drafted for war, to tell others that they should go to war, or tell them that they should not go to war.[22]

In Britain, the Syndicalist stress on local militancy was maintained in the Shop Stewards Movement, many of whose leaders belonged to the SLP. They continued to advocate Industrial Unionism and were, after some initial confusion, hostile to the war effort. However, it was the economic struggle over wages which they regarded as the primary

struggle, and they generally remained silent on the war. The Syndicalist nature of the Shop Stewards Movement was displayed by
J. T. Murphy, then a leading SLP militant, when he wrote that

> none of the strikes that took place during the course of the war
> were anti-war strikes. They were frequently led by men such as
> myself who wanted to stop the war, but that was not the actual
> motive. Had the question of stopping the war been put to any
> strikers meeting, it would have been overwhelmingly defeated.[23]

The stoppages had a different origin and a different motive, economic
rather than political. When the group around John Maclean, an anti-
war Marxist, tried to raise the question of the war at the Clyde
Workers Committee, he was excluded from the discussions. As James
Hinton noted, 'whatever its members might say as individuals, the
Committee itself was neither for nor against the war'.[24]

In thus ignoring the patriotic sense of national loyalty, the Syndicalists failed to confront the force which had crippled their hopes of an
industrial insurrection. The State which conducted war outside its
boundaries would demand peace within, and the Syndicalists were by
their nature a threat to this internal peace. In refusing to court
unpopularity by opposing the war, they ensured that their disruption
to the internal peace would be limited from the beginning. Their
actions also indicated that their differences with labourism, which
similarly accepted national boundaries between the working class,
were much less substantial than appeared on the surface. The Syndicalist challenge to labourism would, as a result, be integrated into the
Labour Party with a startling ease.

THE REACTION OF THE LABOUR PARTY

This similarity was not at first recognised by the Labour leaders, who
reacted to the Syndicalist threat by holding fast to the accepted ethic
of British Socialism. Keir Hardie, while welcoming the labour unrest
which went under the name of Syndicalism, expressed contempt for
Syndicalist theory. Snowden, in his *Socialism and Syndicalism* (1912),
rejected Syndicalism as hostile to authority and political action. Their
militant preaching of class war was inimical to his sense of socialism
as social harmony and order. MacDonald, while marginally less
hostile to the union unrest than Snowden, was similarly horrified by

the Syndicalist rejection of traditional parliamentary politics as defined by Victorian Liberalism.

However, the more alert representatives of British Socialism saw the need to adapt their ideas to take account of the Syndicalist challenge. This was particularly true of the Webbs, the arch-exponents of elitism and representative democracy. Their hostility to the revolutionary aspects of Syndicalism was absolute, but it was the constructive aspects of control by the producers which caught their eye. Up to the advent of Syndicalism, the Webbs had seen the trade unions merely as bodies which would negotiate wages with the employers, but the strike wave of 1910–12 forced them to see the unions in a more positive light.

In a series of articles in the *New Statesman* in 1913, the Webbs argued that democracy, or more specifically representative democracy on the parliamentary model, should be extended from the political to the industrial sphere. The citizen was not just a consumer, but a producer as well and, as such, needed to be represented in all spheres of economic life. In industry, this was to be done by workers' *participation*, by which the Webbs meant the use of the real and vivid knowledge of industry built up by the experience of the unions. 'There is no reason why the fully recognised Trade Unions should not, we do not say merely acquiesce in scientific management, but actually promote the new science.'[25] The unions, an expression of grass-roots democracy, would thus advance from their restrictive role to take their place in the rational movement of historical evolution.

However, to the Webbs, the Syndicalist emphasis on producer control to the exclusion of the consumer and the State was totally unbalanced. Syndicalists were demanding that power be concentrated in a minority of the community, thereby increasing the likelihood that unions would become conspiracies against the public interest. The Webbs argued that 'to base any governmental organisation on Associations of Producers is to negative democracy',[26] and proposed a society based on voluntary associations of consumers as well. Such consumer groups as the Co-operative Retail Societies were, in fact, superior as an instrument of democracy because, unlike trade unions, they had no vested interest to protect and no tendency to restrict membership. The State, based upon these associations, would be an extended co-operative society, supplying national services such as post, museums and libraries. In this way, 'the Socialist State, far from being a centralized and coercive bureaucracy, presents itself to us as a highly diversified and extremely numerous set of social groupings.'[27]

These proposals, elaborated in a modified form in the Webbs' *A Constitution for the Socialist Commonwealth of Great Britain* (1920),[28] are a striking foretaste of the Corporate Socialism that was eventually to emerge as Labour's political thought.They are also an indication that Syndicalism contained within it strands which could be taken out of their revolutionary context to fit a capitalist society in which political organisation needed to be supplemented by social organisation. However, it was not the Webbs who were to absorb the Syndicalist challenge into the Labour Party's thinking. They remained too commited to an elitist Fabianism to adapt themselves to the working-class appeal of the Syndicalists. It was to be G. D. H. Cole, a close sympathiser with the class war ideas of the Syndicalists, who was to blunt their revolutionary challenge and demonstrate their similarity with, and political contribution to, the Labour Party.

6 G. D. H. Cole and the Guild Socialist Response

The response of many on the Labour Left to the new syndicalist doctrines was much more sympathetic than that of MacDonald or the Fabians. Indeed, through their adaptation of syndicalist ideas to British Socialism, they were to play a major part in the evolution of the Labour Party's political thought. This particular inheritance of syndicalist theory has often been neglected by later commentators who recognise only the revolutionary aspects of Syndicalism.

The development of British Syndicalism in the direction of Communism, via the Shop Stewards Movement, would certainly explain this neglect. The Industrial Unionism preached by the SLP was given its fullest radical exposition in William Paul's *The State: Its Origins and Functions* (1917), where the libertarian analysis of the state as rooted in class society closely resembled the analysis put forward in Lenin's *State and Revolution*, published in the same year. Indeed, the similarities of the syndicalist stress on industrial self-government with the actuality of working-class rule through the *soviets* (or workers' councils) in Russia after 1917 won many syndicalists throughout Europe to the support of Bolshevik rule there. They saw Lenin as healing the split between the Marxist orthodoxy of the Second International and the revolutionary spirit of Syndicalism and Anarchism. The destruction of the substance of soviet democracy under the impact of civil war and economic collapse did not quench their belief that Bolshevism was the natural heir to syndicalist ideas, and SLP militants were an important element in the early politics of the Communist Party of Great Britain, founded in 1920–21.[1] Indeed, at the second congress of the Third International in 1920, Industrial Unionists like Jack Tanner and William Gallacher clashed with Lenin on the question of affiliation to the Labour Party,[2] although they later accepted Lenin's argument that Communists should work inside the Labour Party in order to win over Labour's mass working-class support (a policy marked by eventual failure).

However, as has been noted, Syndicalism had other aspects which were to be much more important in Labour's thinking. Its revolutionary form contained an implicit corporatist strain. This was seen most clearly in Italy, where syndicalists constituted the radical wing

100

of Mussolini's Fascist movement. Many Italian syndicalists, rejecting the stultifying effects of parliamentary democracy as the expression of a timid and materialistic bourgeoisie, found it easy to transfer their allegiance from the working class to the nation as an agent of social change. Mussolini himself was relatively uninterested in ideology, but his radical followers like Sergio Pannunzio and Filippo Corradini saw Fascism as a logical consequence of their syndicalist beliefs. The rule of a narrowly based parliament, representing only the bourgeoisie, would be replaced by the rule of economic bodies based on the realities of the social nation. To Pannunzio in 1922, 'syndicalism...is the negation of the old political conception; the negation of the parties, the affirmation of the classes and of their organisation in the corporations or syndicates'.[3] There was an intense struggle between these syndicalists and the more conservative supporters of Fascism after Mussolini came to power, but by 1925 the syndicalists had been victorious. Italy was ready, as Pannunzio put it, 'to be the first to give Europe a real living example of a national state, based on syndicates, which is the ultimate and the primary and essential spirit of Fascism'.[4] The syndical laws which established the corporate state in Italy, organising employers and unions into different economic groups, was hailed as the culmination and fulfilment of the Italian syndicalist tradition.

In Britain, this corporatist strain in Syndicalism was not to take a Fascist form. For all its rhetoric on the equality of classes within the nation, Fascist corporatism was a fundamentally anti-union movement. Their destruction of the freedom of the trade unions to collectively bargain with the employers made the corporate state an empty form, covering a basic social inequality between employer and worker without any mediation. As such, it was *absolutely* incompatible with any strain of socialism which was likely to be accepted by the Labour Party, even if its hostility to parliamentary democracy could be set on one side. However, this corporatist aspect of Syndicalism was to take a peculiarly British form through the evolution of a new type of socialist thinking in the Labour Party. The manner of this evolution was determined by one of the most subtle and complex of Labour's thinkers, G. D. H. Cole.

Cole was deeply moved by the labour unrest which swept Britain before the Great War, and he explained the popularity of syndicalist theory as an indication that Fabian collectivism had had its day. The new claim for freedom from a bureaucratic state was taking form as a demand for a greater degree of self-government than could be granted by the narrow political democracy of the ballot-box. However, Cole argued that Syndicalism was too one-sided to be a suitable doctrine to fit English conditions. It was too rooted in the small, localised trade unions which flourished in France (the US influence was always underplayed by Cole). In Britain, Syndicalism would have to adapt itself by evolving into a new theory based on national and centralized unions. In an article in *New Age* in February 1914, Cole argued that

> syndicalism can only stand by its power to adjust itself to the new situation, and to develop...a new theory grounded on the acceptance of the National Union as the necessary unit of industrial action and organisation.[5]

To point Syndicalism in the direction required, Cole drew on the theories of the English Guild Socialists and, in doing so, provided an important stepping stone in the evolution of Syndicalism from revolutionary socialism to the corporate socialism eventually accepted by the Labour Party.

THE GUILD SOCIALISTS

The theory of Guild Socialism was originally born as the intellectual fantasy of Arthur J. Penty (1875–1937), who had become an architect after working in his father's office at the age of thirteen. As such, he was appalled by the ugly utilitarianism of industrial capitalism and became a disciple of the medievalist ideas of John Ruskin and William Morris. He felt that the human race had become trapped in an industrial system which had corrupted morality and had replaced craftsmanship and imagination by the machine and repetitive drudgery. He was initially a member of the Fabian Society, but by the turn of the century he became convinced that the state socialism of the Fabians and the ILP was merely a new expression of the base evil of industrialism.

Penty advocated another solution in *The Restoration of the Gild System* (1906). He argued that it was necessary to transfer the control of industry from the hands of the financier into those of the craftsmen organised in guilds. There would be a return to the organic society of the Middle Ages, as a closed economy of handicrafts and agriculture would supersede the evil leviathan of factory production. As in the days of yore, craftsmen would serve a local market under the direction of their guilds, which would regulate the hours worked, the prices of the products, and the myriad other decisions made on grounds of profitability in a capitalist society. Competition between the guilds would take the form of quality rather than price, while politics would be transformed as the guilds became the upper house of Parliament. The thorough rejection of existing society was fully recognised by Penty, who pointed out that 'the nature of the reforms is such as to place the centre of gravity of the reform movement outside the sphere of politics'.[6]

These quaint ideas could well have passed by as a pleasant but inconsequential whimsy, if Penty had not been in close touch with A. P. Orage (1873–1934), a member of the ILP whose fascination with the irrationalist philosophy of Nietszche inclined him to consider ideas of a new morality for new men. After first meeting Penty at the Leeds Theosophical Society, Orage came under the influence of his ideas and turned the popular weekly, *New Age* (which he bought in 1907) into a political platform for Guild Socialism. Moreover, the arcadian setting of Penty's theories was removed by the most prominent of the guild theorists to be identified with the journal, S. G. Hobson.

Hobson (1870–1940), born to a Quaker background in Ulster, had written a series of articles in *New Age* between 1912 and 1914 and collected in book form as *National Guilds: An Inquiry into the Wage System and the Way Out* (1914). Hobson attempted to draw out the revolutionary nature of Guild Socialism. He rejected Penty's medievalism, arguing that it was capitalism rather than industrialism which was the enemy of human fulfilment. Under the wage system, labour was a mere commodity, valued at a price, hired and fired according to the needs of profit, and excluded from the management of industry. In the face of this, the narrowly political concerns of the Labour Party and the ILP with capturing state power were laughable – 'political emancipation leaves the worker quite as much at the final disposition of the employer as was the Greek helot'.[7] State socialism was to Hobson merely another name for state capitalism, as labour would be exploited by the state.

It was the wages system which was the cause of labour's troubles, and it would be through the abolition of the wages system that labour would find its real emancipation. This would be done by the trade unions, who must move from their present basis of negotiating wages to the control of industry. This could be done by monopolising the supply of labour to the employer, forcing him thereby to pay labour's wages to the union, which would itself divide them among the workers. In this way, the unions would be in a position to take control of industry in co-operation with the state. The unions would thus become national guilds, based on industry rather than handicrafts, and closely co-operating with other guilds to satisfy the needs of the people. The state would be the final arbiter of conflicts, as it represented the community, but generally Hobson believed that the state should totally disengage itself from economics, restricting itself to the narrowly political concerns of foreign policy, defence and law.

It was obvious that this critique of state socialism (which bore marked similarities to the syndicalist critique) would lead some Guild Socialists to a total rejection of the Labour Party. Hobson was particularly hostile, seeing the failure of the ILP to attack the wage system as a cause of its degeneration into opportunism. Indeed, according to Hobson, even if the Labour Party accepted Guild Socialism, it should be rejected as an agency of change. It was a *political* party, operating in the narrowly political sphere, and thus incapable of effecting the *economic* changes that were required. Hobson, echoing the syndicalists, argued that 'the lesson would have been learnt in due season that the socialist conquest of the industrial system is an economic and not a political operation; that economic power must precede political power'.[8]

It is understandable, then, that many commentators should see Guild Socialism as incompatible with the Labour Party's political thought. As one recent writer has put it,

> Guild Socialists well understood the nature of the British political system and were willing to argue against participation from within on the grounds that such participation must always involve the falsification of ideals and aspirations. For them the political labour movement was wrong at its core simply because it had chosen to work within the system.[9]

If Guild Socialism as a theory was restricted to the works of Penty and Hobson, this would certainly be the case. However, in taking up Guild Socialism as an English answer to Syndicalism, a group of young Fabians around G. D. H. Cole turned it from an interesting theory into a major political force with which to be reckoned. In doing so, they demonstrated the malleability of the Labour Party's political thought, and made an invaluable contribution to its development.

COLE AND GUILD SOCIALISM

G. D. H. Cole (1889–1959) was the son of an estate agent, and was educated at Balliol College, Oxford, where he developed an interest in modern poetry and in Rousseau. He was also converted to socialism by the literary writings of William Morris and joined the Fabian Society. The labour unrest of the pre-war years excited the romantic in Cole, who saw militant class conflict as giving the worker a sense of dignity and vitality of which he had been robbed by capitalism. He attempted to accommodate the syndicalist theories which were then becoming popular into the mainstream of English politics by drawing on the Guild Socialism of *New Age*. In *The World of Labour* (1913), Cole elaborated his own ideas of socialism, expanding and modifying them in books like *Self-Government in Industry* (1917) and *Guild Socialism Restated* (1920). In this task, he was aided by William Mellor (1888–1942), with whom he worked closely throughout the decade. Their frustration in the Fabian Society led them to form the National Guilds League (NGL) in 1915. They found ready ears on the Labour Left, and were to have a major impact in the next few years, influencing R. H. Tawney and Clement Attlee[10] among others.

Cole's ideas were, with some exceptions, close to Hobson's own modernist conception of a guild society. However, he gave the ideas a formidable intellectual weight and pragmatic quality which identified him as *the* theorist of Guild Socialism. Cole's grasp of political theory enabled him to link *New Age* with the participatory democracy of Rousseau and with the pluralist beliefs of J. N. Figgis, whose *Churches in the Modern State* (1913) asserted the importance of social groups in relation to the state. Cole's own fascination with the ideas of the dignity of craftsmanship put forward by William Morris and John Ruskin enabled him to link syndicalist theory with the Ethical Socialist strain in the Labour Party's thinking. Because of his intellectual grasp and ability, Cole's thought represents an important confluence of political theories, merging several different currents into one formidable political force.

The Syndicalist Influence

Rousseau and Figgis had their intellectual attractions for Cole, but it was the syndicalist assertion of workers' management of industry which held his attention. It seemed to be an urgent and concrete expression of the demand of the working class for freedom as well

as bread, clearly demonstrating the inadequacies of the Fabian call
for the abolition of poverty. The collectivists were attacking the
symptom rather than the cause, as the tyranny of the wage system
lay behind the poverty of the working class.

> What, I want to ask, is the fundamental evil in our modern society
> which we should set out to abolish? There are two possible answers
> to that question, and I am sure that very many well-meaning
> people would make the wrong one. They would answer
> POVERTY, when they ought to answer SLAVERY.[11]

It was the slavery of the wages system which destroyed freedom and
individuality in the worker, reduced men to the status of a machine
and treated human beings as a mere means to producing wealth.

Cole saw the labour unrest as a reaction against such a system, and
fully supported the syndicalist calls for a class war in society. The
strike weapon was not merely a bargaining weapon, but an assertion
of Labour's free will, without which the worker would cease to be a
human being – 'the finest thing that can be accomplished by Labour
Unrest is a heightening sense of being alive, an awakening that will
lead men from mere discontent to the positive striving for a better
life'.[12] This occasional exultation in militancy was not merely a
youthful display of aggression, however, as Cole recognised the realities of a class society which made class conflict necessary. Unlike
Ramsay MacDonald whose organic conception of society excluded
class conflict, Cole did not see strike action as selfish. He merely
pointed to the actuality of class struggle, and took his stand on
the belief that he could not be neutral in it. The two classes were not
the same as one another in terms of justice or liberty, because the
capitalist class exploited and the working class was exploited through
the wage system. Thus, Cole called for militant working-class action

> not on the grounds that it is desirable, but on the grounds that it is
> a monstrous and irrefutable fact. The class structure is established
> in our social institutions, and it is only by means of the class
> struggle that we can escape from it.[13]

This view, as can be imagined, did not gain a sympathetic ear from
the more traditional Fabians.

However, Cole was in revolt against the state socialist and collectivist traditions of the Fabian Society. He believed that the failures of

collectivism were bearing fruit in the labour unrest. Collectivism, according to Cole, had carried the anti-capitalist arguments to their logical conclusion in their call for nationalisation, but in so doing had forgotten that socialism was a human proposition as well as a business one. As a result, they had identified the ideal socialist state with the state of the present, falling into the illusion that a mere extension of the existing powers of the state's sphere of action would bring socialism. They saw nationalisation as the panacea for the problems of anarchical competition, and had failed to notice that capitalism itself had eliminated competition by means of creating an even deadlier enemy in the monopoly. By accepting the logic of collectivist socialism, capitalism had entrenched itself more firmly than ever.

The reason for the failure of collectivism, argued Cole, lay in its nature as a theory of the distribution of wealth. The relations of *production* were left untouched, so that there was a mere transfer of ownership from the capitalist to the state. In asserting redistribution, the collectivists denied the humanity of the working class, reflecting the narrow materialism of capitalist society.

> They believe that working class ideals begin and end with higher wages, with the securing of a slightly better standard of material comfort. They do not realise that the foundation of inefficiency in industry lies in the divorce of the mass of the workers from power and responsibility.[14]

To Cole, the transfer of ownership to the state was of secondary importance compared with the question of who controlled industry. His antipathy to state socialism seemed to be a return to Marx's critique of labourism as a theory of distribution which sought to maintain capital while getting rid of capitalists.

In contrast to collectivism, Syndicalism raised once again the point of view of the producers, but in a very one-sided manner. Where the collectivist totally disregarded the producer, the syndicalist totally disregarded everything but the producer. In doing so, it not merely ignored the interests of the consumer, but restricted humanity to a mere economic function. As a purely economic theory, it totally disregarded morality, culture and nationality as important elements in life. Syndicalism thus presented itself to Cole as a vague assertion of producers' power which had never been sufficiently thought through.

In affirming the value of industrial action and of the workers' natural organisation it lays down the true principle of a philosophy of labour; but in taking this doctrine to imply the denial of the state, it goes too far and is led into extravagance and perversity.[15] Cole attempted to extract the constructive aspects of Syndicalism from the narrow economism with which the theory had been presented. 'Syndicalism is strong in what it asserts and weak in what it denies.'[16] The weakness of Syndicalism lay in its economism and its denial of political democracy. However, its strength lay not only in its assertion of class war but in its positive proposals for *social* democracy. It recognised that representative democracy was meaningless if it was restricted to the narrow sphere of politics while leaving the everyday social life of people untouched.

Political and Functional Democracy

Cole accepted that 'the bare ballot-box democracy of the great State'[17] disguised social inequality and injustice, making it a parody of real democracy. The power of the press, dependent as it was for finance on the advertisements of rich capitalists, moulded public opinion into a mood hostile to the radical socialist changes needed in society. The unequal education system, by which the few were trained to rule while the many were trained to obey, extended from the industrial to the political sphere. Working people had neither the confidence, leisure-time, nor wealth to understand the society around them, making the democratic forms of government an empty structure without substance. Moreover, the voters in a parliamentary democracy have no control over their representative on issues that arise in the House of Commons, can change their representative only at infrequent intervals, and have only a limited choice of candidates from which to select. In these circumstances, representative government was in reality misrepresentative since social inequality had the effect of 'perverting and annihilating in practice the theoretical democracy of modern politics'.[18]

Cole wished to supplement political democracy with 'functional' democracy. The totality of a person cannot be represented by any other person, since each of us has many different aspects – at work, in the family, as a consumer, as a citizen – which demand different representatives. If they are to be truly represented, people must be represented through their different functional aspects so that democracy would really require each person to have not one but many votes. Only in this way could society, as a complex of associations, find a full democratic expression – 'all true and democratic represent- ation is therefore *functional* representation'.[19]

Of the many functions in society, however, Cole was particularly interested in the economic function of labour. It was in the factory, by means of the wage system, that despotism was most evident, and the Guild Socialist ideas of Penty and Hobson were to Cole the best machinery by which the producer could be represented. It was also the means by which Cole could link up the syndicalist nature of labour unrest with the traditions of Ethical Socialism so important to the Labour Party's outlook. Guild Socialism always held a fascination for Cole because of its demand for the more harmonious, organic society called for by Ruskin, Morris and Carpenter.

He always used the term 'guild' rather than 'syndicate', because of its medieval associations (though he was adamant that there could be no return to a pre-industrial order). To Cole, the guild idea was essentially a demand for 'pleasure, joy, interest, expression in the works of a man's hand, taken from the worker by Capitalistic Pro- duction and the Industrial Revolution'.[20] Years later, after Guild Socialism had collapsed as a political movement, Cole was to write pessimistically that

men will rightly work far better if their task is made as light as possible, and if they are clearly conscious that it is worth perform- ing. This was the truth behind Guild Socialism, the valuable truth which has outlived its cant.[21]

Guilds and Unions

Cole did not want to restore the medieval guilds by returning to the material conditions of the Middle Ages. He saw the factory as the natural unit of guild life, internally self-governing and the basis of the wider functional democracy. The factory was the smallest and, therefore, to Cole as a disciple of Rousseau, the most intimate centre of an individual producer's working life. Consequently, the principle of factory representation had to be the foundation of the regional and national organs of guild representation. Unless the worker was a positive and active member of a community, the communal spirit which was the motive of the socialist society envisaged by Cole would be absent. Guilds, unlike the modern capitalist factories, were not 'a mere prison of boredom and useless toil, but a centre of free service and associative enterprise'.[22] Therefore, while the regional and national guilds would regulate and co-ordinate the activities of the local guilds, representing them in their external associations with other economic corporations, the factory would remain the fundamental unit of a guild democracy, appointing technical experts through their elected representatives, and developing its own sense of discipline and efficiency.

These guilds were to be the trade unions in the modern conditions of industrial society, rather than the closed and privileged corporations of the Middle Ages. This meant that the unions had to develop much further than their present defensive functions in capitalism, but the structure of the future guilds could already be discerned in the present unions. Their first duty, argued Cole, was to fight the employers, beside which all other activities were secondary and comparatively unimportant.[23] This duty determined the democratic structure of the unions. While the initiative in taking and organising strikes was necessarily local, the finances for strike activity had to be centralised in order to help the wider class struggle. This contrast between local democracy and centralised co-ordination was a perfect reflection of the future guild system. The democratic structure was, however, constrained by the negative approach forced on the unions by their exclusion from the actual conduct of industry. As a result, 'viewed from the standpoint of any theoretical system, the British trade union movement is merely an appalling chaos of contending atoms'.[24]

However, the very fact that unions were the rudimentary defence of the worker against total wage-slavery was reason for hope. At the moment, they imposed negative restrictions on the capitalist, restricting the production of wealth on the grounds of the safety and living standards of the worker. The labour unrest, caused according to Cole by a loss of faith in capitalism, provided the opportunity for this negative power to be turned into the positive power of executive and legislative control.

> Regarded merely as the instruments of collective wage bargaining, the Unions are the most powerful weapons in the hands of labour; if they are in addition the germs of the future organisation of industry as a whole, their importance becomes at once immeasurably greater.[25]

When seen in this light, the unions' functions and structure became as central to the Guild Socialists as they were to the syndicalists.

In analysing this structure, Cole echoed the criticisms of union bureaucracy by many syndicalists, particularly by the authors of *The Miners' Next Step*. He argued that union leaders were, by the nature of their job, efficient clerks rather than people of initiative and originality. They would make good officials if they were the servants of the rank and file, but their increasing respectability divorced them from the viewpoint of workers on the shopfloor, making them a burden on the workers' movement. Consequently, there was a growing breach between the leaders and the workforce, as the leaders forgot their origins and initial sympathies. While the capitalists organised, the unions squabbled amongst themselves in the selfish and sectional approach of fighting one another rather than the real class enemy. The union leaders were interest-bound in maintaining this emotional approach, based as it was on the outmoded craft structure of their unions.

Against this, Cole called for rank and file action to overcome the conservatism of the leadership. This, he believed, would create a 'Greater Unionism'[26] of co-operation between industrial unions, overcoming demarcation disputes and other differences within the working class, and increasing the co-operation of that class. In this Greater Unionism, the unions would be organised industrially as a preparation for their guild role – 'the basis of organization would be neither the craft to which a man belonged, nor the employer under whom he worked, but the service on which he was engaged.'[27] The new, reorganised unions would become the guilds which ran industry. Like the medieval guilds, they would enjoy a statutory and recognised position in society; exercise a monopoly over the market; be an association of masters, because all would be masters; and would stand for the lost morality of pride in craftsmanship.

Guilds and Corporatism

It was the corporatist strain in Syndicalism which had been drawn out by Cole. The guilds, or unions, were to be 'self-governing independent corporations with the widest powers'[28] to run their affairs. These corporations were to be fully democratic, electing their own officials and managers, and free to administer themselves within their own sphere. While ownership was vested in the community, represented by the state, control would normally be in the hands of the unions, or

guilds The character and amount of production would be determined
by the state, but the methods and processes of production would be
entirely in the hands of the guilds. Each national guild would elect an
executive committee, and each year there would be a Guild Congress
(similar to the TUC) composed of representatives from each guild
and working in co-operation with the government. This was seen by
Cole to be as practical as the government's relationship to the armed
forces – with total independence being respected within the limits of
the state as ultimate authority.

If the guilds were to take executive and legislative control of
industrial affairs, this did not mean that they could forget the
limits of their sphere of interest. One of Cole's major disagreements
with the syndicalists lay in his rejection of their narrow, one-sided
economism. The power of the unions might be absolute within
their rightful realm, but outside that realm other functions needed
to be represented. 'The control of industry may be the future
existing destiny of the trade unions; the direct control of the whole
national life is most emphatically not for them.'[29] The consumers
needed representation, too, as the guild idea was a denial of the
sovereignty of the consumers. Cole changed his mind on how consumers should be represented – in *The World of Labour*, he nominated the state as representative of the community, while by the time
he came to write *Guild Socialism Restated* he proposed consumer
associations – but he was adamant about the balance needed between
producers and consumers, so that one fraction of society did not
obtain undue power over others. 'The solution must surely lie in a
rational division of functions, allowing both producer and consumer
a say in the control of what is, after all, supremely important to
both'.[30]

If the citizen needed representation as both producer and consumer, then representation as a citizen of a country was particularly
needed. Cole was aggressive in asserting his nationalism, though it
had a decidedly left-wing stance. As far as he was concerned, national
ties remained of enormous importance in social, moral and political
terms. It was 'still the strongest bond which can tie men together',[31]
uniting them in a common inheritance of history and culture and
transcending class divisions. In 1913 he wrote prophetically that,
while a general strike against war looked very well on paper, in
practice 'there is nothing so certain as that, at the breath of a war
scare, all the peaceable professions of the workers will be forgotten,
and jingoism will sweep like a scourge over the country'.[32] This was

because Britain was a nation based on natural differences, tied together by a common descent which went far deeper than bonds of neighbourhood or class. It was true that the working class were exploited throughout the world, facing the same capitalist enemy, so that the citizen as a worker was cosmopolitan. The difficulty was that the citizen was not merely a worker, but a member of a nation shaped by two thousand years of history. Thus, while throughout the world parliamentary democracy was an illusion as a result of industrial autocracy, 'it does not follow from this, as some Syndicalists would have us believe, that the worker must abjure patriotism, and become a citizen of the world of labour, pure and simple'.[33]

In the light of his rejection of the one-sided economism of syndicalist theory and his assertive nationalism, Cole was led to a pluralist view of politics. As the representative of the geographical group known as the nation, the political state could claim sovereignty, but it was a strictly limited sovereignty. Parliament, representing the citizen, would be elected on a territorial basis, while the guilds, representing the producer, would be elected on an industrial basis. On the inevitable question of whether Parliament or the guilds (or any other association) was supreme, Cole took a libertarian stance. While the state was sovereign in regard to national matters such as defence and foreign affairs, it had no right to interfere with areas such as industry or religion which were *not* common to its citizens. As soon as this pluralist nature of society was recognised, then the role of the democratic state as the first among equals would become clear. As Cole put it,

> the demand for functional devolution is not a demand for the recognition of associations by the state, but a demand that the state itself should be regarded only as an association – elder brother, if you will, but certainly in no sense father of the rest.[34]

While it retained ultimate power, the state had to recognise the restricted limits within which it could operate.

Guild Socialism and War

The outbreak of war in 1914 rendered untenable Cole's peculiar combination of ideological elements, principally his assertion of class war and his libertarian rejection of the strong State in conjunction with an aggressive nationalism. However, Cole continued to act as though his theoretical system could take the strain easily. He was certainly aware of the contradiction forced into his system by the grim reality of war. If he were to call for the continuation of class war, it would be a denial of nationalism; if he were to acquiesce in the wave of jingoistic sentiment which swept the country, it would be a denial of the injustice of a class system. Cole believed that, when national security was threatened, socialists must rally to the aid of their country – 'they cannot logically take advantage of the economic situation for an attack on capitalism, if in so doing they hamper the country in the conduct of the war'.[35] However, he also understood that in such conditions the state would act on behalf of the capitalists by attacking trade union rights.

In these circumstances Cole called on the worker both to serve the nation and to maintain the strength of the unions. He sought to justify this stand by making a distinction between the state and the nation. The former was corrupt and to be resisted; the latter was a fundamental bond which demanded obedience. Thus, Cole argued,

> the class struggle is suspended, or largely suspended, in terms of external strife, not because the State is greater than the Trade Union, but because the individuals in such times transcend the groups through which they ordinarily act.[36]

If the corrupt state were to take advantage of such patriotism, it was to be fiercely resisted. In particular, the state's sovereignty even in times of war was limited by the individual conscience of the dissenter.[37] Nevertheless, when the nation was in danger, the worker must serve even as corrupt an institution as the state.

It was a solution which had more theoretical appeal than common sense. If the nation was in danger, then a class state was duty bound to curb the rights of any group (such as the unions) should they threaten national unity. In such a situation (which did exist in Britain as a result of the 1915 Treasury Agreement), any socialist would be forced to *choose* between nation and class. The state and the nation could not be separated in practice, so that Cole was forced into a metaphysical defence of the right of the existing class state to mobilise its citizens in its defence. He held that 'the State, as it exists today, is a mere parody of the true expression of the national unity; Labour, in giving it allegiance, is offering it service in virtue of what it might be'.[38] His system was saved at the expense of reality. As a result, Cole's political activity in the NGL throughout the war was marked by the refusal, common to many syndicalists, to recognise the existence of war. Politically, Cole was not neutral as much as neutralised.

Cole and Labourism

Cole had performed a remarkable juggling act in constructing his system of ideas known as Guild Socialism. He had balanced Syndicalism and state socialism, Rousseau and Figgis, industrial and political democracy. However, Cole's belief in the renewing power of the trade union movement inevitably forced him to relate his ideas to its labourism and to its political party.

Cole's attitude to the Labour Party in its pre-socialist period can easily be misunderstood. On the surface he seemed to regard it as at best an irrelevancy and at worst as reactionary. He saw the party as incapable of obtaining a parliamentary majority and incapable of knowing what to do if it ever did obtain one. Its narrow reformism could be compared only with the narrowest view of a trade union as a body concerned with obtaining higher wages. As a result the Labour Party could be of no concern to those interested in socialist transformation. Cole regarded it with contempt as 'that sad failure of Socialism, endeavouring, by a trick, to seem stronger than it really is'.[39] It had ceased to fulfil the real needs of the wider labour movement, forcing the working class to turn back to the trade unions as agents of social reconstruction.

Unlike the Labour Party in Parliament, the trade unions could deliver material gains to their members. Their social and economic power stood in marked contrast to the weakness of the parliamentary representatives. The political arena was a mere debating society in comparison with the economic arena, where the real decisions would be fought out. Consequently, the Labour Party could not advance beyond the limits set for it by trade union power. It was a reflection of union struggles rather than a major force in its own right:

> in politics democracy can nibble, but it may not bite; and it will not be able to bite until the balance of economic power has been so changed as to threaten the economic dominance of capital.[40]

However, despite his initial contempt for the Labour Party, Cole was never an anti-Labour politician. The subsidiary role played by the political party in relation to the trade union did not mean that it played no role. On the contrary, he argued that the failure of the

Marxists (both the SDF and the SLP) to gain any working-class support demonstrated the importance of the Labour Party for socialists. Indeed, if Labour could be purged of its non-socialist element it would become the key component in the transformation of society through its political position as a party seeking state power. As the unions rose in dominance through their militant success in strike action, so would the Labour Party become more important in its wake, capturing electoral success as a result of trade union success. Industrial action is thus put in its context as industrial, not political, in its influence. In stark contrast to the syndicalists, Cole argued that 'even if strikes can succeed in raising real wages and in bettering condition, it does not follow that they can ever by themselves bring about the expropriation of the capitalist'.[41] It would not be right if they could, because of the necessarily sectional nature of the unions. Only the state, as the representative of the community, had the right to bring capitalist ownership to an end.

This raised the question of nationalisation. Cole's attitude to state socialism *as a tactic* changed over time, from an early neutrality on the question of state ownership to a position of advocacy by 1917.[42] However, his opposition to the *principle* of state socialism was absolute. It was a denial of self-government and, as such, a denial of the essential freedom of the worker. The state, as representative of the community, must *own* industry, but *control* of industry must lie with the guilds. As a result, state ownership would be a necessary stage in the transition to guild control. State socialism would certainly be a major advance compared with the system of state capitalism, or state intervention to protect the capitalist class, that had evolved during the Great War. To Cole,

> under either system, the power of the State is arrayed on the side of the wage system; but the chance of developing the Guild idea and the Guild demand among the workers seems to me very much greater under national ownership than under State capitalism.[43]

As the political party capable of legally endorsing the transfer of capital to the workers, the Labour Party was inevitably seen by Cole as a critical area for Guild Socialists to capture for their ideas. Cole became much more active in the Labour Party during and after the war, helping to draft the Guild Socialist constitution accepted by the ILP in 1922. However, his theoretical position on the Labour Party and the place of political action remained fundamentally the same as that proposed in *The World of Labour*.[44] He welcomed Labour's 1918 Constitution as a bridge for co-operation between the political and economic wings of the labour movement, but maintained that constitutional activity by itself would achieve little. There was never any chance, given the realities of public opinion in a capitalist society, that the working class would vote as a block for a socialist society, while the power of the middle classes meant that counter-revolution could be easily provoked. Therefore political action, when necessary, was secondary to economic action. The industrial order was the vulnerable point of the existing system, and it was there that the labour movement could be mobilised with a strength which it could not exercise in any other direction. Cole expressed succinctly the relation between industrial and political action, between the unions and the Labour Party, in 1918 – 'In the Commonwealth today, power in the economic field is the key which alone can unlock the gates of real political power.'[45]

Cole's acceptance of the Labour Party did not mean that Guild Socialism fell easily into the framework of labourist ideology. Indeed, Cole continued the syndicalist attack on labourism in several ways. As has been noted, he rejected Labour's politics of merely redistributing wealth, pointing to the need to change the capitalist relations of *production* through the abolition of the wage system. In doing so, he resurrected Marx's challenge to labourism in that he identified capital (as a social relationship), rather than individual capitalists, as the enemy of the working class. Moreover, Cole's rejection of simple parliamentary representation and his views on functional representation seem to put him outside the boundaries of mainstream political thought in the Labour Party. His rejection of the existing state, as undeserving of loyalty compared to the ideal socialist state, seem at first sight to place him on the revolutionary side of the workers' movement.

However, Cole's critique of parliamentary democracy was not as radical as it appeared. Where the syndicalists wished to destroy the political state, replacing it with a social republic, Cole wished to maintain the state. The syndicalists, like Lenin, regarded parliamentary democracy as a sham disguising the realities of class dictatorship. If that dictatorship should ever be threatened, it would react savagely. If the socialists ever came close to capturing parliamentary power, they would find that Parliament would have power taken away from it by capital. This was why their ideas could never be reconciled with the Labour Party's political thought. In contrast, Cole never thought in such revolutionary terms, despite his awareness of the close relationship between class and power. Parliamentary democracy was not so much a sham as an outpost of popular rule which needed to be reinforced by the social democracy of economic associations. The rule of the capitalist through the wage system was seen as an autocracy, but never anything so beyond recovery as a dictatorship. To acknowledge such an extreme view would propel Cole to a revolutionary standpoint which he never wanted to reach. He would go so far, but no further. He would point to the despotism of capitalist rule in the factory:

> in politics we do not call democratic a system in which the proletariat has the right to organise and exercise what pressure it can on an irresponsible body of rulers; we call it modified aristocracy; and the same name adequately describes a similar industrial structure.[46]

However, Cole's solution to this was industrial democracy; not the revolutionary general strike preached by the syndicalists ('a fool's idea of how to run a revolution'),[47] and certainly not the revolutionary party called for by the Leninists.

This was a result of Cole's conception of the state, which was rooted firmly in Fabian thought as much as in Rousseau. He profoundly disagreed with the syndicalist idea of the state as a fundamental instrument of class rule. Cole often criticised the state socialists as identifying the present state with the ideal state, but he ultimately agreed with Shaw's view (in *The Impossibilities of Anarchism*) that the state, no matter how badly used by the capitalists, was capable of being used well if the working class could capture its citadel. Thus, he could point out in 1917 that 'in the Society of today, the State is a coercive power, existing for the protection of private property, and merely reflecting, in its subservience to Capitalism, the economic class structure of the modern world'.[48] He could even go so far as to argue, as he did throughout his ten years as an active Guild Socialist that

> it is of no use for the workers to look to the State for salvation: the State responds only to economic pressure, and the salvation that will be got from it will be strictly in proportion to the economic pressure applied.[49]

However, even in his most enthusiastic celebrations of class war, Cole never forgot the power of the state and its ability to crush the trade union movement in any direct constitutional clash in the sense envisaged by the revolutionary syndicalists. The state was far stronger than any single employer, and the unions must co-operate with it, not destroy it. His view of class war was restricted solely to the economic struggle at the point of production; in politics, he believed that the state stood above class struggles between employers and workers and could be pressured into supporting the unions' cause. To Cole, 'it is in warring with Capitalism that they [the unions] will learn to do without Capitalism; but they must realise their freedom in partnership with, and not in opposition to, the State'.[50]

In rejecting the revolutionary implications of Syndicalism, Cole was able to extricate its corporatist strain which he regarded as its constructive and positive element. He believed that 'syndicalism is strong in what it asserts and weak in what it denies',[51] and that its strongest point lay in recognising that social life in the economic sphere was totally unregulated by the democratic mechanism that governed the political sphere. In this way, Cole made the 'constructive', or corporatist, aspects of Syndicalism more palatable to British Socialism.

Moreover, Cole's acceptance of political, parliamentary action to achieve political ends made his anti-capitalist ideas into a Utopian blueprint, acceptable only to the Labour Left at a certain time. He realised that the state was too powerful to be overthrown by the economic action of a general strike, as advocated by the syndicalists, and hoped that the combination of parliamentary action and union power would bring about a social revolution. In practical terms, it was a forlorn hope, as the growing strength of the unions was emasculated by the economic depression of the 1920s. However, it was a forlorn hope even in Cole's terms of the powerful, repressive state. If the strength of the Labour Party *was* so dependent on the strength of the unions, then there would be no reason for the state to allow a social revolution quietly to gather strength without striking out against it. Any such attack on the unions might, or might not, be successful, but it would certainly involve the sort of extra-parliamentary action envisaged by the syndicalists and deplored by Cole. In this context, Cole's ideas were an intellectual fantasy, with no practical answer to the problem of transition to a guild society. Cole's old friend, William Mellor, recognised as much when he (temporarily) joined the Communist Party. In an article criticising his old belief in Guild Socialism, Mellor argued that 'It hovers in a state of uneasy equilibrium between the mediaevalist and the revolutionary',[52] explaining its contradictions in Cole's own personality.

This criticism is underlined by the startling inaccuracy of Cole's own theory. He elaborated his ideas at a time when the unions were growing in strength, and he simply assumed that this would continue. However, the onset of economic depression in the early 1920s led to a severe weakening of trade union power, though this weakening was certainly not reflected in Labour's political success during the decade. Cole's failure to develop an economic theory *of the present*, as opposed to an economic blueprint for the future, was to impress itself upon him only after the slump had destroyed the National Building Guild, and with it Guild Socialism, in 1922.

However, this is to overlook the importance of Guild Socialism for the politics of the Labour Party. In the short term, it served as an intellectual rallying point for the Labour Left in the immediate post-war period. Until 1918, the ILP had seen itself as the socialist agency inside the Labour Party, whose task it was to push the trade unions in a socialist direction. With the 1918 Constitution, this task was accomplished, while the creation of individual party membership threatened the ILP's organisational existence. The party's search for a *raison d'être* was intensified by the appeal of Leninism and the ideas of Soviet democracy to its own left wing, some of whom helped to form the Communist Party in 1920–1. In these circumstances, Clifford Allen, a leading member of the No-Conscription Fellowship, who identified the guild idea with the nobler aspects of Soviet Communism,[53] fought successfully for a Guild Socialist constitution for the ILP. Written partly by Cole, the constitution as adopted in 1922 called for the achievement of both political and economic democracy, with the internal management of each industry in the hands of its workers and co-operating with the representatives of the consumers. The new constitution accepted that

> the best way of effecting a peaceful change to Socialism by the organization of the workers politically to capture the power of the State, and industrially to take over the control and management of the industrial machine.[54]

It was ironic that this constitution was adopted in the very year that Guild Socialism collapsed as a political force. The distinctive voice for which the ILP was searching in the 1920s would come from another direction.

In the long term, Guild Socialism left a much more important legacy for the politics of the Labour Party. In eliminating the revolutionary aspects of Syndicalism, Cole had made its corporatist strain acceptable to Labour thought. Previously, British Socialism had regarded the unions as purely defensive instruments of the working class in a capitalist society, with the Labour Party alone concerned with the problem of government. Cole had widened the scope of Labour theory, demonstrating the possibility of economic associations such as the unions taking part in the government of the country's economic affairs. The old panacea of nationalisation, contributed to British Socialism by the Labour Marxists, had been found wanting by the Left and a call for the economy to be run by extra-governmental organisations raised.

This should not be taken to mean that Guild Socialism was an early version of the corporate socialism which came to be accepted by Labour in the 1940s. There were many crucial differences, as will be seen. Cole's ideas were too democratic and anti-capitalist to be acceptable to anybody but the Labour Left. However, in raising the question of functional as well as representative democracy, Guild Socialism was an essential transitional stage in the evolution of Corporate Socialism. Cole himself was well aware that Guild Socialism was an eventual ideal, and that a series of stages would be required before it could be attained. State socialism was acceptable to him as such a stage, but so, if necessary, was joint control of industrial affairs by the unions with the state and the capitalists. He was privately ambiguous on the Whitley Council ideas of joint control, while in 1917 he argued that

> the workers must be prepared, if necessary to assume, through their trade Unions, a half share in the ownership of capital, as a step in the direction of National Guilds. They must not, however, accept any joint responsibility with capitalism in return for less than a half-share in ownership.[55]

John Parker even recalled Cole's 'initial sympathy with Mussolini's corporate state.... He saw it as a development of Sorel possibly leading to a form of socialist syndicalism'[56] though he soon recoiled from the Fascist suppression of free trade unions.

These statements demonstrate the extreme flexibility of Cole's use of corporate ideas. He remained a Guild Socialist for the rest of his life, though after 1922 he ceased to regard it as a practical alternative for the immediate future. For the Labour Party, Guild Socialism had a passing effect in the short term, but in the end its corporatist stance was to be resurrected in a new form, with Cole playing an important part in its evolution. However, before this could take place, Labour faced a new intellectual challenge from the Liberal Party on its Right.

7 The ILP and the Keynesian Challenge

Outwardly, the 1920s was a decade of political progress for the Labour Party. With the enfranchisement of working-class men and (after 1928) women, its future electoral success seemed assured. It replaced the fractured Liberal Party as the official Opposition in 1922 and advanced quickly to form minority governments in 1924 and 1929. The belief in the inevitability of gradualism – the slow evolution of capitalism into socialism propagated by the Fabians and Mac-Donald – was being borne out.

However, a different story could be discerned in the economic reality which lay behind the political realm. After an initial post-war boom, an economic depression set in after 1920 which overshadowed all other issues in British society. The decline in British manufacturing in the world market, together with the savagely deflationary measures of a cost-conscious government, led to a fall in industrial production by a quarter in 1920–1. Unemployment rose from 2 per cent of the labour force to more than 18 per cent within a year, while money wages fell by 38 per cent in the four years after 1920. When the economy gradually recovered after the mid-1920s, unemployment remained resolutely high, rarely sinking below 10 per cent for the rest of the decade. The export of capital abroad, which had been the mainstay of British prosperity in the pre-war period, was ceasing to be sufficient to prevent a crisis in the accumulation of capital in the 1920s.

In these circumstances of mass unemployment and shrinking export markets, the trade union foundations of the Labour Party's political power were badly battered. The defeat of the miners and the collapse of the Triple Alliance in April 1921, followed by the defeat of the Engineers in the 1922 lockout, effectively ended the first Shop Stewards Movement. This destruction of the power of the union rank and file strengthened the hold of the union leadership and prepared the way for the defeat of the General Strike in 1926, when the TUC General Council capitulated quickly to the government and the employers as the constitutional implications of the strike became clear to them. The government followed up their victory with a vindictive Trades Disputes Act in 1927, which banned sympathy strikes and made trade union financial support for the Labour Party more difficult. The success of the employers in these disputes, together with the fear of unemployment, led to a drastic decline in union membership, which fell from over eight million in 1920 to under five million by the decade's end. Any realistic hope that progress could be made in the industrial as well as the parliamentary arena was ended for all but a few militants on the Left. Instead, the concern of union leaders like Ernest Bevin of the Transport Workers was with the immediate question of overcoming unemployment within a capitalist society.

However, it was precisely in the question of unemployment that the bankruptcy of British Socialism was revealed. It was able to postulate a morally superior system of co-operation to replace a class-divided society, but it was unable to put forward realistic schemes for the regulation of a trade cycle which was entering into a vicious circle of unemployment and falling productivity. MacDonald seemed more concerned with the minutiae of parliamentary behaviour and court manners than with developing his earlier political ideas.[1]

In response to an ILP campaign, the Labour leadership did adopt a new programme (drafted by Tawney), *Labour and the Nation* (1928), but this contained little more than the old platitudes of British Socialism. A variety of palliatives from higher direct taxes to enlarged powers for the Food Council were proposed, but there was no new political strategy underlying them. A belief in 'the familiar commonplace that "morality is the nature of things" and that men are all, in truth, members of one another'[2] was very uplifting, but hardly met the requirements of the time. It was as if nothing had changed since the days of Carpenter and Blatchford.

It was believed on both Labour's Right and Left that unemployment and poverty would disappear when capitalism had finally ended, a belief which fed the ILP demand that Labour should refuse to govern the country until it had a parliamentary majority to introduce socialist measures. In realistic terms, though, Labour was unable to achieve such a majority in the conditions of the 1920s, and the ILP refused to entertain the idea, equally impractical at the time, of a workers' dictatorship. The real weakness which underlay Labour's electoral progress in the decade was its bankruptcy of economic solutions to overcome the immediate crisis. It was all very well to dream of healthy young boys and girls dancing around camp-fires in the socialist commonwealth, but in the meantime the rent had to be paid and the diseases of malnutrition cured.

An ILP committee around Brailsford and Hobson did produce a set of proposals, *The Living Wage*, in 1926, while Oswald Mosley put forward his solution of protectionism and credit expansion in his 'Birmingham Proposals' in 1925, but both groups were unable to change Labour thinking in the short term. The *Living Wage* proposals were soon submerged in a militant campaign for *Socialism in our Time*, and suffered from theoretical shortcomings. Mosley's proposals gained popularity in certain sections of the Left under the second Labour Government, but were obscured for a time by his own personal ambitions which led him to leave the Labour Party. Moreover, they had more in common with the advanced Liberalism of Keynes, than they had with any socialist programme.

It was, indeed, from Keynes and the Liberal Party with their programme for reviving a capitalist economy that the main theoretical challenge to British Socialism rose in the decade. Keynes was particularly prominent in this challenge. His subversion of neo-Classical economic theory in the early 1930s, known as the Keynesian Revolution, had its foundations in his double challenge to *laissez-faire* and to British Socialism in the previous decade. It was, however, an ambiguous challenge, since Keynes was led, at first implicitly, to identify the lack of 'effective demand' as the main economic problem facing capitalist society. As such, he came to agree partially with the principal Labour economist of the 1920s, J. A. Hobson. The ambiguity of the Keynesian challenge to British Socialism, and the ultimate Labour response to that challenge, must be found in Keynes' criticisms of the Labour economists of the twenties.

THE LABOUR ECONOMISTS

The causes of, and remedies for, unemployment in the Labour Party of the 1920s tended to revolve around the ideas of J. A. Hobson, described by Brailsford as 'the most respected intellectual influence in the Labour movement.'[3] This may seem at first sight paradoxical, as most of his ideas had been formulated while he was an active Liberal.

Hobson

John A. Hobson (1858–1940) was born to a middle-class family in Derby, educated at Oxford and quickly developed a disregard for intellectual orthodoxies, particularly in political economy. Together with a like-minded businessman, A. F. Mummery, he wrote *The Physiology of Industry* (1889) in which Say's law, that supply and demand would always balance, was challenged. Mummery, who was apparently the more original of the two, died shortly afterwards, but Hobson developed their 'under-consumptionist' ideas in a long series of books for the rest of his life. As a Liberal Radical, his bitter opposition to the Boer War led him to write *Imperialism* (1902), in which the vaguely anti-capitalist ideas of the Liberal and Labour parties were given a coherent theoretical form. The book had a major effect on Brailsford's analysis of the Great War, as has already been noted, as well as being a model for Hilferding and Lenin to develop its anti-capitalist ideas in a revolutionary direction. As an anti-war Liberal in the UDC, Hobson decided to join the Labour Party after the Great War, though he regarded the ILP as too extreme. By this time his writings on poverty and unemployment had won him recognition in the labour movement, where both MacDonald and Snowden were adherents of his economic heresies.

Hobson was a radical critic of orthodox political economy, which he regarded as a sophisticated attempt to justify the necessity and finality of an unjust economic system. Their conservatism had prevented economists from developing marginalist theories to cover a consistently human theory of wealth, Instead, they had concerned themselves merely with the determination of prices, failing to lift their horizons above the mean limits of the business world. Hobson pointed to the class nature of political economy, arguing that

> its immanent conservatism recommends it, not only to timid academic minds, but to the general body of the possessing classes who, though they may be quite capable of following its subtleties of reasoning, have sufficient intelligence to value its general conclusions.[4]

In its place, he attempted to revive Ruskin's conceptions of a humanist political economy which would cover the economics of welfare as well as profit. Like Ruskin, Hobson was aware that economics had a human and social, as well as a commercial, importance, and that the principles of justice and health should be the foundations of political economy, rather than the subjective valuations of 'consumers.' Against those Liberals who held to *laissez-faire* and free trade, Hobson pointed out that the growth of cartels and monopolies had severely restricted free competition in industry, leading to much greater profits than were due to entrepreneurs. These profits had totally upset the 'natural' balance of spending and saving, leading to a situation where too much was being saved and not enough spent. This 'surplus' of saving was becoming unearned income, idly accumulated by the rich, rather than flowing along the healthy channels necessary for economic growth. The constant tendency towards gluts and over-production in capitalist society, unexplained by the orthodox economists, could only find a satisfactory solution in recognising the surplus of unearned and excessive incomes incapable of consuming the increased production of industrial society.

The limited consumption of the working class was the other side of the coin of the 'surplus' incomes. As a result of their under-consumption, the working class provided only a limited market for the goods they produced, so that every increase in output would *not* eventually find its outlet in consumption, as orthodox economists claimed. Consequently, the limited market, which had led to the export of capital characteristic of capitalist imperialism, was identified by Hobson as bringing about overproduction, leading directly to deflation and unemployment. The war had made the depression deeper and longer than previous depressions, but it was not the real *cause* of the depression. 'The general shrinkage of effective demand which constitutes a cyclical depression implies a failure of consumption to keep pace with production in the industrial world as a whole.' This normal tendency of production to outrun consumption, experienced by businessmen as a difficulty in selling their produce, was to be ended by increasing consumption through the reduction of the surplus of unearned income. A policy of redistributive taxation and increased wages would raise the consuming power of the working class, who would then provide the expanded markets needed to absorb the increased output.

Hobson's analysis fitted in neatly with the labourist traditions of the British trade union movement. He regarded it as one of his aims to establish 'an intelligible and consistent theory alike of the harmony and the antagonism of capital and labour'. In doing so, he removed the ambiguities in the labour theory of value as propagated by Hodgskin. This theory, that all value was created by labour, had disappeared from non-Marxist economic thought, which excluded the capitalist relations of production from its sphere of concern. Hobson, too, excluded production relations from his analysis. He rejected Marxist economics because it confused the economics of a hypothetical society in which the state, owning all the instruments of industry, need no longer take into account the categories of rent, interest and profit, with the economic analysis of current industry.[5]

This was not really true of Marx, but Hobson rejected the labour theory of value along with Marx. He believed that *all* factors of production, capital and land as well as labour, contributed to social wealth, and that there was consequently an underlying harmony of the interests of capital and labour in the sphere of production.

In a society of free competition, 'a law of natural harmony of interests among the owners of the factors of production determines the distribution'[6] of wealth. If there was no surplus, or if the surplus was fairly distributed between capital and labour, there would be industrial peace. However, the surplus was *not* fairly distributed. Instead, the brute laws of force determined the distribution of wealth among the different social classes, with some obtaining excessive and unearned portions of the surplus. The harmonious relations of production were disrupted by the unequal relations of distribution. Hobson was clear as to the real villains of the piece – 'Among entrepreneurs, the financier or manipulator of fluid capital and of credit is at present in a position of such vantage that his share of the surplus is out of all proportion to his services.' It was the financier, the parasitic *rentier*, who mulcted the wealth created by honest employers and workmen, and who was consequently an enemy of industrial progress and justice. The bankers were the unpatriotic rascals who diverted wealth abroad while leaving British industry starved of capital,[7] and together with the idle plutocrats accumulated their unused surplus.[8]

The trade unions emerged for Hobson as the major force in industrial society working for progress. As economic crisis was caused by underconsumption, then trade union action to raise wages was socially beneficial, enhancing rather than harming the efficiency of the economy. Trade union struggles, through their raising of the level of consumption, were a counterforce to the plutocrats who disrupted the essential harmony of the social classes – 'if capital or ability takes too much, and labour not enough, industrial progress continues to lag, for the healthy march of industry requires a proportionate advance of all the factors'. Therefore, where labour was able to eat into the surplus of unearned income, industrial harmony and prosperity would result. It followed that social reform, whether carried out by Liberal or Labour, should be aimed at strengthening the power of the unions in collective bargaining.

Hobson's economics may well have fitted in with the labourist tradition, but there was nothing particularly socialist about them. Indeed, he was an active Liberal for a large part of his life, collaborating with MacDonald and other moderate socialists in the Rainbow Circle and the UDC. His decision to join the Labour Party after the Great War was more a mark of his recognition of political realities than of any conversion to socialism. Hobson later wrote,

> Though . . . my sympathies have been with the Labour Party, I have never felt quite at home in a body governed by trade union members and their finance, and intellectually led by full-blown Socialists. For neither section of this Labour Party avowedly accepts that middle course which seems to me essential to a progressive and constructive economic government in this country.[9]

He saw his economic theories as seeking a reconciliation between socialism and individualism, which would avoid the disastrous wastes and perils of class conflict and international strife that proceeded from unregulated capitalism.

Hobson believed in a mixed economy because he believed that the acquisitive motive, selfish and immoral though it might be, was the only incentive which could make industry work. It was necessary to modify, rather than destroy, the egoistic motive by directing it into socially useful projects. It was a regulated capitalism to which he directed his energies – 'the industrial system thus envisaged consists, partly of nationalized industries, operated by representative government, partly of private industries working either by automatic competition or by some scheme of profit-sharing.' Hobson thus remained a Liberal, in economics as in politics, yet his analysis was taken up by the ILP, the far Left of the Labour Party in the twenties.

THE LIVING WAGE AND THE ILP

Hobson's economics found early favour in the Labour Party, profoundly influencing MacDonald, Snowden and Brailsford. In particular, it fulfilled the need of the ILP in the 1920s to act as a distinct left-wing body within the labour movement.

As has been noted, the ILP's *raison d'être* had been threatened
by the 1918 Labour Party constitution, which had accepted socialism
as its eventual aim and had created local Labour Parties to accommodate individuals hitherto able to join Labour only through the
ILP or the Fabian Society. The ILP needed a coherent ideology
to attract people who would otherwise turn to a local Labour Party
or to the Communist Party. Guild Socialism had served as a distinctive and attractive brand of socialism, but by the time it was
adopted by the ILP in 1922, the collapse of the Building Guild and
the NGL (National Guilds League) had robbed it of any practical
relevance. The moderation of the first Labour government, with
its emphasis on respectability, appalled the militant Clydeside group
in the ILP and seemed to demonstrate that Labour's acceptance
of socialism had been at best lukewarm. As a result, the ILP felt
that they must still convince the trade unions of the necessity of
socialism and in doing so appointed an economic committee –
Hobson,[10] Brailsford, Frank Wise and Arthur Creech Jones – to
formulate immediate proposals to overcome the crisis of unemployment.

The *Living Wage* document, published in September 1926, was the
result.[11] The demand for a living wage – a minimum wage for all
workers – had become generally accepted in the labour movement,[12]
but the novelty of this latest appeal lay in the terms in which the ILP
economists couched their demand. In this document, profound in its
consequences for Labour's political thought, they pointed to the lack
of 'effective demand' in capitalism rather than private ownership as
the key problem awaiting Labour's immediate solution:

> All of us realise that the low purchasing power of so many millions
> of wage earners is among the most potent causes of the widespread
> unemployment which has cursed our country during the last six
> years.[13]

The ethical argument for a living wage – that the mental and physical
growth of most of the population was stunted by poverty and low
wages – was pointed out, but the main weight of the argument was
based on Hobson's economic theory that low wages limited the home
market. The power of the masses to consume failed to keep pace with
the power of industry to produce, so that the benefits of mass production were withheld and unrealised. 'We produce less wealth than
our technical resources would enable us to create because the mass of

the wage-earners lack "effective demand". The owning class has misused the advantage of its position.'[14]

The immoral selfishness of the 'owning class' was arraigned, but it was the lack of 'effective demand' rather than capitalist relations of production which was singled out as the real obstacle to prosperity. It followed, and these ILP economists recognised the logic, that nationalisation was no real solution to the crisis of demand. The state ownership of declining industries in itself would neither avert unemployment nor prevent wage reductions. While nationalisation, as a measure of reorganisation, might be suited to certain key industries – those governing the pace and direction of economic growth, such as credit, coalmining and transport – it was unsuitable for depressed trades such as engineering, textiles and agriculture The ILP economists argued that 'it would be folly to suggest nationalisation as the appropriate method for reorganizing these weaker trades',[15] and proposed in its stead an Industrial Commission which could take under its survey all industries which were not capable of paying the living wage. This Commission would have the power to suggest and ultimately enforce amalgamation of companies within each industry in order to strengthen them by realizing the economies of mass production.

As the lack of effective demand was the key problem, it was agreed that the solution to economic crisis and unemployment lay in a general and simultaneous increase of the purchasing power of the masses through the policy of the living wage, particularly in introducing family allowances to help working-class women faced with the heartbreaking task of raising children in poverty. This could be done without inflation through the control of credit. At the first signs of a slump, the banks would be forced to expand credit and reduce interest rates, while restrictive measures could regulate a boom. In the slump conditions of the 1920s it was necessary to increase credit even at the expense of inflation, which was regarded as 'a slight evil in comparison with the increase in production and employment which will be brought about.' However, the expansion of credit with such disregard for price rises was to be seen as an emergency measure rather than the norm. This policy of credit control, with the object of maintaining steady prices and employment, could only be effective if the independent powers of the Bank of England were taken away by nationalisation. If the state owned the bank, then nationalisation of the joint stock banks was unnecessary in the short term as they could be controlled quite easily by the central bank.

Once the problem of inflation was mastered through credit control,
the policy of a living wage – based on need and deliberately estimated
as higher than the present level of industrial efficiency – would be
able to stimulate economic growth. In an early formulation of the
multiplier, the ILP economists argued that the new stream of purchasing power generated by the raising of wages would create
new employment, as the engineer, for example, would be able to buy
boots from the hitherto unemployed bootmaker, who would then be
able to provide new employment from his sale, and so on in a ripple
effect. In this way, the unemployed would be absorbed into the
labour force and trade stimulated. The trade unions, which would
maintain their freedom to bargain with the employers, were thus
given an economic as well as a moral justification for negotiating
higher wages.

This document was a remarkable portent for Labour's new economic ideas, but suffered from a number of defects. The problem of
how to reconcile continually rising wages with stable prices was
ignored as inapplicable to a situation of mass unemployment, but the
role of the trade unions could not be so easily shunted aside. The
freedom of the unions to negotiate higher wages was affirmed, but the
ILP economists argued that the unions were incapable of obtaining a
general living wage. Their bargaining power was closely tied to the
trade cycle and the slump of the 1920s had demonstrated their current
weakness. Moreover, even in times of prosperity, the lowest-paid
workers who most needed a living wage found combination in a
union very difficult to achieve without being dismissed. As a result,
it would be through political rather than trade union action that the
living wage would be achieved, though the authors made an almost
ritual obeisance to the idea that, 'in the last resort, it is on the
organised refusal of men to work for less than a living wage that our
hope of securing it lies',[16] a point nowhere explored. In effect, it was
being argued that the negotiation of higher wages should be taken
from the industrial into the political arena. It would be government
representatives, not trade unionists, who were to dictate collective
bargaining. This attitude aroused widespread hostility among the
trade union leaders, with Ernest Bevin warning the ILP leaders not
to interfere with the proper role of the unions by dragging wages into
a political programme.[17]

A further problem arose over the *socialist* nature of the
programme. Oswald Mosley had already asked the 1926 ILP Conference

Could a wage giving a civilised standard be paid until reorganisation had taken place or a credit policy on Socialist lines be operated? How could we win the Socialist Commonwealth by operating the capitalist system of finance?[18]

Mosley had his own interpretation of a socialist credit policy, as will be seen, but his question touched a raw nerve among delegates. Brailsford had to reassure them that

their task was to guide the country in this period of difficulty into Socialism. They must have their clear-cut plan. Every wandering, every irrelevance, meant a waste of effort. ... Their purpose should be not to administer the capitalist system, but to transform it.[19]

It was hard to see how such conclusions followed from the *Living Wage* document, however. It was argued there that, 'by all these conquests, the transition to the further socialisation of industry would be immensely eased',[20] but it was difficult to see how such a conclusion could emerge from the arguments presented. It was argued that nationalisation was *not* a cure for declining industries, and that prosperity could be achieved through an upward movement in wages instead. Once these industries were rising in prosperity, then it would be easier to nationalise them. However, if a well-regulated capitalism could ensure prosperity, then there seemed little *reason* to nationalise industry. The whole question of ownership would become irrelevant from an economic standpoint, though the moral issue of the evil nature of competition and the tyranny of employers remained of some validity.

The reformist implications of the document were quickly buried by the militant campaign of the ILP Left, led by James Maxton and John Wheatley, around the campaign document, *Socialism in our Time*, adopted at the 1926 ILP Conference. In this document, the demands for a living wage and family allowances were seen as part of a resolute socialist policy to carry labour quite quickly into a new society. Fenner Brockway linked the demand to the Guild Socialist ideas of the ILP by arguing that capitalism was incapable of providing such reforms. The campaign for a living wage could, therefore, never be successful under capitalism, serving merely as a propaganda point to win the workers to the recognition that only a fully socialist society could help them. In this way, the living wage demand would have the effect of exerting the fullest pressure of the trade union movement for such concessions as Capitalism can provide, and of revealing in all its bareness the inability of the existing system of society to do justice to the workers.[21]

This campaign was carried a stage further in 1928, when James Maxton and the militant miners' leader, A. J. Cook, issued a manifesto against the increasing trend of the Labour Party and the unions towards a corporate solution to the problems of capitalism. *Our Case for a Socialist Revival* was a full-blooded exposition of Labour Marxism, stressing that socialism could only arrive as a result of class struggle. They rejected the programme of the Labour leaders as an enlightened Liberal programme and argued that the new policy of collaboration with the employing class was merely an invitation to the unions to participate in their own exploitation. Such 'progressive' attitudes would merely lead to an increase in slave-driving as employers used the unions to increase their profits. As for the Labour programme 'if every measure...was carried, then we would not have socialism but rationalised capitalism, in which the main industries of the country remained in the hands of the exploiting capitalist class'. In its stead, Cook and Maxton called for a full-blooded socialist programme, including the abolition of the monarchy and the nationalisation of all manufacturing industry under workers' control.

As a result of this identification with the ILP Left, the *Living Wage* proposals were rejected by the majority of the Labour leadership, which saw them as a mere ploy to challenge their evolutionary socialist policies. Hobson, aware of this, virtually dissociated himself from the ILP campaign in order to save the substance of his proposals. He wrote to Ramsay MacDonald,

> I was asked as an economist, not as a politician, to join the small Committee which drew it up, and am not concerned about the use which may be made of it in the Labour Party and the country... In the Committee, at an early stage, I found some disposition to utilise the minimum wage in a way that seemed to me dangerous. Its present form is not I think at all open to such criticisms.[22]

Hobson's attempt failed as MacDonald and the Labour Right rejected the programme outright in face of the ILP threat, turning instead to the comfortable if vague nostrums of British Socialism in *Labour and the Nation*. It was Keynes, an opponent of the Labour

Party, who was paradoxically to retrieve Hobson's ideas for eventual absorption into the Labour Party's thought.

KEYNES AND THE LIBERAL CHALLENGE

The Liberal Party, which had achieved a fragile reunification of its Asquith and Lloyd George wings in 1923, was in desperate straits during the 1920s, squeezed between Conservatives and Labour. They elected only 40 MPs in the 1924 election, while the shaky coalition of *laissez-faire* free traders and radical interventionists was constantly threatening to tear itself apart, as demonstrated by the bitter acrimony in the 1926 General Strike, when Lloyd George clashed with Sir John Simon by refusing to condemn the TUC without equally condemning the government. It was this desperate situation which forced the Liberal leadership to undertake a major overhaul of its ideas, and in so doing to put its finger on the weakness of British Socialism as an immediate remedy for the economic crisis.

It was Lloyd George who began the great Liberal debate with an article in *The Nation* in April 1924, when he pointed to the need for a great rethinking on the use of national economic resources. It was to be a totally fresh approach, since it was independent of the interests of employers and unions, and of their two parties, Conservative and Labour – 'Capital and labour are alike strangled by vested interests and traditions. Both are capable of producing infinitely more wealth for the benefit of the community than they are doing.' A reply was immediately forthcoming from the Liberal economist, Keynes, who called on Liberals to turn their backs on *laissez-faire* and to endorse state intervention to guide the economy back to prosperity. Lloyd George then used the immense personal funds that he had accumulated during the years to launch a series of Liberal committees and summer schools which, by the late 1920s, had produced several reports, notably on land and industry. It was the Yellow Book , *Britain's Industrial Future* (1928), which was the foundation of the challenge to *laissez-faire* and British Socialism, and it was Keynes who was mainly responsible for it.

John Maynard Keynes (1883–1946) was born into a Victorian background, and was educated at Eton and Cambridge, where he became a member of the elite 'Apostles' (an unofficial academic group which included Bertrand Russell and Lytton Strachey). As a Fellow at Cambridge after 1908, his initial work was philosophical, concerning the logical foundations of probability. However, he made his mark with the public as a result of his *Economic Consequences of the Peace* (1919), a trenchant critique of the Versailles Treaty which ended the Great War. He followed this in the 1920s with a series of books on current monetary policy in which he called for a state-managed currency level and public works to stimulate trade and employment. It was in the following decade, with his *General Theory of Employment, Interest and Money* (1936) that he made his main claim to fame.

This was a major attack on the orthodoxy of the neo-classical economics of Marshall, Jevons and Pigou in which Keynes (and the early Fabians) had been raised. Influenced by a new generation of economists – Joan Robinson, Piero Sraffa and Richard Kuhn in particular – Keynes was impelled by the mass unemployment of the Great Depression of the early thirties to question the normal economic law that the trade cycle was of short duration so that long-term unemployment was voluntary. The general slump conditions of the early 1930s were a glaring disproof of such a theory, and Keynes was led in his attempts to solve the problem to join the economic heretics, whose ideas 'only live on furtively, below the surface, in the underworlds of Karl Marx, Silvio Gesell or Major Douglas'. He came to agree with Hobson and the Labour economists that the problem was one of ineffective demand. The orthodox ideas of the neo-classical economists were held to be true for the special case where capital and labour were fully employed; they were totally unable to grasp the general case of involuntary unemployment due to a vicious circle of falling productivity and prices. To explain the situation, Keynes turned to 'the brave army of heretics.... Mandeville, Malthus, Gesell and Hobson, who, following their intuitions, have preferred to see the truth obscurely and imperfectly rather than to maintain error.' The 'Keynesian Revolution' was launched.

However, this revolution in academic thought in the 1930s, with all its consequences for political economy, had been prepared in Keynes's double challenge to *laissez-faire* capitalism and British Socialism in the previous decade. In terms of his theoretical presumptions, Keynes was firmly trapped in the orthodox economics of Marshall in the 1920s,[23] but his concern with immediate practical problems led him to stretch the orthodox theories to their limits. To all intents and purposes the radical solutions to particular economic problems put forward by Keynes, culminating in his writings for the Liberal Party,

were solutions to a situation of underconsumption, or lack of effective demand.

This was due to his recognition that capitalism had developed well
beyond its golden age of free competition between small entrepreneurs. In such circumstances as the development of cartels and oligopolies, *laissez-faire* had ceased to be a libertarian concept and had
become a disguise for allowing the worst aspects of capitalism to
come to the fore. However, this was precisely the course taken by the
free trade Liberals, fighting on the outmoded battlegrounds of political democracy, individual liberty and free competition. They did not
realise that cut-throat competition was devastating in its effects on
prosperity and industrial efficiency, or that the day of the small
business unit had passed forever. Combination, in the business world
as much as in the world of labour, was the order of the day, and the
Liberal task was to take advantage of it, to regulate it, to turn it into
the right channels. All the mistakes of government economic policy,
according to Keynes, were the result of continuing 'to apply the
principles of an economics, which was worked out on the principles
of *laissez-faire* and free competition, to a society which is rapidly
abandoning these hypotheses'.[24] Keynes may have couched his ideas
in the terminology of Marshall, but he was already in 1925 aware of
the inadequacy of traditional economic nostrums.

However, Keynes was a critic of British Socialism as well as of
laissez-faire. He was explicit in his criticisms of the Labour Party,
which was frankly too plebeian for his tastes. One of his main objections to Marxism had been his refusal to accept 'a creed which,
preferring the mud to the fish, exalts the boorish proletariat above
the bourgeois and intelligentsia who, with whatever faults, are the
quality in life.'[25] The Labour Party was a party where the mud had
ensnared the fish – where the intellectuals who should lead were
dominated by the illiterate trade unionists – and as a result it was
not the party of Keynes. Labour

> is a class party and the class is not my class. If I am going to pursue
> sectional interests at all, I shall pursue my own. . . . I can be influ-
> enced by what seems to me to be justice and good sense, but the
> class war will find me on the side of the educated bourgeoisie.[26]

He did not believe that Labour allowed the educated bourgeois to
lead the uneducated masses, who had no clue as to their best interests.
Instead, it was the ignorant trade unionists – 'once the oppressed,

now the tyrants, whose selfish and sectional pretensions need to be
bravely opposed'[27] – who led the intellectuals behind their banner.

Keynes was to modify his views on the unions, partly as a result of
his work with Bevin, but he constantly pointed to the strength of the
Left, the party of catastrophe which hated the existing order, as the
most dangerous aspect of Labour's class base. The Left's strength
compelled the Labour leaders continually to protect their flank by
appealing to the baser instincts of the working class. Instead of
working out realistic solutions to the immediate problems of falling
productivity and rising unemployment, the Labour Party remained
trapped in the passions of jealousy and resentment of their betters.
They were their own worst enemies, as the only ones to suffer from
their class war rhetoric were themselves. To Keynes,

> the Labour Party has got tied up with all sorts of encumbering and
> old-fashioned luggage. They respond to anti-Communist rubbish
> with anti-capitalist rubbish. The consequence of all this is that,
> whether in or out of office, the business of orderly evolution seems
> likely to remain in Liberal hands.[28]

Such blatantly anti-working class sentiments may at first sight appear
to bar any possibility of the Labour Party being able to absorb
Keynesian thinking in any way, but this would be to ignore the
novelty of Keynes's ideas. The anti-union prejudice which appeared
to cut him off from Labour thinking was superficial, as he entertained
high hopes of the Labour Party as an agent for his ideas if channelled
by Liberal ideas. He recognised even in the mid-1920s that 'great
changes will not be carried out except with the active aid of Labour.
But they will not be sound or enduring unless they have first satisfied
the criticism and precaution of Liberals.'[29] It was up to the Liberals
to become more progressive and more far-sighted than Labour if they
were to mould the future in a beneficial manner. The strength of
Liberal ideas would, for Keynes, far outweigh the great party
machines of Conservative and Labour.

Moreover, many of Keynes's ideas made a particular appeal to
discontented Labour intellectuals. The aristocratic temperament
which led him to reject the working class mud in favour of the
educated fish also led him to a contempt for the vulgar and greedy
materialism of the idle plutocrat and the timid businessman. These
were aspects of the more objectionable features of capitalism which
Keynes felt could be gradually removed. His later calls for 'the

euthanasia of the rentier and, consequently, the euthanasia of the cumulative oppressive power of the capitalist to exploit the scarcity value of capital'[30] could be found in his writings of the 1920s, where he called for the state regulation of such vested interests as the Bank and the usurers. It was not capitalism, but a few capitalists who were to blame for the crisis. It was a small group of conservative and unimaginative men who withheld investment from the economy in case their profits were endangered, causing mass unemployment and the criminal waste of human and economic resources. To Keynes, 'the powers of uninterrupted usury are too great. If the accretions of vested interests were to grow without mitigation for many generations, half the population would be no better than slaves to the other half.'[31] Only the state, as the representative of the whole community, could curb their power and guide the economy in a useful direction.

In his reply to Lloyd George's call for a great Liberal debate on the economy, Keynes wrote that

> we are brought to my heresy – if it is a heresy. I bring in the State. I abandon *laissez-faire* – not enthusiastically, not from contempt for that good old doctrine, but because, whether we like it or not, the conditions for its success have disappeared.[32]

In turning to the state as an agency of economic direction, Keynes was thus aware of the novelty of his ideas for Liberal thought. The New Liberalism at the turn of the century had accepted the state as an instrument of social reform, but had retained the traditional Liberal belief in *laissez-faire* and free trade. Keynes was calling on Liberals to recognise the reality that such a system had turned into a wasteful economic juggernaut of finance houses and monopolies which crushed human hopes and social justice.[33] The state would need to be used to stop such injustice, not merely at the level of social welfare, but also within the economic bedrock of production on which welfare rested. In calling for a system of public works to create employment, and in demanding that the fluctuations of the currency should not be based on gold, Keynes turned in the statist direction which would culminate in the *General Theory*.

He also presented a dramatic alternative to British Socialism. The belief of the Fabians, reflected in the ideas of the Labour leadership of the twenties, was that the state as representative of the community would inevitably supersede the private interests of an unregulated capitalism. In his call for state direction of a capitalist economy,

Keynes was putting forward a formidable challenge to a Labour intelligentsia which abhorred the cut-throat competition of private enterprise while having no realistic solution to the problems of the trade cycle and general unemployment. Keynes agreed with their fears of capitalism while providing an immediate strategy for the pressing problems of the British economy.

However, Keynes was clear that capitalism was to remain. The greater economic role of the state was not to be at the expense of the merits of *laissez-faire*. To Keynes and his fellow Liberal authors of the Yellow Book, private enterprise was an unrivalled method for a decentralised management in touch with local needs, an excellent means of testing efficiency and innovation, and the only practical way in which the various goods and services could be evaluated. These merits should be retained, while state intervention was necessary where privately owned industries failed. This was particularly the case in areas such as slum clearance, canal and dock development, and similar social enterprises:

> it is not a question of choosing between private and public enterprise in these matters. the choice has already been made. In many directions, ... it is a question of the State putting its hand to the job or of its not being done at all.[34]

In this way, state activity could develop and equip the country to meet the challenges of world competition through the existing economic system, leaving the old debates between individualism and socialism behind.

The corporatist nature of the Liberal proposals on the management of public enterprise and the mixed economy was a natural supplement to their rejection of *laissez-faire* capitalism. They rejected syndicalist and Guild Socialist demands for workers' management in favour of a system of profit-sharing and diffused ownership to restore to the worker a sense of dignity. The attempt to create a popular capitalism did not resolve the problem of the management of public industry, which must be firmly geared to economic efficiency (in the commercial, rather than the social, sense). To Keynes and the authors of the Yellow Book,

> our object must be to work out, more consciously than hitherto, the best type of organisation for the great body of public services which have already crept half-unnoticed out of private hands, and

to recruit a class of officials for running them as capable as the General Managers of great industrial companies.[35]

This should be done by means of a public corporation, such as the British Broadcasting Corporation, which would have an autonomy of decision-making within the limits of final accountability to the government or the local council – 'but only in the sense in which a company is responsible to its shareholders'.[36] These ideas of a public enterprise, run on commercial lines, were to have an important future for the Labour Party.

The acceptance of corporate industry was extended to the direction of the national economy. The old division of responsibility whereby the state looked after politics while industry looked after the economy was to be transcended by a partnership of the state, organised capital and organised labour. Trade Boards and Joint Industrial Councils would be responsible for making recommendations on productivity, wages and economic goals for individual industries and trades. A Council of Industry should be established which would be responsible for sanctioning these recommendations, and ready to give authoritative advice to an Industry Minister, whose decisions would be final. This overall Council 'should be so constituted as to represent, and to command the confidence of, the industrial world',[37] and would be supplemented by a series of other boards and councils to guide Britain rationally in the direction of economic revival. Such corporatist agencies were crucial for a capitalist economy in which the State was to play a major role in restoring economic efficiency and profitability.

KEYNES AND HOBSON

The onset of world depression in the early 1930s led Keynes finally to break from his orthodox background in Jevons and Marshall, with their belief that the normal condition of a market economy was a balance between saving and spending. Recognising that this was a special rather than a general case, Keynes pointed to the lack of effective demand as the cause of economic crisis. He was thus forced to come to terms with the economic heresy of Hobson and, in so doing, to sharpen his critique of the Labour economists.

In a series of letters to Hobson in the early 1930s, Keynes admitted an increasing interest in the under-consumptionist argument, but never fully accepted it,[38] He recognised that production lagged behind consumption, and vigorously criticised the belief of the Treasury and the Bank that a policy of thrift and cutting consumption would lead to recovery by way of a balanced budget. On the contrary, such measures would worsen the crisis, hastening the collapse of private investment by taking wealth out of the economy. To Keynes, as to Hobson, 'what we need now is not to button up our waistcoats tight, but to be in a mood of expansion, of activity – to do things, to buy things, to make things.'[39] If such a policy of expansion, particularly in the form of increasing government spending, were carried through, then consumption would revive, and with it would revive investment.

However, it was investment, not consumption, which was the key to economic recovery according to Keynes. This was the essence of his disagreement with the Labour economists. He recognised that production in any economy was the key to increasing consumption, and that in a capitalist economy production could take place only if entrepreneurs could be persuaded to stop saving their capital and start spending it. If the whole of increased investment were absorbed in consumption, employers would not make a profit and would therefore refuse to invest. There must be a certain amount of investment to cover unsold stocks – 'unless there is this amount of investment, the receipts of the entrepreneurs will be less than is required to induce them to offer the given amount of employment.'[40] It was underinvestment of capital, not under-production, which was the real problem to be tackled, according to Keynes.

Consequently, he rejected the demands of the Labour economists for a rise in wages to overcome the cause of unemployment, as he rejected their calls for a redistribution of wealth. He did not believe that wage-bargaining really affected unemployment, pointing to the coincidence of high unemployment and a docile labour force, and called for a reduction of real wages through a monetary policy which would drive prices higher than money-wages.[41] As for redistribution of wealth, Keynes regarded such a policy as unnecessary and harmful to initiative. While the disparities of wealth between rich and poor may be too high, 'for my own part, I believe that there is social and psychological justification for significant inequalities of income and wealth';[42] the money motive was highly valuable for many human activities. For Keynes, an expansion of wealth, rather than its redistribution, should be the aim of any community.

The trouble was that in choosing to overcome the vagaries of the trade cycle by state intervention, Keynes still remained trapped in the shortcomings of orthodox economics. He believed that 'consumption – to repeat the obvious – is the sole end and object of all economic activity',[43] and that for all its shortcomings a market economy was the best regulator of such activity. His economics began and ended with market relations of purchase and sale, and as a result could only indirectly touch on the process of producing wealth which lay behind the market. For Keynes, the problem arose from a gradually declining demand for consumer goods, itself causing a reduction in demand for capital goods. The failure of capitalists to invest was attributed to *psychological* causes of consumer demand. Marx's argument that the real object of capitalist economic activity was the pursuit of surplus value, and his insights into the *social* causes of crises arising ultimately from the subjection of labour to capital through the wages system was lost, as it was to be lost for the bulk of the Labour Party.

The Keynesian challenge to British Socialism was, then, highly ambiguous in its analysis and conclusions. Keynes was a Liberal throughout his life[44] because of his total opposition to state socialism as a tyrannical system which stifled both freedom and efficiency. He disliked the working class base of the Labour Party (although he respected individual trade unionists such as Ernest Bevin, with whom he worked on the Macmillan Committee in 1930), and his support of social inequality flew in the face of the important ethical element in British Socialism. However, his criticism of *laissez faire*, and his call for state intervention in a mixed economy through the stimulation of investment, touched a vital weakness in the Labour Party's political and economic thought. A need for an immediate economic programme to overcome the crisis of unemployment was glaring in the Labour Party of the 1920s and early 1930s, leading the Labour economists around Hobson to propose the living wage. Keynes's critique of Hobson's underconsumptionism, together with his calls for a corporate organisation of public enterprise in a mixed economy, were to sharply divide Labour's Right and Left in the 1930s. Thus, while he never joined the Labour Party, Keynes's ideas were to have a major effect on its thought.

8 The Emergence of Corporate Socialism

Britain had suffered mass unemployment for a decade when she was struck by the ravages of the world depression which began with the Wall Street Crash of October 1929. For forty years, the export of capital had served to cushion capitalist societies from major crises, but the 'Great Slump' of the 1930s seemed proof of the Marxist belief that capitalism was doomed to collapse. Lenin's assertion that imperialism was the final phase of capitalism inspired or terrified many as Europe plunged into protectionist trade wars and social crisis.

In Britain, already suffering from the slump conditions of the previous decade, industrial production fell by a further 17 per cent, while unemployment soared to three million by 1932. The economic crisis and the rising level of unemployment threatened to make a mockery of the ethical demands of British Socialism, demonstrating to supporters and opponents alike that the Labour government had no economic strategy (because it had no economic theory) with which to tackle the crisis. Instead, it fell back on orthodox policies of retrenchment and was eventually swept aside in the financial crisis of August, 1931, unable to put through the anti-working class measures demanded by the bankers and unwilling to fight those bankers. After Ramsay MacDonald deserted the second Labour government to head a National Government of Conservatives and Liberals, the country settled into a relative political stability compared to its rivals. The decimation of the Labour Party after the 1931 elections, when it sank to 46 MPs; the weakening of trade union organisation by unemployment and the industrial defeats of the previous decade; the minuscule size of the British Communist Party; and the dominance of National, mainly Conservative, Governments with large parliamentary majorities throughout the decade, all served to underline the stability of the British state, making the need for a Fascist movement superfluous for most of the patriotic men and women who, had they lived elsewhere in Europe, would have been drawn to the far Right.

However, political stability did not bring about any substantial economic recovery. It is true that the Midlands and south-east England enjoyed a minor burst of prosperity with the development of new, light industries,[1] but the conditions of mass unemployment and poverty persisted in Scotland, northern England and South Wales while, in general terms, the recovery of the economy after the mid-1930s was insufficient to pull these depressed areas into prosperity. The onset of a minor downturn in the trade cycle in 1937–8 was a reminder of the precarious situation of British capitalism in the decade.[2] In this situation, the National Government drifted indecisively after taking Britain off the Gold Standard and ending free trade in 1931–2. Its political cunning was matched by an inability to bring forward any imaginative economic measures.

In other countries, whether dictatorships as in Germany or democracies as in the United States, the state actively intervened to stimulate production and create employment. A major turning point was being reached, as the state now took over the role of staving off capitalist crisis played earlier by the export of capital (although this still continued to play a major part in the determination of investment decisions). The practical policies of state intervention carried out by Roosevelt and Hitler were reflected in the development of Keynesian economic theory, which now argued that a market economy was incapable of sustaining itself without crisis, and needed the state to supplement its activities. Just as the state aided capital at its birth, so now it was required to step in as its nurse and saviour.

The Labour Party, politically immobilised throughout the decade, now came into its own in the realm of ideas. On the surface, Labour now attempted to rid itself of the taint of MacDonald, regarded as a heinous traitor who had deserted the class and party which had placed him in such a high position. The Left were in full cry, as their mixture of traditional radicalism and Marxian rhetoric appeared increasingly justified by social misery at home and the growth of Fascism abroad. Their call for an urgent policy of class militancy and alliance with the Communists led to fierce debate and the temporary expulsion of several left-wing leaders from the Party. However, behind the more spectacular splits and polemics within the Labour Party during the thirties, a solid foundation of unity was being built around a new ideology of Corporate Socialism.

Labour was now able to resolve the problem of ideas bequeathed by the British Socialism of the Party's founders. It was able to provide an economic theory for the present to supplement the ethical ideas which had served the Party during its infancy. The needs of capitalist society, and of the organised working class within that society, were met as the Labour Party incorporated the syndicalist and Keynesian challenges into the general framework of its traditional ideas In doing oo, Right and Left were united on the fundamentals of a minimum programme of social and economic reform which would reshape British capitalism in the 1940s.

THE LEFT AND THE STATE

The ILP and the Socialist League

The failure of the Labour government of 1929–31 appeared to the Labour Left as the fullest justification of all their criticism of Fabian gradualism and elitism. The attacks of the Communists on Labour's acceptance of a parliamentary democracy which was nothing more than a cover for a bourgeois dictatorship appeared very close to the mark in the light of the 1931 crisis, when a Labour government was easily pushed out of power by a bankers' cabal. A drastic reappraisal of tactics and ideas was needed if Labour was to recover its credibility among working-class socialists and an increasingly Marxist intelligentsia.

In this reappraisal, the Labour Left suffered a major reverse with the decision of the ILP to disaffiliate from the Labour Party in July 1932. In formal terms, the ILP secession was concerned with party discipline, but in practice the leadership around James Maxton and Fenner Brockway had become convinced that the time was ripe to build a separate Labour Marxist party based on the class war and unadulterated socialism. Brockway, in *The Coming Revolution* (1932), argued that in the new circumstances of the 1930s even the method of *Socialism In Our Time* had become inadequate. The ILP was not prepared to wait for an election in five years time, during which the misery and deprivation of the working class promised to be intolerable. Brockway called on workers to break with the gradualism of the Labour Party, and with the trade union bureaucracy which had vested interests in that gradualism, in order to step up extra-parliamentary activity.

The language was revolutionary, but it was mere rhetoric. Brockway's view of extra-parliamentary action had more in common with pressure-group activity (on the lines of tactics already demonstrated as futile during the General Strike) than it had with a threat to the State. His pacifist views led him to ask the ILP 'to contribute to the revolution a technique in which the main method will be, not armed conflict, but action by the working class to take control over industry in their disciplined strength.'[3] It was certainly a view too extreme ever to gain a majority against the entrenched interests of the union leaders, but it was not incompatible with Labour Party membership. The ILP's belief that it could strike out on its own was the factor dividing it from the Labour Left, not its ideas. It was a false belief; ILP membership dropped from 17 000 in 1932 to 4 500 by 1935, and it ceased to have political significance, a chilling reminder to the Labour Left of Keir Hardie's belief that socialists must subordinate their socialism to their labourism if they were to survive.

Under E. F. Wise, the ILP dissidents who remained within the Labour Party joined with dissident Fabians in 1932 to form the Socialist League, which sought to continue the grand ILP tradition of converting Labour to socialism from within. It was this body which served as the fount of left-wing initiatives for a reappraisal of tactics and ideas on Labour's part. Its opposition to the Labour leadership – expressed in its *Programme for Action* (1933), a call for an Emergency Powers Act and increased public ownership – was largely ineffective, since the League inherited from the ILP a lack of trade union support, but its attack on the gradualism of MacDonald had wide echoes in the movement after 1931.

R. H. Tawney, who had drafted *Labour and the Nation*, now called upon Labour to rediscover the reasons for its existence. Labour's hesitancy under MacDonald could not be remedied by a reorganisation or by new programmatic proposals. It was a weakness of political philosophy – an indecisive conception of what type of society Labour wanted. Tawney's conception was now one of radical rather than mild reform; it was 'to abolish all advantages and disabilities which have their source, not in differences of personal quality, but in disparities of wealth, opportunity, social position and economic power.'[4] This was certainly radical, though hardly revolutionary, and Tawney maintained his rejection of class hatred in favour of sentiments more suitable to a socialist commonwealth. Nevertheless, the 1931 crisis had convinced even Tawney that devious counter-attacks could be expected from the plutocracy which could be more effective than Labour had hitherto anticipated, and he too called for emergency powers to attack the citadels of private wealth as a priority above the immediate relief of economic distress. He now argued that 'onions can be eaten leaf by leaf, but you cannot skin a live tiger paw by paw; vivisection is its trade and it does the skinning first.'[5] It was a view of capitalism which came uncomfortably close to that of the Marxists.

Cripps

Stafford Cripps, who became Chairman of the Socialist League on the death of Frank Wise in 1933, came to be seen as the embodiment of the Labour Left's attack on moderation. Cripps (1889–1952) was the nephew of Beatrice Webb, and after the usual upper-class education at Winchester and Oxford made his name as a constitutional lawyer with a knack for mastering very complicated documents and evidence. A firm Christian and political moderate, he was induced to join the Labour Party by Herbert Morrison and was almost immediately appointed Solicitor General in 1930. His class background and political moderation led MacDonald to ask him to join the National Government in 1931; however, Cripps did not merely decline but performed an astonishing political somersault to become one of the most militant spokesmen of the Left.

His logical mind had led Cripps to grasp the implications of the 1931 crisis quickly. In a letter to William Graham immediately after the formation of the National Government, he argued that

> it seems absolutely necessary to throw off once and for all the attitude of compromise which was impressed upon us by reason of the minority position in which the Labour Government found itself.... We must, I feel, completely divorce ourselves from the past.[6]

This he proceeded to do in his analysis of the undemocratic nature of the British ruling class, in a Marxist style which concealed his Christian socialist outlook. He believed that the 1931 crisis – 'the clearest demonstration of the power of capitalism to overthrow a popularly elected Government by extra-parliamentary means'[7] – was proof that the capitalists and plutocrats would go to any lengths to defeat Parliament.

If there was to be any hope of the peaceful parliamentary change called for by Labour, then the dangerous power of the capitalist enemy had to be recognised and defeated quickly. A Labour government, democratically elected, must proceed to take power away from capital, in the lifetime of a single Parliament. This could only be done if an Emergency Powers Bill to control capital was passed on the first day of office to give Ministers extraordinary powers, similar to those granted in 1914. If the House of Lords rejected the bill, the government would ask the Crown to create enough peers at immediate notice to ensure eventual passage; if the Crown refused, the government would either resign or rule unconstitutionally, disregarding the Lords entirely. If the armed forces intervened on behalf of wealth and privilege, then the government must be prepared to become a temporary dictatorship. There must be no time allowed for the anti-democratic forces of capitalism to gather and to exercise their subtle influences on the legislature before the strong points of private wealth had been transferred to the state.

With these arguments, Cripps rapidly became the *bête noire* of the British establishment, especially when he hinted darkly at possible opposition from Buckingham Palace. He made it clear that he was referring to Court circles rather than the Crown itself, but this was not enough to prevent a storm of abuse descending on his head, including censure from a Labour leadership terrified of being seen as anti-royalist and unconstitutional. In fact, Cripps merely envisaged action to protect parliamentary democracy against any illegal moves from the ruling class. He was, given his belief that the National Government was introducing Fascism into Britain,[8] excessively constitutional, willing to wait on an eventual Labour majority which he believed to be inevitable. He did envisage trade union action to protect Labour against any armed attempt to unseat it, but this was hardly unconstitutional given the right of any government to protect itself against undemocratic action.

Laski

The attack on gradualism had major implications for Labour's conception of the nature of the State. Ever since the early Fabians, Labour had regarded the State as an essentially neutral instrument which happened to be in the hands of capitalist parties but which could be wrested from them by the workers' party through democratic elections. The 1931 crisis had led many of Labour's radicals to doubt whether this was in fact the case, and Harold Laski, the political theorist who sat on Labour's National Executive during the decade, set about reformulating the theory of the State. In doing so, he demonstrated the limits of the radicalism to which the Labour Left could go without becoming Leninist. Laski flirted with the Leninist theory of the State in order to frighten the British ruling class but ultimately he refused to grasp the revolutionary implications of his flirtation.

Harold Laski (1893–1950) had been born into an Orthodox Jewish family in Manchester and educated at Oxford, but had rejected his background to write for the *Daily Herald* during the syndicalist unrest. After a period teaching at Harvard University (1916–1920), he returned to an active role in the Labour Party as well as an academic job in political science at the London School of Economics. During the 1920s he had adopted a federalist approach to society, based on the pluralism of J. N. Figgis, and elaborated his theories in *A Grammar of Politics* (1925). However, in the aftermath of the 1931 crisis, he quickly recognised the grave constitutional implications of the formation of the National Government. A party which had been elected by the people, with a larger number of seats than any other at Westminster, was unable to carry its principles into practice because it was frightened of how the investing public might act. The refusal of international bankers to grant a loan to the Labour government was 'an announcement that finance-capital will not permit the ordinary assumption of the constitution to work if these operate to its disadvantage'. In other words, grave doubts had arisen as to whether a socialist society could come about by constitutional means. In these circumstances, Laski felt that the Left should go beyond the constitutional measures sought by Cripps to make a radical reappraisal of the nature of the State which would ascertain whether the Labour Party, born and nurtured within the framework of the British constitution, was capable of transforming society.

In doing so, Laski moved a considerable distance away from the pluralist ideas put forward in his *Grammar of Politics* (1925). In a new preface to that book, he made it clear that he had not rejected the libertarian principles first laid down there – indeed, time had reinforced their truth – but that he had overestimated the ease with which such a society could emerge. He now believed that only Marxism could explain the naked force which had come to the fore in Nazi Germany and which lay implicit in capitalist Britain. In the face of this, his pluralism was not discarded as much as submerged in Marxism – 'I now recognise...that the pluralist attitude to the State and law was a stage on the road to a Marxist understanding of them.'[9] In doing so, he reduced the importance of all the ethical and philosophical grounds on which the State demanded the allegiance of its citizens to concentrate on the ugly, but unavoidable, realities of power and violence. Lenin's theory that the State was nothing but armed bodies of men existing to protect the ruling class was now accepted by Laski, who then proceeded to test it against the traditional liberal theory of the State.

This liberal conception was a philosophical one in the worst sense of the word, existing in ideas only without any relation to reality. It saw the State as an expression of reason, existing to promote the good life of its citizens by curbing the excesses of individualism. Obedience was based on the recognition of self-interest, as argued by Hobbes, while the right of rebellion was allowed whenever the State threatened this self-interest. The liberal tradition, as a result of this of rebellion, was a perpetual challenge to tyranny and repression, but it could not be divorced from the men who created and exploited it. It could be traced in a decisive shift in economic power from the monarch to the middle class property owners in the seventeenth century, when the ideas of liberty were put forward by John Locke to defend a bourgeois Parliament from royal encroachments. The rights of property were the reality behind the empty and legalistic notions of liberty and equality. In the real world, the formal doctrine of equality before the law was confounded by the social inequality between rich and poor, who had very different access to court protection because of the costs of legal action. If the poor sought to end their exploitation, they would find the forces of the State arrayed against them to protect the legally entrenched interests of the rich exploiters.

To Laski, it was 'the first duty of a political philosophy to examine the character of the State in its actuality rather than in its idea.'[10] It was in what the State did in practice, and not in its formal claims, that its real nature lay. In practice, the State existed in a society distorted by class relations, and would do everything in its power to protect the ruling class. This was not merely a question of the personnel of administration, law and the military being drawn from the upper classes; it was the belief of the ruling class that they were the natural and justifiable rulers of a social hierarchy which would lead them to identify any threat to property as an evil conspiracy to subvert a traditional and law-abiding community. Their long rule had blinded them to the class nature of their society, just as the liberal theory of the State concealed the central nature of the property system which lay behind it. This economic factor was the bedrock on which social and political institutions were built, as demonstrated whenever a threat arose to property. Racial or religious antagonisms might alter or determine the personnel of the State, but did not threaten its unity in the same way that class antagonisms did. When a socialist movement threatened the ruling class, then it subtly deflected the threat, as in Britain, or turned to Fascism as in Italy or Germany, to protect itself. Thus Laski, like Marx and Lenin, saw the State as 'an instrument, not of the community as a whole – that is an abstract entity devoid of intellectual expression – but of the class which owns the instruments of economic power.'[11]

With this view of the State as an instrument of the ruling class, Laski attempted to investigate parliamentary democracy in Britain to ascertain the possibility of a peaceful transition to a socialist society. The success of representative government in Britain had been due to particular historical causes – a unified nation free from foreign invasion; a sense of liberty after the seventeenth century revolutions; economic, military and imperial success; and, above all, a sense of security. If the capitalist economic system on which representative government rested could provide security for the vast majority of the people, then the State could command allegiance from its citizens, no matter how grudging. In its phase of expansion, capitalism could afford to be tolerant; to grant suffrage to the propertyless and women; and to offer a better standard of life to all its citizens. However, the class nature of British society remained constant through all the flux of liberal reform; the justice and wisdom of the reforms were determined by their effect on the existing order.

As capitalism plunged into economic crisis, and was faced with a socialist threat, all the gifts of political and social reform were called into question. Indeed, when two parties which differed over the fundamentals of property and class power confronted one another, the Constitution itself was placed in jeopardy. To Laski, 'Constitutional principles and forms do not operate in a vacuum of abstract reason',[12] and the manifest failure of the economic system to provide security for a growing number of its citizens placed representative government itself in the dock. The performance of the second Labour government had made it clear that socialist measures might not be compatible with a generally accepted democratic government. The fall of that government had been an admission that, whatever the will of the electoral majority, the owners of economic power were the permanent masters of the Constitution – 'the State is their State; and its supreme coercive power can only be directed to those objects of which they are willing to approve'.[13] Should the Left take power, it would face a loss of confidence on the Right; there would be economic strains, a flight of capital and a halt to investment. This withdrawal of confidence would shatter the consensus on which the unity of the State rested, so that representative government was losing its meaning in the British Constitution. This would present a challenge to any government, forcing it either to retreat or to attack the power of capital in a much more fundamental and urgent manner than had been envisaged by Fabian gradualism.

To Laski, 'the British Constitution... is the expression of a politically democratic government; it is not the expression of a democratic society.'[14] In politics, universal suffrage and the party system ensured frequent elections and peaceful changes of government. In society, a good education was generally reserved for the rich, while access to the civil service, the legal profession and the military establishment was denied to the working class. For men and women who had the misfortune to be born into the working class, their lot was a poor education, toil tempered by mindless entertainment, and the misery of a tiny pension at the end of a life spent working for capital. The schools, the press and the Church were geared to teaching obedience and acceptance of a proper station in life, while those socialists and trade unionists who did not bow to capitalist rule were denounced as unpatriotic agitators. The whole British social system was based on the fear and hatred of the ruling classes for their inferiors, disguised as a patronising liberalism which could easily turn into a ferocious repression if the rulers were threatened.

It was the possibility of repression which profoundly disturbed Laski. The British Constitution was so vague and shifting -- 'a matter of understandings and ideas and sentiments that are always half-articulate rather than explicitly expressed'[15] – that repression and suspension of democratic rights could take place without abuse of the law. When capitalism enjoyed prosperity and the political climate was calm, a generous interpretation of the Constitution could be allowed. At a time of economic and political crisis, the interpretation was likely to be strict and authoritarian. The House of Commons was procedurally slow; the Lords could hamstring legislation for two years; while the Crown, the reserve power of the Constitution, could always add legitimacy to any suspension of democratic government and legal rights.[16]

Despite this pessimistic analysis of parliamentary democracy within the capitalist State, Laski rejected Communist revolution on the grounds that it was a futile appeal to the irrational in human nature.[17] Violent resistance to a dictatorship might be morally justifiable, but the slightest possibility of peaceful change must be exploited to the full to avoid violence and a dictatorship of the Left. In a capitalist democracy, Laski had no doubt that the scales were weighed against socialist change, but 'I believe that it is the duty of the citizen to exhaust the means placed at his disposal by the constitution of the State before resorting to revolution.'[18] The development of military technology and the efficiency of the modern State made successful revolution, rather than a fearful blood-bath, extremely difficult, if not impossible. As a result, Laski advocated constitutional change through the Labour Party. He pointed out that Britain could escape violence as a result of its historical traditions and its capacity for tolerance, but his pessimism and grave doubts as to the democratic convictions of the ruling class make his constitutionalism appear as a forlorn grasping at straws. In looking at the profound differences between the parties on the question of property, Laski believed that 'the prospect of solving them in terms of reason, instead of terms of power, becomes a matter of extraordinary difficulty'.[19]

This raises the question of the nature of Laski's Marxism. In one sense, it came close to the revolutionary theory of the State held by Lenin. Laski attempted to denigrate the liberal theory of politics as an exercise in logic rather than in life, and pointed to the violence and power relationships which stood behind the ethical and philosophical defence of State power. Like Lenin, he saw the State as a coercive instrument of class rule, ready to turn to armed force as the capitalist economy went into crisis. His concentration on *realpolitik* rather than philosophical justification thus marked a major evolution of Laski's thought from the previous decade.

However, its resemblance to Marxism was more superficial than real.[20] Unlike Marx and Lenin, Laski continued to see the State in fundamentally moral terms. He accepted that it was an instrument of coercion, but held that it did have a purpose and a justification – to satisfy the demands of its subjects. Indeed, 'the fulfilment of the state-purpose can only be accomplished when the incidence of its actions is unbiased'.[21] The State in capitalist society was biased, but the State in a socialist society would be unbiased. It was a utilitarian theory, not a Marxist one. Where Marxism sought finally to abolish the State, Laski was attempting to rescue the liberal theory of the State from its capitalist trappings.

The dabbling in Lenin by Laski, Cripps and a large section of the Labour Left aroused strong opposition in the rest of the party. In 1933, Labour's National Joint Council issued a manifesto, *Dictatorship versus Democracy*, in which Communism and Fascism were equated as sinister evils threatening the democratic state. Clement

Attlee (who became leader of the Party in 1935) rejected the belief that capitalism was inevitably anti-democratic and ready to reject the Constitution. He acknowledged that Britain's rulers had become more callous and ruthless than they had been in his youth, but believed that the long tradition of personal and political freedom, together with universal suffrage, would safeguard the democratic process. Attlee argued that

> there is nothing more misleading than to try to apply to all countries a cast-iron theory of historical necessity and to argue that Britain must go the Moscow road unless she follows the example of Berlin or Rome. The theorists at the end of the eighteenth century might equally well have argued that Britain must go the way of France unless she was prepared to align herself with Austria and Prussia.[22]

Attlee was undoubtedly right in his arguments against the dogmatism of many on the Left, but he was himself too sanguine on the resistance of the ruling class and the extreme flexibility of the British Constitution, which could be used against any real threat to their power. He held that, while Labour's acceptance of the Constitution relied on its opponents' similar acceptance, 'as long as the workers have it in their power to achieve their ends by the use of the ballot-box, they have no right to seek to obtain them by any other means'.[23] In the actual conditions of the 1940s, this resistance did not materialise, but then again there was no real threat to capital as a social system by the structural and social reforms of that period.

Foreign Policy and the State

The deepening international crisis in the 1930s brought to the fore the confusion felt by the Labour Left about the class nature of the British State in a much sharper form than that posed by the Great War. In the earlier crisis, the ILP had refused its support to the war effort on anti-capitalist and pacifist grounds, but refused to go as far as Lenin in denying the authority of the State by a policy of revolutionary defeatism. In the 1930s, the Left's dilemma was sharpened by the fact that the German threat was also a Fascist threat, with both a record and a promise of anti-working class measures much more vicious and far-reaching than those of the Kaiser.

It was George Lansbury (1859–1940) who gave the old pacifist answer to the crisis. Lansbury had become leader of the Party after the 1931 election. He was chosen because he was the most senior figure to survive the electoral rout, but he was also a Christian pacifist whose views became increasingly embarrassing to the other party leaders once the problem of national defence came to the fore. At the 1935 party conference, Lansbury opposed the use of sanctions by the League of Nations against Italy, which had invaded Abyssinia, on the grounds that they may lead to war. In doing so, he presented a coherent connection between the Party's domestic and foreign policy, as he had long rejected the militant doctrine of class war as a solution to the dire poverty and distress among the working-class people to whom he had devoted his life. He declared,

> I have no right to preach pacifism to starving people in this country and preach something else in relation to people elsewhere. And that has been a fundamental state, it has not been something of an expediency. It has been a belief that we should sooner or later in the world win our way with waiting.[24]

This sentimental pacifism was not seen as very realistic against the armed might of ruthless fascists. Lansbury was swept aside at this conference, while the Left realised that the new situation required very different answers from those given twenty years earlier. Cripps and the Socialist League called for a distinct policy which was as fundamentally opposed to the National Government in foreign affairs as it was in domestic affairs. On the grounds that workers should have nothing to do with wars caused by capitalism, the Left opposed rearmament for a Tory government, which might well use its weapons against Soviet Russia rather than Germany. As Cripps told the 1935 conference, 'To me, the central factor in our decision must turn not so much upon what we as a country should or should not do, but upon who is in control of our actions.'[25] The League of Nations was rejected as a viable instrument for world peace on the grounds that it was warped and neutralised by the conflicting interests of the imperial powers. Indeed, Cripps went far towards a denial of the nation-state in declaring that

> it is impossible for us to serve two masters – our own selfish interests as British imperialists and our desire for peace as world

citizens. The interests of the British Empire and the world are not identical.[26]

The distinct foreign policy presented by the Left called for an alliance of a socialist Britain with other socialist powers, including the Soviet Union, in a quarantine of the Fascist powers,[27] though the exact policy to be carried out should Britain became involved in war before it became socialist was not investigated. Instead, the immediate policy of the Left was a domestic alliance of progressive forces against fascism as a preparation for government. This demand for a united front of Labour, the ILP and the Communist Party was later extended to a call for a popular front of all progressives, including Liberals and anti-appeasement Conservatives. It was reinforced by the success of the Popular Front in Spain and France, and when Spanish generals attacked the Popular Front, the resulting civil war was transformed in left-wing thinking into a defence of democracy against Fascism. All talk of specifically working-class defence against capitalism was dropped, along with any demands smacking of socialism, in the interests of unity between all classes in the nation against the Fascist threat.[28] The Popular Front policy sealed the fate of the British Left; the Socialist League was disaffiliated from the Party in 1937, while Cripps and two of his lieutenants were expelled in 1939 (to be readmitted during the war).

Their policy of fundamental opposition to the government on foreign policy never really stood any chance of being adopted by a constitutional party with the political traditions which made up the Labour Party. In rejecting both Lansbury and the Left, Labour reaffirmed that the needs of national defence stood as a priority above the class divisions in British society. Clement Attlee (1883–1967), who succeeded Lansbury as party leader in 1935, rejected the Cripps policy as breaking up this national unity.

> If a Capitalist Government is in power, the workers must resist everything that the Government does. If a Socialist Government is in power, the Capitalists will do the same. The result is that the country ceases to count as a factor in world affairs. It is immobilised until the class struggle is resolved.[29]

When Cripps turned to the Popular Front strategy, the Labour leadership was even able to expel him on the grounds that he was resurrecting the MacDonald policy of class collaboration with the Liberals.

Despite the difference over foreign policy and the populai fiont, the Left and Right of the party ultimately remained united in the thirties as they had in the Great War. Just as the ILP had been unwilling to take up Lenin's call for revolutionary defeatism then, so the Socialist League was unable to echo the call of Trotsky (taken up momentarily by Orwell as a result of his experience fighting with the Spanish Anarchists)[30] that the 'progressive' elements of the middle class were just as much enemies of the working class as the Fascist elements. It was too uncompromising a position in its logic, and to have taken it up would have involved a total denial of loyalty to the State. On the other hand, the Left were unwilling to accept the bi-partisan policies of the Labour leadership, implying as they did a fundamental trust in the ruling class. As a result, they fell between two stools, seeking to deny the Government the means to arm itself against a foreign threat while unable to take this denial to its logical conclusion. They were neither revolutionaries nor patriots, finding themselves instead in a position of moral righteousness and occasional flights of fantasy which became increasingly untenable and finally impossible as war approached. The collapse of the Left's 'independent' foreign policy at the outbreak of war demonstrated that, when the decisive moment came, for the Left as much as for the Right, the forces which divided Britain were seen as less important than the forces which united her.

THE LABOUR KEYNESIANS

Until the Great Depression of the 1930s, Labour economic thinking had been based on the underconsumptionism of J. A. Hobson. It was believed, on both Right and Left, that trade union successes in obtaining higher wages and a policy of redistributive taxation would increase both working-class and national prosperity. The ILP, in its living wage policy, sought to use Hobson's economic ideas to force the pace in the transition to socialism, but MacDonald and Snowden were no less committed to the underconsumptionist 'heresy'.

However, the economic policy pursued by Snowden in government in 1929–31 was marked by a respect for orthodoxy worthy of any Tory Chancellor. His acceptance of Hobson was combined with a belief in the Quantity Theory of Money – the theory that any increase in purchasing power without any corresponding increase in productivity would cause inflation. That prospect was terrifying for any

Chancellor for whom the recent hyper-inflation suffered by Germany in 1923 was a dark reminder of the consequences of dabbling in wild experiments. Snowden had this in mind when he rejected radical ideas in an address to the 1929 Labour conference:

> in the control of credit and currency, the administration of the control must be kept free from political influences. . . . I have seen and I know something of the danger of the control of credit and the means of starting an inflation policy, and it might be highly dangerous in the hands of a Government that wanted to use this means.[31]

In other words, the incorruptible socialist, Snowden, was forced to uphold the market and the bankers as the forces determining financial policy. The result was financial crisis and the desertion of Labour by Snowden and MacDonald.

Alternative policies were already being presented as the Keynesian challenge to British Socialism was making itself felt. Keynes did not fully work out his theories, particularly his modification of the Quantity Theory of Money through the multiplier, until the early 1930s. However, his calls for the state management of credit and currency markets had been quickly absorbed into the Labour tradition by the agile mind of Sir Oswald Mosley.

Mosley

Mosley (1896–1980), who became a Unionist MP in 1918, took into politics the values of comradeship and heroism which his experience as an officer in the trenches had taught him. He became an Independent in 1920, in protest at the unheroic terrorism of the 'Black and Tans' against the Irish, and gradually moved to the Labour Party, attracted by the Guild Socialist ideas of the ILP. By the mid-1920s he had grasped the implications of Keynes's criticisms of Treasury policy to develop an economic policy distinct from the living wage proposals of the Left. He later wrote that 'the background of my economic thinking was first developed by a study of Keynes – more in conversation with him than in reading his early writings.'[32] As a result, he elaborated his new thinking in a pamphlet, *Revolution by Reason*, in 1925.

Arguing that the economic crisis made evolutionary socialism out of date, Mosley called for an emergency policy of credit expansion through nationalisation of the banking system. The state banks would, through their bold and vigorous use of monetary policy, reverse the crisis of a lack of demand in the home market, They would ensure that the new credit go into the hands of the working class, so that the purchase of necessities rather than luxury goods would lead to a reverse of the decline of Britain's staple industries. Social justice and economic sense would go hand in hand in reviving the national economy.

In calling for an expansion of credit, Mosley remained committed to the orthodoxies of the Quantity Theory of Money, but was much more imaginative about it than the timid Labour leadership. The evils of inflation were recognised, but Mosley argued that they could be overcome by a vigorous adoption of state planning – 'Here our Socialist planning must enter in. We must see that more goods are forthcoming to meet the new demand.'[33] This point was elaborated after he became Chancellor of the Duchy of Lancaster in the 1929 Labour government. He called for a bold programme of public works to create enough goods to accommodate an expansionary credit policy. Dissatisfied with the lack of response to his proposals, and calling for a strong central direction of unemployment policy, he resigned from the government in May 1930, and then left Labour to form the New Party in February 1931. His subsequent career as a fascist obscured his importance for introducing Keynesian ideas into the labour movement, demonstrating as he did that as a short-term remedy for unemployment they were far from incompatible with state planning of the economy. His support from the Left (Arthur Cook, the militant miners' leader, and Aneurin Bevan were among the signatories of the Mosley Manifesto) indicated the forthcoming unity in the Party on economic issues.

Durbin

However, the Left's commitment to the underconsumptionism of J. A. Hobson led to a great reluctance on their part to accept the Keynesian challenge. It was a Labour moderate, Evan Durbin (1906–48), who grasped the significance of Keynes's differences with Hobson.[34] In his book *Purchasing Power and Trade Depressions* (1933), with which Hugh Gaitskell collaborated, Durbin set about a criticism of underconsumptionist theories of the economy from a Keynesian point of view. He put his finger on the fundamental difference with Hobson when he wrote, 'I share Mr Keynes's view that all the existing theories of underconsumption have failed to take account of the importance of the activity of investment in the solution of the problems of monetary income.'[35]

Durbin attacked Hobson's theories directly by pointing out that an excess of saving as a result of low consumption was not necessarily disastrous. On the contrary, the growth of industrial capitalism in the nineteenth century was direct proof that a restriction of competition promoted the accumulation of capital for investment in new industry. While saving could check industrial expansion if it was in the form of a hoard, it could positively promote growth of the economy if it was in the form of investment. An increase in investment, through its power to increase physical productivity, would increase consumption in its wake. Thus, 'the investment of the savings has brought into existence new capital of a type which enables costs to be reduced on the average'.[36] The need to reduce incomes could in this way be removed by new investment, which would allow general wealth to grow rather than redistributing the existing wealth. It was not an attack on the ruling class that was needed, but a concerted policy to increase the general wealth.

If Durbin rejected the traditional radicalism of the Labour Left, he also made it clear that the market system was not able to increase social wealth. The failure of a planless economy to respond to a rise in savings by converting those savings to investment would cause a general depression, since the hoarding of capital would lead to a contraction of consumption goods and, therefore, capital goods (which Durbin believed to be totally dependent on the market for consumption goods). This would bring about a general contraction of the economic system, leading to unemployment and social insecurity. Only a planned socialist economy – where government, banking, industrial and trade union action was centrally co-ordinated – would be able to overcome the trade cycle of boom and slump which had come to characterize capitalism.

However, Durbin rejected the Mosley policy of relying on a bold policy of credit expansion as much as he did the Labour Left demands for a raising of incomes. Both policies would lead to inflation, according to Durbin, because price stabilisation was not possible in a market economy, or even in the transition to a planned economy, as it was impossible to control fully the effect of credit expansion. There was no real certainty in such a situation that any saving of capital would not be hoarded rather than invested. In a socialist economy, the State could control the direction as well as the

size of the new credit flow, but practical difficulties meant that such
an economy could only be established gradually.

As a result, Durbin argued for a mildly expansionary monetary
policy through the use of low interest rates, a discriminatory tax
policy to encourage private capital investment, and a firm commitment to check inflation by imposing higher taxes. His main hope in
preventing the inflationary consequences of cheaper money lay in an
agreement by the unions to maintain stable incomes, avoiding what
would later be called 'cost-push' inflation. Only in this way could
unemployment be gradually reduced in what was bound to remain a
semi-planned economy for a prolonged period. Durbin believed that
Labour's economic policy

> must be based upon the necessity of making a large quantity of
> *private* industry expand its demand for labour, at the existing level
> of wages, and upon the demand of the Trade Unions for the
> maintenance of money wage rates.[37] [*Durbin's italics*]

In this way, as incomes for all consumers remained constant, more of
the fall in prices would go to capital for investment and the economy
would gradually move towards a stable prosperity.

Dalton

Durbin's adoption of Keynesian policies was echoed by other prominent Labour figures, particularly Bevin and Dalton. Hugh Dalton
(1887–1962) was born into an upper-class family – his father was
Canon of St George's Chapel and tutor to the Royal Family – and
was educated in economics at Cambridge by Keynes. He joined the
Fabian Society at his University, and entered politics in 1922 after an
academic career at the London School of Economics. He was a
leading moderate on Labour's National Executive during the 1930s,
where he was instrumental in securing eventual Labour acceptance of
the policy that only the Bank of England, not the joint stock banks,
should be taken into state ownership. In doing so, he was closely
advised by the XYZ Club, a group of Labour sympathisers from the
City. The participation of Durbin and Gaitskell in this club ensured the
conversion of Dalton to the new Keynesian economics, as seen in his
Unbalanced Budgets (1934) and *Practical Socialism for Britain* (1935).

Dalton argued that the world crisis had arisen purely and simply as
a result of the conservative policies of bankers. In Britain, the 1931

crisis was a 'banker's ramp', after a small group of plutocrats had taken the decision to deflate the economy without public discussion or parliamentary sanction. As unemployment and the faltering of investment had unbalanced budgets throughout Europe – by reducing the number of companies and individuals from whom revenue could be taken from the State in taxes – the bankers had totally sacrificed the need to fight social inequality and a better distribution of wealth in favour of the sacred task of balancing the budget. In the face of the conservative economic policies successfully imposed by these financiers, Dalton concluded that 'the world-wide crash in the price level since 1929, with all its disastrous consequences, is a bankers' achievement'.[38]

To remedy this situation and pull the nation out of slump, Dalton advocated a control of the financial institutions through a nationalised Bank of England, enforcing public direction of economic policy, which would be given the purpose of benefiting the whole community rather than a few profit-making individuals. Monetary policy would thus be determined by the State, rather than the anarchical forces of the market or the rigidities of the Gold Standard. It would be used to move gradually towards a prosperous planned economy by means of a controlled expansion of credit, avoiding the twin evils of inflation and deflation. Such a policy must, however, ensure that the new wealth generated in what would at first be a mixed economy would accrue to the working class as well as forming a reserve for new investment. As he put it to Labour's 1932 conference, 'in a period when productive power is increasing you must be increasing purchasing power equally with productive capacity, and therefore...more purchasing power is distributed to our people.'[39] This concern that the plan should be for the benefit of the working class differentiated the Labour Keynesians from Keynes himself, who, while not averse to reducing unfair inequalities of wealth, maintained a patrician and disinterested attitude to the labour movement.

Dalton distanced his own ideas from those of Keynes by arguing that an expansionary fiscal and monetary policy could not take place in a capitalist economy, which was geared to the private pursuit of profit rather than the public good. He argued that the capitalist system was unsuited to large changes in the value of money and, while admitting his technical agreement with the Keynesians, believed that

> their policy, in order to be effective, needs to be pushed a good deal further than most of them seem willing to push it. I believe that

freedom from the plague of recurrent booms and slumps can only be found in a planned economy.[40]

Therefore, to control the capital markets which could thwart Keynesian policies, Dalton advocated a National Investment Board, which would be able to licence and direct new investment in industries, mobilising national resources in a rational and co-ordinated manner. He saw the creation of such a board as a major step towards the creation of socialist financial institutions, able to deal both with the immediate problem of unemployment and the longer-term need for a planned development of industry and the economy.[41]

Bevin

The position of Ernest Bevin in the labour movement during the 1930s made him a particularly influential figure in Labour's gradual absorption of Keynesian economics. Bevin (1881–1951) had been an illegitimate child, born in a Somerset village and orphaned at eight. After working as a farm boy, he took a series of unskilled jobs in Bristol before becoming an official in the Dockers' Union in 1910. The industrial unrest of those years strengthened his labourist politics, and he was never able to escape the dualism of a profound hostility to employers and a recognition of the value of negotiating with them. As the first leader of the powerful Transport and General Workers Union from 1922, Bevin played a major part in trade union politics, and was a dominant influence in the TUC General Council, and thereby in the Labour Party, which was very much under union control in its weakened parliamentary condition of the 1930s.

As a member of the Macmillan Committee on Finance and Industry in 1930, Bevin worked closely with Keynes, learning the new economics quickly as the Treasury and Bank officials were subjected to close and critical questioning, and becoming one of the few union leaders to earn Keynes's respect. He had none of Snowden's awe for the guardians of financial orthodoxy, and asked Montague Norman, the Bank's governor, whether it was not possible

to have some direction through public bodies, municipalities, of the whole operation of credit, and therefore while you restrict one form of credit you maintain the volume of home credit, to prevent the blow falling upon the workpeople.[42]

He believed that if incomes had to be so reduced, the burden should not fall on the working class to the exclusion of the wealthier sections of society. However, Keynes was demonstrating that a resolution of the crisis need not be at the expense of Bevin's members and, having grasped this, Bevin went on to attack the financial orthodoxy which upheld the Gold Standard and respected the private nature of the Bank of England.

In a series of pamphlets, Bevin called for an end to the reign of the financial autocrats, with their belief in balanced budgets and their infliction of misery on the labour movement. Instead, there should be a recognition that people are the only genuine subjects of economic concern:

> We are being congratulated on a balanced budget and the possibility of a surplus, but if we approach the question of balance correctly we must not do so in terms of money only, but in terms of life, health and opportunity.[43]

A budget surplus was not to be valued if it was achieved at the expense of a deficit in health.

Against orthodox economic policies, Bevin called for state intervention in the world of high finance, so that increased investment through the creation of credit would lead Britain away from the vicious circle of low investment and high unemployment. As a minimum programme of reform within capitalism, he argued that 'we must socialise the Bank of England, as other countries have socialised their Central Banks, in order to be free to pursue an expansionist monetary policy on the basis of a managed currency'.[44] However, like the other Labour Keynesians, Bevin believed that the only real solution to the crisis lay in public control of industry. Only in a planned, socialist economy could Keynesian techniques work.

However, this planned economy was to take place in a national context. Bevin, steeped in the labourist traditions of the British working class, saw the protection of the workers of his own nation as taking a priority over the workers of other nations, just as he saw the interests of workers in his own union as taking precedence over the interests of workers in other unions. Under his influence, the TUC Economic Committee rejected free trade in favour of trade within the economic bloc of the British Empire, rich as it was in resources and geared by its imperial tradition to supplying Britain itself. This labourist trait of Bevin was strikingly demonstrated at the 1930 TUC:

What I say is this, and I am not afraid of saying it. I sit on a Colonial Development Committee under an Act passed by the Labour Government, and I see the expenditure of millions of pounds going on for the development of areas where native races have not yet begun to be industrialised. You talk about the coal trade. Ought there not to be some control against the possible development of coal in Tanganyika and in East Africa, which might come into competition with your coal here at a time when the world does not want it?[45]

At a time when trade wars were about to begin, it was a recipe which neatly combined a commitment to his own workers with a commitment to the British State and its Empire.

It was this belief in a planned economy of publicly controlled industry and finance which provided a bridge to the Left for the Labour Keynesians. The Left were initially suspicious of Keynes. They were not just objecting to reforms of a capitalist economy, since their support of the living wage proposals and the Mosley manifesto demonstrated their awareness that immediate measures to relieve distress had to be taken. Their objection was more fundamental, as they felt that the Labour Keynesians, in identifying capitalism with the free market and socialism with planning, were ignoring the whole question of class power. If Keynes was correct, there would be no need to redistribute wealth from the rich; in contrast, Hobson's theories of economic surplus and underconsumption had the maldistribution of wealth between social classes at their very centre.

Cole

It was G. D. H. Cole who attempted to reconcile the Left to Keynes. He remained a Guild Socialist, but the collapse of the Building Guild and the militant trade union movement in the 1920s had left him politically impotent and isolated. As a result, he abandoned the abstract heights of socialist theory to engage in a series of concrete studies of practical social and economic policies. He took Hobson as his guide in these matters at first,[46] and attempted to counter the Keynesian Liberal proposals of the late twenties with his *The Next Ten Years* (1929). Here, he accepted the Liberal assertion that capitalism had, through abandoning *laissez-faire*, succeeded in increasing production, but argued that its class nature had prevented it from resolving the problem of distribution of the wealth produced. As a result, the market was unable to buy all the new goods, leading to a crisis of overproduction and resulting in mass unemployment.

A different method was needed, if the market was to be expanded to buy these new goods. He adopted the Liberal plan for a National Investment Board, but hoped to use it to replace capitalism eventually. To Cole, the Liberal proposals 'are far too timid and hesitant, but they indicate clearly the line of advance'.[47] In socialist hands, such a board must have much greater powers, such as the control of all private loans. Moreover, as the State would lend money to all private firms, it was only reasonable to insist on some form of state control, such as state representatives on the company board of directors. In this way, the State would be able to increase purchasing power through an expansion of credit and public works. Moreover, Cole differed not only from the Labour Keynesians, but also from the *Living Wage* authors, in calling for the nationalisation of all banks. Public ownership of the Bank of England could give a socialist government control of the *amount* of credit, but it was also necessary to control the *direction* of this credit. The commercial banks would have to be brought under state ownership if that was to be done. However, the objective was social justice, not merely the increase of economic efficiency. The need for public works was because

it is fatal, in the modern world, to make the possession of purchasing power conditional on the ability to find employment, and to keep those who cannot find it alive in idleness out of the produce of those who can.[48]

Cole was very much open to Keynesian economics, but was only prepared to accept the theories with critical qualifications. In 1933, he edited a collection of Labour Keynesian articles, *What Everybody Wants to Know About Money*, in which he stressed the possibilities of escaping from the iron implications of the Quantity Theory of Money. Cole now accepted the Keynesian argument that an increased supply of money could only cause inflation under the unusual circumstances of full employment. In a situation of economic depression, an expansionary monetary policy would bring the idle economic resources into play through the multiplier process. Any inflation that occurred would not only be temporary but desirable – 'if reflation starts from slump conditions, in which prices are out of adjustment with the current debt and income structure, it will usually be desirable that prices should be durably raised to some extent'.[49] However, he did not believe that the State could maintain full employment by using Keynesian techniques unless it could control the size, timing and costs of industrial production, as well as the broad distribution of purchasing power.[50]

Cole attempted, then, to make a Hobsonian Socialist out of Keynes. He always felt that the credit for the new economics should have gone to Hobson, rather than Keynes, and at the end of his life wrote that 'for me, at any rate, what is commonly known as the Keynesian revolution was much more the Hobsonian revolution in economic thought'.[51] Indeed, Hobson was more important, because he recognised the importance of class, whereas Keynes was seen by Cole as a mere technician, whose economics could somehow fit either a state capitalist or a socialist economy. In his enthusiastic response to the publication of Keynes's *General Theory* in 1936, Cole argued that Keynes's capitalist conclusions were extraneous to his main theories. They were 'but briefly sketched in his closing chapter and...not a necessary deduction from this analysis'.[52] The economist in Cole was attracted to Keynes, but his ethical ideal of socialism would not allow him to accept Keynes as a whole.

This reconciliation of Keynes and Hobson was crucial to the fundamental differences on economics between the Labour and Left. Where the Labour Right stressed the necessity of making the economic cake bigger by a policy of state intervention and direct planning, the Left placed a stress on the re-division of the cake. The Left were much more aware of social class – it was part of the Labour Marxist legacy – and sought to use state intervention to aid the organised labour movement *against* the capitalists. However, in accepting the analysis of Hobson and Keynes, they ensured the effective burial of the revolutionary insights of Marx's labour theory of value.

Thus, in different ways, Keynesian economics came to be accepted as an integral part of Labour thinking. The more militant parts of the Labour Left remained hostile for many years,[53] but the bulk of the Labour Party recognised that it was a practical and immediate response to the difficulties of a capitalist economy. It was much clearer than Hobson's economics, because it recognised the role played by investment in developing an economy. Moreover, it involved state intervention in the sphere of production, rather than distribution, and through this the Labour Keynesians from Durbin to Cole saw the necessity of replacing an unplanned market economy with a planned socialist economy. It was through their call for a much more thoroughgoing plan than the Keynesian Liberals had proposed that the Labour Party was able to evolve British Socialism into the practical world of administering industry. The acceptance of Keynesian economics was thus crucial in the emergence of Corporate Socialism.

PLANNING AND CORPORATE SOCIALISM

In order to escape from its precarious position, capitalism required more than financial planning. The fine-tuning techniques of Keynesian economics, geared to regulating a trade cycle which was causing so much social distress, had to be supplemented by state intervention into the very heart of the productive process. There had to be a major restructuring of industry in Britain (and the other capitalist powers) to place the nation in a more efficient and competitive position in the world market. This restructuring required not merely an encouragement of new industries, but a political and social regulation of industries which had grown to a size and power much greater than the enterprises of the *laissez-faire* economy.

The need to regulate the great corporations which corresponded to economic and social reality had a profound effect on political activity. While the State was drawn increasingly into the economy, its monopoly of political life was being undermined. The powerful (if unequal) corporate pressure groups of the economy – the bankers, industrialists, trade union leaders – were gradually drawn into the decision-making process so that the State was on the way to becoming 'first among equals' in its relations with these institutions (a parallel decline in importance of other non-economic pressure groups, from the churches to the professions, was also taking place). A regulated, or semi-planned, capitalism was emerging, with important consequences for a party which sought major social change on behalf of the labour interest.

Mosley, Labour and Corporatism

While the moves towards corporatist politics were accelerated by Fascist governments in Germany and Italy, and by a liberal Democratic administration in the United States, it was to be the Labour Party which was to take the main initiative in Britain.

Interestingly, it was Oswald Mosley who introduced corporatist ideas into the Labour Party, just as he had introduced Keynesian ideas. Mosley was initially attracted to the Guild Socialism of the ILP, with its allusions to the regulation of trade by the old medieval corporations. He quickly developed these ideas of extra-parliamentary administration in 1930 to call for a small economic general council which would regulate and plan trade, a proposal which won much left-wing support. After leaving the Labour Party, Mosley was able to develop fully the corporatism implicit in such proposals to call for a corporate state, with the producers as the basis of national life and with the powers of finance guided in the national interest. The state would direct the whole economy through the machinery of a central economic plan. To Mosley, 'the main object of a modern and Fascist movement is to establish the Corporate State. In our belief, it is the greatest constructive conception yet devised by the mind of man.'[54]

However, unlike his former Labour allies, Mosley saw such a planned economy as eliminating class conflict through destroying the freedom of the employers and unions to negotiate their economic contract. He opposed any section of the nation which was free of state control and called for the suppression of any vested interest which claimed allegiance to any body but the State. The occupational franchise on which a social Parliament would be based – so similar in form to syndicalist and Guild Socialist proposals – would not be based on free associations (just as the unions in Nazi Germany and Fascist Italy were so completely integrated with the State that they ceased to be representative of their members). Mosley argued that, through the machinery of government control,

> existing organizations such as trade unions and employers' federations will be woven into the fabric of the Corporate State ... instead of being the general staff of opposing armies, they will be joint directors of national enterprise under the general guidance of corporative government.[55]

These were incompatible with any corporatist proposals acceptable to the Labour Party, geared as the latter were to the different conditions of British political and social life. Formed as a party representing the rights of labour in capitalist society, the Labour Party was in the 1930s adapting its ethical brand of British Socialism to meet the changing social and political requirements of the unions in a new type of corporate society. The corporatism being evolved by Labour theorists was one based on *free* trade unions – free from state control – which would bargain with similarly free employers' associations in conjunction with a tolerant state. It was a flexible system of 'corporate bias',[56] rather than a corporate state in the rigid sense adopted in Europe.

It was prefigured in the Mond–Turner talks of 1927–28, when TUC leaders met with progressive employers to discuss an agreed solution to the crisis in industrial relations. Ernest Bevin, who took a leading part in their negotiations, saw them as a major pointer to the future.

> For the first time in history, the representatives of organised labour have been invited to meet a group of important industrialists to discuss the finance and management of industry. ... I look forward to the time when the General Council will be coming and laying before this great Parliament of its own creation annual reports on the discussion of great economic problems. ... Thus and only thus will the movement be really intelligently dealing with the great economic problems of our times.[57]

The talks failed, but they remain highly significant as a pointer to the more subtle and flexible forms of institutional co-operation between State, industry and unions which could exist.

Cole

Just as Labour had incorporated the Keynesian challenge into its framework of ideas, so now it incorporated the syndicalist challenge which elsewhere had evolved into either Communist Parties or Fascism. As has been seen, the revolutionary implications of Syndicalism had been removed by the Guild Socialists, who attempted to bring out the corporatist strain of functional representation into Labour thinking. While it had succeeded in being adopted by the ILP, Guild Socialism had proved both too radical and too irrelevant for the Labour Party of the 1920s. However, the idea that social and economic groups outside the formal political sphere of Parliament should have their say in government was now coming to the fore in discussions on the nature of socialist planning. It was none other than G. D. H. Cole, the leading Guild Socialist theoretician, who took a major part in these discussions. His isolated position after the collapse of the guild movement did not lead him to renounce the

ideal of the regulation of industry and trade by workers' guilds, but
the ideal became even more distant. The early attempts to stress the
necessity of state intervention as a transition to the guild ideal were
stressed more than ever and the working class nature of the guilds
was gradually reduced in importance. In a series of books beginning
with *The Next Ten Years* (1929), Cole proceeded to outline a structure
of economic planning in which the different interest groups would
have some participation in decision-making. The Keynesian economic
techniques proposed by Cole were a necessary supplement to such a
structure, as both were expressions of an active economic State.

Cole, more than most British political thinkers, was extremely
sensitive to developments in foreign socialist thought and seized on
the *Plan du Travail*, proposed in the early thirties by the Belgian
Socialist, Henri de Man, as a prototype of a Labour plan. Rejecting
left-wing calls for a fully socialised economy, de Man had put forward an anti-crisis plan calling for the immediate establishment of a
mixed economy – with the State running finance, monopolies and
public service industries, while private enterprise was to run the rest.
Cole grasped quickly the significance of the plan[58] and called on
Labour to institute a similar model in which the state controlled the
commanding heights of the economy, as it was later to be called. He
proposed a series of planning agencies to guide the economy in a
socially useful and competitive direction, changing Britain's trading
and industrial patterns to produce more for the home market. Since
capital was essential as a spur to production, its direction by the
government was also essential, and Cole called for an Economic
General Staff, backed by a National Investment Board, to do this.
A National Labour Corps would be established as one proposal to
clear up unemployment, though Cole argued that this should not be
used to undercut wage rates.

The important change underlying Cole's proposals for a planned
economy lay in the major retreat from his earlier ideals. Twenty years
earlier, he had marked out freedom for the working class as the major
concern of socialism; in the 1930s it had become industrial efficiency.
He had come to the conclusion that 'the ideal society that matters is
not the Utopia of our dreams, but the best sort of society we can hope
to help build out of the materials that lie ready to our hands'.[59] It was
more a defeatist than a realistic attitude, and it led Cole to see
socialism as a pragmatic scheme which would certainly involve
nationalisation of a large number of monopolistic and socially
necessary industries and enterprises, but hardly the universal public

ownership of a Communist economy. It was not the ownership or administration of industries and services but the control of policy by the State which defined socialism for Cole at this point.

In a major modification of his ideas, Cole now called for industry to be run by experts rather than the workers themselves. The worker as a consumer was only interested in getting the world's produce supplied at the lowest price and in the quickest time, and as a result he 'will find his best interest in getting industrial administration into the hands of those who are most competent to conduct it'. The administration of industry by experts on powerful public boards and commissions would need to be controlled by an independent department of inspection and audit to prevent bureaucratic rule, but the full-blooded workers' rule called for by Cole in 1913 had been watered down to works councils representing the interests of the workers in regard to wages, conditions and dismissals. It was a poor echo of his earlier proposals which challenged the industrial power of the capitalist class. Now, 'the object of this...policy, let it be made quite plain, is to bring about a radical redistribution of the productive forces of British industry in the light of a changed and changing economic situation'.[60]

This change from concern with class power to concern with economic efficiency led Cole to advocate a mixed economy, where the continuation of private enterprise was left to the ability of the industry or service concerned to serve its part in the economic life of the nation. The State needed to serve a direct role in production to secure both a correct distribution of wealth and balance of employment. While the state sector would be wide-ranging, 'this does not mean that it is necessary to nationalise everything – heaven forbid'. It did mean that the public sector 'of industry must be large enough to set the tone for the rest, leaving private industry to operate within a framework of public interest, rather than the other way round'.[61] However, in basing his arguments on efficiency, Cole left himself open to the argument that the achievement of economic prosperity by a regulated capitalism applying Keynesian policies would make a bureaucratic economy of public corporations and enterprises totally unnecessary.

He also ignored the class nature of the state which was to intervene in the economy. In the predominantly private economy accepted by Cole for the short term, the dynamic of capital accumulation was geared to profit, and any state intervention in such an economy would usually aim to restore profitability (which was, after all, only a name for efficiency in a market economy). Cole assumed that the state was fundamentally neutral and beneficial to the labour movement if directed by a Labour majority in Parliament, a slight shift in the dualistic approach to the state which he had adopted in his Guild Socialist days. The fact that a Labour government might be called upon to attack working class living standards if it was to intervene in a regulated capitalist economy was left unresolved, for Cole as for the Labour Party in general.

Morrison

It was Herbert Morrison who was to be instrumental in imposing a corporatist view of nationalisation on the Labour Party, as he was later to be responsible for imposing it on the economy. Morrison (1888–1965) was the son of an alcoholic London police constable, and overcame the handicaps of an elementary education and an eye infection to become a minor journalist. After a brief flirtation with the SDF before the Great War, he became prominent in the London Labour Party, where he immersed himself in the local problems of transport, health, education and housing. He was Minister of Transport in the 1929 Labour Government, where he prepared a London Passenger Transport Bill (later passed by the National Government); and became Labour leader of the London County Council in 1934.

Morrison applied his experience in local government, and as Transport Minister, to bring the debate on nationalisation to a sound business level. Rejecting the utopian platitudes of pre-war British Socialism, Morrison concerned himself with the down-to-earth problems of management of the wide range of industries due to be nationalised. Like Cole, Morrison's object was the maximum wellbeing of the public, and the protection of working class living standards, which he did not see as identical with the destruction of wage-slavery. On the contrary, socialist industry was to Morrison merely a more efficient form of capitalist industry, carried on according to the sound commercial principles of the more responsible private corporations. He scorned any high moral purpose which blurred the realities of the business world, and argued that the ethical ideal of socialism could only be realised through a sensible and orderly administration of public enterprise. To Morrison, 'it is essential that Socialism should be sound public business as well as being healthy in its social morality',[62] since only the competent rule of a dedicated elite could ensure the prosperity of the nation.

Morrison saw the public corporation on the model of the Post Office and the BBC as the best form of administration of industry, combining as it did public ownership, public accountability and sound business management. It was superior to direct management by the government, since Ministers tend not to be experts and, in any case, should not immerse themselves in the minute detail of commercial enterprise at the expense of keeping a general strategy in sight. It was also superior to the workers' control advocated by Syndicalism and Guild Socialism, since that had a tendency to concentrate on the interests of the local workforce at the expense of the general interest of the enterprise and the community. The same problem ruled out administration by the technical experts, whose sphere of concern wastoo narrow for the purpose of the enterprise in serving the community.

To Morrison, the management of the Boards of directors who would run the public corporations should not be chosen by ministers purely on the grounds of favouritism or a narrow concern with the particular industry, and should have the public rather than any sectional interest in mind. Managers would be offered salaries above the Civil Service level to find the people – Morrison would have no truck with the older socialist ideas of equality, as put forward by Marx in *The Civil War in France* – and should be able to make the industry pay its way in the new 'socialist' business world. They should also have the fullest possible autonomy from ministerial intervention consistent with final governmental responsibility, as an interfering Minister could easily ruin any business project. Only in this way, argued Morrison, could socialised industry prove its competence and superiority over private enterprise.

Morrison's conception of corporate public enterprise – of Corporate Socialism – was a logical consequence of adopting the syndicalist and Guild Socialist ideas of functional government to the Fabian ideals of administrative elitism inherent in British Socialism. In doing so, the ideals of the freedom of the working class from wage slavery, which distinguished Syndicalism and Guild Socialism as separate ideas, was eliminated. This was not to say that Morrison was not oblivious to working-class aspirations to government, but he saw such aspirations in individual rather than class terms. He wanted workers to be appointed to the Public Boards which would run their industry on the basis of ability, not merely because they were workers. Their personal business sense would enable them to meet the other board directors as equals, and not as inferior beings chosen for ideological reasons. As Morrison put it to the 1932 Labour conference,

> We ought, therefore, to say unhesitatingly that real ability – not the technician only, nor the expert – but real business ability, of which the Labour movement has its share, shall be the test of appointments to Boards of this kind.[63]

The idea that workers should no longer be a commodity had vanished in the 'commonsense' talk of commerce.

Wootton

The case for a corporate plan with the aim of achieving social equality and full employment was cogently argued by Barbara Wootton (1897–1988). Eventually to become the first woman to enter the House of Lords, she was educated at Cambridge and fought against male prejudice to obtain an academic career after the death of her husband in the Great War. Her influential book *Plan or No Plan* (1934) attempted to meet the arguments of political economists that a planned economy would destroy the balance between supply and demand, regulated as it was by price in a market economy. She argued that these economists held an incorrect notion of the workings of a capitalist economy. The result of private ownership was that supply became governed by the need for profit, and not by any price mechanism. Moreover, the maldistribution of wealth and the social injustice of unemployment totally distorted demand, so that essential goods were left to rot while people in desperate need of such goods were hungry because they were unable to afford them.

Wootton pointed to the success of the Five Year Plans in the Soviet Union as an example of the superiority of a socialist over a capitalist economy, though she abhorred the lack of political liberty there. In Britain, which enjoyed a much firmer economic base of political wealth than Russia, a planned economy would not need any political change. Parliamentary democracy could co-exist with a series of regulatory commissions headed by a Planning Commission, which would determine the general questions of wages and prices, the building of new factories, and the closing of outmoded ones. The corporate nature of such an economy would not destroy political democracy, since the role of Parliament was not to administer industry but to set general guidelines on which the planners would be able to act. Her Fabian notions of administration determined her views of Parliament as 'at best an assembly, not of experts on everything from cost- ccounting to maternal mortality... but of guardians of common human interest'.[64] In this way, the dangers of over-centralisation would be avoided, as public enterprise would gauge supply and demand much more efficiently than a market price.

The experience of nationalised industries, in the Soviet Union and Britain, has demonstrated the incorrect nature of such a view. The destruction of price as a regulator of demand and supply in the USSR led to such a gross inefficiency in production and distribution that it dealt a deadly blow to ideas of planning, while in the public enterprises in Britain commercial objectives have proved to be opposed to social welfare objectives. Preobrazhensky, the Soviet economist of the 1920s, discussed the need for democratic planning to gauge the co-ordination between demand and supply, but the discussion was vague, confusing as it did the Communist Party and the working class, and he disappeared in the Stalinist purges of the 1930s. Wootton did not make the distinction between bureaucratic and democratic planning either – it would have been alien to her corporatist thought – and saw problems of co-ordination as being perfectly soluble in the light of planning by the experts.[65]

This disdain for democratic management in favour of corporate planning led Wootton to endorse the rejection of workers' control by Morrison and the Labour leadership. The need for discipline at work would be ignored under workers' control as was demonstrated in Russia in the early days of the Revolution, and there could be no room for such anarchical propositions. She pointed to Lenin's imposition of an appointed management to replace the workers' committees which had initially run much of Russian industry, and concluded that internal management of industry should be in the hands of foremen and managers. The workers would, of course, be free to choose the job they wished, guided by the different pay and prospects offered by alternative occupations, but this did not imply any say in management. The rule of an industrial elite was unaffected by the question of whether business was conducted under a planned or an unplanned economy, according to Wootton. She conceded the possibility of representative works' councils to discuss the effects of management proposals on staff welfare, but they were to be advisory only:

it is not the business of staff to decide major issues of policy concerning the amount of goods to be produced, or the prices at which they are to be sold or the wages payable to those engaged in their manufacture.[66]

Unlike Lenin, who saw appointed management as a necessary transition to a Communist society, Wootton saw it as an end in itself. The socialist vision of a free society was dismissed as just a vision. The possibility that democratic planning might be more efficient than corporate planning was not even considered.

Dalton

The similarity of the corporatist proposals with the institutions of Fascism was recognized by Hugh Dalton. In his editorship of *Unbalanced Budgets* (1934), in which the economies of Fascist Italy and Nazi Germany were studied to assess the possibilities of state planning, Dalton speculated about the economic superiority of such systems over the *laissez-faire* policies of Britain. The suppression of political and trade union liberties was abhorred by Dalton, but this did not blind him to the similarities of institutions like Mussolini's IRI (Italy's version of an industrial development board) with the proposals of the Corporate Socialists of the Labour Party. As a result, he wondered

> whether modern Italy is not moving along a path which will lead, not only to Economic Planning, but to Socialism. This suggestion is repugnant to most Italian Fascists and to many Socialists.... Yet it is not to be ruled out as unthinkable, not even as improbable.[67]

In the light of this conception of socialism, Dalton endorsed the Morrisonian ideal of a public corporation as the usual form of management of nationalised industries. Prices and output would be set by a central planning authority, as in the Soviet Union, but competition between public bodies such as gas and electricity services should flourish. He believed that, far from abolishing competition, socialism would be its most perfect realisation. The State would 'institute planned public competition, in place of unplanned private competition, and plan to avoid the waste and misdirection of resources which, under capitalism, are a chronic disease'.[68] This was not merely a major modification of the Ethical Socialist ideal of a co-operative commonwealth, but a false distinction between capitalism as a system of private ownership and capitalism as a market economy based on competition between different enterprises. A market economy based on a mix between public and private enterprises, or even on public enterprises alone, would be a severely distorted market rather than a planned economy. The conflict between commercial profitability and social welfare which would occur, and the whole question of whether profit or a plan should be the regulator, were left in a highly confused state.

Dalton did believe that the corporate plan should be used to fight against poverty, insecurity and unemployment. It would be the expression of a welfare state, directed by a Supreme Economic Authority, responsible ultimately to the Cabinet. The task of this Authority would be to co-ordinate the sectional plans put forward by local and industrial authorities into a national investment plan with the immediate aim of conquering unemployment through public works, reduction of the hours of labour, a raising of the school leaving age, and a lowering of the retirement age. A policy of equal opportunity in industry, the professions and education would be encouraged in the interests of comradeship and morality. In this way, the initiative and ability present in many working class children would be freed from a caste-divided society to take a major part in social and economic life.

Dalton's corporatism was thus definitely linked to a model of social welfare, as opposed to the Fascist view of corporatism in serving the needs of national superiority. His firm adherence to the traditional liberties of British society, leading him to reject the paranoid talk of the Labour Left that Fascism was being introduced into Britain, was a reinforcement of the specific difference between Socialist and Fascist corporatism.

Corporatism and the Left

The ideas of Corporate Socialism put forward by Bevin, Morrison, Wootton and Dalton met with vigorous resistance from the Socialist League. Much of the Labour Left's Marxism may have been mere rhetoric, but their recognition of the importance of class conflict alerted them to the elitist notions of the public corporation. The working class was to be effectively excluded from industrial power by new socialist businessmen, a notion inimical to the syndicalist and Guild Socialist ideas which had become part and parcel of the Left since the war. However, their vocal opposition disguised an underlying agreement with the Labour Right about the nature of planning

which was to serve as a basis for an agreement among all sections of
the Party on the fundamentals of a socialist state.

Harold Clay, the deputy leader of the Transport Workers Union
and a member of the Socialist League, called on the labour movement
to remember the lessons of the syndicalists and Guild Socialists on
the need for workers' control. He criticised those socialists who
wished to place the trade unions on the same basis as employers,
consumers and others in industry. If such views were taken in, the
Labour Party would 'accept the permanence of the commodity status
of labour and deny the possibility of an effective partnership of the
workers in socialized industry'.[69] However, Clay accepted the public
corporation as a major step towards a socialist society,[70] objecting
only to Morrison's exclusion of the unions from representation on the
Public Boards. This exclusion would lead, according to Clay, to an
unrepresentative bureaucracy without any check to their power. His
opposition helped to defeat the Morrisonian idea at the 1933 party
conference, but thereafter the notion of workers' control all but
disappeared from sight, and by 1937 Morrison's ideas were tacitly
accepted by the Party.

The similarity of the proposals of the Corporate Socialists to
Fascism led to attacks from the Left, who argued that only workers'
control could prevent the country from drifting in the same direction
as Italy. G. R. Mitchison, a prominent Socialist Leaguer, counterposed the socialist planning embodied by nationalisation under
workers' control to the corporate state that he saw emerging. He
argued that

> the Tory party is being driven, by force of circumstances, from the
> unregulated and individualist capitalism of Victorian times, via the
> trusts and employers' associations of a later period, to a system of
> producers' corporations on Fascist lines.[71]

However, in identifying corporatism with Fascism, the Left failed
to recognise the subtleties of 'corporate bias' that was emerging, nor
their essential agreement with the assumptions of their Labour
opponents.

The direct democracy of the working class advocated by the revolutionary syndicalists had been watered down by the Left to representation of the union leadership on the Public Boards of the
nationalised industries. The syndicalist ideal of self-government was
rejected along with the Morrisonian view of corporations free form

political interference. It was not the corporate form of public enterprise that was wrong, but the autonomy and expertise of management. The League called for a National Economic Council composed of trade unions, experts and representatives of the public Boards of other industries. In this way, they sought to make industry 'subject to considerations of public policy and to co-ordinate all the industries concerned in accordance with a general Plan directed by the working class movement.'[72] It was not corporatism, but its right-wing form, to which the bulk of the Labour Left objected.

Their sympathy with the bureaucratic planning of the Soviet Union and their reliance on the trade union movement as expressing the economic interests of the working class, led the Left to accept the idea of centralised planning by a small body of experts,[73] adding only the need for trade union representation. As Ben Pimlott has observed,

Though the Socialist League increasingly adopted the rhetoric of Marxism, its heritage included a body of ideas whose source was closer to Keynes than Marx, and which it shared with politicians of the centre and right. This it never acknowledged, but the links were strong.'[74]

It was G. D. H. Cole who served as the intellectual link between the older class-based politics of Labour and the efficiency-orientated idea of corporatism. He was able to supplement Keynes with Hobson to provide a redistributionist aspect to Keynesian economics acceptable to the Labour Left, and he was able to develop the ideas of functional representation of the syndicalists and Guild Socialists to the notion that employers and unions were political powers in their own. Cole chaired an interesting series of discussions between leading academics, civil servants, employers and union leaders under the auspices of the Nuffield College Reconstruction Survey in 1941-3 in which each group came to a general agreement on the necessity of state intervention to create a mixed economy of nationalised industries and private corporations based on the fundamental cooperation of capital and labour. A new era of corporate consent was about to open.

An ideology of Corporate Socialism had evolved by the 1930s, in the sense of 'corporate bias' as defined by Keith Middlemas (and, in a more radical interpretation, by Leo Panitch).[75] Corporatism in Britain was at that time beginning to develop in the vague and non-contractual form which was to be predominant after 1940. In this

way, the employers' and trade union groupings were to be brought
into the processes of government consultation on social and economic
affairs, in an attempt to curb the tendencies to class conflict in
Britain. In the Labour Party in the 1930s, it became accepted that
politics could not be restricted to the parliamentary sphere, but must
incorporate the great economic corporations of labour and capital
into the hitherto sacrosanct realm of the State. For both the Labour
Right and Left, behind the political pyrotechnics of the struggles over
emergency powers and the Popular Front, an underlying unity had
emerged.

The emergence of Corporate Socialism in the 1930s had been the
result of an integration of the twin challenges of Keynesian Liberalism on the Right and revolutionary Syndicalism on the Left. The
economic theories of Keynes were generally accepted as superior to
the underconsumptionism of Hobson, but in the process it was changed from a call for the state regulation of a capitalist economy to a
policy for the financial planning of a mixed economy in which the
'public sector' was to be predominant. In the same way, the revolutionary attitude of Syndicalism had been eliminated by the Guild
Socialists, who had attempted to make the idea of extra-parliamentary, functional representation palatable to the Labour Party. They
failed to do so, but had bequeathed (directly through Cole) the
corporatist strain in Syndicalism to the new notions of bureaucratic
planning which emerged as a necessary supplement to the economics
of the Labour Keynesians.

In its final form – nationalised enterprises on the Morrisonian
model, planning for welfare, and Keynesian economics – Corporate
Socialism was to reshape British society in the 1940s. The early belief
of the Left that they would run into effective opposition from the
bourgeoisie turned out to be generally untrue, though they hardly
challenged the social relations of capitalist society. On the other hand,
their very success in generating economic prosperity was paradoxically to lead to a major crisis for the reforming influence within the
Labour Party.

Part IV
The Revisionist Challenge

Introduction to Part IV

The entry of Labour into the Coalition Government in 1940 began a decade of social and economic change for Britain. As a coalition partner of the Conservatives and then, after its 1945 electoral triumph, as a government in its own right, the Labour Party carried the ideas of Corporate Socialism into practice. In doing so, they took the major steps needed to restructure capital after the war at the same time as their welfare measures sought to ameliorate working-class distress. The decade of the 1940s thus created the preconditions for a general prosperity never before seen in Britain. The old cycle of boom and slump was replaced by a state-regulated capitalism which appeared to banish forever the scourges of poverty, insecurity and unemployment.

However, the very success of Labour in power created new and unforeseen difficulties for the party. It had always been a coalition of different interests and ideals grouped around the social power of its trade union base, and the admission of the unions as a formally equal partner with government brought to the fore the tensions between labourism and their desire to serve the national interest. These tensions were mainly reflected within the unions themselves, especially when the union leaders accepted a policy of wage restraint in the late 1940s, and were eventually to take institutional shape in the conflict between the union bureaucracies and a new shop stewards' movement. In the political party of the unions, such tensions were at first concealed by the size of the administrative tasks facing the Labour government, but as the middle classes turned back to their Conservative allegiance the debates on whether Labour was to be a national or a class party began to intensify. When Labour was forced into opposition in the 1950s, the Labour Right took the initiative in attempting to force the party to sever its connections with the cloth-cap image of British Socialism and present itself as a 'modern' national party.

The call to present Labour as more than a labourist party had been made from the beginning, as seen in Ramsay MacDonald's desire to promote the party as the true heir to Liberalism and his attempt to draw the middle-class intelligentsia into its leadership. In one sense, the revisionists of the 1950s were in a direct line of continuity with MacDonaldism, but the new circumstances of affluence and Cold War gave them a particular characteristic differentiating them from the old right wing of British Socialism. They were marked by the debates of the 1930s on Keynes and planning, and felt that Labour had somehow to move on from Corporate Socialism by reawakening its reforming impulse in the very different conditions of a successful capitalism. The old demand for a socialist society directed by the working class was challenged by a new conception of socialism, a conception which would eventually move into direct conflict with the corporatist nature of Labour's political thought.

9 The Revisionist Forerunners

It seemed more important to carry through major social and economic changes than to theorise about them in the circumstances of the 1940s. The party created to protect the unions was in power throughout the decade remoulding society in the forms thrashed out in the arguments of the 1930s. The debates in the country over the social security demands of the Beveridge Report of 1942, or the Keynesian pledge to full employment embodied in the White Paper on *Employment Policy* of 1944, were merely echoes of the process of policy development which Labour had already evolved. As a result, the Labour electoral landslide of 1945 was the culmination of both a national[1] and party preparation over fifteen years.

The administration of corporate socialism shunted aside any major developments in Labour's political thought. Under Herbert Morrison, the champion of public enterprise, many of the staple, loss-making industries (coal, electricity, rail and road transport) were taken into public ownership with generous terms of compensation. Trade unionists were appointed to the Boards in a number of cases, but always in the light of the Morrisonian ideal of business ability – they ceased to be trade unionists, and became business executives, once they accepted their positions. Under Hugh Dalton at the Treasury, the Bank of England was nationalised painlessly, with the merchant and high-street banks left in private ownership and subject to overall control by the central bank. In addition, the state maintained a close scrutiny of the private sector through rationing and a series of planning controls which eventually proved too cumbersome and bureaucratic for the smooth running of the economy. After 1947, Labour economic policy shifted away from a reliance on direct physical controls to the Keynesian techniques of 'fine-tuning' the economy through fiscal and monetary policy. The Government also completed the efforts of previous administrations in creating the Welfare State. The establishment of National Insurance to cover illness, unemployment and old age was accompanied by the creation of a free national health service by Aneurin Bevan, the left-wing Minister of Health who successfully out-manoeuvred the selfish opposition of the British Medical Association.

In foreign affairs, the appointment of Ernest Bevin as Foreign Secretary ensured a tough anti-Communist stance. Bevin's fierce labourism, nurtured in his struggles against employers and Communists in the Transport Workers Union, was transmuted into a close alliance with the Americans against Soviet Russia, Britain's wartime ally. Bevin cast his arguments in trade union terms, denouncing left-wing opponents as equivalent to 'scabs' and likening the world struggle against Russia with his own struggle against the Communist attempt to take over 'his' union – 'You have built the Soviet Union and you have a right to defend it. I have built the Transport Union and if you seek to break it I will fight you',[2] as he put it to the Soviet Foreign Minister in 1946. He was a major figure in the development of the Cold War and in building the anti-Soviet NATO alliance in 1949. Elsewhere, after granting a messy independence to a partitioned India in 1947, the Labour government presided over vicious wars against the Communists in Greece and Malaya.

Labour's reforms took place on the basis of a capitalist economy, however. The Marxist strand within the Labour Party remained generally quiescent, since they believed that a further major push towards a statified economy would be undertaken soon, but in this they faced major opposition from the Right, around Herbert Morrison. Morrison accepted the need to extend the public sector significantly, but believed that both Government and the electorate required time to consolidate the gains already made before any further steps could be taken. As Morrison put it to the 1948 party conference:

> The mere transfer from private ownership to public ownership is the beginning of the business, it is not the end. An enormous amount of work needs to be done in adapting, consolidating, and, if need be, reforming and changing the organization of social-ist industries...you must expect the new programme to be of a somewhat different character and a somewhat different tempo from the last, for we have to embody in it proposals for the consolidation of existing achievements, proposals for laying still more firmly the economic foundations of society.[3]

Labour's electoral defeat in 1951 made the whole question irrelevant in terms of government, but the first attacks on a free health service by a Labour Chancellor (Gaitskell) in April 1951, were an indication that the Labour dream of a socialist health service was an illusion if it continued to be based on a capitalist economy.[4]

The political debates that took place in the 1940s remained generally confined to the conceptions and ideas formed over the previous forty years. Morrison's belief that Labour should appeal to the middle classes as a national party, together with the movement away from direct planning controls on private investment to more orthodox Keynesian economic policies, were indications of change on the Right, however. It was the first stirrings of a revisionist challenge to Corporate Socialism – a challenge whose outlines could already be discerned in the writings of two major Labour theorists, Evan Durbin and Douglas Jay.

EVAN DURBIN

E. F. M. Durbin (1906–48) was the son of a clergyman who managed, after an elementary education, to win a scholarship to Oxford. Together with Douglas Jay and Hugh Gaitskell, he worked closely in the 1930s with Hugh Dalton and the XYZ Club of Labour sympathisers in the City to fight the underconsumptionist ideas of Hobson then prevalent on the Labour Left.[5] His *Politics of Democratic Socialism* (1940) stands out as one of the earliest revisionist presentations of political and social ideas, though his wish to write a companion volume on the economic principles of democratic socialism was cut short, firstly by his work as a junior minister in the Attlee government and then by his untimely death in a bathing accident in Cornwall.

Durbin's reaction to the rise of Fascism and Communism in Europe in the 1930s was not merely an echo of the Labour leadership's rejection of the Popular Front. He extended it to an attack on Labour Marxism, and proposed a much more gradual change in society which would appeal to the middle classes as well as the trade unions. Where the Left pointed to the class nature of the State and the need to strike at the financial power of the ruling class, Durbin argued that the political democracy of British capitalism was far too valuable to risk any rapid social change. The ruling class and the working class, for all the social philosophies which divided them, had much more in common in the need to preserve parliamentary democracy.

Durbin saw Marxism as a lack of balance in the human mind, which had led to a stress on the competitive and coercive aspects of human nature. The cruelty released by extremism of any kind was a result of the attribution of the cause of social frustration to human will – whether Nazi identification of the Jews as the incarnation of human evil, or the Marxist belief that the capitalist class was the cause of all the ills in the world. The adult powers of imagination and reason were used for aggressive purposes, leading to a peculiar and dangerous fetishism of ideas – 'Men will die like flies for theories and exterminate each other with every instrument of destruction for abstractions'.[6] The fact that men and women could turn to Communism in reaction to capitalist crisis or the rise of Fascism appeared foreign to Durbin's way of looking at the world. Instead, he understood the Communist who thrived on violence in the terms of psychology – the use of Freudian terminology such as 'projection' and 'displacement' were freely sprinkled through the argument. In a manner which tended to betray Durbin's Oxford background, he wrote of the Marxists that

> it is, of course, no argument to call one's intellectual opponent a cad. And yet . . . [they] are conditioned . . . by the necessities of their emotional life and by an overpowering desire to find a scapegoat on which to lay their own aggression. Fanatics, extremists and persecutors of all ages are such as these – men of blood and men of hatred. Their underlying desire for suffering is not hidden by a pair of spectacles or a high-pitched voice.[7]

None of us are perfect, of course, and democratic governments have not been averse to cruelty and torture against their opponents, but Durbin's emotional revulsion was an indication of the political hatred the revisionists were to feel for Marxism.

Durbin saw Marxism as totally alien to the British way of life. The Communist call for proletarian dictatorship as a temporary instrument of workingclass rule had frozen into a totalitarian nightmare of rule by one party. Durbin pointed out that even the working class taken on its own requires choice between its parties – in Britain there was the Labour Party, the ILP and the Communists – and asked why only one should be allowed to represent workers. Just as the Russians had eliminated opposition, so the Communists in Britain would destroy any dissent from their rule if given the chance. The Communists abused liberty by choosing themselves as the vanguard of the proletariat, and crushed other parties because they recognised that, given the choice, they would be rejected in free elections.

The peaceful changes of government in Britain, where Attlee was not threatened with execution nor Baldwin with imprisonment if either lost an election, stood in stark contrast to the cruelty and oppression of the police state under Nazi and Communist rule. There, the opposition was totally at the mercy of the government and was ruthlessly dealt with in travesties of natural justice. The Communists, like the Nazis, governed by terror and force, not law and consent. If economic injustices had been lessened, the prevalence of political injustice nullified any claims by the Soviet Union that it was socialist (Orwell had a similar hatred of Stalinism reinforced by his experience fighting with the Anarchists in Spain, though his calls to transform England made in *The Lion and the Unicorn* in 1940 distance him from Durbin's gradualism).

The other side of Durbin's hostility to Marxism was his conception of parliamentary democracy as a necessary cushion against rapid social change, a conception dependent on R.G. Bassett's *The Essentials of Parliamentary Government* (1935). Bassett, whose sympathy with Ramsay MacDonald had led him out of the Labour Party in 1931, believed that consensus and cooperation between the parties was essential for parliamentary democracy to function at all, so that ultra-conservatives or politicians who were too radical were a menace to the British system of government. Durbin took up this idea to attack not only Communists, but also Labour Marxists like Laski and Cripps.

He defined democratic government as a particular *method* of arriving at decisions, rather than a style of life. The freedom of the people to choose a government and the freedom to oppose the government without being persecuted were essential to this method, but there also had to be an implicit understanding between the parties not to persecute the other – 'Mutual toleration is the keystone of the arch and the cornerstone of the building'.[8] If a Conservative government believed that Labour was aiming to break up and destroy the Conservative Party, it would naturally move to defend itself. In such circumstances, democracy would become impossible, as no government would willingly surrender power to such an enemy. A solution of profound differences which was too radical, such as that proposed by the Marxists, would mean a social strain which would eventually lead to force, and then the country would be on the slope to terror and civil war.

Since parliamentary democracy as a *method* of resolving class differences thus involved compromise, then the policy of a Labour government should not be so extreme that it would drive the Opposition to illegality and violence. If a Labour Marxist government carried through extreme measures, then Britain could forget about peaceful and democratic change for at least a generation. However, this did not mean that a Labour government should have its policy dictated by the Conservatives. In the real political world, a reforming party's policy should not be so moderate that it would drive the party's activists to more extreme parties. These activists, intolerant and partisan as they often appeared to Durbin, were recognised by him as the moving force of the party system on which democracy rested. The balance between progress and national consensus was the narrow path on which any democratic socialist party must tread.

Parliamentary democracy was thus seen by Durbin as both more important than and integral to any social change. It was part and parcel of any socialist achievement – 'in so far as we are democratic we are already, in some degree, socialist, and to betray democracy is to betray socialism'.[9] It was, of course, a highly restrictive and conservative definition of democracy and socialism, but its implication that the Conservatives are in some way more socialist than the Communists because they adhere to parliamentary forms is logical. Durbin believed that both Conservatives and Labour, capitalists and workers, belonged to the same nation, bound together by an emotional unity that was far deeper than divisions of social class. Democracy was the only institutional framework within which this emotional unity could be expressed, since it allowed for the mutual toleration of differences.

The Communists, like the Fascists, were outside this emotional unity of the nation, since they denied freedom of speech and opposition – the fruits of the democratic method. As a result, Durbin argued that such anti-democrats had no democratic rights, a much more openly illiberal proposal than most politicians of any party would contemplate. Durbin argued that to allow those who seek the destruction of democracy to gather strength would be a sign of weakness, not freedom.

We should constantly remind ourselves that the enemies of democracy have no moral right to the privileges of democracy; and that a time may come when, to defend ourselves, it will be necessary to suppress their political organization.[10]

Such an open statement of intent to drive the Communists underground was only more honest than many politicians (the Fascists were, after all, effectively suppressed during the war), but in terms of the internal politics of the Labour Party amounted to an outright declaration of war on the radical socialists and Labour Marxists who saw democracy as a means to the rapid transformation of society, and who were sympathetic to united work with the Communists.

The Marxist argument that Parliament was merely a political facade disguising a bourgeois dictatorship was dismissed by Durbin, who pointed to the major changes in the democratic capitalist economies of Britain and the United States. The existence of political democracy in these countries had meant that the State had been forced to curb the vices of *laissez-faire* capitalism. In a confused but irresistible manner, the common people had gradually pushed the State to regulate capitalism so that *both* labour and property were able to benefit. The growth of the unions to protect workers against low wages and the arbitrary tyranny of the employer in the factory had been a prelude to political action. State planning to regulate the trade cycle and the use of taxation to protect the individual from the main dangers of economic life – unemployment, illness, old age – were due to a vigorous democracy responsive to popular needs.

Moreover, the changes in capitalism had led to changes in its class character which greatly weakened the Marxist case for a proletarian revolution. The proletariat, far from being impoverished, had taken small property-holdings for itself in the form of savings – a humble but psychologically important state in society, which had led to a mentality derided by Marxist as 'petty-bourgeois'. The middle classes themselves, far from disappearing as Marx had predicted in *The Communist Manifesto*, had risen enormously in numbers, with the growing army of technicians, 'white-collar' workers and suburban householders. Capitalist property itself had changed, as the growth of the private corporation had led to a dispersal of owners among a large number of shareholders and a divorce between ownership and control. The upper bourgeoisie was no longer a single class deserving expropriation, but a variety of groups, from a parasitic class of property-owners without any function to the salaried managerial class which administered company affairs on a daily basis.

Durbin believed that Labour should move out from its old trade union base to win over the new middle classes. The Marxist element in the equation of British Socialism had become irrelevant and potentially anti-democratic, and needed to be replaced by a more classless outlook. Moreover, the major redistribution of power within the private corporations would enable Labour to turn the new managerial class against the other, useless sections of the upper bourgeoisie. The rentiers and property-owners had become parasites on the shoulders of the managers, while the company directors who took the strategic business decisions behind closed doors were 'an irresponsible, self-recruiting, nepotic oligarchy'.[11] Their real functions of management had been lost, leaving them on the same useless level as the property-owners. The rejection of Labour Marxism, and the appeal to the new managerial and middle classes, were to be taken up by the revisionists.

Durbin's view of politics as psychology was based on false reasoning – he assumed what he needed to prove. He believed that democracy could only survive if the emotional life and character of a nation lent itself to gradual change and toleration. The roots of democracy in his sense of the word were neither rational nor intellectual – 'it is fundamentally a consequence of psychological health and the absence of neurosis'.[12] The British were, of course, the nation which Durbin had in mind. He took the characteristics of British culture (cleansed of blemishes such as Chartist risings, the mass strike wave before and after the Great War and the repression of nationalist resistance to its Empire) and assumed it to be free of neurosis. It was a very insular view, leading Durbin to a contemptuous rejection of other national models such as France, and to an over-sentimental view of the Empire.[13]

Just as Durbin accepted the orthodox view of British political culture as a model of mental health a little too glibly, so his identification of Marxism with neurosis and sadism borders on the self-righteous. It was not merely the fact that he identified Marxism much too easily with its Stalinist form – understandable in the 1930s, though the diversity of Marxism could not be contained within such a narrow frame – but the superficiality of the analysis. The fact that capitalist crisis or war may lead sincere people to Stalinism obviously has a psychological aspect, but no more than any other response to such harrowing times. Many radical psychologists would argue that we are all living in a neurotic society anyway, and that nobody is in a position to moralise. In the light of uncertainty on the scientific status of psychology, Durbin's emphasis on mental health and the lack of it seems on the same level as those dogmatic Marxists who once glibly dismissed all twentieth century ideas not in conformity with their own as unworthy and 'petty-bourgeois'.

In pointing to the changes in capitalism and the working class, Durbin prefigured much later revisionist writing. However, his belief that the rise of the managerial and middle classes meant that 'we are living in a society whose class composition is shifting steadily against Marx's proletariat'[14] gravely underestimated the ability of Marxism to adapt and evolve to explain new developments in capitalism. His own Keynesian beliefs prevented Durbin from recognising any virtue in the labour theory of value (which was more than ever seen as a bizarre anomaly in economic thought) and to assume that the economy could be painlessly turned away from crisis. In such circumstances, there was no *real* need for radical change, a belief that he would pass on to other revisionists.

Durbin was a major forerunner of revisionist thought in political ideas, but his belief in a centrally planned economy prevented him from breaking out of corporate socialism. He believed that a socialist society – defined as 'fundamentally a demand for social justice ... for economic freedom and social equality'[15] – was not possible in an economy run on the profit-motive. Any attempt to end social inequality or to extend the social services would lead to higher tax burdens on capitalist companies, leading to a crisis of investment. Only a central planning authority and state direction of capital were compatible with a just society. Thus, 'while the institution of some form of planning is not the object, it is the indispensable preliminary means for the attainment of the new society'.[16] It was to be Douglas Jay who was to point to later revisionist developments away from Corporate Socialism.

DOUGLAS JAY

Douglas Jay (b.1907), after enjoying the usual education of the upper middle classes at Winchester and Oxford, was closely associated with Durbin and Gaitskell in the XYZ Club. It was his book *The Socialist Case* (1937) which marked him out as a forerunner of revisionist thought.

Like Durbin, Jay was not interested in questions of class power, but in the inequality and injustice that existed as a result of an unfair system of distributing wealth. This system was the major cause of the poverty that blighted working-class existence, preventing the enjoyment of all that is valuable in life. If poverty was an enemy which could be cured, it was necessary to strike at inequality – 'one of the chief reasons that the poor are very poor is that the rich are very rich'.[17] While perfect equality could be ruled out, as the loss of incentives which would result would cause even greater poverty, it was necessary to reduce the wide disparities that did exist.

Jay's own conception of socialism as concerned with equality and security, rather than class power, was a result of his belief that a regulated market economy was a fundamentally sound economy which was accidentally distorted by unequal rewards. He ridiculed Marxist economics for failing to grasp that the rewards to the different factors of production were all essential and necessary, and used the orthodox arguments of neo-Classical economics to demonstrate that the reward of interest to stockholders was to induce the capitalist to part with his capital for the length of time needed to pay for the plant and raw materials required for production; rent the reward for persuading the landowner to have his property for one use rather than another; and profit the reward for the risk taken by the entrepreneur. To each function a fundamental and necessary economic service corresponded. The price mechanism determined the allocation of the wealth produced by these factors so that, in theory, a balanced equilibrium would result from a just and orderly system.

In practice, Jay pointed out, this elegant system stood in sharp contrast to the unjust and disorderly world of reality, disfigured as it was by gross inequality, extreme poverty and criminal waste. The reason for this, according to Jay, was that the price mechanism 'ignores entirely...the absolute difference in consumers' needs... between the need for bread of a man who has got enough and the need for bread of a man who has not got enough'.[18] It ignored the reality of social inequality between the classes.

Land, capital and enterprise were certainly essential services, but this did not mean that their rewards were *earned*. Jay argued that the capitalist performed the economic function of capital, but did not really earn the reward of interest. Saving involved a negligible sacrifice, and waiting hardly a sacrifice at all for people who owned an enormous amount of property. The 'abstinence' of the Rothschilds or the Rockefellers was hardly abstinence in any meaningful sense, while their business caution and timidity in investing their capital could lead to a serious crisis in the market economy. In effect, Jay argued that most capitalists enjoyed unearned income, as it arose from waiting rather than working.

To counteract these social inequalities, and the monetary and economic crisis resulting from them, Jay called for state intervention,

in particular the nationalisation of the Bank of England. An unregulated price mechanism ensured that the real needs of the poor
were sacrificed, while an unregulated monetary system ensured permanent unemployment and insecurity. The regulation of capitalism –
the redistribution of wealth by means of a taxation policy which
would gradually abolish inheritance, and a managed monetary policy
to regulate the trade cycle – was Jay's solution to the flaws he had
detected in the market economy.

However, they were *flaws* rather than fundamental defects. Jay saw
nothing inherently wrong with the price mechanism as a regulator of
demand and supply and, while rejecting the social philosophy of a
capitalist society, he saw nothing wrong if state regulation could
correct its abuses. The fact that poverty and insecurity exist in capitalism did not validate the radical calls of the Labour Left. To Jay, 'we
must emphatically not run to the opposite extreme and assume that
the price system is worthless. . . . We have merely shown that there are
blemishes in its sacrosanctity'.[19] All the flaws in the price mechanism
were connected to inequality of income, and would disappear as that
inequality disappeared. Jay, like the neo-Classical economists,
believed that the market economy enjoyed a *fundamental* equilibrium,
and saw state intervention as restoring the conditions in which that
equilibrium could be regained.

In diverting the attention of socialists from questions of class
power, Jay pointed to a definition of socialism which had more in
common with the New Liberalism at the turn of the century. Unemployment and poverty were no longer seen as caused by a market
economy, so that nationalisation ceased to be crucial to the achievement of socialism. Jay was challenging the Labour Party's notions of
Corporate Socialism when he wrote that

> the tendency of socialists lately to think less of the dispossession of
> property and more of organization, 'planning', efficiency and so
> on, is in many ways unfortunate. What society fundamentally
> needs is not so much planning as socialism.[20]

The identification of planning with socialism was denied by Jay, who
saw socialism as bringing about the suppression of unearned income,
not the abolition of the market economy or the destruction of the
social power of the ruling class.

Thus, where the corporate socialists looked to agencies of planning
and debated the best form for nationalised industries, Jay attempted

to look for safeguards for private enterprise against state intervention. He accepted the call for the nationalisation of natural monopolies like gas or rail transport, but demanded that both small companies *and* large well-established industries which were efficient under private ownership should be free from state control. He argued that nationalisation was usually wrong, in that it would create a monopoly which would extract a monopoly profit from the public and which would fail to reduce costs. Such a monopoly, whether state or private, was a conspiracy against the public health – 'To organise such a conspiracy has almost been the first instinct of producers throughout history, from the days of the guild to those of the "Corporative State." '[21] To safeguard consumers, the price system had to be left intact from state intervention, and competition within the public enterprises and between public and private companies should be encouraged to aid efficiency and customer service – for example, Jay argued that a nationalised rail company should compete with private road transport companies. Planning was desirable only where inequality and insecurity could be diminished without too great a loss of consumer freedom and without the creation of unnecessary state monopolies in industry.

In his criticism of nationalisation as a creation of an unhealthy monopoly rather than a panacea for the evils of capitalism, Jay pointed to one of the weaknesses of Corporate Socialism. Planning by the State – whether through public ownership or state direction of capital – could not in itself bring social equality or economic security. Indeed, the inevitable creation of a bureaucracy to run the extended economic powers of the State could very well hinder the development of a just society, creating the new inequalities of state patronage and privilege, as was occurring in Stalinist Russia. Jay realised that the coordination of demand and supply could not be achieved by centralised planning – it was his main disagreement with Durbin – and looked instead to the traditional price mechanism.

However, in divorcing the distribution of wealth from the wage system and locating it in the old Fabian distinction between earned and unearned income, Jay was retreating back to the market economy, regulated as he wished to make it. The consequences of the acceptance of Keynesian economics by the Labour Party had been grasped most acutely by these forerunners of revisionism. The need for class struggle to defend workers against the ravages of a capitalist society, and the belief that there was a fundamental weakness in the market economy, were denied by political thinkers who saw only the surface reality of capital without probing to the authoritarian and degrading system of wage labour which lay behind it. Jay, in seeking to eliminate the unacceptable face of capitalism while maintaining the essentials of the system, was pointing the way for the revisionist challenge to Labour's Corporate Socialism.

SOCIALIST COMMENTARY

The administration of the nation in the 1940s absorbed the critical energies of many on Labour's Right. Jay, Gaitskell and Durbin all worked in the Civil Service during the war and had ministerial duties in the 1945 Labour government. The policies of Labour in power – the public ownership of loss-making industries, the extension of social security, and an anti-Soviet foreign policy – were not such as to arouse rebellion on Labour's Right, while the direct physical controls on industry had been made necessary by the emergencies of war and were gradually lifted.

However, the development of the line of thought begun by Durbin and Jay was not totally at a standstill. The Socialist Vanguard Group criticised the corporatist nature of Labour proposals and sought to provide ideological backbone for opposition to the Soviet Union through their journal, *Socialist Commentary*. Their criticisms were greatly strengthened by the addition of Dr Rita Hinden to their team. Hinden (1909–71), a close friend of Gaitskell, had been born in South Africa and, after being educated at the London School of Economics, joined the staff of the Fabian Colonial Bureau in 1940. Her background gave her a special interest in colonial affairs which proved influential in the Labour Party as the process of dismantling the British Empire proceeded.

The hallmark of this journal was anti-Communism, which extended to an opposition to any policies which smacked of Marxism. *Socialist Commentary* hailed a mixed economy as a third alternative to Russian Communism and American *laissez-faire* capitalism.[22] However, in any conflict between the two bigger systems, it called for Labour to recognise the superiority of capitalism:

> Wherever the Russian controlled world expands, democratic social-ism and all the values for which it stands are doomed to perish, whilst present-day American capitalism, for all our misgivings about it, at least leaves room for free institutions to flower and survive.[23]

Their anti-Communism suffused the group's attitude to the British colonies. In common with the Labour leadership, they opposed independence for Britain's African colonies, believing that the principles of social justice and equality would be best granted by a benevolent Britain. At one conference in April 1946, Rita Hinden clashed with the Ghanaian nationalist Kwame Nkrumah – 'When Mr Nkrumah said "we want absolute independence" it left me absolutely cool. Why? ... British socialists are not much concerned with ideas like independence and self-government, but with the ideal of social justice.'[24] When she came to accept ultimate independence (after a visit to Nigeria in 1948), she remained convinced that Britain needed to guard such inexperienced countries from the evils of Communism by the establishment of representative institutions in the colonies before independence. These institutions, she declared in an editorial on colonial policy in *Socialist Commentary*, should be centres in the fight against Communist propaganda. The fact that she saw the colonies as remaining outposts of British influence was admitted in the same editorial, where she declared that

> we have not the intention, and we know it, of sacrificing our standard of living for the sake of colonial development; we do not contemplate an evening out of wealth; we know too, that our development plans are partly inspired by our own needs. We must say this quite frankly.[25]

Her real attitude to representative institutions in the colonies was demonstrated when she persuaded the Labour Party to support the dismissal of Cheddi Jagan's pro-Soviet government in British Guiana in 1953.

The anti-Communism which determined the colonial policy of *Socialist Commentary* expressed itself in demands that Labour should loosen its ties with the unions to become more of a national, and less of a class, party. They argued, in support of Herbert Morrison's desire to establish Labour's appeal among the middle classes, that the achievements of the 1945 Labour government had finally given the working-class movement an equal social status in society. The time to recognise that the demand for social justice had burst beyond the narrow divides of any class or section of the community had come, and *Socialist Commentary* was much more forward than Morrison in identifying the left-wing demand for more nationalisation as the obstacle to this recognition. Echoing Douglas Jay, *Socialist*

Commentary called for a movement away from planning to a vision of socialism as concerned with welfare and equality:

> It has repeatedly been argued ... that nationalisation is not an end, but a means – one means among others – to achieve certain social objectives. No betrayal of social principle is involved if, compared with the past, it figures less prominently today, when the key industries are already in the hands of the community.[26]

It was a demand that was to be taken up with increasing frequency in the new boom conditions of the 1950s.

10 The Revisionist Heyday

By the time that Labour's huge parliamentary majority had been all but eliminated in the 1950 election, its programme for transforming British society had been completed. The State had taken a leading role in restructuring capitalism through the policies of nationalisation, fiscal and direct planning and welfare, while the decline of Britain as a world power was partially disguised by the tough foreign policy of Ernest Bevin.

However, Labour had exhausted itself, in ideas as much as energy. It had succeeded only too well in implementing its policies, and was in real danger of becoming a rudderless, conservative party. Its ageing leadership drifted, harmed by the retirement of Cripps, the death of Bevin, and the resignations of Bevan and Wilson, until Labour's defeat in the 1951 election. This defeat began a period of thirteen uninterrupted years of Conservative rule, who won three successive elections in the decade, each one with a larger majority than the last. The Labour defeats of 1951 and 1955 could be blamed on bad party organisation or on the ferocious divisions between the Left, led by Bevan, and the Right, led by Morrison and Gaitskell. However, the unity of the party under Hugh Gaitskell's leadership after 1955 did not prevent an even greater defeat in 1959, leading to speculation on the possibility of Labour's survival.

It was the long economic boom which helped the Conservatives. After an initial set-back, the British economy entered the most sustained period of prosperity in its history, enjoying a boom which raised production figures, incomes and standards of living to heights thought impossible before the war. Unemployment virtually disappeared, as economic growth and political stability began to be considered the norm throughout Europe. Interruptions in economic prosperity, as in 1952 and 1957, were brief and easily overcome by government policy, apparently destroying the Marxist belief of the Depression years that capitalism could not survive and grow. It was fondly imagined that a theory and a practical policy had been found which would ensure the boundless expansion of the mixed economy, while the limits of that expansion were concealed by optimism and the very length of the boom.

There were danger signals even in the halcyon days. The economic boom was accompanied by a creeping inflation, but at an average of

3 per cent a year in 1952–65 this was explained as a necessary and minor consequence of full employment. The decline of Britain's share of world markets from 1954 in the face of increasing competition from Japan and West Germany was a genuine cause for concern, but this too was more than offset by the general rise in world trade, which grew at the phenomenal rate of 6 per cent per year in the 1950s and 7.5 per cent in the early 1960s. The continuing decline of the manufacturing capacity of British capitalism was concealed by general prosperity in the capitalist world. It was, however, a prosperity which witnessed the further concentration of capital in oligopolies and monopolies – 180 firms employing one-third of the British labour force accounted for half the net capital expenditure of Britain in 1963; 74 of these firms, with ten thousand or more workers each, amounted to two-fifths.[1]

The boom led to major changes in working-class expectations with worrying consequences for the Labour Party. Until the late 1950s, few workers had cars and even fewer had telephones, but the prospect of a continually rising prosperity was always in view. With the sudden access to a range of commodities previously regarded as luxury goods, from washing machines to television sets and cars in the late 1950s, the image the working class held of itself began to change. The change was often exaggerated by observers at the time,[2] but there was a real trend for working-class families to cease identifying with the labour movement as closely as once had been the case. However, the real position of the working class as tied to alienating work and long hours did not change. It expressed itself in a new shop stewards' movement and a series of unofficial strikes which were short lived and usually successful. Their increased bargaining power at a time of full employment gave the unions a renewed sense of industrial power, although this made them intensely unpopular with the middle classes.

NEW FABIAN ESSAYS

The economic prosperity also led to a rising revolt against Corporate Socialism within the Labour Party by the 'revisionists'. These leading figures in the party took their name from the German Social Democrat Eduard Bernstein, who attempted to 'revise' Marxism at the turn of the century by expunging its revolutionary conclusions. Just as Bernstein wanted the Social Democrats to bring their revolutionary theory into line with their reformist practice, so the British revisionists wanted to force Labour to bring its socialist pretensions into line with its acceptance of a 'mixed', mainly private enterprise, economy. They believed that Labour's ideology of Corporate Socialism had achieved its objective of creating prosperity, leading Labour to lose its reforming impulse, and they hoped to revive the radical traditions of the party by cutting out the shibboleths and Marxist rhetoric which made Labour appear a relic of the past.

The exhaustion of ideas in the Government had already led to a certain amount of re-thinking within the Labour Party Research Department, where Stephen Taylor was questioning the nature of socialism once physical controls had been set aside, and once the redistribution of wealth had led to a more prosperous society.[3] A concern with the rights of citizenship within a modern social democracy was articulated in the late 1940s by the influential sociologist, T. H. Marshall, who argued that a social form of citizenship had grown up in the twentieth century to complement the civil and political concepts of citizenship which had grown up in earlier years.[4] This new citizenship, tied to an erosion of class privileges and inequalities, gave its members certain social entitlements such as claims for social protection against destitution and illness. Marshall's concern about the class inequalities which were so essential for generating economic growth within a capitalist society, and the nuances of his approach to class, were very influential with the revisionists, especially Crosland.

Revisionism emerged into full development, however, out of a revival of the Fabian Society by G. D. H. Cole as a research centre and intellectual sounding-board for both Right and Left in the Labour Party. It was a Fabian conference in 1949, chaired by Cole, which decided to produce an updated version of the original *Fabian Essays in Socialism*. The result, in *New Fabian Essays* (1952), was a series of contributions from Bevanites such as Ian Mikardo and Richard Crossman as well as revisionists, but the bulk of the authors had served their intellectual apprenticeship in *Socialist Commentary*.

The revisionists pointed to the need for the Labour Party to find a new and radical direction now that it had achieved its programme. Tony Crosland, in his essay, 'The Transition from Capitalism', pointed out that the prognoses of the Labour Marxists had been dramatically disproved by events. Far from collapsing, capitalism was expanding, bringing with it a rising standard of living for the working class. Crosland argued that Labour must face up to the new realities – 'it is now clear that capitalism is undergoing a

metamorphosis into a quite different system, and that this is render-
ing academic most of the traditional socialist analysis.'[5] A new definition of socialism was required if Labour was not to become the party
of the *status quo*.

Public ownership as an instrument of socialist planning was questioned by the revisionist essayists, who pointed out that the equation
of socialism with planning was profound misunderstanding. As
Britain was a planned economy, through nationalisation and state
direction of the private sector, it followed under the narrow definition
of Corporate Socialism that nothing more needed to be done to
change society. In fact, argued the revisionists, a class-ridden and
inegalitarian society like Britain was far from socialist in the sense of
the traditions of Ethical Socialism. Roy Jenkins, in his essay 'Equality', argued that public ownership should be egalitarian in motive,
rather than merely looking to efficiency. It should be 'an essential
prerequisite of greater equality of earned incomes and an inevitable
concomitant of greater equality in the ownership of property'.[6]
Jenkins was pointing to a redefinition of socialism in his call for
workers to share in the ownership of property – a form of democratic
capitalism, as had been advocated by the Liberals in the 1920s –
and pointed out that public ownership need not be outright
nationalisation as argued by Corporate Socialists. Instead, Jenkins
saw cooperative or part-control by the State as preferable alternatives
to the bureaucratic model pressed by Labour since the 1930s.[7]

Austen Albu went further in his essay 'The Organisation of Industry' in his attack on Corporate Socialism. Nationalisation had not
satisfied the need for a democratic sense of responsibility called for by
Tawney. Planning for full employment, the redistribution of wealth
and the increase in industrial efficiency were being achieved by other
means than the traditional model of public ownership. However, the
notion of socialism as a sense of democratic participation was still
unsatisfied. The model of the public corporation as the model for
efficiency needed to be modified, according to Albu, by worker
participation if Corporate Socialism was not to degenerate into a new
managerial autocracy, distant and manipulative rather than selfish
and brutal. It was, of course, to be participation with management
rather than the outright self-management demanded by the more
class-conscious syndicalists, whom Albu thought of as primitive.

The *New Fabian Essays* was a tentative document, pointing out the
need for a redefinition of socialism while making only cautious sallies
in that direction. A common element among revisionists was the need

for a classless society, but by this was meant a society without the indignities and inequalities of caste rather than the abolition of the wage-system called for by Marx or the Guild Socialists. However, its rejection of social revolution did not mean that it was a conservative movement – it was Morrison who represented the conservative tendencies in the Labour Party – or even just a desire to curb bureaucratic excesses. The revisionists were in revolt against Corporate Socialism and wished to release the radical energies locked up in the Labour Party by an outmoded class outlook. As Roy Jenkins put it in his book *Pursuit of Progress* (1953),

> The first duty of a party of the left is to be radical in the context of the moment, to offer a prospect of continuing advance and to preserve the loyalty of those whose optimistic humanism makes them its natural supporters.[8]

The process of elaborating the new definition of socialism took a major step forward with the publication, in 1956, of John Strachey's *Contemporary Capitalism* and Tony Crosland's *The Future of Socialism.*

STRACHEY

John Strachey (1901–63) was born into a Conservative family – his father was the editor of the *Spectator* – but joined the ILP at Oxford University. He was closely associated with Mosley, leaving the Labour Party with him in 1931 to help form the New Party. Mosley's increasingly Fascist tendencies soon led Strachey to leave the New Party, and during the 1930s he came to be seen as the symbol of the Marxist intelligentsia who closely sympathized with the Communist Party. His books *The Coming Struggle for Power* (1932) and *The Nature of Capitalist Crisis* (1935) presented the traditional Marxist arguments that capitalism was doomed to collapse and that the ruling class would react with violence.

However, his reading of Keynes modified his earlier views and he became increasingly convinced that state direction of the economy could overcome capitalist crisis. He then played a prominent part in the Labour Party, becoming Minister of Food in the 1945 Government, where he was embroiled in a notorious abortive scheme to grow groundnuts in East Africa. After the 1951 defeat, he contributed a paper to *New Fabian Essays*, where he acknowledged the influence of Keynes and Douglas Jay in winning him away from Marxism. However, it was in *Contemporary Capitalism* (1956) that Strachey most fully presented the revisionist case against the Marxism he had once espoused.

He argued that Marx had, in fact, correctly analysed nineteenth century capitalism in pointing to the concentration of capital and the increasingly severe cycle of booms and slumps. If left to itself, capitalism would undoubtedly have ended in poverty, class war and social revolution. Marx made his error in his failure to recognise that capitalism was capable of change – 'he under-rated the element of liberty and over-rated the element of necessity in man's condition even within a given social and economic system. His categories were altogether too hard and fast.'[9] In fact, capitalism had been able to change its nature to regulate the trade cycle and to overcome unemployment. The working class, far from becoming 'immiserated' as Marx believed, had increased their stake in society as they grew increasingly affluent.

The social mutation which had occurred in capitalism, according to Strachey, was the ability of the new managerial class to consciously control the economy rather than be controlled by it. The divorce between ownership and management, present through capitalism, had reached a new stage as the joint companies had grown to their present size, leading to a management based on competence and ability to avoid the crisis which had hitherto wrecked hopes of a stable business environment. It was the control of prices which was the key to the situation, according to Strachey. In a competitive economy, prices were outside the control of firms, set by the market conditions of demand and supply; in the economy of large firms and oligopolies of contemporary capitalism, the firms could set their own prices, as they controlled the market.

> Prices, from being objective data which move automatically in accordance with no man's will, became things which may be moved, within certain limits, by the conscious decisions of groups of men. Such a change nullifies some of the basic principles of capitalism,[10]

bringing a planned market economy into the realm of possibility. The key function of accumulation had taken on a semi-collective character, while the automatic self-regulating character of the economy was eroded as it came under conscious control.

The present problem of capitalism was not instability but the question of whether a few oligarchs or the people were to benefit from the economy. If production was left to the capitalists, they would be prevented by the profit motive from investing their capital where the social good required it. However, most businessmen and economists were agreed that the economy could not rest on such a flimsy basis as the selfish decisions of individuals, and that the State itself must become increasingly associated with the economic process.

Strachey called for the new capitalism to be controlled in the interests of the population rather than a few oligarchs. He believed, like Durbin and Jay, that democracy had been the central force in modifying the harsh brutalities of early capitalism, and that democracy was the answer to the present problems of a managed capitalism. Through economic democracy, as expressed in the separation of the managers from the owners, decision-making power had been placed in the much more responsible hands of disinterested managers who would invest to avoid a slump. Through political democracy, state intervention could guide the economy in response to the needs of the electorate – the people. As a result, according to Strachey, the question of whether capitalism would become more stable or less stable depended on the democratic pressures brought to bear on a changing system.

The importance of Strachey's book lay in its rejection of the traditional left-wing opposition to capitalism which he had once espoused. Such views, Marxist and syndicalist in origin, were still powerful in the Labour Party, but Strachey insisted that they were based on an old-fashioned view of a society which had generally vanished. However, the book still expressed the ideas of the 1930s. The questions of economic stability and efficiency, rather than equality and social justice, pervaded his writings, which failed to go beyond Keynes. The positive presentation of revisionist socialism was presented by Crosland in a much more radical break with the concerns of Corporate Socialism.

CROSLAND

Tony Crosland (1918–77) had been a tutor at Trinity College, Oxford, before entering Parliament in 1950. He had written for *Socialist Commentary*, the main right-wing periodical, and had contributed a major essay on the new capitalism to *New Fabian Essays*, but it was *The Future of Socialism* (1956) which established his place as the main exponent of revisionism in the Labour Party.

Crosland's redefinition of socialist priorities sprang from his belief that the economic problems which had absorbed the Labour Party's attention for a generation had been resolved. The collapse of capitalism widely expected by many on the Left in the 1930s had not occurred, as unemployment had been overcome and total output was rising. The economy was behaving in a buoyant and productive manner in the mid-1950s, and working-class living standards were on the increase as national wealth was reaching new heights. The old capitalist enemy had lost its power to the State, which used fiscal and monetary policies to aim for full employment, a more equitable distribution of wealth, and high economic growth. It had become a *welfare* state, interested in helping business only in so far as this helped the economy on which the community depended.

Crosland noted, as did Strachey, the managerial revolution which had transformed the old cut-throat capitalism of self-interested entrepreneurs into a mixed economy where decisions were no longer in capitalist hands. However, he did not regard it as being peculiar to capitalism, as the growth of managerial power could be detected in all industrial societies of a certain size and complexity.

> The new managers (like the capitalists before them) pursue the goals of growth, profits and personal wealth. But such broad statements are true of any industrial system; as true, for example, of managers in Kharkov as of managers in Birmingham or Detroit.[11]

There had, however, been a major change compared with the old capitalists, as the managers had a different relationship to property. Where the old capitalists had made their business decisions on the basis of maximum profits for the companies they owned, the new managers were merely salaried workers who were more concerned with social status and stability than with the single pursuit of profit. They had much more social responsibility as a result, and took a major interest in welfare schemes and good labour relations.

Crosland admitted that profit still played a major role in the private sector, but he called on socialists to forget their prejudice against the moral overtones of the term and to take a dispassionate look at the real functions of profit in all industrial societies. He argued that it is a mistake to think that profit, in the sense of a surplus over cost, has any special or unique connection with capitalism. On the contrary, it must be the rationale of business activity in any society, capitalist or socialist, which is growing and dynamic.[12]

The precondition of economic growth was the ability to take aside part of the firm's output in order to improve the means of production or to invest in expanding areas of the economy. This was as true of Russia as of Britain, regardless of how the extra output was created or who decided where it should be directed. The old socialist argument that it should not be expropriated by the capitalist was made out of date by the mixed economy, where democratic institutions could be used to ensure that profit created in the private sector could be used for re-investment rather than privileged consumption.

Crosland argued that it was the changes which had taken place in the working class which posed the greatest dangers for the Labour Party (a theme which he took up with even greater urgency after the 1959 defeat). It appeared grossly absurd in the conditions of growing affluence to think of the working class as wage-slaves, or of the unions as the powerless representatives of the underprivileged. In fact, the conditions of full employment had given the unions a new and much greater power. It was a sellers' market for labour power, in which the employer was in a poor negotiating position if his labour force was not to be lost to a competitor offering higher wages. It could be argued that profit was still being squeezed by the workers, but this was indirectly determined by government management of the economy rather than the greed of the employer. The workers were no better off in this respect in the nationalised industries (or in the collectivist economies of Eastern Europe), and affluence made a nonsense of any grievance that might otherwise be felt.

However, while prosperity and social security were softening the hostility between the classes, and the militant language of class war was passing out of use, the Labour Party remained trapped in the past. The traditionalist conservatism of the labour movement and the dogged persistence of class antagonisms among a minority of British workers were responsible for a poor image of Labour with the voters. The Labour Party owed its whole existence and historic growth to the trade union movement yet, ironically, this unique identification was a clear political liability, for the simple reasons that the old industrial working class was both shrinking in size and growing in material comfort. Crosland pointed out the clear political implications here for the Labour Party, which would be ill-advised to continue making a largely proletarian class appeal when a majority of the population is gradually attaining a middle-class standard of life, and distinct symptoms even of a middle-class psychology.[13]

In the face of these changed conditions – a buoyant economy which could no longer be meaningfully described as 'capitalist', and a gradual disappearance of class antagonisms – Crosland called for a re-statement of socialism if Labour was to be a credible government in the second half of the century. The old objectives of socialism had either been achieved, as with full employment and social welfare, or had become irrelevant, as with the need to abolish private property or to increase the power of the proletariat. The old shibboleths were increasingly absurd in the new age, and the traditions which dominated Labour's language and thinking had to be left behind. 'Keir Hardie cannot provide, any more than can the Gracchi, the right focus with which to capture the reality of the mid-20th Century world.'[14] Sweeping away the conservative stagnation which threatened to clog up Labour's channel of radical energy, Crosland sought a new socialist philosophy for an affluent age.

In doing so, he concentrated his criticisms on the belief of the Corporate Socialists that public ownership and planning were fundamental to socialism. This belief was based upon a confusion between means and ends. Nationalisation was merely a means to achieving the goals of socialism, not the goal itself. In justification of this, he pointed to the post-war experience of public ownership, which had belied all the hopes held by Labour in the 1930s. It did not lead to an expansion of planning, because the public corporations were as independent of government control as the private companies. The State was able to exercise control over the whole economy, but this depended on the willingness of the government to use fiscal and monetary controls rather than ownership.

Moreover, Crosland argued that the creation of state monopolies had led to restrictions on individual liberty, encouraged sloth and prevented individual initiative. An unresponsive bureaucracy, remote from the workforce and generally deaf to consumer interests, had hardly led the country nearer to a socialist society. In this situation, competition should be seen in a more favourable light by socialists, who should cease planning any further extension of public ownership, at least in the traditional form of the public corporation covering a whole industry. The basic utilities had already been placed under State control, while the remaining large industries – cars, aircraft, chemicals, shipping and others – were neither private monopolies nor inefficient. Any further programme of public ownership should be strictly governed by the fixed criteria that economic improvement could take place by no other means, and that competition would be encouraged by such means as part-state ownership. Whatever the form of future state intervention, Crosland was clear that the old confusion between nationalisation and socialism should be jettisoned:

> State ownership of all industrial capital is not now a condition of creating a socialist society.... What is unjust in our present arrangements is the distribution of private wealth; and that can as well be cured in a pluralist as in a wholly state-owned economy, with much better results for social contentment and the fragmentation of power.[15]

Just as nationalisation was generally rejected by Crosland, so the faith of the Corporate Socialists in planning was called into question. He accepted, of course, the Keynesian prescriptions for state intervention to regulate the trade cycle and to create full employment, but the direct physical controls advocated by Labour in the 1930s should be rejected. According to Crosland, such planning was detrimental to any expansionist economic strategy. It denied the consumer a free choice of goods, was highly unpopular, and needed a cumbersome and insensitive bureaucracy to administer the industries concerned. He agreed that certain industries did require direct state intervention to help them in certain circumstances – for example, they might need an exceptionally large amount of capital, or to be directed to a region of high unemployment – but, generally, planning in the form envisaged by the Corporate Socialists was no longer viable.

Having pushed aside the dogmas of nationalisation and direct state planning which had confused people about the real nature of contemporary socialism, Crosland pointed to the positive values which still needed to be attained. These concerned, above all, the questions of welfare and equality. On the first, Crosland pointed out that the aim of the welfare services was not social equality, but the relief of social distress and hardship. There was still an enormous amount of suffering, despite the welfare state, due to genuine parental ignorance in regard to the care of their children, and to the disintegration of the

family unit as a result of increased occupational mobility and of the
development of new housing estates, which had led to the neglect of
the old and unmarried. Above all, there were the special cases at the
fringes of society – the mentally ill, neglected children, the blind and
the chronically sick. As economic prosperity rose, socialists should
ensure that society concentrated on increasing the amount of its
resources towards these special cases.

Indeed, as the impoverished nature of the welfare services became
more apparent, Crosland later saw the major task facing socialists
as the closing of the appalling gap between private affluence and
public squalor, as it had been put by the American economist
J. K. Galbraith. In 1962, in *The Conservative Enemy*, Crosland
pointed to the outdated and bleak hospitals; overcrowded school
classes; the shortage of university places; the uncivilised mental
hospitals; and the oppressive ugliness of the industrial towns as
examples of public squalor. The worst area was housing, where
overcrowded slums and decaying sub-standard houses spelled out
misery and a lack of hope for the future, particularly for the newly
married. This was particularly vulgar, given the general rise in prosperity – 'we are now rich enough for the uncivilised state of the social
sector, so deadening to happiness and vitality, to stand out as un-
endurable.'[16]

The reason for this stark contrast between private wealth and
public poverty could not be traced to the profit motive of capitalism,
according to Crosland. The private sector did not determine the
amount of government expenditure on health or education. This was
determined by the *political* decisions of the government in power on
the amount of taxation and the direction of public spending. It was
natural, then, for a Conservative government committed to the philosophy of private affluence and selfishness to spend as little as
possible on welfare services. It should be equally natural for a Labour
government to be morally obliged to increase the proportion of the
national income due to the social services. It was, according to Crosland, a distinguishing mark of socialist values to relieve social distress
and hardship on the grounds of compassion and human concern, not
on the grounds of equality. Indeed,

> the relief of this distress and the elimination of this squalor is the
> main object of social expenditure, and a socialist is identified as one
> who wishes to give this an exceptional priority over other claims on
> resources.[17]

The other pillar of socialism concerned social equality, identified by Crosland as the aspiration towards a classless society. In view of his understanding of post-war capitalism, Crosland quite naturally rejected the Marxist view of class – the relationship between capital and labour – as much too narrow. Ownership had become irrelevant and social classes had grown more complicated with the growth of a managerial and white- collar class. To Crosland, caste had become mixed in with class, as he pointed to the multitude of factors – income, occupation, job hierarchies, lifestyle, accent and perception – which went to create a division between 'superior' and 'inferior' people. Taking class in this wider sense, he saw a rigidly defined class structure as pervading national life:

Class, in the sense of class consciousness and the existence of clearly defined classes, is an exceptionally marked phenomenon in British life. The hierarchies of education, occupational prestige, and style of life all show pronounced breaks; and these breaks broadly coincide.[18]

This class system had to be challenged by socialists despite the absence of class violence. It created frustration, resentment and envy, leading to the collective manifestations of discontent seen in strikes and to the suspicion and antagonism between management and workers in British industry. This antagonism could not be traced to poverty, falling wages or unemployment, which hardly existed in Britain by that time. It had a social, rather than an economic cause. Moreover, there was an understandable element of merit in this feeling of resentment, as working class parents were just as anxious as middle class parents that their children should not miss out on the opportunities available at a time of rising prosperity, and were prepared to use their bargaining power to the full to ensure that this would not happen.

Inequality was, moreover, both wasteful and inefficient. The tight restrictions on social mobility between the classes meant that genuine social communication within the country was lacking. People born into the working class with a genuine capacity for leadership or with a real talent to contribute towards society were, unless they were lucky enough to win a scholarship, condemned to a life of frustrated ability. On the other side of the coin, people born into a ruling elite which had become hereditary and self-perpetuating became the leaders of society though they might be totally unsuited to the task.

Above these practical arguments against the British class system, Crosland also pointed to the question of social justice. He admitted that this involved a moral judgement, which was not subject to proof or disproof, but it was a moral judgement which distinguished socialism from the selfish philosophy of the Conservatives. To socialists, people had social *rights*, such as equality of opportunity and equal dignity. Moreover, the ability of people to inherit enormous wealth to flaunt in the face of their fellow citizens was seen as morally abominable.

Nevertheless, Crosland qualified his argument by pointing to the educational system to prove that equality of opportunity, as advocated by the Tories in the 1950s and 1960s, was not enough. The creation of a meritocracy, an elite based on merit rather than birth, would merely change the personnel of a class-divided society, not alleviate class inequalities. If the public and grammar schools were opened to all purely on grounds of merit, the gulf between the superior style and education of Eton and that of a secondary modern school would still engender frustration and resentment among those left behind. Indeed, the one comfort working-class children had, that they would *really* have succeeded if the system was not weighted against them, would be removed. Crosland concluded that 'if the inequality of rewards is excessively great, the creation of equality of opportunities may give rise to too intense a competition, with a real danger of increased frustration and discontent.'[19] To overcome this, he called for a non-segregated comprehensive school system; the gradual abolition of the eleven-plus examination system; a greater opening of university education; and ensuring that public schools enrol a wide cross-section of the community.

Finally, Crosland pointed to the changing arena of political conflict as material standards of living rose and economic problems faded from the popular consciousness, to be replaced by problems of leisure and privacy which did not directly concern socialism. However, socialists should take a special interest in the intolerable moral restrictions on abortion, divorce, homosexuality and censorship. There was a need for more liberty and even jollity which would eventually, he believe, prove more important than the need for higher exports. In the new and happier age that was arriving, Crosland called for the demand for liberty to be championed above all by socialists, 'in whose blood there should always run a trace of the anarchist and the libertarian, and not too much of the prig and the prude'.[20]

Crosland's analysis of the changes in capitalist society were criticised by the New Left on the grounds that the new 'managerial' class were still capitalists because they owned large numbers of shares in their firms, and that consequently they were still guided by the profit motive. The attributes of 'welfare' capitalism noted by Crosland, such as the concern with good labour relations and welfare schemes, had been present in the 1920s, pioneered by Henry Ford in the interests of squeezing more productivity out of his workforce. However, such criticisms were not really relevant to Crosland's analysis, as he believed that state direction of the economy would force private enterprise to behave in a socially responsible manner. It was this indirect control of private enterprise which was the essential difference from the old cut-throat capitalism of the days of *laissez-faire*, according to Crosland, and as such the whole question of ownership was succeeded by one of political *will*. The decision on whether welfare and education or private affluence should take priority was dependent on the political complexion of the government.

However, Crosland's dismissal of nationalisation and direct planning as only one means to achieve socialism, and an inadequate one at that, had the effect of dismissing the power of capital. In one sense, Crosland could correctly point out that the paranoid predictions of the Labour Marxists that capitalism would thwart socialist policies had been proved wrong by the success of the 1945 Labour Government (though Marxists could respond that the basis of capitalist power had never been challenged). Moreover, the ability of capital to pay for welfare *and* to achieve the economic growth needed to pay for welfare was just assumed by Crosland. The Marxist analysis of the laws governing capitalism appeared to be discredited by events, of course, and all the empirical evidence in 1956 suggested that capitalism had overcome its tendency towards crisis, but Crosland's failure to investigate the conditions of prosperity further seems, in retrospect, as short-sighted as it was understandable. Welfare and equality were treated as though they had nothing to do with the power relations which underlay the mixed economy, and the consequences for socialism of the possible failure of Keynesian economic policies were ignored.

This seemed perfectly justifiable in the full employment conditions of the 1950s, and the publication of *The Future of Socialism* was soon followed by the ideological victory of the revisionists within the Labour Party. Crosland himself helped to write *Industry and Society* (accepted by the 1957 Labour conference as official policy), which called for the public ownership of individual firms rather than whole industries, and stressed the preference for state purchase of shares in those firms rather than outright nationalisation.

However, it should not be thought that this heralded a more conservative Party. In rejecting nationalisation and direct planning, the revisionists hoped to release the radical energies of the Labour Party to direct it to progressive social policies. Crosland's book inspired a number of radical criticisms of contemporary capitalism which were more perceptive and prophetic than many of the old Corporate Socialists'.

TITMUSS AND THE RADICALS

This was demonstrated clearly with the publication of *Conviction* (1958), a series of essays edited by the journalist Norman Mac-Kenzie. They were expressions of faith in the moral values of socialism against the acquisitive nature of private affluence. MacKenzie (b.1921), in his essay 'After the Stalemate State', called for a return to the socialist creed of William Morris and the Ethical Socialists in protest at a society which 'is in many ways more moral, more humane, than any society we have known, and yet it has made too many of us morally indifferent.'[21] Brian Abel-Smith (b. 1926), in his essay 'Whose Welfare State?', was critical of the mean-minded hypocrisy of the middle classes who carped at the welfare services while actually taking advantage of them more than the working class and the needy. Like Crosland and Galbraith, he pointed to the contrast between the poor quality of education and health, coexisting with the palatial prestige offices, new factories and superstores of private enterprise. Together with Peter Townsend (b. 1928), Abel-Smith undertook much valuable work in uncovering the poverty and suffering which lay hidden behind the protective facade of the 'welfare' state.

It was Richard Titmuss who exercised a major influence on Labour's social policy. Titmuss (1907–73) worked in an insurance office from the age of 18, using his time and experience to write on poverty, ill-health and family planning. His *Problems of Social Policy* (1950), part of the official *History of the Second World War*, established his reputation and he was appointed Professor of the new Department of Social Administration at the London School of Economics, despite his total lack of any university experience.

In a series of books and essays starting with *Essays on the Welfare State* (1958), Titmuss drew attention to the major social problems in Britain which had been concealed by myth and ignorance. The built-in tendency of capitalism to cause unemployment may have been cured by Keynesian economics, but the social problems of the working class and the forgotten people at the margins of society were put forward as the new concerns for socialists. In doing so, Titmuss took a much more class-conscious view of society than Crosland (though he acknowledged the importance of Crosland's own analysis for a new socialist thinking).[22] Thus, he used an empirical study of wealth and income to disprove the general belief that the rich and poor were becoming more equal, a belief which was based on selective statistics chosen by intellectually narrow-minded sociologists. The growth of tax advisers and pension consultants meant that cash in hand was less important than trusts, overdrafts and other forms of wealth for the middle class. Moreover, by confining their studies to individuals, the major changes in the family life and status of women in wealthier classes went unexamined.[23] He concluded that, far from becoming a more integrated society, income inequalities had been growing in Britain since 1949.

The disguised improvement of middle-class living standards at the expense of the working class in the provision of welfare was pointed out by Titmuss in his influential essay 'The Social Division of Welfare', which had a major effect on Labour's social policy, changing it from concern for a floor of benefits and services to an extension of middle-class benefits to the working class.[24] He pointed out the mythical nature of right-wing complaints that working-class scroungers were impoverishing the middle classes. In fact, a close look at the social administration of welfare revealed that it was the middle classes which were the main beneficiaries because of their exemption from the full weight of taxation as a result of fiscal and occupational benefits. To Titmuss, such benefits tended 'to divide loyalties, to nourish privilege, and to narrow the social conscience'.[25]

It was the continuing pattern of class divisions and snobberies in Britain which concerned Titmuss in his studies of the welfare state. The social services had been created at the beginning of the century in accordance with middle-class expectations of how the working classes were supposed to behave, so that the social problems of family and environmental life were treated as cases of individual failure. Real insight into the problems of poverty and insecurity were lacking, as outside observation by the 'better' classes could never be the same as genuine acquaintance with working-class reality. Many institutions formed at the time of the Poor Law survived into the modern welfare state with few modifications in structure, bringing fundamental problems of ethical values to the service. Thus, as the emphasis shifted to a higher quality of service in education and health, there was a clash with the elitist values of the old administrative structures, which were too inflexible and conservative for a democratic age. The resolution of the conflict would depend on how 'needs' were to be defined, and that in itself depended on *who* defined them.

In this respect, Titmuss was particularly worried about the bureaucratic nature of the social services. The growth of specialisation and professionalism had given those groups with an exclusive knowledge the power to decide the fate of others, and the influence and prestige of these groups was rising with the growth of scientific and technical knowledge. 'As the social services become more complex, more specialised and subject to a finer division of labour they become less intelligible to the lay councillor or public representative.'[26] The changing role of the family, the social emancipation of women, and a longer life span all required new and, above all, *intelligible* changes to the social service, yet this new professional elite were as distant from ordinary people as they ever were.

The consequences of this for democracy were spelled out by Titmuss in a Fabian tract, *The Irresponsible Society* (1960), a full-scale attack on the corporatist nature of society which was in many ways akin to that made by the New Left. Using the example of private insurance companies which catered for the wealthier classes, Titmuss pointed to the amount of power 'concentrated in relatively few hands, working at the apex of giant bureaucracies, technically supported by a group of professional experts, and accountable, in practice, to no-one'.[27] He argued that the moral values of society were being warped by these directors, managers and professionally trained advisers who made the decisions which shaped society. They saw only the technical administration of the economy, industry and services, without being aware of the social use to which rising prosperity must be directed, and they imposed policies without democratic discussions or consideration of moral consequences. This elitist rule had combined with the success of Keynesian economics to strengthen conservative governments committed to inequality and privilege, while a decline in the quality of Royal Commissions and the use of distorted statistics had created a myth that social protection had extended to all under the auspices of a benevolent welfare state. In such circumstances, it was necessary for Labour to rediscover its ideology, and to set an example of moral leadership and social responsibility. It should attack the centralisation of decision-making in social administration which had led, paradoxically, to less spending for welfare and to an accelerating inequality in society.

It was a radical attack on Corporate Socialism, similar to that of Crosland, on the grounds that centralised elites in the social sector were a menace to the values of socialism. Titmuss wrote, 'to me, the "Welfare State" has no meaning unless it is positively and constructively concerned with redistributive justice and social participation'.[28] It was a sense of community rather than an order of command from a faceless few, or an undignified hierarchy of snobbery and hypocrisy. It was this sense which fed his belief that social policy was concerned with altruism and the reclaiming of the lost and forgotten into a warm-hearted fellowship. It was fitting that his last book, *The Gift Relationship* (1970), should be concerned with social welfare as a gift of strangers, thereby denying that they were strangers. It was a study of the recent decline of the voluntary gift of blood in the United States, and the consequent rise in the commercial value of blood. Titmuss saw this as a horrifying sign that the primal bonds which knit society together were breaking up, and pleaded for social policy to be concerned with 'the unquantifiable and unmethodical aspects of man... [and to] promote an individual's sense of identity, participation, and community'.[29]

Titmuss demonstrated the radical nature of the call by the revisionists to forget about the outmoded ideas of nationalisation, and to concentrate instead on promoting a classless society concerned with welfare for all its inhabitants. He was more aware than Crosland of the dangers to democracy posed by the new managerial class, but did not really present any viable structural alternative to their rule. He overestimated the role played by political and moral will in changing social values and attitudes, and underestimated the social and economic realities of class society. Like the revisionists, Titmuss was confident that the economic success of Keynesian policies would be uninterrupted, yet it was to be the re-emergence of economic crisis which would lead to major attacks on the inadequate social services by Labour as well as Conservative governments.

GAITSKELL

It was the success of Hugh Gaitskell which ensured the triumph of revisionism in the Labour Party in the 1950s, just as it was his character which drew a limit to that success. Gaitskell (1906–63) had come from an upper middle-class background – his father was an official in the Indian Civil Service – and received the conventional education at Winchester and Oxford. He joined the Labour Party at the time of the General Strike, and was a lecturer for the Workers Educational Association at Nottingham. His direct experience of the bloody repression of the Socialist rising in Vienna in 1934 instilled a sense of caution into his politics, and this was reinforced by his close association with Evan Durbin, with whom he helped to develop Labour Keynesianism in the 1930s and whose untimely death in 1948 seems to have shaken Gaitskell particularly badly. After entering Parliament in 1945, Gaitskell's career advanced rapidly, and he succeeded Cripps as Chancellor of the Exchequer in 1950. He soon succeeded Morrison as the standard-bearer of the Labour Right in the bitter struggles of the early 1950s, and his election as Labour leader after Attlee's retirement in December 1955 was a major victory for revisionism.

Where Attlee was a great conciliator of the different factions within the party, Gaitskell believed that clarity and decisive leadership were necessary if Labour was to lose its cloth-cap image and become a credible political force. He appeared unable to distinguish leadership of a party from leadership of a faction, but this arose from his belief in his own ideas and a fear that Labour would be badly harmed if those ideas were not carried through. This ensured a stormy period for the Labour Party. As one of his colleagues recalled,

> Integrity, absolute integrity, that was the essential quality of Hugh Gaitskell's character. When he considered it was his duty to say or do something, nothing could stop him. The sharp edge of intellectual integrity would cut through all barriers.[30]

He had early set his sights on the target of nationalisation, arguing in a Fabian tract, *Socialism and Nationalization* (1956), that the experience of state monopolies had been one of bureaucracy and remote management which had proved frustrating to producer and consumer alike. Indeed, in 1959, he went so far as to call for the deletion of Clause IV – which called for 'the common ownership of the means of production, distribution and exchange' – from the party constitution. He argued that, while the State must preserve the right to intervene to end monopoly and inefficiency in the private sector, the Labour Party must recognise in theory as it already recognised in practice that nationalisation was not the first principle and aim of socialism.

> We have long ago come to accept, we know very well, . . . a mixed economy, in which case, if this is our view – as I believe it to be of 90 per cent of the Labour Party – had we better not say so instead of going out of our way to court misrepresentation.[31]

This attack on the shibboleth of nationalisation was an attempt to release the critical impetus within the Labour Party, for Gaitskell as for other revisionists. He wanted Labour to stand for a view of socialism as public morality against the acquisitive values of traditional capitalism.

This became clear soon after Gaitskell became Labour leader, when Gamal Abdel Nasser, the Egyptian nationalist leader, nationalised the Suez Canal without compensation, leading to an abortive Anglo-French military expedition in November, 1956. Initially, Gaitskell stood firmly behind the government, echoing its comparison between Nasser and the Fascist dictators of the 1930s, but as the government defied United Nations resolutions by taking military action, he led the party into opposition. He believed that the armed intervention not only damaged the whole notion of collective security but took world attention away from the simultaneous Soviet invasion of Hungary. As he argued in the Commons,

> Do not Hon. Members appreciate that, at this time above all, when the news of Russian intervention in Hungary is coming through, it is an immense tragedy that the moral strength of this country, and of the United Nations, because of our action, is so gravely damaged?[32]

The combination of moral aptitude and anti-Communism expressed Gaitskell's approach to policy issues.

The moral aptitude certainly came to the fore on the question of race, which was becoming increasingly important as immigrants from the old Empire began to arrive in Britain, which was at that time desperately in need of labour. The white community, especially those working-class areas of the cities where immigrants congregated, did not take kindly to this intrusion by people over whom they once felt they had ruled. A race riot in Notting Hill in 1958, which was accompanied by a minor revival of Fascist activity, led to racist calls for controls on immigration, which was seen as a threat to the nation. These calls found a response among Labour as well as Conservative MPs, and the Labour leadership were quick to affirm their opposition to all immigration controls on Commonwealth subjects.[33] Gaitskell's anti-racism was allowed full play on this issue, particularly when the Conservative government caved in to backbench pressure by introducing a Commonwealth Immigration Bill in the autumn of 1961.

In what he regarded as one of his most important Commons speeches, Gaitskell attacked 'this miserable, shameful, shabby Bill' as 'a plain anti-Commonwealth measure in theory and . . . a plain anti-colour measure in practice.'[34] he accused the Tories of wanting to forget about the former Empire of which they had been so proud, yet in doing so they were striking at the central principle of non-discrimination against race on which the Commonwealth was based. He attacked the myths that immigrants were 'scroungers' on the social services, had a high birth rate, were diseased or criminal, using official evidence to contradict the falsehood, and pointed to the natural anomalies of a newly arrived group to explain other allegations. He pointed out that those who called for immigration controls as the only way to prevent racial friction were admitting a shameful failure to fight racism wherever it existed in Britain. The acceptance of such defeatist arguments would place Britain on the level of the US South, and the government should have the courage to fight racism rather than to appease it. Gaitskell's arguments were based on the belief that racism weakened the moral strength of Britain, and he recognised that immigration controls were necessarily racist, despite all the economic and social arguments cobbled up by the control lobby.

His moral approach was firmly based on the nation state, however. He was profoundly concerned about the impact of racist measures on Britain's image in the Commonwealth. He appealed to the government to remember that the West Indies, from which a large proportion of immigrants arrived, 'are still our Colonies. We are responsible for them, and they think of themselves, as anybody who has been there knows, as British people. Oh, yes, they do. It is rather moving.'[35] It was this same nationalism which led him to break with many other revisionists by opposing entry into the European Common Market. The economic arguments for entry did not appear too pressing in the early 1960s, so that Gaitskell could base his decision on the grounds of opposition to political union with the other European countries. As he told the 1962 Labour conference,

We must be clear about this; it does mean, if this is the idea, the end of Britain as an independent European state. I make no apology for repeating it. It means the end of a thousand years of European history.[36]

This combination of morality and nationalism could be radical when applied to questions of the welfare state and domestic racism, but in terms of foreign affairs it became a conservative defence of Britain's alliance system. Gaitskell particularly believed that the important issues which divided the parties on home policy should be held in check by a fundamental consensus·on the basic questions of national defence and parliamentary democracy. He followed his friend Evan Durbin in arguing that 'a certain basis of consent, a willingness to compromise, to accept the rules of the game is absolutely essential'.[37] This sense, combined with his deeply felt anti-Communism, led him to place his leadership on the line in opposition to the Campaign for Nuclear Disarmament, which called for Britain to set a moral example to the world by unilaterally renouncing nuclear weapons. The 1960 party conference endorsed this demand, despite a challenge by Gaitskell that he would 'fight and fight and fight again' to save the Labour Party from such extremism.

His arguments against unilateralism were based on the *realpolitik* of power, not the moral righteousness with which he approached most other questions. The retention of nuclear weapons gave Britain an independent voice in the world, while unilateralism would severely weaken NATO against the threat of Communism. It was because Gaitskell, in the revisionist tradition established by Durbin, believed that Soviet Communism was an aggressive and immoral force which recognised only brute force that he defended the frightening concept of the 'balance of terror', the belief that Russia would not use nuclear weapons if faced with an annihilating nuclear response. As he put it to the delegates,

I do not believe that Mr Khruschev has any intention of deliberately starting an aggressive war in present circumstances ... but I do believe that if you give them the opportunity of advancing the cause they believe in without cost or risk to themselves, they will not reject the opportunity. I ask you, bearing in mind all these things, and reflecting on the events of recent years – what they did in Hungary ... to say that it would not be wise for us to take the risk.[38]

It was a coherent argument, but it was based on the Cold War paranoia against Russia which continually set a limit to the radicalism of the revisionists. The weakness of their opponents' case could not disguise the basic agreement of the revisionists with all the conservative circles in Europe and the United States who were convinced that the Communist threat to the national identity was a far greater evil than any of the problems of poverty and inequality within that entity.

HEALEY

This was particularly brought out by Denis Healey (b.1917) who, after a youthful membership of the Communist Party in the 1930s, became one of the clearest and toughest followers of the foreign policy of Ernest Bevin. As Secretary of Labour's International Department after the war, Healey was in a good position after his election to the Commons in 1952 to rise to become Labour's Defence spokesman. His views on foreign policy as *realpolitik*, and his attacks on the neutralism then becoming popular in the Labour Left, were expounded in his contribution to *New Fabian Essays*, and in pamphlets such as *Neutralism* (1955).

Healey argued that foreign policy could not be governed by traditional socialist ideas of welfare. The element of power in politics became the crucial factor in the international arena which tended to override the traditional moral approach of simple co-operation and brotherhood preached by Labour between the wars. International politics was determined by the threat of force, or even by brute force itself. This did not mean that Healey totally rejected morality in foreign policy, merely that he pointed to its limitations. He argued that 'power, of course, is not the only reality in world affairs. But it is a pervasive reality which has its own laws and fixes the limits within which moral criteria can operate.'[39] The ability of modern nuclear weapons to wreak a devastating havoc on the world made the moral case for international co-operation greater, but this moral case had to be tempered by realism if it was not to end in the very war it sought to avoid.

On this basis, Healey rejected the Left's attempts at neutralism as Utopian and gullible. A neutralist foreign policy was suitable to anyone who refused all political commitments as inconsistent with a fine spiritual life, but it was unacceptable to anyone who had a sense of responsibility. In the real world of power, Britain must recognise the necessity to ally with the United States against Russia. He took

up Durbin's argument that the USSR was not socialist because it was
not democratic, and compared totalitarian communism with the
democracy of the United States, where state intervention since the
New Deal had promoted social progress and made capitalism more
acceptable. Moreover, when it came to accusations of imperialism,
Healey felt that the Russian denial of independence to its own subject
nationalities compared most unfavourably with the peaceful ending
of the British Empire and the reluctance of the United States to take
up many political responsibilities. He certainly had a point on Russian oppression, but his ability to overlook US intervention in countries from Guatemala to Iran in the early 1950s, as well as Britain's
ability to resist by military force any nationalist resistance which
appeared dangerous to British interests, whether in Guiana or
Malaya, is breathtaking. Nevertheless, given his basic premises, Healey concluded that 'only the most absolute pessimist about political
action as such can remain morally neutral in a struggle where the
totalitarian state is opposed by a state with less pretentious claims'.[40]

Healey was quite clear on the result of any conflict between the
needs of defence and those of welfare, as were other revisionists. It
was Gaitskell who, as Chancellor, imposed health service charges in
1951 to help pay for an increase in arms expenditure caused by the
Korean War, an increase which led to the resignations of Bevan and
Wilson from the government. Healey rejected Bevanism as the confusion between wish and reality. The Left made no attempt to assess
the nature and extent of the military danger which must decide the
nation's level of armament. Against their wish to concentrate on
welfare, Healey argued that 'all the will in the world is worthless if
we have another war. False teeth and spectacles are small comfort to
a corpse'.[41] It may have been a brutal way of putting it, but it was
undoubtedly true. The point was how to avoid a nation of corpses,
though Healey's prescription of the Western Alliance did not strike
everybody as the best way. The fact that socially progressive causes
took second place to defence against Communism indicated the conflicts within the revisionist call for social reform, though few wished
to be as blunt as Healey in pointing them out.

REVISIONISM AND LABOURISM

The political ideas which had gained ascendancy in the Labour Party
in its first fifty years had all generally fitted into the framework of

labourist ideology. Some political tendencies enjoyed a tenuous relationship with labourism, such as the Labour Marxism of Tom Mann and James Maxton, or the evolutionary socialism of Ramsay MacDonald, but in general the realities of the political and social power of trade unionism ensured the subordination of any elements in their thinking which lay outside labourism. When those elements could not be subordinated, as with MacDonald's belief in 1931 that Labour's class interests should be subordinated to the 'national' interest, the result was their secession or marginalisation.

The revisionists gained ascendency in the Labour Party in the 1950s as a result of trade union support – Gaitskell was fervently backed Arthur Deakin of the Transport Workers, Will Lawther of the Miners and Tom Williamson of the General and Municipal Workers – but their relationship to labourism was less congenial than any other political tendency in the preceding half century. Ramsay MacDonald had wanted Labour to be both a national and a class party, and in doing so had fallen foul of the party he had helped to create, but he had always seen the working class as socially outcast from the nation. He had, indeed, joined the ILP in 1894 precisely because of the anti-working-class prejudices of the Liberals, and had seen the Labour Party as the means by which the trade union movement would find its rightful place in the nation. The revisionists shared with MacDonald the belief that Labour must become a national party, but went much further than he did in seeking to divest Labour of its class image.

This was clearly expressed by Crosland, who argued that the changes in the standard of living and in the very composition of the working class must force Labour to face a new electoral reality. He summed up his view of Labour's dilemma in pointing to the historic link between the party and the movement:

> The Labour Party owes its whole existence and historic growth to the working class; one cannot think of one without the other. Yet, today, ironically, this unique identification is a clear political liability, for the simple reason that the working class is shrinking in size.[42]

Unless a steady decline was to be its fate, the Labour Party must become a broadly based national party. It was an extension of the message of Ramsay MacDonald, but in the prosperous conditions of the 1950s, it appeared to strike a meaningful and inspiring call.

However, it was a message which struck at the heart of labourism. The fundamental belief that the working class must organise itself separately from the employing class was pushed aside as irrelevant by the revisionists, who called for an end to the class antagonism present in British industry. Where MacDonald saw Labour as *both* a national and a class party, the revisionists wanted Labour to be *merely* a national party. They believed that the capitalist system which had led the unions to form their own political party was dead, and that the task of any progressive lay in radical social and cultural policies to help the poor and the forgotten at the margins of the existing system. That system itself had to be justly administered, not changed, and its just administration required a rejection of the old talk of class in favour of a role of partnership in industry and the services.

This attack on labourism was the real issue which lay behind the controversy over nationalisation and Clause IV after the 1959 election defeat. Immediately after the defeat, Douglas Jay wrote an article for the periodical *Forward*, calling for Labour to sever its links with the unions and to accept the mixed economy as permanent. As Gaitskell's biographer has pointed out, 'Jay's bugbear was the party's working class image, and he brought up nationalization only as an afterthought.'[43] Gaitskell himself rejected such anti-labourist talk as politically suicidal – Labour needed the unions for finance and support – and, at the special party conference after the 1959 defeat, said,

> I have always looked upon the Trade Union Congress and the Labour Party as part of the same great Labour movement, and our close integration as one of our greatest strengths. I see no reason to change my mind.[44]

However, his call to drop Clause IV from the Party constitution was couched in terms of its unattractiveness to an electorate which was ceasing to identify itself as working class. It was a symbolic move which was sought by Gaitskell, just as the main opposition came from trade unionists worried at the implications for the class nature and purposes of the Labour Party. Gaitskell succeeded in getting Labour to accept the mixed economy as one of its basic aims, but trade union opposition thwarted his attempt to drop Clause IV from the constitution.

The anti-labourism implicit in revisionist thinking could co-exist, if sometimes a little uneasily, with the political realities of the Labour Party as long as the economy was booming and the union leaders comparatively free from the pressure of their members. In the prosperous conditions of the 1950s, the unions could combine free collective bargaining and regular consultation with relatively friendly Conservative governments. They were growing stronger in numbers and, apart from a few left-wingers, the union leaders were less willing to appear partisan than they had for decades (a trend exemplified by George Woodcock, the TUC General Secretary, who was anxious to distance the union movement from identification with any one political party). In such circumstances, the revisionists seemed to be much more in tune with events than a dogmatic Left which appeared not to notice that capitalism had changed, or with the ideological stagnation of the Corporate Socialists.

In fact, the revisionist success could only be temporary, as it was predicated on the solution of the old problem of boom and slump which had bedevilled the economy before the war. The post-war boom disguised the fundamental conflict between the labourism of the trade unions and the revisionism of the Party leadership. If the boom had been as indefinite as the revisionists then believed, the radical and progressive nature of their ideas would have been allowed to blossom. As it was, the gradual ending of the long post-war boom spelled out a limit to their radicalism, and brought into the open their antagonistic relationship to the labourism of the unions. It was significant that, in an introduction to the 1964 edition of *The Future of Socialism*, Crosland should note

> Were I completely revising the book, I should substantially alter only one major argument, that relating to economic growth. Here I was too optimistic – not about the *capabilities* of the Western-type mixed economy... but about the performance of the Anglo-Saxon economies in particular.[45]

The performance of these economies was to have dire results for Crosland's revisionism.

11 Revisionism in Crisis

THE CALL FOR DYNAMISM

It was the beginning of the 1960s which witnessed the dawning realisation that the comparatively sluggish growth rate of the British economy, manifesting itself in low investment and a worsening balance of payments, was making an increase in state investment necessary. The belief that Britain had a stagnant economy because of its stagnant social institutions led to a renewed questioning, often cheaply satirical, of British society and politics. It also led the government to seek entry into the European Common Market; to intervene in wage bargaining by means of a 'pay pause' in 1961–2; and to establish the National Economic Development Council (NEDC) in which the corporatist tripartism between the state, the employers and the unions was institutionalised.

In this situation, the crisis in revisionist thought came to the surface. The promise of higher social spending and greater social equality had always been dependent on a high economic growth rate, and the stagnant growth in the British economy in the early 1960s presented itself as the most pressing problem facing any radical who sought change within the mixed economy. The deep schism which emerged within the revisionist camp over the Common Market was the most dramatic demonstration of its crisis. Where Roy Jenkins called for entry as the best means of overcoming the weakness of the British economy and as an excellent chance for Britain to find a new role in world affairs, Douglas Jay and Hugh Gaitskell opposed the government on the grounds that Britain could solve its economic problems outside Europe.[1] The French veto on British membership in January, 1963, ended the debate abruptly, but it would return.

The increasing sense that measures needed to be taken to overcome economic stagnation presented a major chance for the Corporate Socialists. The revisionist belief that 'fine-tuning' the economy had resolved the old problems of unemployment and economic growth seemed increasingly problematic as the traditional fiscal techniques of Keynesian economics were unable to push the economy forward. As a result, the accession of Harold Wilson to the Labour leadership after Gaitskell's sudden death in January 1963, presented the opportunity to reunite the Labour Party by integrating revisionist ideas with the old Corporate Socialist calls for direct planning. The divisions which had torn Labour apart for a decade were healed by a technocratic appeal which sought to obliterate ideological debate by posing a pragmatic solution to Britain's problems.

Harold Wilson (1916–95) was a perfect representative of this trend. Ambitious and shrewd, he had moved from an academic career at Oxford to a political career at Westminster in 1945 and, at thirty-one, became the youngest cabinet minister in the government as President of the Board of Trade. He presided over the 'bonfire of controls' in 1948 which heralded a move of the government away from the concerns with direct physical planning to indirect guidance of the economy through Keynesian techniques, though his corporatist commitment to the state was cogently expressed in 'The State and Private Industry', a paper written with Christopher Mayhew for a meeting of ministers in May 1950 as part of the debate about the future direction of the government. His resignation from the Cabinet in April 1951 and his subsequent association with the Bevanites gave him an appeal to the Left, while his willingness to desert Bevan by taking the latter's place in the Shadow Cabinet in April 1954 and then to support Gaitskell for the leadership in 1955 established both his refusal to be closely linked with any faction and a reputation for duplicity. He was, in fact, concerned above all other matters with electoral victory and saw party unity as the key to that victory. His primary emphasis on corporate planning sets him apart from the revisionists, while his distrust of the divisive nature of theory led him to see Gaitskell's conflicts with the Left on Clause IV and defence as both dangerous and fundamentally irrelevant. In a revealing discussion with John Junor, then editor of the *Sunday Express*, Wilson pointed to the success of Harold Macmillan in reuniting the Conservatives after their Suez debacle, saying,

> The man's a genius. He's holding up the banner of Suez for the party to follow, and he's leading the party away from Suez. That's what I'd like to do with the Labour Party over nationalisation.[2]

It was this contempt for theory and public debate which makes it difficult to weigh Wilson's contribution to Labour's political thought. He was too responsive to party and popular moods while in opposition to have many fixed principles, while his concern with administration in government gives his record in office a sense of endurance rather than innovation. However, in the early 1960s, he caught the

national and party mood in his appeals to a technocratic, classless
society as the solution to Britain's problems. Like the revisionists, he
identified the social privileges of the establishment as the barrier to
socialism, but he was not a revisionist – he did not identify socialism
in terms of equality and welfare. The establishment was a cause of
Britain's stagnation, and a barrier to the basic dynamism in the
British economy waiting to be unleashed. To Wilson, 'we are living
in the jet age but we are governed by an Edwardian establishment
mentality'.[3] The old boy network of connections through birth and
wealth were clogging up the vital arteries of Britain's economic
system. The commanding heights of the economy had been taken
over by the State, but the old aristocracy still remained in control. As
a result, the scientific revolution had passed Britain by, leading to
stagnation – 'in science and industry we are content to remain a
nation of Gentlemen in a world of Players'.[4]

Wilson's solution lay in the new meritocratic class of scientists and
professionals who would bring purpose to Britain's stagnating economy and society. Only they could competently apply the latest
statistical and analytical techniques to the problem of economic
expansion. This was, of course, the very class against which Titmuss
had warned in *The Irresponsible Society*, condemning them as elitist
administrators with neither morality nor compassion, but to Wilson
they were the harbingers of a new age of technology and scientific
planning. The difference of Wilson's vision of socialism from that of
the revisionists was concealed by a general agreement that the British
economy needed to escape from stagnation. This was why Wilson
could unite the Labour Party with his arguments that

> Socialism, as I understand it, means applying a sense of purpose to
> our national life: economic purpose, social purpose, moral purpose.
> Purpose means technical skill – be it the skill of a manager, a
> designer, a craftsman, a nuclear physicist, or a doctor, a nurse, a
> social worker.[5]

He was making it clear that the social radicalism of the revisionists
could only be satisfied if the economy could recover its dynamism.

It was the tried and tested ideas of Corporate Socialism, not
revisionism, on which Wilson relied to do this, and it was to economists like Thomas Balogh that he turned for the application of these
ideas to the Britain of the sixties. Balogh (1905–85) was a Hungarian
who had taught at Balliol College, Oxford, since 1939. He had served

as an adviser to various governments and to the United Nations, and was to serve as economic adviser to Wilson's Cabinet from 1964 to 1968. Long before, in *The Economics of Full Employment* (1944), Balogh had endorsed the Corporate Socialist interpretation of Keynes, accepting that a market economy would lead to instability and unemployment if left to itself. By the early 1960s, he had come to identify Britain's economic stagnation as due to 'a deep-rooted failure to acquire technical and scientific dynamism',[6] which had led to an uncompetitive situation in world markets and a fall in investment. The insufficient growth rate in the economy which had resulted had undermined social growth in schools, hospitals and housing, and had led trade unions to demand higher wages to prevent a fall in their members' living standards. The wage inflation caused by this had led to a further decline in investment, and so the vicious circle continued.

In seeking a solution to stop this process, Balogh admitted that wartime planning had failed because of its rudimentary, crude and negative nature. Moreover, planning had been thrust on a reluctant bureaucracy by the particular needs of the war. However, the Conservative rejection of planning had also failed through a tragic waste of Britain's resources in private consumption. This was hardly surprising, since a non-planned economy was one where businessmen and financiers were simply unaware of the implications of their investment decisions for their own prosperity. The real solution lay in neither of these alternatives, but in a fully planned economy, with industrial modernisation being given a priority by a more powerful NEDC. It was not the *principle* of Corporate Socialism which was wrong, but its inadequate *application*. The Development Councils set up to plan individual industries under the post-war Labour government should be revived, but this time they should be free of business domination. Moreover, it must be an economy which was centrally planned, not a compartmentalised series of competing plans – 'a mechanism is necessary which would elaborate, and implement, a set of coherently chosen targets enforcing social priorities in a plan which takes into account the effects of the totality of investment projects'.[7] The technical management of such an economy need require no fundamental changes in private ownership – though Balogh wrote, 'I doubt whether the moral or psychological handicaps could be overcome without extending public ownership'[8] – but it *did* need a conscious co-ordination of the process of decision-making.

Balogh was nothing if not consistent, and his call for a planned economy necessarily involved a planning of incomes. He did not go so far as to advocate direct state interference in the process of free collective bargaining, based as it was on the invaluable knowledge of employers and unions, but 'what is needed is to add to this sectional knowledge, a due regard for the requirements of the general economic position'.[9] An Arbitration Board, for example, could decide a dispute between employers and unions where both sides agree to apply. He acknowledged the natural hostility of the Labour Party's trade union base to an incomes policy, but the requirements of a planned economy overrode all sectional considerations. Moreover, he believed that the economic success of planning would in itself win the co-operation of the unions, and argued that

> the sacrifice will not be in vain, that the restraint on wages on which the restoration of British industry depends would in the due – and not too distant – future yield positive results in increased living standards.[10]

It was in the light of this strategy that the 1963 Labour conference unanimously passed a resolution calling on the party to develop an incomes policy in association with the trade unions, and that the Labour government elected in October, 1964, prepared a National Plan to bring about a 25 per cent increase in output in five years. Neither Balogh nor the Labour Party asked themselves what would happen to wages and the unions if the hoped for growth did not take place.

In fact, the Labour government of 1964–70 failed in its economic objective and, thence, in almost every other. The strategy of planning was a miserable debacle with George Brown's National Plan still-born. The balance of payments crisis dominated government policy from beginning to end, forcing it into a series of stringency measures which fell on its own working-class constituency. The failure of a statutory incomes policy in the summer of 1966 was followed by the failure of the chauvinist policy of maintaining the value of sterling, signalled by the devaluation of the pound in November 1967. The growing opposition of the unions to government policy led to tre-mendous strains within the labour movement, rising to a head with the government's attempt to curb the unions by legislation in 1969. The failure of the government even to introduce a bill as a result of the opposition within the parliamentary party and the unions marked the final failure of Labour's economic policy, underlined by the rise in unemployment to over half a million after 1967, and by a series of strikes in 1969–70 which destroyed the effects of an incomes policy. The attainment of a surplus in the balance of payments in 1969–70 was due more to the restraint on working class demand than it was to any drastic restructuring of British industry.[11]

If the government's record marked a failure of Corporate Socialism, it was also a failure for revisionism. The hopes of liberal reform were kept alive by the tenure of Roy Jenkins at the Home Office in 1965–7, when a series of social reforms on censorship, abortion and homosexuality were pushed through the Commons with Jenkins's active support. However, James Callaghan, Jenkins's successor as Home Secretary, was generally seen as a disgrace by revisionists.[12] He capitulated, for example, to racist demands to restrict the entry of Kenyan Asians in 1968. John Mackintosh expressed revisionist feeling when he told the Commons,

> I do not know who has put the wind up the Home Office and destroyed the reputation of the Labour Party for non-racialism by suggesting that we could not absorb 26,000 people this year into a humane and reasonable society. I will certainly not listen to any more speeches from either Front Bench advocating multi-racialism in other countries. I feel humiliated to have to stand here and make this speech.[13]

Revisionist frustration was particularly marked by Labour's failure in social policy, the area they had marked out as their own. While there were certainly innovations in a progressive direction – official support for comprehensive education, and the introduction of a system of wage-related social security contributions and benefits. for example – the savage cutbacks in social expenditure and the increase in unemployment more than balanced them. The growth in spending on health, education and social security merely kept pace with the increased demand for and cost of basic services. The distribution of wealth and social privilege was left untouched, while poverty may well have worsened.[14] However, a number of revisionists were in leading positions in the government – Jenkins was the Chancellor who reimposed charges for health prescriptions – and it had always been assumed that reforms depended on a healthy economy.

At the 1968 Labour conference, Roy Jenkins told delegates that the revisionist hopes of social reform had to mark time on economic success:

until we get that success, we cannot achieve our other goals except by mortgaging the future. For success here is the key to a higher and more secure level of unemployment. . . . It is the key to a steady and satisfactory rate of growth, and with such a . . . rate of growth, but not without it, new horizons in social policy would open up.[15]

The government's record was a failure of revisionism as much as it was of Corporate Socialism.

REAPPRAISAL

The failure of the 1964–70 Labour government led to a mood of doubt among the revisionists. Harold Wilson himself could point to the machinations of speculators and subversives as the cause of his government's failure,[16] but many revisionists felt that a much less superficial reappraisal was needed, a belief which was intensified by the growing strength of the Labour Left after the 1970 defeat.

Tony Crosland attempted to come to terms with the failure of the Labour Government in a Fabian tract, *A Social Democratic Britain* (1971) and in *Socialism Now* (1974). He argued that there was no need to redefine socialism as concerned with equality and welfare, but the *means* had to be reappraised in the light of the government's disappointing failure to modify class differences. Britain in the early 1970s was as class-divided as ever, with poverty and homelessness increasing. In spite of trade union strength, the working class was still inferior in terms of income, status, fringe benefits and job security. The growing wave of strikes stood as a stark reminder that Crosland had been premature in once dismissing class divisions as outmoded – 'the labour issue continues to dominate our society, and class relations in industry are characterised by a mutual distrust amounting often to open warfare.'[17] Above all, the economy was beginning to deteriorate, bringing into doubt even the wisdom of state spending, so crucial to revisionist thought.

However, Crosland was unwilling to reject his original belief that capitalism in itself was no longer an enemy for socialists. While capitalist industry had certainly increased in size, he did not detect any increase in capitalist *power*. On the contrary, the strength of the unions and the sharper competition from abroad had made the private sector more precarious than ever. He was not worried about

the growth of the multinational corporations either, as their investment had increased the real income of British workers. He did recognise their potential dangers – to the balance of payments, or to the
revenue, as a result of evasion – but argued that these dangers could
be met by government action on a national and international level.
Nationalisation was still seen as a weapon of the last resort, since the
ability of governments to legislate, tax, police or embargo large
companies could be just as effective. In view of this, and in view of
the general failure of nationalisation to achieve equality, Crosland
wrote, 'I see no reason to alter the revisionist thesis that government
can generally impose its will (provided it has one) on the private
corporation.'[18]

In the face of this, Crosland pressed once again the revisionist
argument that the broad objectives of any Labour government must
be to help the poor and deprived, and to promote greater social and
economic equality. He was also forced against the fact that high
economic growth was necessary to attain this, albeit with a strict
social control over the environment to prevent pollution and the
destruction of rural beauty. The problem was the failure of the
Labour government to attain the increasingly elusive goal of higher
production levels.

This was ascribed by Crosland to its deflationary policies, caused
by its original obsession with maintaining the parity of sterling. There
were, of course, deeper reasons for the general decline in the vitality
of the British economy during the century, ranging from the faulty
structure of British industry to the public-school system, but he
believed that this decline could be halted by government will. Crosland held that a Labour government should choose its priorities and
stick to them, refusing to be blown off course. If a problem arose with
the balance of payments, it should choose a policy of flexible
exchange rates rather than a cut in social welfare. If the problem was
inflation, then the government should choose an incomes policy, on
the basis of agreement with the trade unions, rather than let low paid
and poorly organised workers get left behind in a wages free-for-all. If
the government could do this, then radical policies to reduce poverty
and redistribute wealth could be successfully undertaken. Crosland
could then conclude from the failure of the 1960s that

a move to the left is needed, not in the traditional sense of a move
towards old-fashioned Clause IV Marxism but in the sense of a
sharper delineation of fundamental objectives, a greater clarity

about egalitarian priorities, and a stronger determination to achieve them.[19]

This was a theme taken up by Roy Jenkins in *What Matters Now* (1972), a series of speeches largely written by David and Judith Marquand. Jenkins (b.1920) had a dry urbanity and upper-class life-style which disguised his working-class origins and which earned him much unpopularity with the increasingly powerful Left, and his liberal tenure at the Home Office had been fatally marred by the deflationary measures he had taken as Chancellor of the Exchequer in the late 1960s, and by his enthusiastic support for the Common Market.

In the aftermath of the 1970 defeat, Jenkins followed Crosland in returning to revisionist fundamentals. He called on the next Labour government to make the elimination of poverty as a social problem its central aim. To Jenkins, poverty and inequality remained the principal barriers to the freedom of human choice sought by the democratic Left. The impoverished tenant of a sub-standard flat with only a pittance left to live on after the rent and costs of keeping alive had been paid was a standing insult to a humane society, and to talk of the freedom to choose his or her own way of life was a cruel joke for such a person. Jenkins held that a voluntary incomes policy agreed between Labour and the unions, combined with the old Labour demand for a national minimum wage, would be enough to produce a more just and free society. Of course, such a policy could be held to infringe *economic* freedom, but Jenkins held that this was no bad thing:

Ironically, many Conservative MPs who so strongly proclaim the virtues of individual freedom in the economic field, where it can do great harm to others, have bitterly resisted the growth of greater legal tolerance in the field of personal conduct, where individual behaviour rarely interferes with the rights of others.[20]

Both Jenkins and Crosland refused to question their own Keynesian beliefs. The increasing inability of the State effectively to combat economic crisis by the use of techniques of fine-tuning was ignored by them, and they called for a greater use of such techniques to eradicate poverty and inequality. The fact that Keynes had written at a time of high unemployment and low prices, whereas the decade of the 1970s was a time of rising unemployment *and* rising prices, did not lead them to revise their original ideas. Instead, they held that inflation could be kept in check by an incomes policy. Apart from the fact than an incomes policy faced enormous difficulties in its operation and produced inequities of its own, it was a solution to the wrong problem. The wage is merely a price – the price of labour power – and to believe that rising prices are caused by rising prices is to fall into tautology. The demand for higher wages was itself caused by rising prices, and incomes policies invariably failed to control other prices from rising, thereby leading to renewed labour discontent. The revisionists had failed to grasp that the root cause of inflation lay in increased state expenditure and credit to meet the rising demands of a problem-beset economy.

Jenkins himself faced increasing political isolation in the Labour Party, largely as a result of his enthusiasm for the Common Market. His support, consistent for over a decade, was based on the belief that Britain could only shake off the stagnation which had settled over her and regain a sense of purpose in economic activity and in world affairs by joining with her natural European allies. This belief was out of touch with the mood of the Labour Party of the early 1970s, and Jenkins resigned as deputy leader in April 1972, in protest at the party's decision to hold a referendum on whether Britain should withdraw from the Market. It was evidence of a decline in revisionist influence in the party, and the advance of a new Left which was succeeding in winning Labour to a policy of increased public ownership and hostility to the Common Market.

It was in protest at the rise of this Left that the call to go beyond revisionism was raised. John Gyford and Stephen Haseler in an influential Fabian pamphlet, *Social Democracy: Beyond Revisionism* (1971), called on the old Gaitskellite wing of the party to adopt a new and more populist strategy which would come to terms with the new desire for participation. They called themselves Social Democrats to differentiate themselves from the old revisionists, and emphasised that inequality in power and status should be reduced by a more local, grass-roots approach. This call was taken up by Dick Taverne, who resigned from Parliament in protest at left-wing activity and was elected as a Democratic Labour MP in the Lincoln by-election in March 1973. In his book *The Future of Labour* (1974), he called on Labour to break its links with the big unions and cultivate community politics and small business. He wrote that, 'when in doubt, we should favour the small. Indeed, our guiding principle should be "small is beautiful", that variety provides for independence, and that independence provides for greater security and freedom.'[21] It was an appealing message, in touch with popular sentiment, but it was combined with the call for the followers of Jenkins to form a new party. To Taverne, Labour had become too left-wing and union-dominated to be capable of reform.

The Labour government of 1974–9 was another disappointment for revisionists. Its initial sensitivity to the Left and the more militant unions was replaced from the summer of 1975 by yet another lurch to more conservative economic policies as inflation rose to 25 per cent and unemployment to over a million. There were hints of a new type of politics – as seen in the abortive proposals for devolution to Wales and Scotland, or the pointer to a centrist government from the pact Labour made with the Liberals in 1977–8 – but generally the failure of the government only reinforced the glaring need for a break with the revisionist politics of a bygone era. This was underlined by the ultimate failure of the 'Social Contract', the voluntary incomes policy agreed between Labour and the unions. The inability of the union leaders to control the militancy of the rank and file in the 'winter of discontent' in 1978–9 sealed Labour's fate and brought to power a Conservative government of the militant Right. The electoral liability of the Labour Party's links with the trade unions was evident to many revisionists by this time.

It was during the lifetime of this government that the most able of the revisionists, John Mackintosh, began the radical reappraisal that was needed. Mackintosh (1929–78) had been born in India and educated at Edinburgh and Oxford. He wrote *The British Cabinet* (1962), a major study of the institution, and enjoyed an academic career in Nigeria and Edinburgh before his election to Westminster in 1966. His fierce independence won him no love from the Labour leadership, and he never obtained a ministerial post. The failures of Labour in power convinced him that the revisionist politics of the 1950s to which he had adhered were outdated and irrelevant, and he was working on a restatement of revisionist socialism when he died.

By the late 1970s, Mackintosh had come to the conclusion that revisionism was inadequate because it had no economic understanding of or prescription for the mixed economy. The revisionists had merely assumed that their programme could be implemented once the Tories, seen as the cause of economic stagnation, were removed. Mackintosh now admitted,

I had not thought about or appreciated how far the views of what is now called the social democratic section which was then dominant in the Labour Party depended on the kind of growth we had claimed was possible once the Tories were out of office.[22]

There had been no adequate theory of how the mixed economy should work and, despite the different twists and turns of every government since the early 1960s, a long-term economic revival still evaded the country. The Wilsonian explanation that this was due to a series of accidents which blew the country off course seemed much too superficial, failing to explain the sheer persistence of government failure, or the ability of other countries like Japan and West Germany to escape such 'accidents'. To Mackintosh, there had to be a search for much deeper causes if Labour's failure was to be understood and remedied.

The adversarial politics of Conservative and Labour were partly to blame, but Mackintosh eventually rejected this cause, too, as insufficient. There had been drastic policy changes on trade union legislation, incomes policy, administrative reforms of health and local government – which had a disruptive effect on industry, but this was a result of the stagnation of the economy, and not its cause. The party system had been around a long time, and there was no reason why it should permit industrialisation to take place at one point and then cause its decline at another. In fact, the parliamentary system had been very responsive to the needs of industry, moving to stem an irreversible decline.

Mackintosh traced the defects to the very growth of corporatism which Labour had done so much to bring about, leading as it did to a feeling of impotence and indifference in the electorate and its Parliament. He argued that the extension of the vote to a new working-class electorate with major social needs had upset the old Westminster model of checks and balances between the executive (constitutional monarch, Cabinet) and legislature (the parties, the Commons). Power had shifted from Westminster to the Cabinet, imposing a tight discipline on the party system and increasing executive control over the legislative process. While the outward features of government and Parliament remained the same, the reality was very different as the ability of the Commons to force policy changes on governments and significantly amend legislation had generally disappeared.

The adoption of a referendum to decide complex policy issues such as membership of the Common Market merely underlined the trend towards a plebiscitary democracy, where the government could bypass Parliament to appeal directly to the electorate in a form which could be easily loaded in the official favour.

This had been paralleled by the rise of corporate pressure groups, mainly the Confederation of British Industry (CBI) and the TUC, which had come to exercise the power once held by the Commons. These groups had been able to claim the primary loyalty of their members, as demonstrated by the successful defiance of the Industrial Relations law by dockers in July 1972, and as a consequence had denied the legitimacy of Parliament.

> The denial of legitimacy is a clear consequence of two concepts. First, that passage by the House of Commons is not itself an adequate indication of the consent of the community, and second, that prior consultation with recognised groups has become an essential part of the legitimising process.[23]

This growth of corporatism had led the Commons to become a mere registry for the wishes of the pressure groups, who had grown so powerful that they had become able to disregard the will of governments successfully. The House of Commons was excluded from the essential information needed to judge decisions properly, while the Cabinet and the pressure groups consulted one another on the major issues of the day in an atmosphere of secrecy and reticence.

Revisionism had itself contributed to this devaluation of parliamentary democracy, according to Mackintosh. Crosland's libertarian rejection of nationalisation had not gone far enough, and he had been unable to break adequately from the statist approach of the Corporate Socialists and the Fabians in his demands for welfare and equality. He did not realise that mere changes in social and economic institutions by the State could not in themselves change the social attitudes of the people. As a result, the whole social, political and industrial atmosphere in Britain had contributed to a feeling of impotence against the vested interests of big business and organised labour which really ran the country, and of contempt against a Parliament which only pretended to rule. The dangers to democracy were only too clear to Mackintosh, who wrote 'It is, I fear, basically unhealthy for a country to depend on a political system which is not backed by positive conviction and understanding, and whose original principles have become corrupted and confused.'[24]

In this context, the task of the social democrats in the Labour Party was clear. The importance of parliamentary democracy and the

independence of the individual Member of Parliament must be reaffirmed against the power of the Cabinet, while the evolution of
political responsibility to the regions and the locality must revive the
feeling of participation and citizenship essential if the whole nation
was to revive its faith in democracy. This would inevitably mean a
fight against the corporate interests which ran the country, including
the trade unions on which the Labour Party depended. However,
Mackintosh did not let party considerations prevent his

> primary emphasis on putting the mass of community before the
> interests of those with a monopoly-hold on economic power, be
> they financiers, multinational corporations, or unions controlling
> key sectors of the labour force.[25]

Mackintosh was an exceptionally able thinker who was experienced
in both the theory and practice of politics, and his elaboration of a
new social democratic doctrine was still in the process of transition at
his death. He was able to pinpoint the weakness of revisionism as its
lack of an economic theory which could stimulate growth, but was
himself unable to dig deeper than the political manifestations of
corporatism and the decline of Parliament which had accompanied
the mixed economy. The economic causes of economic decline – lying
in the process of production itself – were ignored as Mackintosh
attempted to combat the feeling of impotence and indifference
which had once settled over once-mighty institutions like Parliament.
The fact that this mood may have been created by economic decline
as much as by corporatism was not really investigated, but the
solutions of devaluation and a revival of the independence of Parliament would fall into the same trap as Crosland – the belief that
institutional changes would lead to a change of attitudes. The fact
that power over an ailing economy would be held by Westminster
and regional assemblies would not necessarily be more inspiring than
the exercise of power by the Cabinet or the corporate pressure
groups.

Moreover, Mackintosh made the mistake of treating organised
labour as an evil similar to organised capital. The unions had definitely grown in numbers and their leaders were regularly consulted by
government on the important industrial issues of the day, but this
does not necessarily imply that they were equal in power and status to
the leaders of industry in an economy desperate for investment by
those leaders. It was true that the unions denied the legitimacy of

Parliament by defying the Industrial Relations legislation of 1972, but they had done so many times before, most notably in 1834 when workers were deported for attempting to form a union. When a law is aimed at a section of the community, there should be no surprise when that law is defied. In overlooking this, Mackintosh and his supporters overlooked the limits to legitimacy of parliamentary legislation marked out by the founders of liberal political thought like John Locke.

In his attacks on the corporate power of organised labour, Mackintosh was developing the anti-labourism implicit in revisionist thinking to a new and more dangerous stage. The social democrat wing of the Labour Party, as it was now called, was reaching a point where the revisionists could find no home in the Labour Party.

THE SOCIAL DEMOCRAT BREAK WITH LABOUR

The failure of the 'social contract' in a series of strikes in the 'winter of discontent' in 1978–9 sealed Labour's electoral fate. It also appeared to be a final proof that the party's unique relationship with the unions was not capable of delivering the incomes policy felt to be essential by the social democrats. The power of the Left, growing throughout the decade, was making the existence of the old revisionist wing increasingly uncomfortable, and the displacement of sitting moderate MPs by their local parties was making it intolerable. The conditions for a major schism were present, and it was Roy Jenkins who set the final process in motion.

Jenkins had been increasingly alienated from the party during the 1970s, and his failure to win the Labour leadership after Wilson's retirement in March, 1976, may finally have convinced him that he had reached the end of the road in British politics. He withdrew from Westminster to become president of the European Commission, the archetype of the 'Eurocrat' so hated by the Labour Left, but he had not finished with British politics. The final failure of the Labour government, paving the way for the tough and divisive regime of Mrs Thatcher, made him aware of the possibility of a new party, committed to the concerns once praised by Evan Durbin. The strength of the Left in the Labour Party, and the rise of the New Right in the Conservatives, indicated to him that an important political vacuum had grown in the centre which would hold the support of the majority of the electorate.

It was at the Dimbleby Lecture in November, 1979, that Jenkins put forward his new views. His acceptance of the present contours of the mixed economy, with a rejection of any further public ownership, was less startling than his call for a major change in the political system. The fixed two-party system was a century old, yet during that century the society on which it rested had been transformed. Britain had seen its world power and status gradually disappear, while the strict social divisions which had characterised a class society had become weaker than ever before. The disparity between the stable political system and the changed society was emphasized by Jenkins, who argued that the stability had become a mark of political ossification.

> Traditionally, this British stability was considered a major national asset. Now the question is whether the stability has not turned into political rigidity, whether the old skin is not drawn too tight for effective national performance.[26]

Jenkins traced the decisive changes to Suez, which had marked the end of Britain as a world power, and the formation of the Common Market without British membership. The result had been an isolated Britain which failed to enjoy European economic growth and prosperity, and suffered instead an inexorable decline into one of the poorest powers in Europe. By the time the country finally joined the Common Market, it was too late to take part in Europe's thriving economic boom, which had finally exhausted itself. The political system had failed to halt Britain's economic decline, despite their wildly enthusiastic promise by the major parties that it was they which held the keys to prosperity. The result was a decline in the prestige of the House of Commons and a growing desire for a third party by an increasing number of the electorate.

The answer to these problems given by Jenkins was for an end to the ideological politics which was coming to characterise the party system. Mackintosh had, of course, defended the party system, believing that adversarial politics was a result rather than a cause of the crisis, but to Jenkins it was a major threat to the consensus celebrated by Durbin and Gaitskell, a consensus which had presided over the long post-war boom. Such intense political partisanship only harmed the economy, as controversial legislation was repealed and then passed again, while conflict on the shop floor between workers and employers was only encouraged by the sight of the two parties bitterly attacking one another. Jenkins did not present any proof of this point – it was not only Marxists who believed that employers and workers might have different economic interests – but he did believe that a change in political attitudes towards a sense of harmony and conciliation would have a major effect for the better on industrial relations. It was, then, a call for a politics of the *centre* which was made by Jenkins:

> The vocation of politicians ought to be to represent, to channel, to lead the aspirations of the electorate. These aspirations, not on every issue, but in essential directions, pull far more towards the centre than towards the extremes.[27]

To attain this 'politics of the centre,' Jenkins called for institutional reforms, particularly in the electoral system of 'first past the post,' which grossly distorted the wishes of the electorate, preventing the political expression of popular alienation from the two parties. The fact that the Liberals could only take 2 per cent of the seats at Westminster from more than 18 per cent of the vote in October 1974, was merely the latest proof of the inequities of the system. The old argument that the current electoral system ensured stable and coherent government had been manifestly disproved in the last two decades, argued Jenkins, while he pointed to the old Labour Party as a combination of liberal social democrats and responsible trade unionists to demonstrate that coalition politics could be a healthy phenomenon. However, he held that 'the great disadvantage of our present electoral system is that it freezes the pattern of politics, and holds together the incompatible because everyone assumes that if a party splits it will be electorally slaughtered'.[28]

It was an ominous warning that the arguments about electoral reform were basically an attempt to ensure the survival of a social democrat break from the Labour Party. Labour had once called for electoral reform, too, only to forget the inequities of the system once it enjoyed the fruits. Jenkins appeared to have remembered that the 'first past the post' system was unfair only when it became necessary to unfreeze the system.

Moreover, his call for a 'politics of the centre' was a mark of the crisis into which revisionism had fallen. In the hands of Crosland, the rejection of nationalisation had gone hand in hand with a desire to unleash the radical impulse within the Labour Party. There was a desire to attack the citadels of wealth and privilege, and to transform capitalist and materialist values into the socialist values of compassion and welfare for the poor and the outcast of society. The failure to achieve economic growth had ruined this radical impulse in revisionism, which was now in danger of degenerating into a politics of moderation and accommodation to the existing social system.

Many social democrats rejected the moderate centrism of Jenkins and, during 1980–1, as the need and preparations for a new party took shape, attempted to revive the original radicalism of the revisionists to a form more suitable to the eighties. In doing so, they looked to the ideas of decentralisation becoming popular as part of a general reaction to the elitist rule of corporatism. Taverne and Mackintosh had pointed to this tradition, alive in the earlier writings of Cole and Tawney before Corporate Socialism had established its sway within the Labour Party, its roots lying deep in a radical and commonwealth past. The political atmosphere among middle class activists was certainly ripe for such politics, prepared by the local concerns of Liberal populists, ecologists, and even the ideas of direct 'participatory' democracy which had become popular in sections of the radical Left.

Shirley Williams (b.1930) and David Owen (b.1938) proved themselves adept at taking up the new ideas, ecological and communitarian, then coming to the fore. The daughter of the feminist writer, Vera Brittain, Shirley Williams had been active in the Labour Party throughout her life, participating in the Gaitskellite Campaign for Democratic Socialism during the unilateralist crisis of 1960–1, and serving as General Secretary of the Fabian Society before entering Parliament in 1964. A charismatic personality, she was a member of Labour's National Executive Committee throughout the 1970s, and served in the Labour Government of 1974–9, first as Prices Secretary, and then as Education Secretary. Her defeat at Hertford and Stevenage in the 1979 election freed her for the rethinking necessary to write *Politics is for People* (1981), although she was to leave the Labour Party after the constitutional victories of the Left in 1980–1.

Williams took the revisionist critique of Corporate Socialism elaborated by Crosland to the logical conclusion that state socialism must be rejected altogether, leading her to sharply differentiate the social democratic tradition from the Labour Marxists and those on the Left who flirted with Marxist ideas. While the goals of equality and the abolition of poverty may have been common to social democrats and Marxists, they could not bridge the gulf separating these two strands of socialist thinking. Marxism was, according to Williams, basically hostile to parliamentary democracy because of its rejection of the mixed economy, and led inevitably to the bureaucratic privileges and vicious repression of dissent seen in the Soviet Union. She drew the distinction with social democracy clearly in her argument that 'a pluralist democracy complements a pluralist economy; a monolithic political system complements monolithic economic ownership and control'.[29]

She then proceeded to attempt to incorporate the new decentralist ideas which had arisen in the previous decade, particularly in the ecological movement. Unlike the political extremists, whose forefathers she traced back to Stalin and Hitler, these ecological romantics were concerned with the quality of life, more important to them than any economic system or careless talk of class oppression. They saw industrialism, not capitalism, as their main enemy, and recognised the need for 'a sense of belonging , of being cared for, of being wanted, of being part of a network of relationships with people and also with objects'.[30] It was a need which led to a resentment against the impersonal nature of the State and technology which threatened the fragile ecology on which we all depend. It was a need which led to the demand for the preservation of the small community from the encroachment of the ugly cities, and demanded the right of ordinary people to run their own affairs. It was a movement that she felt political parties must learn from, and which would respond to the old libertarian traditions of social democracy. To her, 'Owen and Tawney are to political thought what Vaughan Williams was to music; pastoral, gentle and humane'.[31]

The formula of local democracy was seen as a panacea for the problems of British society, though Williams maintained that public schools should be abolished on the grounds that freedom of choice was outweighed by the profound harm inflicted on society by a segregated education. The need to increase spending on social services, once at the heart of revisionist thinking, had now been reduced in importance to the problem of making the existing welfare services less bureaucratic and remote, throwing the administration of schools, hospitals and housing open to the community. The problems of staffing could easily be met by imaginative thinking – for example, voluntary service could be encouraged as unemployment and early retirement provided a pool of people 'willing to participate in working in it for nothing'.[32] The consequences of this for the labour force as a whole in posing the danger of lower wages was not raised, however.

The radical nature of the break with revisionism was brought out in her call for a modest and self-sustaining economic growth to be led by the small firm. The revisionists had always regarded the large corporation as a progressive step compared with the cut-throat competition which had characterised the small capitalists, and regarded the economies of scale enjoyed by large firms as crucial to the high rates of economic growth needed to pay for social reform. However, Williams rejected such large firms as a cause of rigidities in the working of the economy. 'The history of natural selection tells us that size is irrelevant to survival. What matters is functional efficiency. The dinosaur proved to be an evolutionary dead end; the fish and the bird survived and flourished.'[33] The obsession with size shown by post-war governments had contributed towards the impersonal elitism which has denied people a sense of responsibility, and had led towards the general crisis in which Britain now found herself. Williams argued that the government should cease concerning itself with state monopolies or big business, and look instead to the small firm as its primary concern. Unfortunately, this exaltation of the small-time capitalist tended to ignore the harsh economic climate and stiff competition which often force small businesspeople to reduce costs by the very unromantic methods of the sweatshop and appallingly low wages.

The call for a new, decentralised socialism tied to modest economic growth was echoed by David Owen, who had been a research doctor at St Thomas's Hospital until his election to Westminster in 1966. He had risen rapidly to become, on Crosland's death in February 1977, the youngest Foreign Secretary since Anthony Eden. After the defeat of the Labour government, Owen rapidly established himself as one of the leading social democrats in the party and, in *Face the Future* (1981), he still attempted to link the new ideas to older traditions in the labour movement.

He argued that Labour was facing the 1980s with the old formulae of 1945, with their calls for more centralisation and state control. In fact, these formulae had turned into the very problems which needed to be confronted. It was the undemocratic nature of corporatism, where decisions were taken by unrepresentative pressure groups like the CBI and the TUC, which had succeeded capitalism as the real enemy of socialists. These corporate pressure groups were insensitive to individual cases, and their very size discouraged the initiative and innovation so needed by Britain. The smaller business firms, like the homeless and workers not in unions, found themselves excluded from the political and economic decisions which concerned them. To Owen, 'Britain cannot be revived unless corporatism is rejected and democracy allowed to flourish in its place.'[34]

However, the Labour Party was identifying itself more closely with the centralised politics of corporatism, moving out of step with popular sentiment. Owen traced this to the pursuit of equality at the expense of freedom. This pursuit of equality was certainly worthwhile, as there was much evidence that inequality and poverty were closely linked, but the problem of how to overcome inequality was becoming particularly difficult at a time of low economic growth when all social classes held on to their existing wealth. He did accept the need to continue egalitarian measures, but his advocacy of tax reform and the raising of social benefits hardly amounted to a major assault on the bastions of social privilege.

In fact, according to Owen, 'what is needed is a socialist philosophy outside the restrictive confines of much of the present polarised political debate, which asserts the radical democratic libertarian tradition of decentralised socialism'.[35] It was a tradition with an honourable lineage, stretching back to G.D.H. Cole and to William Morris, concerned with freedom from the tyranny of the State rather than the Fabian anxieties about poverty and inefficiency. Moreover, Owen linked this concern with a growing movement on the European Left which took up the rights of workers in the workplace, demanding that they be treated as human beings rather than mere cogs in a factory. This was the motive behind the demand for *autogestion* (workers' control) put forward by Michel Rocard, a leader of the moderate wing of the French Socialist Party. This old demand, abstracted from the anti-capitalist terms in which it was once couched, was now taken up as an alternative to the old panacea of state intervention.

It was this hostility to the State which Owen took up as he attempted to change the revisionist concerns for poverty and equality to a new concern for freedom. He accepted state intervention in the marginal sense of providing finance for new capital-intensive industries such as computers and the micro- chip, but generally the corporate state stood in the way of the development of a participatory democracy and wider ownership by the community. As a result, he called for more open government and an end to the secrecy traditionally shrouding the processes by which decisions were taken in Britain. The evasion of parliamentary control by corporate organisations such as the CBI and the TUC, which had succeeded in curbing democracy by arrogating decision-making to themselves, would be ended by an increase in the parliamentary powers of scrutiny and the authority of the backbench MP. To Owen, as to Mackintosh,

> Parliament cannot cease to be the forum for the representation of a wide variety of views and must never accept being the endorser of traditions curbing the individual rights of citizens that are taken by departments or Ministers without specific parliamentary authority.[36]

Members of Parliament must rediscover and reassert their rights as the traditional practitioners of government.

In common with Shirley Williams, Owen took the revolt against Corporate Socialism to a new phase of positive encouragement of private enterprise. Attacking the Labour Left as centralisers who were unable to reconcile themselves to the freedom and initiative of the private sector, he called for a much more resolute and clear-headed approach to the mixed economy. The Corporate Socialists had never considered the market sector of the economy to be worthy of any other study than that of cutting its size, while the revisionists were more concerned with equality and welfare than the economy on which any policies had to rest.

Owen clearly differentiated social democratic ideology from both Corporate Socialism and revisionism by pointing to the failure of the mixed economy. This failure was due to an inversion of values, as private corporations willingly looked to the State for financial aid to compensate for their lack of enterprise, while the public corporations acted as though they were commercial companies in search of a profit rather than services to help industry and the community. The social democrats, in advocating a mixed economy, should be prepared to accept the consequences of a market sector, which should be free from the detailed restrictions of central government control, to find scope for private initiative and thereby make its full contribution to the economy. Private firms had become commercially irresponsible, refusing to confront militant unions or dismiss workers who had become unnecessary. They looked to fiscal benefits from the State, rather than normal commercial criteria, as the basis for the siting of new firms. A *realistic* commitment to the mixed economy would involve a recognition that the private sector must not be emasculated by the public sector. It involved a questioning of 'the extent to which inducing a sense of social responsibility in the private sector is compatible with the economic dynamic that should come from the private entrepreneur'.[37]

If Owen and the social democrats (who included such prominent thinkers as David Marquand and James Meade) wished to break away from both revisionism and Corporate Socialism in their hostility to the State, they remained committed to the restrictions on incomes sought by the Wilsonian technocrats. Freedom for the small business enterprise did not extend to collective bargaining as the social democrats reaffirmed the need for an incomes policy. Owen argued that 'full employment, reasonable price stability and free collective bargaining are all incompatible',[38] and called for an incomes policy which would avoid the rigidity which had led to the collapse of previous attempts of the past two decades. To the social democrats, it was not the principle of state restrictions on incomes which was wrong, but the will and the intelligence to carry that principle through to the end. This belief was shared by many others on the Labour Right, but the social democrats felt much more independent of trade union interests in elaborating their policy.

In the final analysis, it was mass unemployment – which climbed to three million by 1982 – which was to act as the force which restricted the unions' power to bargain with the employers. As in the 1930s, a large reserve army of labour served as an excellent weapon with which to frighten a suddenly insecure workforce. The social democrats were, of course, opposed to such a weapon, but they were unable to demonstrate how their advocacy of an incomes policy would have any other effect than cutting living standards. The abeyance of wage-militancy in the mid-1970s did not curb inflation, as increased wages were not a cause of inflation. As has been argued, the wage is merely a price – the price of labour power – and to argue that rising prices are caused by rising prices is to fall into a tautology. When workers struck for higher wages, it was an attempt to maintain living standards. It was a result, not a cause.

Just as social democrats called for a continuation of the attempts at incomes controls, so they saw themselves as continuing the traditions of revisionist foreign policy. Where the Left was becoming committed to calls for a withdrawal from the Common Market and a unilateral renunciation of nuclear weapons, the social democrats remained passionate defenders of the Western Alliance and a more positive approach to Europe. Owen himself, an ex-Foreign Secretary, rejected the pacifist tendencies of a renewed CND as a council of despair in the face of the Soviet military build-up. The CND's call for Britain to take a moral lead in the world by a policy of disarmament was seen as absolutely unrealistic, given the ruthless Soviet contempt for weakness and their refusal to heed moral considerations when their power was threatened, as seen in their occupation of Czechoslovakia and Afghanistan.

The social democrats called themselves internationalists to distance themselves from the perceived insularity of the Left. This was a little unfair, however, as their internationalism was defined in terms of support for NATO and the Common Market. In this sense, the old imperialists before the Great War could be seen as internationalists because they supported the *Entente* with France and Tsarist Russia. In fact, they shared with others on the Labour Right the *realpolitik* approach to foreign affairs put forward by Bevin and Healey. The difference between the social democrats and the rest of the Labour Right – the bulk of which, around Denis Healey and Roy Hattersley, remained committed to traditional revisionism – lay in domestic, not foreign policy.

The upshot of these differences was a break with the Labour Party. A Social Democratic Alliance had been founded in 1975, but its McCarthy-style accusations against the Left limited its effectiveness, and it was finally proscribed for preparing to stand candidates against official Labour candidates. However, the inexorable advance of the Left in the constituencies, threatening to unseat moderate MPs, led the Right to organise more seriously – in the Manifesto group of MPs and the Campaign for Labour Victory in the constituencies, both formed in 1977. The return of Roy Jenkins to the political fray, together with a series of Labour conferences in 1980–1 which made far-reaching constitutional changes to the party and severely weakened the Right, finally led to the decision to quit. In March, 1981, the Social Democrat Party (SDP) was launched by Jenkins, Williams, Owen and William Rodgers in a flurry of media publicity.

SOCIAL DEMOCRACY AND REVISIONISM

Social Democracy grew out of the revisionist movement of the 1950s in terms of ideology and even personnel. Shirley Williams, William Rodgers and Dick Taverne had been prominent figures in the Campaign for Democratic Socialism, a Gaitskellite group launched to fight unilateralism in the early 1960s, while Roy Jenkins had been prominent in the revisionist cause since *New Fabian Essays*. However, the differences between revisionism and social democracy, often reflected in differences between Jenkins and the new leaders, were profound.

The commitment of the revisionists to welfare and equality had been an attempt to rescue the Labour Party's radical impulse from what they regarded as the dead hand of semi-Marxist ideas. The commitment had always been dependent on high economic growth and general prosperity – in the belief that capitalism had basically solved its major problems – but the long period of almost uninterrupted boom in the 1950s had seemed to be manifest proof that a new technique had been found which could guarantee precisely the growth rates required.

However, the history of Britain from the beginning of the 1960s was one of consistent failure to achieve economic growth. It has not been a failure which could be ascribed to any one party, as it occurred under both Labour and Conservative governments. It has not been a failure of political or social institutions – as Mackintosh argued, the parliamentary system has always been particularly sensitive to the needs of industry, while the corporatist nature of politics since the 1940s thrived during the post-war boom. The causes of economic decline must be located in the economy. There has been a failure of Keynesian economics – the old techniques have ceased to work for more than a limited period, as the new conditions of 'stagflation' and then 'slumpflation' made a mockery of the economic experts who had believed that capitalism had found a means of overcoming its problems. Keynes had called for an expansionist policy to overcome mass unemployment and falling prices, but such a policy was grossly inappropriate at a time when prices were constantly in danger of rising to alarming levels. Capitalism had found itself unable any longer to offset crises, and the revisionists were powerless to solve or even understand them.

The Social Democrats were the heirs of this failure of Keynesian economics. Unable to find new prescriptions for economic prosperity, they called for the community to adapt to an era of much lower economic growth than the revisionists had once expected. They were not *against* growth, which they recognized as essential to any social progress, but they accepted the need for *lower* growth. As a result, the radicalism of the revisionists, who wanted to attack the bastions of social privilege and caste snobbery, was muted. The old concerns with welfare and equality were shifted away from the foreground of Social Democratic thought to be replaced by new concerns with decentralisation and ecology. The old demands for equality were replaced with new demands for freedom, and the old belief in economic growth led by large and socially responsible corporations had been replaced by the new belief that 'small is beautiful.'

It was Tony Crosland, never one to respect cant, who had pointed out the middle class bias of these demands. As he wrote about the new ecologists of the 1970s,

> They are highly selective in their concern, being militant mainly about threats to rural peace and wildlife and well-loved beauty spots; they are little concerned with the far more desperate problem of the urban environment in which 80% of our citizens live.[39]

The working class had lived in ecologically unhealthy and overcrowded conditions since its birth, but the new concerns of ecology have only arisen as the middle class have been threatened with the pollution and urban crowding that they have always expected others to accept peacefully. The new-found belief in lower economic growth and ecology was a mark of the Social Democratic appeal to a comfortable middle-class constituency which had rarely demonstrated any concern for the problems and aspirations of the labour movement.

It was in their calls for freedom that the specific nature of the Social Democrats was revealed most starkly. In harking back to the decentralist traditions of G.D.H. Cole and William Morris, they were throwing a veil over the class nature of those traditions. Both Cole and Morris were aware that freedom could not be divorced form the social conditions within which people behaved towards one another. In a society where the majority of the population were forced to sell their labour-power to others in order to live, it was a travesty of ideas to talk of individual freedom without relating it to *social* freedom. This was why Cole, in his activist days as a Guild Socialist, called for a militant pursuit of the class war by the labour movement. It was not because he believed class war to be a commendable state of affairs, but because class struggle was a *normal* condition of a capitalist society. If labour refused to fight this struggle, they would be defeated by capital and *social* freedom would be pushed aside as a viable alternative. William Morris saw Parliament as a representative institution of the enemy of the working class, and warned that the propertied classes would kill to preserve their privileges. Both Morris and the young Cole were passionate believers in a pluralist and libertarian socialism, but it was hardly the same sort of socialism as that of the Social Democrats.

In contrast, the Social Democratic calls for freedom were expressed in the conservative calls for more small business firms and voluntary social work. To David Owen, the market sector had become *too* socially responsible in its attitudes to dismissals and wage bargaining, and had prevented the mixed economy from working as a result. His response that the market should be freed from the fetters of state control was an indication of the retreat from the revisionist values of social equality and welfare. It was an almost inevitable result of the divorce of freedom from its social context of a class-divided society.

In alliance with the Liberals, the SDP were to pose a major election threat to Labour throughout the 1980s before Kinnock's leadership destroyed their electoral chances and led to their absorption into the Liberals (with the exception of a small and short-lived rump under Owen) after the 1987 election. Their direct political influence was relatively short-lived, but in the longer term the new ideas of Mackintosh, Williams and Owen, elaborated by writers such as David Marquand, were to exert a major influence over New Labour theory.

Part V
The Challenge of the Left

Introduction to Part V

The reaction against Corporate Socialism on the Right of the Labour Party was not at first echoed on the party's Left. Indeed, the Bevanite Left of the 1950s remained in many ways trapped in the role of guardian of an ideology which was no longer inspiring and looked increasingly like a conservative support of the *status quo*. At a time of increasing prosperity, the Bevanites remained committed to a cloth-cap image of the manual working class, symbolised by their leader, the ex-miner Aneurin Bevan. At a time of Cold War, they advocated a foreign policy which smacked to many of neutralism. At a time when it was becoming clear that nationalisation was not bringing in the New Jerusalem, they remained committed to an extension of public ownership on the same corporatist lines.

It was in reaction to this that the New Left began to gather strength after the twin shocks of Suez and Hungary in 1956. Disillusioned with Stalinism and uninspired by Bevanism, they heralded an intellectual renaissance for the Left in Britain in their stress on the need for a more democratic culture and a more radical conception of politics than that held by the Labour Party. They appeared to be part of a popular radical movement as tens of thousands mobilised around issues of unilateral nuclear disarmament and then the Vietnam War, and the failures of the 1964–70 Labour government led many on the New Left into a romantic revolutionism which rejected the Labour Party with contempt.

However, the impact of New Left thinking on the Labour Left, especially through groups such as the Institute of Workers' Control, was to lead to a break with Corporate Socialism. Gradually at first, under Michael Foot in the late 1960s, and then more radically under Tony Benn in the 1970s, the Labour Left was revitalised by an absorption of New Left ideas on direct democracy which was eventually to lead them to their greatest victories within the party. The height of their success was the 1981 special conference when the independence of the parliamentary party from the party in the country – an independence which Gaitskell and Wilson had used to thwart previous conference victories by the Left – was finally curbed.

The break with Corporate Socialism had its limits, however, The increasing failure of the mixed economy – a failure which led to the victory of the Thatcher, pro-market wing inside the Conservative Party – did not lead to a break with Keynesian economics among the Labour Left. The need for reappraisal was recognised, but the Left's commitment to the expansion of demand in the economy remained unshaken. The failure of the Labour government of 1974–9 to implement the expansionist proposals of its manifesto was seen as a failure of will, while the economic constraints of a simultaneous rise in inflation and unemployment – conditions which Keynesian economics was not equipped to face – were underestimated.

12   The Bevanite Left

The entry of Labour into the Coalition Government in 1940 shattered the major assumptions built up by the Labour Left in the previous decade. The Left had never fundamentally disagreed with the leadership on the nature of Corporate Socialism (with the exception of industrial democracy), but had argued that Labour should not underestimate the resistance of the ruling class to any government trying to put Corporate Socialism into practice. They had called for an uncompromising resistance to the National Government and the preparation of emergency measures in the likelihood that the capitalists would take every advantage of delay.

Suddenly, the emergency of war had ranged Labour on the side of that ruling class so deeply distrusted by the Left, while the new Coalition Government was forced by military disaster to organise the nation on lines very similar to those elaborated by the party in the 1930s. The very ruling class which was supposed to be drifting towards Fascism had now militarised the whole nation, capital and labour, in a struggle to the death with Fascism. The ruling class which was supposed to be contemplating the destruction of the labour movement had welcomed Labour as equal partners in the coalition and, as the war progressed, was drawing up reconstruction plans of its own which would involve major benefits in health, education and employment for the working class.

Harold Laski, because of the clarity of his quasi-Marxist analysis, was most aware that reality was making that analysis redundant. In his *Reflections on the Revolution of Our Time* (1943), he was forced to come to grips with the fact that the ruling class was not playing the pro-Fascist role he had initially envisaged for them. He held that it was the fact of war which had transformed the situation, awakening the dominant nationalism of Britain's rulers as they realised that German victory meant economic ruin as well as national enslavement for them. To Laski,

> In the summer and autumn of 1940 there was something that is not difficult to describe as a regeneration of British democracy. The character of the struggle was defined in terms which made the identities between citizens a hundred times more vital than the differences which had divided them.[1]

Laski had not totally given up his previous distrust of the ruling class, however. While capitalists and workers were united against the fascist threat, their inherent conflicts of interest had not been resolved. Capitalism and democracy were ultimately inconsistent, as had been demonstrated in the 1930s when Hitler had been financed by German monopolists as the strongest opponents of the workers' movement. It was true that Fascism had developed into a despotism which was nearly as harmful to capital as it was to Labour, but Laski argued that fear could still drive the British ruling class to turn to Fascist solutions when the end of the war had removed their need to rely on working-class support. If reason could prevail, then there would be no cause for concern, but Laski was apprehensive at the possibility that fear for their privileges would still lead Britain's rulers to contemplate the suspension of parliamentary democracy.

It was this suspicion of Conservative promises of social reform after the war that led Aneurin Bevan to launch major verbal attacks on the Labour leaders whenever they appeared to subordinate the interests of the working class to those of coalition unity. In *Why Not Trust the Tories?* (1944), Bevan pointed to the betrayal of Lloyd George's pledge of a 'home fit for heroes' after 1918, and warned workers that they were about to be duped once more. He held that, because the workers existed to protect the property and privileges of the rich,

> honest politics and Tory politics are contradictions in terms. Lying is a necessary part of a Tory's political equipment, for it is essential for him to conceal his real intentions from the people. This is partly the reason for his success in keeping power.[2]

Bevan's belief that the ruling class had not changed its spots, and was preparing to resist a socialist government by fair means or foul, impelled him to furiously attack the Labour leaders whenever they contemplated a continuation of the coalition after the war.

In fact, the 1945 Labour government finally laid to rest the fears of the Labour Left. The natural leaders of the Left, Cripps and Bevan, were taken into the Cabinet, the former to impose a policy of austerity on the working class after 1947 as Chancellor of the Exchequer, while the latter won the hearts of the Left by instituting a free national health service. A programme of nationalisation, planning and welfare was put into practice with a minimum of overt resistance on the part of the capitalists. The point was rubbed in by Hugh Dalton, who wrote,

> Once, in some Left Book Club circles, I had listened to the tedious theory that the capitalists would resist, if necessary by force, a Socialist Government which tried to nationalise the Bank of England.... Impatiently, I had replied: 'Make me Chancellor of the Exchequer and give me a good Labour majority in Parliament, and I will undertake to nationalise the Bank of England over a dinner party.' And now no dinner party had been necessary; only tea for two.[3]

KEEP LEFT

With a Labour Government actually carrying through its measures of corporate socialism, the Left after 1945 was a much tamer echo of the ILP Left which had harried Ramsay MacDonald. It was often unorganised and, apart from foreign affairs, found itself in fundamental agreement with the government. The main organised opposition of the Left coalesced around a critical amendment to the Address by 57 Labour MPs in November, 1946. A number of these produced *Keep Left*, a manifesto mainly written by three left-wing MPs, Michael Foot, Richard Crossman and Ian Mikardo, in April 1947. This was an early formulation of what came to be called Bevanite policy.

In domestic affairs, this *Keep Left* group acknowledged the achievements of the government, calling only for a much greater sense of urgency in the socialist measures already begun. To these left-wing backbenchers, 'present difficulties are not the result of socialist planning; they are the result of not enough boldness and urgency, and too much tenderness for vested interests. You can't make socialist omelettes without breaking capitalist eggs.'[4] What was needed included an effective incomes policy in the form of differential real wages, in which taxation would favour the incomes of workers essential to the export drive. Such a policy would, of course, be linked to a national profits policy in which taxation would be lighter on those firms seen as essential to the national interest. In addition, the group proposed a negative direction of labour, by which they meant the prevention of inessential firms from increasing their workforce without a licence. In general terms, their domestic proposals amounted to a much tighter control over capital and labour by the State rather than the all-out

assault on the citadels of capitalism called for by the Socialist League
thirteen years earlier.

It was in their attitude to foreign policy that the Keep Left group
emerged as both distinct and portentous. They denounced the anti-
Soviet policy of collective security being pursued by Ernest Bevin as a
counsel of despair, assuming an unbridgeable gulf between the Soviet
Union and the West which was in danger of becoming a self-fulfilling
prophecy. They argued that while Russia was a totalitarian police
state, it could not be seen in the same light as the expansionist Fascist
powers, as the Russians had no economic motives for aggression such
as the relief of unemployment. Moreover, the anti-Soviet policy
pursued by Britain and the United States was merely fanning Soviet
suspicion of Western motives. The *Keep Left* authors called on the
government to remember that Communist Russia had suffered enormously as a result of the Western invasions in the wars of intervention
which had followed the Bolshevik Revolution, and in the recent war.
The current state of cold war could only deepen the suspicions har-
boured by the Soviet leaders and prepare the way for a new world war.

As an alternative, the Keep Left group called for a third way,
distinct from both Soviet Communism and American capitalism. This
would be a socialist foreign policy which would establish a moral
leadership for Britain in the new world of power politics, a leadership
which would soothe antagonisms and ensure that the world would
not have to endure another and more terrible war.

> The task of British Socialism must be, wherever possible, to save
> the smaller nations from this futile ideological warfare and to heal
> the breach between the USA and the USSR. But we cannot do this
> if we ourselves have taken sides either in a Communist bloc or in an
> anti Bolshevik axis.[5]

Instead of turning to either of the great powers, the *Keep Left* authors
argued that Britain should look to Europe instead (though, ironically,
they were to be the most virulent opponents of the Common Market
at a future date). They called for an Anglo-French alliance to be used
as the basis for a European Security pact powerful enough to be
independent of Soviet–American rivalries. In this way, Britain would
again be a distinctive voice in the world.

In looking at the moral lead which could be given in world affairs,
the Keep Left group showed themselves more aware of the military
aspects of imperialism than its economic roots. For example, they

argued that 'the oil of the Middle East is a legitimate British interest. But the British army in the Middle East does not in the long run make our oil supplies any safer or ward off the Communist menace.'[6] Consequently, they called for the withdrawal of British troops as their presence stirred major feelings of resentment which could prove fertile ground for Communism. The sincerity of Britain's socialist intentions demonstrated by such a withdrawal was seen as the best defence of Britain's oil reserves – rather than a recognition that the oil did not actually belong to Britain.

This belief of the Left in a more humane Empire was even more manifest in the case of Africa, where the *Keep Left* authors called for more schemes of capital investment by the colonial power rather than political independence for the colonies. To the post-war Labour Left,

> We have the opportunity in Africa to make good the ravages of a hundred years of Western imperialism and exploitation. By developing the vast resources of manpower and material and by raising the standard of living, we shall do a great deal more to confront Communism than we shall achieve by an attempt to hold the Empire by force.[7]

It seemed only to be the military consequences of imperialism, rather than imperialism itself, which was at fault.

The success of Labour in the 1940s had thus taken its toll of the Left's distinctive analysis. The class basis of its ideas in the 1930s had in the main disappeared from view, as the calls for emergency measures to quickly strangle ruling class power were succeeded by demands for tighter state controls and direction on capital and labour, while the demand for a Popular Front with the Communists was replaced by plans for a moral combat against Communism.

Moreover, the distinctive demands for workers' control were diluted or dropped in these years. The *Keep Left* authors saw the issue in terms of increased efficiency rather than class power, arguing that 'industrial democracy is not so much a matter of machinery as of attitude',[8] and seeing an extension of joint consultation committees between capital and labour as an excellent supplement to the higher level of discussions between the TUC and the employers. Harold Laski recognised the problem of bureaucratic management in the public sector as a major source of inefficiency. He wrote, 'It is disturbing that we have not yet found the proper forms through which to associate the trade unions with the management of a nationalised industry in a way that makes their relation democratically effective.'[9] However, he rejected workers' management on the grounds of efficiency, arguing as an alternative the education of workers in citizenship and skills. Stafford Cripps, one-time doyen of the Left, said in one speech in October, 1946,

> from my experience there is not yet a very large body of workers in Britain capable of taking over large enterprises...until there has been more experience of the managerial side of industry, I think it would be almost impossible to have worker-controlled industry, even if it were on the whole desirable.[10]

Finally, the liquidation of non-Stalinist parties in Eastern Europe in 1947–8 led to a retreat from the only distinctive ideas on the Left – the moral third way. The Left's main weekly, *Tribune*, founded to support the United Front, now supported the ban on Communists holding positions in the Transport Workers Union. The formation of the anti-Soviet military alliance NATO in 1949 led to a split in the Keep Left group. While Mikardo continued to argue for a neutralist policy, Foot now accepted that the democratic way of life made a British alliance with the United States inevitable. To Foot,

> the choice was not the result of some similar plot or some betrayal of Socialism contrived by Ernest Bevin. It was the inexorable consequence of the combined Soviet challenge to the British Commonwealth, American capitalism and democratic Socialism.[11]

The publication of *Keeping Left* in January 1950,was a mark of this shift in left-wing thinking.

In his posthumously published book *The Dilemma of Our Times* (1952), Laski was left to bemoan the disappearance of any radical alternative to the Soviet–American conflict, and facilely blamed the whole post-war tension on Churchill's anti- Communist intransigence. The political torpor which had settled over the Left was shattered by the resignation from the Government in April 1951, of Aneurin Bevan.

BEVAN

Aneurin Bevan (1897–1960) was born into a South Wales miners' family, and his ideas bore the imprint of his working-class background throughout his life. He became a miner at 14, and was steeled in the militant class conflict of the years before and after the Great War. He imbibed the syndicalist doctrine of James Connolly and Noah Ablett, combining them with membership of the Labour Party, and learned an abiding hatred of the capitalists through his experience of the ruthlessness of the mine-owners. The defeat of the 1926 General Strike convinced him that trade unionism as such had no chance of success. The absurdity of the notion that political victory could be obtained simply by making industry idle was obvious at a time of mass unemployment, when most workers were idle anyway.

Instead, Bevan turned his attention to Westminster as the seat of real power. His election to Parliament in May 1929, opened a tumultuous career in which he was a thorn in the side of the Labour leadership as much as he was against the Conservatives. He was a born rebel, signing the Mosley Manifesto, supporting the Popular Front, and attacking the Labour leaders in the Coalition Government during the war. However, he was only too aware of the fate of political isolation reserved for the ILP and the Communists, and refused to break his links with the Labour Party no matter what the provocation. He was expelled from the party in January 1939, for his open support of Cripps and the Popular Front, but he rejoined before the year was out (unlike Cripps, who maintained a steadfast independence from Labour for six years after his expulsion). His 'loyal dissidence' and his ability led to his appointment as Minister of Health in 1945, and he cleverly manoeuvred the British Medical Association into accepting a free National Health Service. When that service was cut in order to meet the rising cost of armaments, he resigned from the government in protest, together with Harold Wilson and John Freeman. In doing so, he revived the Left as a major source of fractious discontent against the leadership, stamping on it his style and ideas.

These ideas were basically a restatement of Labour Marxism, but presented in a manner appealing to the emotions of labourism. Bevan's own working-class background made him the epitome of the proletarian base and purpose of the party, and his attacks on Hugh Gaitskell as a 'desiccated calculating machine' and on the Conservatives as 'vermin' were designed to point out the middle-class nature of the opposition to Bevanism. Against these intellectuals, isolated by background and social life from the interests and feelings of the labour movement, Bevan wished to recapture the socialist strain in the working class from which he had sprung. He believed that

It is among the solid artisan classes that you will find the most tolerance and the least bellicosity. Their attitude corresponds most closely with democratic socialism. Their lives are rounded by the consciousness of acquired skills and by the rhythm of daily labour.[12]

It was, perhaps, a romantic view akin to Tolstoy's belief in the nobility of labour, but its appeal was undoubted and was apparently authenticated by Bevan's own experience.

This emotional labourism underlay Bevan's restatement of Labour Marxism. He argued that the two major social forces in British politics were private property and poverty, and that democracy was the mediating factor in their struggle. Private property, the foundation of competitive capitalism, had been the force which had transformed society into a modern industrial economy, but it had failed to provide either security or moral values for the individual. Its credo was too grossly materialistic and its social climate too much based on the fear of failure for it to produce anything but misery and poverty. The size of the bank balance was its highest value, while its momentum broke up families and perverted the national sense of compassion and comradeship in people.

Poverty – the awareness of unnecessary deprivation – stood opposed to property. It was this awareness which led to a growing discontent with private wealth and the class which had monopolised that wealth. To fight that class and to defend itself, the working class had created the Labour Party and looked to it for a transformation of society in its own interests. It was their only real alternative, as the individual strivings of personal ambition characteristic of the middle class were absurd to those who worked in the steel mills, the foundries and the mines. The question of how to rise in the social hierarchy was certainly present, but 'the texture of our lives shaped the question into a class and not into an individual form'.[13] The social conflict between poverty and property was thus, for Bevan, the compelling question facing British politics.

Parliament was the arena in which that conflict was being fought, as Bevan held that democracy was the third force which mediated between the other two. Parliament had, of course, existed long before democracy, functioning as an assembly where the ruling class had resolved their differences without resort to armed force. It was only in 1928, the year before Bevan's own election to Westminster, that democracy had really arrived in the form of a universal franchise for men and women. With the weapon of the ballot box, Bevan held that the working class had stepped on to the public stage of history. However, they had chosen to give their democratic backing to the propertied class; the Churchills and the Cecils continued to rule the country as they had done before democracy because 'the people have not clothed the bones of political democracy with the flesh of economic power'.[14] As a result, Parliament was a passive assembly which acted as the servant of social privilege and private property.

This was a major danger to democracy, as the failure to meet public grievances would discredit Parliament itself. Acting as the apologist for the miseries inflicted by capitalism, Parliament had responsibility, but no power; monopolising the disposal of the economic surplus and thereby disfranchising the people from the outset on the use of that surplus, property exercises power while free from all responsibility. In such circumstances,

> democratic parliaments under private property, under capitalism, are the professional public mourners for private economic crimes. So long as parliaments divest themselves of economic power, then democratic institutions are bound to be always the whipping-boys for private enterprise.[15]

It was Parliament itself which would suffer from the selfish pursuit of private profit at the expense of the social good by the tiny class which controlled the commanding heights of the economy.

Against this threat, Bevan called on Labour to turn Parliament – 'a sword pointed at the heart of the property-power'[16] – into an active assembly fighting the class struggle on the part of the labour movement. Wealth used parliamentary democracy to persuade poverty to use its political freedom merely to maintain the rule of wealth; the task of labour was to use the same weapon to expose the social privilege and selfish immorality of wealth to the attack of the people. Bevan called on his party to fight against the sense of parliamentary tradition which in countless ways impressed upon Members the customs and procedures of those who had ruled Britain for hundreds of years. They must remember that Labour's ancestors had tended sheep or ploughed the land, shut out from the colourful pageantry and glory of English history, enduring poverty and short lives uncomforted by recognition or leisure. The time had now come when the common people would make their voice heard, and the time must not be wasted. 'The issue therefore in a capitalist democracy resolves itself into this; either poverty will use democracy to win the struggle against property, or property, in fear of poverty, will destroy democracy.'[17]

Bevan's hostility to capitalists, couched though it was in Marxist language, did not lead him to the perspective of a communist society. He accepted the mixed economy as a permanent feature of British society, rejecting Communism as a Utopian dream whose unrealistic nature was incompatible with any constitutional political party seeking power. Thus, he argued that

> the victory of socialism need not be universal to be decisive. I have no patience with those socialists, so called, who in practice would socialise nothing, while in theory they would threaten the whole of private property. They are purists and therefore barren. It is neither prudent, not does it accord with our conception of the future, that all forms of private property should live under perpetual threat.[18]

This belief in the mixed economy was in perfect accord with the main traditions of the Labour Party's political thought. It was one of the characteristics which excluded a full-blooded Marxism from ever being accepted into the Labour mainstream.

The revisionists were to seize such statements to demonstrate that the whole party agreed in its heart of hearts on the need to reject wholesale nationalisation measures, but in doing so they overlooked a fundamental difference separating them form Bevan. He was interested in *power* for the labour movement, and always saw power as the main instrument which could secure welfare and equality. He supported private ownership in a mixed economy, but was always aware that the planned sector must be the dominant sector. At the 1959 Labour Conference, Bevan distanced himself from the revisionist attempt to reject Clause IV in arguing that

> if we managed to get a majority in Great Britain by the clever exploitation of contemporary psychology, and we did not get the commanding heights of the economy in our power, then we did not get the priorities right. The argument is about power, because only by the possession of power can you get the priorities correct.[19]

Where the revisionists believed that the old arguments about capitalism were outdated, Bevan held that the domination of the economy by capitalists or by the State was still the crucial element determining all other socialist aims.

He thus firmly upheld the difference between Corporate Socialism and the Keynesian challenge to state ownership. In the debate on the 1944 Employment White Paper, Bevan had rejected the Keynesian neutrality towards public ownership expressed in the Coalition Government's proposals. In holding that full employment could be achieved in either a market or a planned economy, he held that Keynesian economics was denying a fundamental principle of the Corporate Socialism evolved by Labour:

> This party did not come into existence demanding socialism, demanding the state ownership of property, simply because there was some special merit in it. This party believes in the public ownership of industry because we think only in that way can society be intelligently and progressively organised. If private enterprise can deliver all these goods, there will not be any argument for socialism and no reason for it.[20]

In rejecting the Keynesian challenge to nationalisation, he was at one with Labour Keynesians as different as Durbin and Cole. Bevan did hold, with Keynes, that ineffective demand was the key to overcoming the economic crisis[21] (he had been one of the signatories of the Mosley manifesto as early as 1930), but he was much closer to Hobson in his belief that this was due to the privileges of the capitalists and the underconsumption of the working class. The nationalisation of industry was thus infinitely superior as a method of control to the indirect fiscal policies advocated by Keynes. Public ownership reduced the dangers of evasion by private vested interests, and made industry available as an instrument of the direct planning of production and consumption. Bevan's roots in Syndicalism and labourism thus led him to a very different analysis from that of the revisionists. Where Crosland and Gaitskell saw the inefficiency of the market economy as characteristic of a by-gone capitalism, Bevan saw the social power of private property as the persistent danger of a capitalism which was very much alive.

However, he remained trapped within the confines of Corporate Socialism. He was not really interested in the demands for direct management by the producers which had been at the centre of syndicalist thinking, and which had found a faint echo in the Socialist League of the 1930s. As far as Bevan was concerned, the total weakness of Labour in power had not lain in its strategy, but in the lack of will with which that strategy was ineffectively applied. He objected to the corporate boards which ran the nationalised industries on the grounds that they should be fully accountable to Parliament, not to the direct democracy of the ruling class. He did not see industrial democracy in terms of workers becoming managers, but in terms of a spirit of co-operation between workers and managers. In his view,

the advance from State ownership to full Socialism is in direct proportion to the extent that workers in the nationalised industry are made aware of a changed relationship between themselves and the management. The persistence of a sense of dualism in a publicly owned industry is evidence of an immature industrial democracy.[22]

Even the old worries of the Left on the constitutional measures necessary to overcome capitalist resistance found no echo in Bevan's political ideas in the fifties.

He was above all a parliamentary socialist, stressing the importance of Parliament as an agent of social change with all the intensity of a man whose old syndicalist faith in the unions had been shattered by the defeats of the 1920s. He was certainly aware of the continuing importance of the unions,[23] but they were now seen in terms of voting power at conferences rather than industrial muscle which would sustain a socialist government against unconstitutional measures. It was Parliament, not the unions, which had become the most formidable weapon of the class struggle for Bevan. It was the ultimate repository of political power, as he once argued in the Commons:

When I got older, I said to myself: 'The place to get to is the Council. That's where the power is.' So I worked very hard and...I got on the Council. I discovered when I got there that the power *had* been there, but it had just gone. So I made some enquiries, being an earnest student of social affairs, and I learned that the power had slipped down to the County Council. That's where it was and where it had gone to. So I worked very hard again and I got there and it had gone from there too.[24]

Power always seemed to elude Bevan, near enough to see but never near enough to grasp. When he finally became a Cabinet Minister he proved unable to bring the free welfare state into being for any length of time. Its basis was chipped away almost from its birth, and the health service was always to be one of the first victims of any recession in the capitalist economy from which it was ultimately financed.

For Aneurin Bevan, 'the belief that a nation's foreign policy must be shaped by domestic necessities, that the two could never be disentangled, was an axiom of politics'.[25] This was true of the 1930s when his hostility to the pro-capitalist policies of the government was linked to his support of a popular front against Fascism throughout Europe. It was also true of the 1950s, when his concerns for world peace and social progress at home were two sides of the same coin. The difference lay in the degree of his fear of the domestic and foreign threats to the working class. In the 1930s, the threats were direct and aggressive; in the 1950s, they seemed more elusive and difficult to combat effectively. It was no longer the Fascists, with their pledge to crush all traces of Marxism and the workers' movement, but the Soviet Union, professing Marxism and the cause of the liberation of the working class, who stood as the main enemy of the nation. It was the United States, democratic home of capitalism and in the grip of a reactionary 'red scare,' which presented itself as Britain's ally.

Bevan resolved the dilemma by taking up the demands of the old Keep Left group that Britain take a third road which would heal the difference between the major powers by demonstrating the superiority of non-aggressive social reform. To Bevan,

> we have allowed the Russian threat to divert us from the one policy that might help to pacify the world. The answer to social evil is social amelioration, not bombing planes and guns; yet we are making the latter on such a scale that we have no resources left for the provision of the industrial equipment which the underdeveloped areas of the world must have.[26]

Communism fed on the poverty and discontent of these areas, yet the West was choosing the short-sighted course of a military policy which would lead to more poverty and discontent. The military response to Communism was both superficial and ultimately self-defeating, according to Bevan. The only effective reply to the Soviet Union was a social and economic policy of development and equality, and for this there had to be a re-examination of social attitudes.

With this analysis, Bevan hailed the development of non-alignment championed by Jawaharlal Nehru of India, Josip Tito of Yugoslavia, and Achmed Soekarno of Indonesia. In the third world, societies which had been dormant for centuries were awakening to national independence and an awareness of a new role in the world. This was as true of Communist powers like China (which Bevan acutely perceived as a national power independent of Soviet control) as it was of non-Communist nations. Bevan argued that the West could not take these powers for granted as natural allies. Their history of exploitation and cruelty suffered at the hands of Western imperialism made them naturally wary of Western overtures and more prone to sympathy for the anti-colonial record of Soviet Russia. If the West posed as a militarist force in the world, it would turn nationalism in a Soviet direction. Instead, Bevan called on the West to accommodate the new nations in a general pattern of world cooperation. The proportion spent on arms in Western budgets should be reduced to be replaced by aid in a new plan for world economic development.

Bevan's attitude to armaments has often been misunderstood. His old opposition to giving arms to a bourgeois government in the 1930s had been considerably modified by the 1950s, though his mistrust of the Tories' intelligence and sincerity was still strong. He maintained that the Soviet military threat must be countered by military force from the West if fear was not to rule world affairs – 'no-one who is not a pacifist or a partisan of the Kremlin would argue that military strength is not needed'.[27] It was not effective national defence against Communism which was wrong, according to Bevan, but the paranoid fear of the USSR which had led to the building of vast war machines far out of proportion to the threat posed. It was not Western rearmament (caused by the Korean War) which was opposed by Bevan, but the level of rearmament, threatening as it did social reforms such as a free health service. He made this crystal clear in his 1951 resignation speech,[28] and he underlined it a year later when he wrote,

> Against the background of mounting tension, it is idle to talk of general disarmament. People are not, and never have been, prepared to throw their guns away while they feel unsafe.... This applies as much to atom bombs as to more primitive types.[29]

It should have come as no surprise, then, when he rounded on the advocates of unilateral nuclear disarmament – the bulk of them his supporters – at the 1957 party conference. It was perfectly consistent with his view of politics as *power* rather than a seminar on moral philosophy or a Quaker sermon. Bevan had been consistently opposed to militarism, but he had recognised the reality of nuclear weapons as a new phase of military destructive power which could not be reversed by morality. In this sense, he held the unilateralists to be guilty of an emotional spasm, born of moral self-righteousness and fear, and called for multilateral disarmament negotiations. The alternative was

> to send a British Foreign Secretary, whoever he may be, naked into
> the conference chamber. Able to preach sermons, of course; he
> could preach very good sermons. But action of that sort is not
> necessarily the way in which you take the menace of the Bomb
> from the world.[30]

Such sentiments were not an opportunistic betrayal, nor were they a
result of his sympathy for Stalinism;[31] they were a logical consequence of his basic political ideas on pacifism and defence.

In another sense, however, it is one more example of his softened
militancy compared with the 1930s. At that time, Bevan and the rest
of the Left had been aware of the imperialist antagonisms between the
major powers, and attempted to draw attention to the class nature of
the state which was determining foreign policy. By the 1950s, this
awareness had virtually disappeared, at least on Bevan's part. He
opposed the militarist language and postures of the Cold War, but
the belief that Britain and the United States were imperialist powers
directed in the interests of the ruling class was now absent, regarded
as belonging to a view of the world held by partisans of the Kremlin.
In its place, a British Foreign Secretary was conceived as capable of
negotiating peace between West and East as though the antagonisms
dividing them were irrational rather than fundamental. Bevan's old
class outlook, formed and tempered in his syndicalist days, had
become softened by the 1950s to one based on reconciliation.

THE CRISIS OF BEVANISM

There was something peculiarly inappropriate about Aneurin Bevan's
ideas on the struggle between poverty and wealth in the boom conditions of the 1950s.[32] The existence of class divisions remained
fundamental to British society, but the impression given by Bevan
was one of a society frozen in the political and social attitudes of
twenty years before. The revisionists seemed to have the edge in
theoretical terms as well as in terms of political power during the
decade. His Labour Marxism belonged to an earlier age than that of
washing machines, televisions, and rising living standards. Moreover,
the power of Bevan's own personality appeared to dominate the rest

of the Left. The political development of the Bevanites was measured more by personal loyalty to Bevan himself rather than by political ideas, as seen in the cries of treachery which greeted the reconciliation of Harold Wilson and Richard Crossman to the Labour leadership in 1954–5. There remained a conflicting set of political tendencies on the Left – pacifists and 'fellow-travellers' vied with neutralists in the '57 varieties' of MPs who followed Bevan in the early 1950s – and, on the issue of German rearmament, the Bevanite revolt brought out an anti-German xenophobia which was not always welcome. However, Bevan himself was the epitome of the Labour Left and, when he was finally reconciled to Gaitskell's leadership in 1957, the coherence and strength of the Left appeared to be shattered.

Bevan himself had not changed his views on disarmament or public ownership, but the conciliatory tone adopted represented a softening of what seemed essential in Bevanism – its style of revolt. Where Gaitskell highlighted political differences in his assault on Clause IV in 1959, Bevan swallowed his personal anger to argue that nothing fundamentally divided the party. He himself made clear his continued Labour Marxist convictions in his only published comment on the issue, when he wrote,

> the controversy is between those who want the mainspring of economic power transferred to the community and those who believe that private enterprise should still remain supreme but that its worst characteristics should be modified by liberal ideas of justice and equality.[33]

The socialist ideas remained the same as those of Keir Hardie, but they were more like the echoes of a man reluctant to surrender the dreams of his youth. He had once said that if private enterprise could provide security there would be no need for public ownership, yet that was precisely what private enterprise appeared to be doing , at least in Britain. Bevan, whose economics were derived from Hobson rather than Marx, was unable to present any convincing analysis of why the disruption involved in social change should be undergone.

Richard Crossman was one of those Bevanites who was aware of the need to develop a new analysis more suited to conditions of prosperity. Crossman (1907–74), after the near-obligatory education at Winchester and Oxford, had been a tutor in political philosophy at Oxford. He was active in the Oxford Labour Party in the late 1930s at a time when that party supported a Popular Front candidate in a

by-election and, after a period as a Director of Psychological Warfare, had been elected to Parliament in 1945. There he quickly established a reputation as an intellectual who listened to the dictates of his
own reasoning process at a level which was too abstract for the more
sordid mechanics of the real political world.

As one of the authors of *Keep Left*, Crossman was a natural ally of
Bevan on the latter's resignation. Much of his writing in the early
1950s was a reflection of Bevanite ideas, but he was already aware of
the sterility of merely repeating the old nostrums of Labour Marxism
as though nothing had changed since the days of Keir Hardie. In his
contribution to *New Fabian Essays* (1952), Crossman had agreed with
the revisionists on the need for the Labour Party to regain its sense of
direction after its post-war success. The achievement of its programme had placed Labour in danger of becoming the Conservative
Party of the *status quo*, concealing from it the corporatist dangers of
the new society. Unlike the revisionists, however, Crossman's critique
of Corporate Socialism concentrated on social and political power.
He argued that

> the planned economy and the centralisation of power are no longer
> socialist objectives. ... The main task of socialism today is to pre-
> vent the concentration of power in the hands of *either* industrial
> management *or* the state bureaucracy – in brief to distribute re-
> sponsibility and so to enlarge freedom of choice.[34]

This belief separated Crossman from the centralist ideas of Bevan
and many others on the corporatist Left. Crossman was the intellectual in politics, extremely sensitive to the currents of thought which
were beginning to emerge on the New Left and determined that
Labour should not be frightened by the series of electoral defeats
during the 1950s into jettisoning its old commitments to public ownership. When Gaitskell sought to eliminate Clause IV after the 1959
defeat, the whole of the Left recognised the importance of the debate
for the basic orientation and philosophy of the party. Frank Cousins,
the left-wing leader of the Transport Workers Union, argued at the
1959 Labour Conference that 'we have all accepted in the past that,
whilst we can have nationalization without socialism, we cannot have
socialism without nationalization',[35] while Barbara Castle attempted
to remind delegates that the old enemy of private enterprise in which
'economic might has become social right and the Devil has taken the
communal interest'[36] remained as immoral as ever. However, Cross-

man went much further in attempting to rethink the old corporatist arguments for public ownership.

He called on the Left to recognise that the old Marxist nostrums were no longer appropriate at a time when Keynesian economic techniques had made unemployment and economic crises nightmares of a past never to return. However, while Keynes had made the economic case for socialism redundant, the political and moral case had grown stronger than ever. It was Marxism, not the socialism of the Labour Party, which had been discredited by economic prosperity. For Crossman,

> Labour's real dynamic has always been a moral protest against social injustice, not an intellectual demonstration that capitalism is bound to collapse; a challenge to capitalist privilege, not a proof that these privileges must inevitably be replaced by a classless society.[37]

In the light of this moral ideal, Crossman was able to argue that while the basic economic problems of capitalism had been solved, a new political problem of an irresponsible oligarchy protected by government had arisen. The vulgarity and wastefulness of capitalism remained as strong as they had ever been, as J.K. Galbraith demonstrated in *The Affluent Society* (1958), but it had been supplemented by the growth of corporatism. In both the private corporations and the nationalised industries, a managerial oligarchy had arisen which was a direct threat to freedom and democracy. This was particularly damaging in the nationalised industries, where remote centralised boards outside the sphere of parliamentary investigation or control operated to the detriment of efficiency and the interests of the producers and consumers. These boards, created according to the Morrisonian ideals of Corporate Socialism, had become a major bureaucratic burden on the industries of the public sector, discrediting public ownership and socialism itself. The answer to these problems, however, was not the revisionist demand that public ownership itself should be dropped. Nationalisation remained for Crossman the only means by which freedom could be enlarged against the selfish abuses of free competition. Instead, he called on Labour to admit the mistakes of Corporate Socialism and call for decentralising the power now held by their oligarchies.

Public ownership must be subjected to the control of Parliament and to the workers themselves if it was to remain socialist in motive and operation. Labour must

seek to make economic power responsive both to the community as
a whole (the consumer) and to the worker in any particular industry (the producer). Plans for Nationalization which do not satisfy
the aspirations towards workers' control are the technocrats' per-
version of our socialist ideal.[38]

In taking up the call for a libertarian socialism based on industrial
democracy rather than jettisoning its socialist principles for short-
term electoral considerations, Crossman believed that the Labour
Party would hold true to its radical traditions, establishing itself as
a fighting opposition rather than a mere alternative government.[39]

Crossman himself was in many ways a political dilettante flitting
from idea to idea without ever really considering the full practical
consequences of committing himself fully to fighting for them. His
anti-technocratic ideas were dropped when Wilson became leader as
quickly as he changed his mind on unilateral disarmament. However,
in distancing himself from the rest of the Bevanite Left in an ideological attack on the corporatist nature of public ownership, he both
heralded and reflected a new movement of ideas, originating outside
the sterility of the established parliamentary Left, which was to have a
major impact on the Labour Party's political thought.

13 The Challenge of the New Left

As the Bevanites attempted to defend the ideas of the 1930s against the revisionist onslaught, a new movement was emerging to the Left of the Labour Party. The rumbling of revolt in Eastern Europe after Stalin's death had finally erupted in Hungary in 1956, leading to a major crisis in the British Communist Party as intellectuals and workers suddenly broke from Stalinist orthodoxy.

Since the demise of Syndicalism, the Communist Party had virtually monopolised political activity on Labour's Left. After early attempts at independence from Soviet control in the 1920s, the Communists had been frozen in the grip of Stalinism, concerned with the defence of the Soviet Union, the workers' homeland, rather than with the furtherance of international revolution. In so far as they represented a country in which the working class had seized power, the Communists could always depend on an emotional reservoir of sympathy and support on the Labour Left. This was particularly the case when the Soviet Union was seen as the main bulwark against fascism, as in the days of the Popular Front, or when the gigantic Soviet war effort against Hitler presented a spectacle of heroism and sacrifice. Moreover, the Party was a home for frustrated Marxist intellectuals and for those workers who felt the need for a more radical break with capitalism than that represented by the Labour Left.

In 1956, the changes in the Soviet bloc following the death of Stalin shook British Marxism out of the torpor which had allowed Bevanism and Stalinism to be the only viable alternatives for the Left. The denunciation of Stalin's crimes by the Soviet leader, Khrushchev, at the Twentieth Congress of the Soviet Communist Party led to a major crisis of conscience throughout Western Communism. The culmination of East European reform movements in the Hungarian Revolution of October–November 1956 – when workers set up independent workers' councils[1] and were crushed by Soviet tanks – led to a major exodus of intellectuals and workers from the ranks of British Communism. The Soviet Union was no longer the lodestar of revolution and many, such as the trade unionists Les Cannon and Frank Chapple, rejected Marxism altogether.

279

However, the British military attack on Suez in November, 1956, seemed to many others proof that imperialism had not changed its spots. The evident degeneration of the Soviet Union did not make capitalism any better as a social system, nor did it invalidate the insights of Marxism into class power or the superiority of socialism. The Labour Left did not offer an attractive alternative for these Marxists, particularly as Bevan himself was absorbed into the Labour leadership. They looked for a different cause, more relevant to the new age of cold war and growing consumer affluence than the alternatives then on offer. Some turned to the Trotskyists, finding in *The Revolution Betrayed* a powerful Marxist explanation of the degeneration of the Soviet state. They helped to form the Socialist Labour League in 1959,[2] but after a promising beginning found themselves in a new trap of orthodox formulae bearing little relation to the outside world.

One group, around John Saville and Edward Thompson, found a different solution. As Marxist intellectuals, they sought to establish a New Left, separate from both Bevanism and Stalinism, seeking to give a political expression to the new cultural and social trends emerging in an affluent Britain. They founded the *New Reasoner* after leaving the Communist Party in 1957, and worked closely with dissident Oxford intellectuals grouped around the *Universities and Left Review*. These papers combined in 1960 as the *New Left Review*, under an editorial board including E. P. Thompson, Stuart Hall and Raymond Williams.

It was E. P. Thompson (1924–93) who expressed their ideals most clearly when he called for a libertarian socialism in tune with the traditions of English working-class radicalism, romantic yet pragmatic in its collective attitudes and actions. As an ex-Stalinist, Thompson was aware that Marxism had been cut off from this tradition by becoming 'Russified', leaving the field wide open to liberal social democracy. The result had been frustration, disillusionment and apathy on the Left, which could offer no alternative to the division of Europe into two sterile ideologies, Stalinist and 'Natopolitan', which were actual Eastern and Western perversions of both Marxism and freedom. The horrors of Stalinism had created a cultural default among the Western intelligentsia, who had generally surrendered their radical inheritance in a tired acceptance of the *status quo*. The anger of the middle-aged and disenchanted intellectual establishment was reserved only for their own disillusionment with the Communism of their youth.

Thompson, with his New Left comrades, looked to the socialist humanism which had emerged among Marxist dissidents in Eastern Europe after Stalin's death. This form of 'Marxism with a human face' (as it was later to be called) seemed to the New Left to be a liberation of thinking from the sterile dogmas imposed on them by the Communist Party. The stress on alienation found in the writings of the 'young' Marx was revived by these 'socialist humanists' (who tended to discount the economic writings of the 'old' Marx as irrelevant to an affluent society). It presented the possibility of a rekindling of moral and intellectual passion in the British labour movement, steering it away from the narrow bread-and-butter questions which had so stunted working-class initiative. Thompson was particularly keen that dissidents in both East and West should rediscover the common ideals and principles which had been buried by the Third International. He wrote that 'this does not constitute a conversion of sections of the Western labour movement to Communist orthodoxy, nor of disillusioned Communists to liberal social democracy. It represents, rather, a rejection of both orthodoxies.'[3] The New Left sought the best elements in both traditions in an attempt to understand and criticise a contemporary, affluent capitalism which was defying the old Marxist theories.

Their criticisms of affluence belonged firmly to the cultural ferment of the 'Angry Young Men' in Britain in the fifties. John Osborne's play, *Look Back in Anger* (1956), and John Braine's novel, *Room at the Top* (1957), began a cultural assault on the vulgar materialism and narrow obsession with success which seemed to dominate British society. It was a moralistic critique of capitalism which was developed by the 'angry young men' of the New Left in *Out of Apathy* (1960). They expressed a disgust at its vulgar commercialism rather than a warning of its economic weakness. They pointed to the contrast of its bright advertising and attractive packaging with the reality of a neglected and meagrely financed system of education and health care. The desolate landscape of cultural creativity was compared with the perverted scale of values which made material wealth and commodities symbols of success. The apparent solution of its economic problems, far from making capitalism a desirable system, had exposed the ugly and selfish nature of the market economy, making a return of the labour movement to the old ideals of a cooperative commonwealth more necessary than ever.

It was the democratic strain which Thompson saw in English radicalism which was used as the yardstick by which the New Left measured contemporary capitalism. They saw a society with democratic forms of government, but not a democratic way of life. As a consumer, the citizen was a hero of modern capitalism, free to buy and equal to all other citizens in front of the bargaining counter. However, it was an illusory freedom and a sham equality. The genuine needs of any citizen for security of employment, adequate health care, or a worthwhile education were denied, while artificial needs based on material affluence and competitive success were created and inculcated by advertisers in order to sell their goods. The consumer was subjected to a debased form of persuasion and manipulated by an authority outside any democratic control. It was this capitalist power structure which lay behind the contrast between private affluence and public squalor being described by Crosland and Galbraith. As Stuart Hall noted, they were not incidental problems – 'they are central to the system itself; they are *structural* faults and weaknesses which have survived the managerial and corporate "revolution" in capitalism, and come out of the other side, unresolved'.[4]

The result of this undemocratic system was a general apathy which paralysed any possibility of change. Social grievances had been transformed into apparently personal problems, while private ambitions of career success and social superiority had replaced the social aspirations for a new society. The democratic processes themselves had been drawn into the maintenance of the *status quo*, making a mockery of Chartist and radical beliefs that universal suffrage would ensure popular control of government. Instead, the great corporations which controlled capitalism had entwined themselves with government to rule the country in their own interests, while fewer and fewer people felt it worthwhile to express their needs through an increasingly bureaucratic political system.

To Thompson, a 'Natopolitan' culture of quietism and social atrophy had smothered the old impulses of a labour movement which had once longed for higher goals than consumer satisfaction. Instead, the Keynesian techniques which had solved the economic problems of capitalism had also removed the social motor of dissatisfaction which had driven the radical movement. A bipartisan acceptance of demand management – known as 'Butskellism' after Butler and Gaitskell, two Chancellors of the Exchequer who epitomised consensus politics – had replaced the socialist challenge of William Morris and the pioneers of the labour movement. To Thompson,

economists are forever 'priming pumps', politicians 'meeting consequences', trade union leaders keeping up with the cost of living index. The most challenging issue is reduced to a nice choice of expediencies. At the heart of a disintegrating imperial system, with weapons of annihilation poised over the earth, the Natopolitan walks carefully down well-known streets, putting his faith in his securities in the bank.[5]

Thompson's own desire to elaborate a radical alternative led him to write the classic, *The Making of the English Working Class* (1963), in which the popular democratic movements of the past were masterfully portrayed in order to demonstrate the hidden potential of the present.

CULTURE AND POLITICS

The importance of culture for the New Left was a natural reaction to the Stalinist orthodoxies which had straitjacketed many of them before 1956. Indeed, the first issue of the *New Left Review* editorialised about the influence of cinema, television and teenage music in society. The old left-wing concerns about unemployment and the unplanned anarchy of the capitalist production process may have become redundant with Keynes, but the cultural desert of modern capitalism, containing within it a subterranean youth culture which was potentially subversive of existing social values, had replaced economics as the concern of the New Left. As the first *New Left Review* put it, the new cultural concerns of the young 'are directly relevant to the imaginative resistances of people who have to live with capitalism. . . . The task of socialism is to meet people where they *are*, where they are touched, bitten, moved, frustrated, nauseated.'[6]

It was Raymond Williams (1921–88) who was the main exponent of cultural politics for the New Left. He had risen to an academic career in literature at Oxford and Cambridge from a Welsh working-class background, and had been an editor of the journal *Culture and Politics*, just after the war. His books *Culture and Society* (1958) and *The Long Revolution* (1961) had a major influence, along with Richard Hoggart's *The Uses of Literacy* (1957), in awakening an interest in the cultural domination of the British working class by their rulers.

In doing so, Williams veered away from the old Marxist distinction between economic structure and cultural superstructure, rejecting its consequent absurdities such as the definition of modern poetry as capitalist poetry made by the Marxist, Christopher Caudwell. Raymond Williams accepted the importance of economic and social organisation in shaping and transforming social experience, a factor which had to be taken into account in moral and intellectual life. However, the moral and artificial reduction of all culture to economics or social organisation was indefensible, and would lead to the cultural totalitarianism which had descended on the Soviet Union under Lenin and, particularly, Stalin. Indeed, Williams held that the final importance of the economy (a qualification to the old model of historical materialism made by Engels) was impossible to measure or judge, and called on radicals to look at society and culture *as a whole*. He held that

> a Marxist theory of culture will recognise diversity and complexity, will take account of continuity within change, will allow for change... but, with these reservations, will take the facts of the economic structure and the consequent social relations as the guiding string on which a culture is to be understood.[7]

This would be a far more fruitful approach than the forcing of cultural and intellectual life into a rigid socio-economic grid.

In concentrating on culture, Williams sought to expose its nature as a force of domination. The communication of the ruling class with the educated bourgeois was fundamentally different from their communication with 'the masses', which they regarded as gullible and herdlike. This contempt for ordinary people, found in the style and content of advertisers and journalists, was a keynote of popular culture as it was developing in an age of the mass media. As Williams put it,

> If our purpose is art, education, the giving of information or opinion, our interpretation will be in terms of the rational and interested being. If, on the other hand, our purpose is manipulation – the persuasion of a large number of people to act, think, feel, know, in certain ways – the convenient formula will be that of the masses.[8]

The institutions of education and communication were created *for*, and not *by*, working people, with the intention of moulding public opinion in the ideas of the dominant social images – the eternal nature of the social hierarchy, the organised market, the natural distinction between an expert elite and an ignorant mass. In this way, dignity was stripped from the working class, whose members absorbed the inferior status accorded to them by a dominative culture.

The reaction of the despised 'masses' to this dominative culture was, to Williams, highly dangerous for democracy. The only means for working-class people of asserting dignity seemed to be the strike or the riot, but Williams saw the inertia and apathy which had shrouded the British working class since the defeat of the General Strike as an equally dangerous reaction. There was something profoundly degrading about the way British people calmly submitted to the manipulation of their rulers, making a mockery of the democratic processes of government by refusing to take an active part in them. They accepted their place in a profoundly undemocratic culture by a withdrawal of interest and a sceptical disbelief in the information given to them. It was a mood which was disastrous for British society, where a degree of common interest and mutual effort was necessary.

The answer, however, did not lie in exhortation, but in the destruction of the dominative nature of culture. Williams argued that communication should be seen in democratic terms, an offering to equals rather than a proclamation from above. An elitist class culture which stressed the hierarchy of individual success and esteem must be replaced by a democratic culture in which the working class were accorded the dignity and respect which they deserved. It was Williams's own regard for his father, a Welsh signalman with quiet pride in his family, leisure interests and work, which suffused his democratic solution to the insensitive and insulting society around him. In looking at modern tragedy, Williams pointed to

> the life of a man driven back to silence, in an unregarded working life. In his ordinary and private death, I saw a terrifying loss of connection between men, and even between father and son: a loss of connection which was, however, a particular social and historical fact: a measurable distance between his desire and his endurance, and between both the purposes and meanings which the general life offered him. I have known this tragedy more widely since[9]

– in the conditions and habits of millions of working-class people whose lives mean nothing to their rulers. If they were recognised as genuine equals in a democratic society, the great creative fertility which lay within men and women would be truly released.

THE NEW LEFT, CND AND LABOUR

With its belief in the need for an alternative radicalism to that of Labour and the Communists, and with its call for a democratic cultural politics, the New Left was a movement of intellectuals with no immediate consequences for practical politics. However, it was intimately connected with a popular, middle-class movement[10] which rose in the late 1950s to protest against the frozen divisions and thermo-nuclear terror of the Cold War.

The Campaign for Nuclear Disarmament (CND) was formed in February, 1958, by a diverse collection of radicals, Bevanites and Christian pacifists to set a moral lead in the world community by unilaterally renouncing its nuclear weapons. As an expression of the 'third way' in international politics, CND naturally attracted the traditional Left, and Michael Foot, an author of *Keep Left*, was one of its founding members. However, in its mobilisation of thousands of young people in demonstrations and marches, it also expressed the New Left call for an end to apathy by a mass democratic movement. New Left clubs were set up throughout the country, putting forward the distinct view that there was a need to break from the orthodox politics of the Eastern and Western establishments. While CND was certainly active in the traditional Left, as seen in its temporary success in winning the Labour Party to unilateralism in 1960, its emphasis on extra-parliamentary agitation separated it from previous post-war radical movements. The militancy of the Committee of 100, set up in 1961, with its tactics of non-violent direct action, was much more in tune with New Left thinking than the less spectacular pressure-group activities of CND.

The New Left eagerly took up CND as a sign of the radical change in politics for which they had been looking. Stuart Hall (b.1932) called for a policy of *active* neutrality in which Britain would be able to lead Europe away from the two armed blocs of NATO and the Warsaw Pact. In *Breakthrough* (1958), he argued that the militarist Cold War rhetoric of the NATO powers was preventing democratisation in Eastern Europe, solidifying the hold on power of Stalinist bureaucracies who could always defuse any threat to their rule by pointing to the Western threat. Moreover, the Western Alliance had helped to keep reactionary regimes in power throughout the 'free world' from Portugal to Latin America simply because they were anti-Communist. This reactionary role into which the West had let itself be trapped had forced many progressive movements of national liberation into the Communist camp.

Hall drew out the unilateralist implications of this analysis by arguing that a break from the alliance system was necessary in order to save the world from war. The existence of two armed camps led inexorably to an accelerating arms race which would one day bring about the war it was meant to prevent. The theory of the balance of terror, whereby the very nature of nuclear weapons would deter any government from launching an attack, was sound in logic but terrifying in reality. At some point the bluff would be called, and the world would be plunged into the horrors of thermo-nuclear destruction.

Hall argued that Britain was in an excellent position to break the alliance systems of East and West. Her position as both a strategic pivot of NATO, and as a possessor of the H-bomb gave Britain a major opportunity of forcing the leading powers to the disarmament table by renouncing nuclear weapons and becoming a leader of the non-aligned Third World. He did not call on Britain to leave NATO, though he later changed his mind on the grounds that

if it is wrong for Britain to manufacture, store and test her own weapons, then it is surely wrong for her to be an active partner in a military alliance which is based on the use of nuclear weapons.[11]

He did not specify, however, the exact manner in which the renunciation of nuclear weapons would have the practical effect of forcing politicians to any disarmament table or, if they finally got there, to an ending of the antagonisms which lay behind the arms race. The importance of moral persuasion was stressed by Hall, who wrote that 'what we need most of all is not military shields, but moral imagination; for we are in one of those peculiar situations in which moral and political considerations are one'.[12] The New Left, like CND, appeared often to have overestimated the role of morality in politics, as though statesmen who in the past have been able to kill millions in the world wars have suddenly become different because of the possession of terrifying weapons.

The later demands of both CND and the New Left to break from NATO had major implications for their relationship to the Labour Party. It was a Labour government which had established NATO, and Labour as a party was fully committed to the Western Alliance against Soviet Communism, though Gaitskell and Healey had been putting forward plans for a demilitarised central Europe as a first step towards *multilateral* disarmament. CND was itself highly ambiguous with regard to the Labour Party. As a pressure group, they wanted to remain free from identification with any one political party, but they could hardly hope for the Conservatives to embrace unilateralism. Canon Collins, one of the CND leaders, has written that 'the balance of those in the spearhead of CND was not political as such ... certainly the bulk of the Executive ... were left of Toryism – but it was [based] on moral principles uncompromisingly.'[13] This dissociation between morality and party politics could not be held as a practical proposition, however, and Ian Mikardo was merely expressing political reality in writing that 'the *only* political force capable of effecting such a change was the Labour Party.... It was the only arena in which the Campaign could ride.'[14] In 1960, the Labour Party actually adopted unilateralism as its policy, but the refusal of Gaitskell to accept unilateralism made the political nature of the party crystal clear. There was no way in which the party could control its leader, who appeared to be generally free to ignore conference as long as he enjoyed the support of the parliamentary party. Indeed, the Labour revisionists fought successfully through the Campaign for Democratic Socialism to have the unilateralist policy reversed at the 1961 party conference.

The New Left had as ambiguous an attitude to the Labour Party as did CND. On the one hand, Labour under Gaitskell appeared to be hopelessly compromised with the Establishment, obsessed with electoral victory to the exclusion of any democratic challenge to the existing order. Hugh Gaitskell's call in 1959 for Labour to shed its working class image in order to fit in with the new way of life portrayed in television and the newspaper colour supplements only confirmed the tendency of the New Left to reject Labour as an adequate instrument of social change. Stuart Hall expressed the general feeling of his comrades in his protest:

> Has the Labour movement come through the fire and brimstone of the last fifty years to lie down and die before the glossy magazines? Has Labour no sense of the capacities, the potential of a society more various, more skilled, more literate, less cramped and confined, less beaten down and frustrated?[15]

Its failure to comprehend the cultural nature of capitalist rule had absorbed Labour into the very social order which it should attack, leaving it as indifferent or even hostile to any challenge to that order.

However, the New Left could not afford to distance itself totally from a party which still commanded the electoral support of the bulk of the working class. The Labour Party, like the trade unions and the co-operative movement, was seen as a creative achievement of working people, founded to establish new social patterns of co-operation and equality. In spite of the pressure on these organisations to adapt themselves to a subordinate role within a competitive and unequal society, they still remained as expressions of potential hope and aspiration for their class. As Raymond Williams put it,

the choice as it presents itself [for Labour] is between qualified acceptance in a subordinate capacity or the renewal of an apparently hopeless challenge. The practical benefits of the former have to be balanced against the profound loss of aspiration in the loss of the latter.[16]

The possibility that Labour could still be an effective instrument of socialism determined the degree to which the New Left distanced itself from the party. After the unilateralist victory at the 1960 Labour Conference, the *New Left Review* argued that CND must recognise the importance of fighting within the *labour movement*, which was much wider than any party machine, and fighting within the Labour Party itself. Scarborough both generalised and politicised the issue of nuclear weapons, and

either the members of the CND who are in touch at any point with the organised life of the Labour movement put the case for unilateralism there, or it will go by default.[17]

The New Left committed itself to a fight on two fronts, within and outside the Labour Party, through resolutions *and* demonstrations, to win the unilateralist case. It was an ambiguity which was to continue after the defeat of unilateralism at the 1961 party conference.

It was Ralph Miliband (1924–94) who constructed the most powerful critique of the Labour Party. In a series of articles culminating in his book, *Parliamentary Socialism* (1961), he argued that Labour's commitment to parliamentary democracy disqualified the party from ever becoming a socialist party. Turning Labour's claim to be a non-ideological party against them, Miliband argued that of political parties claiming socialism to be their aim, the Labour Party has always been one of the most dogmatic – not about socialism but about the parliamentary system. Empirical and flexible about all else, its leaders have always made devotion to that system their fixed point of reference and the conditioning factor of their political behaviour.[18]

It was a commitment which prevented Labour from ever mobilising its working class support in extra-parliamentary agitation to supplement any parliamentary attack on capitalism, as was seen in the isolation and destruction of the Labour Left in the 1930s when the constitutional position of the monarchy and parliament *was* called into question. As a result, any Labour government was doomed to be the working-class manager of capitalism, as in 1945–51, or would be actually forced out of office, as in 1931. Without the countervailing balance of working-class agitation, Labour was condemned to absorption into the existing system.

To Miliband, Labour had become a necessary part of the capitalist system. Its policy of state intervention was perfectly in accord with the needs of capital for a corporate society in which labour would participate in the search for greater profits. Its very nature as a *labour*, rather than a socialist, party made the Labour Party an ideal instrument for this. 'Social democracy, for most of its existence, has been primarily engaged in political brokerage between labour and the established order. This is a function which is of crucial importance to modern capitalism.'[19] The trade unions were unable to carry out this function, as their role was restricted to the sphere of collective bargaining. Only the political party of the unions, offering the promise of a socialist future if the working class was prepared to endure the present, would be able to fulfil this part.

Miliband did leave open the possibility that Labour might change by adopting a more class-conscious, socialist outlook which would survive initial electoral defeat by providing a genuine opposition which would enlist the devotion and support of its members, and which would eventually win real power for social change. He had not made a *fundamental* attack on Labour as a party, as he recognised that its conservative past did not preclude any radical change on its part. He was merely criticising its acceptance of corporate capitalism as an eternal, natural order. He wanted Labour to recognise that in such a society the working class could never be more than a subordinate partner, without any power to make decisions and subject to movements of capital which would dramatically alter its freedom of manoeuvre. Labour's failure to challenge this system had led it, and would lead it, to attack its own working class base in the interests of capital. However, while Miliband recognised Labour's weakness, he was not able to prove the weakness to be a fundamental and permanent condition. In Miliband's analysis, the potential for change would always be present as long as Labour was tied to the working class, and his later pessimism proved to be highly superficial.

THE CHANGE IN THE NEW LEFT

In terms of ideas, the New Left had a distinct contribution to make to British Socialism, but as a political movement its fortunes were intimately bound up with CND. When the unilateralist cause collapsed, the New Left collapsed with it. The huge Aldermaston march at Easter 1963, was a spectacular but final manifestation of CND support. As the whole of the Left rallied around a rejuvenated Labour Party under Harold Wilson in the hope that unity would end more than a decade of Tory government, the unilateralists were forced to place their hopes in an abortive Labour commitment to scrap the Polaris missile. The political incoherence in CND's ranks – ranging from radicals and Christian pacifists to anarchists and Trotskyists – had always made its strength more apparent than real, while the *detente* between Russia and the United States following the Cuban missile crisis of 1962 removed the international tension on which it had risen.[20]

It was in the early 1960s, coincident with the decline of CND, that the *collective* contribution of the New Left to socialist thought ended. In 1962–3, in a move which is still shrouded in some mystery, the eclectic, libertarian approach of E.P. Thompson and Stuart Hall which had hitherto marked the *New Left Review* was replaced by the less anglicised, more rigorous Marxism of a new editorial board led by Perry Anderson. There was, apparently, much acrimony involved, as was demonstrated by a furious attack on the new editors by Thompson. In an article in the 1965 *Socialist Register*, Thompson defended the original radical democratic notions of the first editors by arguing that they were in touch with the English traditions of humane and libertarian socialism. Anderson's conviction that the New Left should be concerned with the debates within Western Marxism on the correct relation between structure and superstructure or the best tactics on a revolutionary seizure of power had resulted in a narrow-minded dogmatism which had done great harm to the movement. Thompson characterised Anderson as 'a veritable Dr Beeching of the socialist intelligentsia. All the uneconomic branchlines and socio-cultural sidings of the New Left which were, in any case, carrying less and less traffic, were abruptly closed down.'[21] The new orthodoxy was a sectarian form of Marxism which looked at classes as categories rather than human beings, and which considered power while ignoring morality.

Thompson had reason to feel angry. As the impetus of the original New Left declined (with the exception of the *Socialist Register*, edited by Miliband and Saville), there remained little trace of any further collective action. The *May Day Manifesto*, issued in 1967 by Thompson, Hall and Williams as a protest against the betrayal of the Wilson government, was a final glimmer. Its call for more radical policies to be followed at home and abroad was merely one manifestation of the growing left-wing dissatisfaction with Labour. Thereafter, the original New Left engaged in their individual contributions to socialist academia – Williams in literary criticism, Thompson in history, and Hall in the sociology of culture – until a much later rise of CND in the early 1980s put Thompson on the political map once more.

The New Left developed considerably after 1962, developing well beyond the boundaries of *New Left Review*. The attacks on working class living standards by the Wilson government, particularly after the 1966 wage freeze, disaffected a growing section of the Left from the Labour Party. The success of revolutionary struggles in the Third World, especially in Cuba, combined with the ugly excesses of the American war in Vietnam to create an extra-parliamentary Left throughout Europe (mainly among students, though it momentarily appeared that workers in France had become infected with revolutionary fervour in May 1968). The disgust of this Left with the consensus politics of social democracy – the 'Great Coalition' between Christian Democrats and Social Democrats in West Germany, the cautious and discredited Stalinism of the French Communists, the overt reformism of the Italian Communists, and the conservative pro-Americanism of the British Labour government – helped to fuel the discontent of young people who looked to Trotsky and Rosa Luxemburg as the idols of a romantic vision of revolution.

In Great Britain, the *intellectual* expression of much of this ferment was channelled into the *New Left Review*. The abstruse and florid theories of Lukacs, Althusser and the Frankfurt Marxists were important in the history of the Marxist intellectual tradition, but in the conditions of Britain they remained merely the mark of a well-educated person rather than a positive contribution to the ideas of the Labour Party. The technical neologisms and academic style characterised the *Review* as an offshoot of a European tradition which was unable to take root in British conditions, sacrificing clarity of language to a rigour best expressed in geometrical imagery. Their attacks on the conservative nature of British culture[22] may have been to the point, but merely underlined their isolation from the labour movement.

FEMINISM, THE NEW LEFT AND THE LABOUR PARTY

The recognition of the needs for a cultural criticism of civil society made the New Left a natural home for the first manifestations of socialist feminism. Feminism has even now to make a major impact on Labour's political thought, though its growing influence cannot be doubted.

The social rights of women had been a perennial issue in the labour movement since the days when Isabella Ford had called for an alliance between the suffragettes and the Labour Party. However, there had been little development of feminist political thought *within* the party since, so that the arguments about family allowances and birth control took place within the confines of acceptance of the traditional family.[23] Similarly, regular attempts to organise working women in trade unions seem to have aroused little thinking on the relationship between women and the labour movement outside the traditional framework of labourism. The women's section of Labour's National Executive Committee was elected by the whole conference (i.e. the unions), in contrast with the constituency section; women MPs and, even more, women ministers were a rarity.

Shirley Williams summed up traditional Labour thinking on women's emancipation in 1980 when she accepted that women could not enter politics because of the demands made on them by the raising of a family, as well as by a general lack of confidence. The reason for this lack of confidence was not ventured because Williams felt that the main political achievement of women had already been attained in the success of the suffragettes. The social oppression of women was covered up by their political emancipation. To Williams, the woman's vote has reshaped the geography of politics much more fundamentally than the election of a handful of women to Parliament. MPs of both sexes now spend a great deal of time discussing welfare questions, health, care of the elderly, maternity services, education, abortion, and so on.[24]

The victory of the suffragettes had been vital for this, and no other major campaign for emancipation seems to have been contemplated by her.

This was not good enough for the radicals of the New Left. They were much more open to intellectual influences from abroad, and the writings of Simone de Beauvoir (*The Second Sex*, 1948) and Betty Friedan (*The Feminine Mystique*, 1963) shaped their thinking in a very different mould. They were aided by the major social disruption in the traditional family in the long period of the post-war boom, as the number of working women increased dramatically and the limited development of contraception and abortion rights led to a slackening of a restrictive sexual morality. The general conditions for a rebirth of feminism were being prepared, and the New Left were among the first and most influential in pointing the way.

It was Juliet Mitchell (b.1940) who acted as the intellectual catalyst for the women's movement. In a seminal *New Left Review* article, 'The Longest Revolution' (1966), she pointed out that the emancipation of woman, once regarded as a major socialist project, had become marginal and neglected. The reason for this lay in the original Marxist analysis which had related women's oppression to capitalism and had assumed that it would be automatically overcome by the advance of socialism. It had been a formal analysis which had not investigated the specific manner in which women were deprived of their social and economic rights by men, and had lapsed as concentration had shifted exclusively to class questions in the narrowest sense. Now, as then 'the liberation of women remains a normative ideal, an adjunct to socialist theory, not structurally integrated into it'.[25] Mitchell sought to restore the question to its rightful place.

In doing so, she began an important debate which owes much of its contours to its origins in the New Left. The rejection by modern feminists of the 'economism' of the traditional Left – by which is meant its concentration on economics as the source of all other human activity – is an echo of Gramsci and Althusser; their emphasis on cultural forms of oppression has its roots in the original writers of the New Left who sought to break from the philistinism of their old

Stalinist politics; and the new emphasis on Freudian psychology, as witnessed in Juliet Mitchell's *Psychoanalysis and Feminism* (1974), can be traced to the libertarian Frankfurt Marxism of Adorno and Marcuse as much as to French structuralists like Lacan. However, the women's movement became a highly influential movement of its own accord, seeking to define Marxism in its own image[26] or even to separate itself from the 'male' Left altogether.[27]

Despite the increasing tendency of feminists to join the Labour Party, it must be said that feminism remains external to the Labour Party's political thought. The trade union movement, the base of the party, has occasionally shown tendencies to accept some of the feminist demands that it change its language (substituting 'chairperson' for 'chairman') but its primary interest in organising women necessarily lies in the oppression of working women by individual (male and female) employers, not in their oppression by men. The problems of male oppression lie outside the general wage-relationship, and it is difficult to see how the Labour Party can take them up as anything more than subsidiary to their main task of defending the labour movement within capitalist society, especially given the almost exclusively middle-class nature of the women's movement.

MIDDLE-CLASS RADICALISM

The New Left has come under sustained attack for its over-intellectualised language and its failure to connect itself to any political movement.[28] In a sense, such criticisms are unfair, as the New Left consciously sought to clarify and modernise radical and Marxist theory by distancing itself from practical politics. Its experience of the theoretical strait-jacket imposed by Stalinism, which prostituted theory to serve as a mere justification for its every twist and turn, has given it ample justification for such an approach, despite its obvious limitations. The sectarian approach to theory expressed by many of the revolutionary groups to which much of the New Left turned in the late 1960s only confirmed the need for a certain independence in theoretical work.

However, it was the *theory* of the New Left which remained stamped by its middle-class milieu. In a study of the CND, Frank Parkin has written sympathetically of middle-class radicalism, which he differentiates from the more selfish goals of the old working-class radicalism. Parkin wrote that middle-class radicals are more typically concerned with issues of a moral or humanitarian nature – as, for example, Anti-Apartheid, the campaign against capital punishment... CND, and so on. These goals are intrinsically different from those pursued by working class movements in that they offer no particular benefits to those that support them.... The main pay-off for such activity is in the emotional satisfaction derived from expressing personal values in action.[29]

This is not quite accurate, as working-class movements *have* occasionally had 'altruistic' goals of a better society as part and parcel of their own material aims. Moreover, middle-class movements have tended to separate humanitarian and moral aims from the general context of a society divided by social class, while middle class intellectuals have often had the tendency to be obsessed with fashionable trends.

The New Left have always been aware of a society divided by class – theoretically, at the very least – but they have often seemed open to intellectual fashion for its own sake. The constant flirtation with a semi-Marxist language has often disguised a fundamental rejection of basic Marxist categories. The labour theory of value which lies at the heart of Marx's critique of capitalist society has been generally replaced by the more fashionable 'neo-Ricardian' theory of value, while Marx's analysis of capitalist crisis as a falling rate of profit has been at least modified.[30] This is partly the consequence of the replacement of Lenin by Gramsci as the ideological mentor of the Left, so that the concern with cultural and political questions has often been to the exclusion of the socio-economic dynamics of accumulation which have driven capitalism forward. The absence of a theory of crisis in the original New Left has been as influential as its stress on culture and radical sociology.

Nevertheless, within these limits, the New Left did present a powerful ideological challenge to the variant of Corporate Socialism which had come to be held by the traditional Labour Left. The demand that men and women should take control of the decisions which govern their lives by a struggle against the establishment was to be applied to the workers' movement with major consequences for the Labour Party.

14 The Bennite Left

The ideas of the New Left were absorbed into the Labour Party as the long post-war boom was coming to an end. The Keynesian policies of state intervention in a mixed economy which had been introduced in the 1940s were ceasing to be adequate as a means of overcoming economic crisis, and the financial basis of the welfare state itself began to appear increasingly shaky. As unemployment and inflation began to grow together, contrary to all the established theories of the mixed economy,[1] the State began to intervene in society in an increasingly coercive manner.

It was the effect of the slowly growing economic crisis on the hopes and policies of the Labour government of 1964–70 which opened the way for a rethinking of strategy by the Labour Left. The government's initial hopes for an extension of socialism through a National Plan proved stillborn, and thereafter it found itself increasingly locked into a series of measures aimed against the labour movement itself. The attempt to restrict working-class living standards through successive incomes policies and the failure of the government's strategy of maintenance of the value of sterling after the devaluation crisis of 1967 was followed by the first cutbacks in the welfare state itself, the most prized gain of the labour movement. By the time the government unsuccessfully attempted to bring collective bargaining under state control through its abortive White Paper *In Place of Strife* (1969), the whole labour movement was beginning to mobilise in its own defence.

In these circumstance the political ideas of the Bevanite Left began to seem increasingly dated to many socialists, who did not accept the hostile attitude to the Labour Party cultivated by the New Left in the late sixties. Michael Foot (b.1913), one of the *Keep Left* authors and the natural heir of Nye Bevan as the leader of the Labour Left, was certainly open to the strategy of CND (which he helped to found), and was implacably opposed to the Labour government's attack on working-class living standards. However, his political thought appeared to be trapped in the past. In an interview with *New Left Review* in 1968, Foot argued that there was no reason to change the strategy of state ownership, welfare and Keynesian economics which had guided the Labour Party since the 1930s. Indeed, he accepted the economic analysis of contemporary capitalism put forward by the revisionists:

I think Strachey's account of what has occurred in modern capitalism is correct. Keynesian economics plus democratic pressures
have, in fact, greatly improved the standard of life for the majority
of people. Strachey did not provide a satisfactory programme for
the future, but I think that his account of what has happened to
modern capitalism is much more accurate than what I suppose
might be regarded as a Marxist account.[2]

It was not the original policies of Corporate Socialism which were
at fault, but the will of the government to pursue those policies which
had led to the retreats and compromises of the late 1960s, according
to Foot. The Labour Party's pledges of increased state intervention in
the economy had collapsed in the face of opposition from international bankers. These bankers had taken control of Britain's
economic destiny, and Foot saw the planning policies of the labour
movement as the only means of regaining national independence. As
Labour's failure was a failure of will, rather than one of policy, Foot
saw no need to re-examine Labour's political and economic ideas.
Instead, he merely called for a return to the original strategy. As he
wrote in *Tribune*,

> it is not true that the only choice left to the country in its economic
> affairs is between the orthodox Treasury doctrine with trimmings
> ... or the atavistically-deflationary jungle-law onslaught on the
> unions which Messrs. Heath and Powell have now persuaded
> Messrs. Macleod and Maudling to approve. There is the Third
> Policy, the expansionist-plus-state-interventionist policy on which
> Labour was elected ... which offers the best hope of saving the
> Labour Government from its failures and timidities.[3]

Instead of attempting to conciliate the bankers, the old enemies of
Labour, the government should return to the principles of the Attlee
Government. The brilliant pamphleteering style concealed an atro-
phied political approach which convinced many on the New Left that
the future no longer lay with the Labour Party.[4]

THE INSTITUTE FOR WORKERS' CONTROL

However, the ideas of participation and direct democracy current in
the New Left were already being incorporated into the Labour Party

by many who refused to wander into what they believed to be a self-righteous political wilderness. Under the auspices of one Labour journal, *Voice of the Unions,* the Institute for Workers' Control (IWC) was set up in 1964 by a group of academics and socialist journalists. By the late 1960s, the IWC was beginning to arouse a major interest in the trade union and labour movement, and the election of a prominent IWC member, Hugh Scanlon, as head of the Engineers' Union in 1967, was a major fillip to its campaign. When Jack Jones, another advocate of workers' control, became head of the giant Transport and General Workers Union in 1969, it was becoming obvious that a new Left was moving to the fore in the Labour Party, which differed from the old Bevanite Left in a specific rejection of Corporate Socialism.

It was Ken Coates (b.1930) who emerged as the principal inspiration behind the IWC. Through books and pamphlets, he tirelessly argued the case against the Morrisonian model of the public corporation accepted by the Labour Party since the 1930s. The traditional programme of public ownership adopted by Labour had to be revised in the light of the experience of nationalisation since the war. The state sector of the economy had become a form of businessmen's syndicalism, serving the private sector in a strictly subordinate role. The management of the nationalised industries had become a bureaucratic oligarchy, seeing the workforce only as subjects of manipulation. The hopes held by the labour movement that nationalisation would be a panacea for economic ills and an embodiment of the New Jerusalem had turned into a bitter disillusionment among the working class, endangering the hope and determination which had kept the socialist ideal alive.

In reaction to the corporatist form of nationalisation, Coates and the IWC sought to recapture the traditions of Syndicalism and Guild Socialism, which had asserted that the producers themselves should run their industry. Coates pointed out that wage-slavery was still the predominant social relationship in Britain, a fact which all the glossy advertising and claims to affluence made by consumer capitalism could not conceal. Most people still had nothing to sell in the market but their labour power, and were totally dependent on the whims and decisions of their employers. The workers were not free to fix the rhythm of their work or rest-breaks, were subject to deafening noise, and frequently suffered physical mutilation as a result of their poor work-conditions. Throughout industry, men and women expended their labour power on an increase in the power, prestige and wealth of others.

To Coates, the struggle for workers' control was a struggle to overcome the power of one person over another. As the first step in overcoming the alienation of the workers from their product highlighted by the young Marx in his Paris Manuscripts, the control of industry by the direct producers would be a major step towards the full dignity of freedom in the economic sphere. Coates argued that

> workers' control brings back into the working class ... all that tremendous weight of self-esteem, of self-recognition, of self-respect, which has been stripped away by years of bureaucratic intrigues and manoeuvres in political institutions. A man who wants workers' control is a man who's aware of his fundamental humanity ... men who are convinced that they're not merely 'hands', that they're not merely 'cogs', but that they have human dignities and rights.[5]

It was a direct call to the libertarian tradition of socialism, which stressed the attainment of freedom rather than the alleviation of poverty as its aim.

However, workers' control was not the same as workers' management of industry. Coates and the IWC pointed out that control meant constraint on the power of employers to act against the interests of the worker. If such control was put into effect, the educational effects on the workforce as they realised the superfluous and unnecessary role of the capitalist would lead to the demand for an end to capitalism and a full role in the management of their enterprise. The demand for a 'social audit', an analysis of the social costs and benefits of local and national economic policy which would involve opening the books of capitalist firms, was the means by which this process of educating workers in the need for socialism was to be achieved. Apart from the educational role of workers' control, it had the added advantage of avoiding the corporatist solution of participation in management.

Workers' participation was rejected by the IWC on the grounds that it was merely an aid to the capitalist search for higher profits. The adoption of such a policy would merely lead to the absorption of the unions into a role hostile to the workforce they were supposed to represent, and a sophisticated means of self-exploitation by the workers. It would be a corporatist, not a socialist, solution to the problems of industrial relations, in that it left intact the present real distribution of wealth. Ernie Roberts, an Engineering Union official who later became a Labour MP, argued that the aim of workers' control must be the immediate issue of protection of workers' rights, particularly with regard to job security and working conditions. Any participation with private management would merely be an excuse in class collaboration. To Roberts,

> the reason for the existence of the Labour movement is to bring about a redistribution of... wealth in the interests of those who create it. When we think of planning our economy, this again depends upon real ownership and control of the economy.[6]

Without this control, workers' participation would be an anti-working-class measure.

The rise to prominence of the IWC was a consequence of the changed circumstances of workingclass organization in an affluent society. The conditions of prosperity and labour shortage in the 1950s and early 1960s had led to the consolidation of rank and file organization around a new shop stewards' movement. As the union bureaucracies became ever more 'integrated' into the corporatist institutions of the State,[7] so the immediate demands of union members expressed themselves in a series of short and often successful unofficial strikes led by these shop stewards. It was the type of grassroots democracy which was seen as a symbol of hope by the New Left[8] and an indication of disruptive anarchy by governments and many union leaders. The IWC rested their hopes for workers' control on the dynamics of this new shop stewards movement, and were amply rewarded by the election of Hugh Scanlon, an avowed defender of rank and file organisation, to the presidency of the Engineering Union.

Scanlon (b.1913) represented the attack on Corporate Socialism within the trade unions. He believed that

> the leadership of the trade union movement is now almost a part of the – establishment – more important still, is a recognised part of the establishment. That wasn't as apparent during the thirties and during the war. It's more a phenomenon of full employment and employers utilising the trade union leadership rather than the heavy stick of unemployment.[9]

He saw the trade union movement as the crucial element which would reunite the trade union leadership with the rank and file, ending the days of corporate consensus in which the unions had forgotten their fundamental task of defending the working class against the capitalists.

Scanlon identified the cause of workers' control with the shop stewards' movement. In a sense, as he pointed out, the workshop bargaining already taking place constituted a certain control over managerial functions, though it fell far short of the effective voice in management which was needed. Moreover, workers' control would find itself constantly frustrated without an extension of the state sector of the economy. As long as industry remained privately owned, workers would find themselves faced with a brick wall of evasion and secrecy because of the capitalist need to make a profit at the expense of the workforce. It was in the public sector where the real movement could take place, as it was only through nationalisation that planning for need could be made effective. Workers' participation in the management of publicly owned firms – in the form of representatives elected by the workshop or the department with the powers of appointment, promotion and dismissal – would avoid the corporatist form imposed by Morrison.

BARRATT BROWN

The corporatist nature of capitalism and Labour's role in managing the economy against the interests of the working class came under a closely argued attack by Michael Barratt Brown, a councillor of the IWC and a particular influence behind the Tribune group's alternative economic analysis in the late 1960s. Barratt Brown located the failure of the 1964–70 Government in its pursuit of corporate solutions in a society characterised by class conflict. He took over the Ricardian conception of profit as determined by the wages of workers, so that the if the minimum subsistence level which constituted the basis of wages was raised, it would

> jack up the whole pyramid of earnings at the expense of profits ... So long as there are pressures upon private companies to maximise profits if they are to survive and grow in the economic system we have, just so long will there be equally strong pressures to keep real wage increases under control.[10]

In returning to challenge corporate capitalism, the Labour government had found itself obeying the dictates of the capitalist to increase profitability by driving down wages. It was the inevitable consequence of managing an economy with an in-built structural hostility to Labour, and electoral unpopularity was the government's reward for sacrificing the interests of its supporters.

In *From Labourism to Socialism* (1972), Barratt Brown sought to analyse the changes which had taken place in capitalism since the war. He pointed to the new industrial revolution by which technological innovation in every branch of the economy was threatening eventual mass unemployment unless the State intervened with a strategy for maintaining full employment. Such predictions had been made since before the time of the Luddites and had proven false, but Barratt Brown was more interested in the social forms in which this new industrial revolution was taking place.

He argued that the control of Britain's economic destiny was being taken over by the development of the new, giant transnational companies which had been established on a world scale as the concentration and centralisation of capital proceeded. As a result, 'the rivalry today is not so much between capitalist *states*, in which finance capital is integrated with the state machine, as between transnational *companies*'.[11] These companies no longer relied on a home base, but were able to operate through plants established throughout the world. Their size and strength were a major threat to national sovereignty, dictating the whole economic structure and strategy of development of Third World countries. They were also able to undermine the political and economic structures of developed countries like Britain through their effect on the balance of payments, the national taxation system, and the scale of investment needed to regulate the economy. To accept the corporate system through which these transnational companies exercised their power would be to acquiesce in the surrender of national sovereignty to small groups of people interested only in their own profit.

In such circumstances, Barratt Brown argued for an end to the consensus of 'Butskellism'. It had been a fated consensus from the start, based as it was on a compact between two irreconcilable classes of capital and labour, and had amounted only to an agreement by labour that the system of private ownership should operate with its acquiescence. In the circumstances where the ability of the State to manage the British economy was under increasing danger from the transnational companies, it was only a radical socialist platform which could regain the initiative for the Labour Party. The revisionist politics of Crosland had proved useless in its analysis, as capitalism retained all its old anarchical and anti-social tendencies. Barratt Brown sought a return to the fundamental analysis of socialism:

> Socialism is not primarily about equality, as Crosland insisted, not even about liberty, important as reforms in these directions may be; it is about the eradication of class, about social control and production for use, instead of profit, for socially formulated needs in place of privately managed markets.[12]

Unless the Labour Party agreed to end the politics and economics of consensus, it would find all its hard-fought gains eaten away as the private capitalists increasingly called for an end to public expenditure on welfare and full employment.

It was in the grass-roots democracy of the working class and in the growing demand for workers' control that Barratt Brown saw the hope for change. In the 1971 work-in at the Upper Clyde Shipbuilders (UCS), he saw a growing trend by which 'working class organisations can and will increasingly establish checks and controls over capitalist economic power'. On this basis, a radical Labour government would be able to use its potential power *against* the transnational companies. It would be able to rally national sentiment against such undemocratic groupings as the Common Market, symptomatic as it was of the power of international capitalism. It would be able to impose Keynesian policies of demand management, backed by the strength of the organized working class, on a world scale by cornering the markets of the Third World. The adoption of a policy of direct physical controls on prices, capital flows and imports was an alternative method of curbing the economic crisis in Britain.

Despite the Marxist language employed, it was a nationalist as much as a class policy which was being proposed by Barratt Brown. Just as his analysis of class conflict was Ricardian rather than Marxist, so his grasp of the role played by the working class was only superficially similar to Marxism. It was a *national* alliance led by the working class to regain British sovereignty which he envisaged, and not that of class conflict *within* the nation-state. He justified this by referring to the changes within the old ruling class brought about by the transnational corporations. The old national capitalist had been replaced as the enemy by the international financier, just as the usurer replaced the hardworking manager for the Fabians in the late nineteenth century. Barratt Brown argued that 'the division emerging in the ruling class in the 1970s is between the giants of industry and finance with international connections and the pygmies in the national market'.[13] In exploiting these divisions, Labour, as the party of the working class, would be able to rally the nation behind its banners.

LEFT ON THE OFFENSIVE

Through the IWC, the ideas of democratic control and an end to corporate socialism were being demonstrated as relevant to the Labour Party in the changed circumstances of the late twentieth century. Where the New Left were agnostic or hostile to the party, believing it from the late 1960s to be incapable of change, these representatives of New Left politics inside the Labour Party argued that decades of work must not be thrown away in an emotional wave of 'ultra-leftism'. Ken Coates, himself expelled from the Labour Party in 1965 for his opposition to government policy on Vietnam, fought successfully for reinstatement and called on the new revolutionaries to rejoin the 'natural' party of the working class.

In an article in the 1973 *Socialist Register*, Coates poured scorn on the talk of 'hegemonic' aspirations which ignored the practical need of workers to defend their own interests. When the Left deserted the Labour Party they were deserting the working class, leaving them to the ideological and political lead of the Right in exactly the same way as the SDF secession from the LRC in 1901 had left the field clear for the Fabians. He pointed to the fate of the ILP, which had collapsed as a political force after it left the Labour Party in 1932, as a chilling lesson for those who wished to found a new socialist party. Against the New Left, Coates argued that the right-wing bureaucracies which ran the labour movement were not impregnable, nor its leaders irreplaceable. The old, corporatist trade union leaders could be and, indeed, had been replaced, as seen in the victories of Scanlon and Jones. He wrote that

> whatever else British socialists may be doing, whatever experiments they feel meet to conduct, either in community action or trade union agitation, the one thing they should *not* do is to turn their backs on the official Labour movement.... It would be time enough to talk about defeat if the battle were over, assuming our

victories left us time, but it is quite, quite wrong to concern ourselves with it now, as the battle lines are just beginning to form.[14]

It was a powerful appeal which appeared to be borne out as a wave of
militant strikes and demonstrations against the policies of the Heath
Government of 1970–4 carried the Labour Party to the Left. The
demands of the IWC for a 'social audit' were placed at the centre of
political debate when workers occupied the yards of the Upper Clyde
Shipbuilders (UCS) in 1971 to begin a work-in, demonstrating to all
that workers could run an industry without the capitalist usurers. The
ability of a parliamentary government to rule against determined
working class opposition was itself called into question after the
successful miners' strike of January–February 1972, followed by the
government's capitulation in the face of a threatened general strike in
July 1972 over the arrest of five pickets under the new Industrial
Relations Act. This period of working class militancy reached its
height when the Heath government was forced to call an election in
February 1974 when faced with a new miners' strike.

The leader of the Yorkshire Miners (and later of the national
union), Arthur Scargill, emerged as the symbol of the renewal in
syndicalist politics, trusting more in the trade union movement than
in any political party. He told one interviewer that

> it appeared to me that, irrespective of what I did politically in
> the... Labour Party or the Communist Party or any other political
> organisation, the *real power* – and I say that in the best possible
> sense – the real power lay either with the working class or the ruling
> classes. Now the working classes were obviously identified with the
> trade union movement and not directly identified with the Labour
> Party which in my opinion had, and indeed still has, lost complete
> contact with the basic problems of the movement and the rank
> and file.[15]

However, even Scargill was aware of the need for *political* action by a
political party, and worked within the Labour Party as it moved to
the Left after its defeat in 1970.

The corporatist, undemocratic nature of British society was the
main object of attack for the Labour Left in the 1970s. However,
where the New Left were highly suspicious of Labour as a parliamentary party hostile to extra-parliamentary activity, the new Labour Left
saw no reason why parliamentary *and* extra-parliamentary activity

could not go together hand in hand. The assertion by Ralph Miliband that Labour was too immersed in parliamentary practice to support action by the labour movement was disproved in practice as Tony Benn marched arm in arm with UCS workers, and as the IWC reminded Labour that it had a tradition older than the Morrisonian and Fabian stress on the expert. The criticisms of the Labour Party by the New Left were nullified as Miliband's call for a broader strategy of action was integrated into Labour thinking.

As the party of the trade union movement, Labour could not escape the ferment in the rank and file in the early seventies. The passage of the Industrial Relations Act in 1971 and Britain's entry into the Common Market in 1973 served as a focus for the Left to urge their rejection of corporatism on the Labour leadership. One of the emerging leaders of the Labour Left, Eric Heffer, urged Labour to return to its working class origins. In *The Class Struggle in Parliament* (1973) Heffer pointed to the trade union base of the Labour Party as the reason why there could be no other party of the working class. If Labour remained true to the first principles of defending that class, then its radical potential could not be lost.

These principles, enunciated in the ideas of British Socialism at the turn of the century, were embodied in *Labour's Programme, 1973*, adopted at that year's party conference. Calling for an extension of public ownership and a measure of industrial democracy, that *Programme* stated Labour's main aim was 'to bring about a fundamental and irreversible shift in the balance of power and wealth in favour of working people and their families'. The Labour leadership was well aware of the need to avoid a repetition of the disastrous split with the unions of 1964–70, and a Social Contract with the TUC was arranged, whereby Labour agreed to push for radical economic measures such as a wealth tax in return for trade union co-operation. The extent of the Left's advance was seen in the composition of the Labour government formed by Wilson in March 1974, with Michael Foot as Employment Secretary and Tony Benn as Industry Secretary.

HOLLAND

It was Stuart Holland who proved to be one of the principal sources of theoretical inspiration behind the 1973 Programme. Holland (b. 1940) had worked as an economic assistant to the Cabinet Office and then to the Prime Minister in 1966–8, and his studies of the

Italian models of public enterprise fed his work on the various sub-committees set up by the Labour NEC to work on its radical programme. It was in defence of this programme that he wrote *The Socialist Challenge* (1975), and his ideological prominence on the Left ensured his election to Westminster in 1979.

Holland developed the analysis already begun by Barratt Brown by pointing to the erosion of the Keynesian foundations of modern Labour economic thinking. The old Keynesian nostrums were suited to an age that was quickly disappearing, as capitalism moved to a new phase of development. The Labour Keynesians had distinguished between the micro-economic capitalist firms and the macro-economic policy of the government, which was able to regulate those firms through demand management. However, the development of the multinational economy had created an intermediate or meso-economic sphere between the two traditional sectors of the economy. To Holland, 'the new giant companies have created a new mode of production, distribution and exchange in the heartland of the British economy',[16] undermining the traditional control exercised by the State. Through their sheer size, they were able to enjoy a near monopolistic power, so that the competition beloved of Tory ideology had degenerated into a competitive struggle between these multinational trusts over the takeover of smaller firms. They enjoyed smaller profits which they were able to use to their own advantage against smaller firms, and their ability to transfer debt and payments allowed them to declare lower profits (for tax purposes) than those actually made.

As a result, these large multinationals had advanced to the centre of the economy, pushing the small firms to the periphery. In doing so, they had pushed the *British* government and *British* firms into a subordinate position. The government was becoming less and less able to control their meso-economic power, and was actually increasing this power – through public subsidy. Thus, the attempt of government to encourage regional investment and technical efficiency through its fiscal policy ended up by merely giving money to multinationals who would set up branches in deprived areas, often without creating much employment as they were mainly capital-intensive projects. The result was merely to worsen the regional problem of unequal distribution of resources in the economy.

The development of this meso-economic power was totally undermining the Crosland thesis that capitalism had developed into a democratic economy through the managerial revolution and the ability of a larger number of people to buy shares. In fact, argued

Holland, personal shareholders were increasingly becoming a capital-ist anachronism as the institutional shareholders – the pension and investment trusts – increased their share of ownership of the large firms. Personal shareholding did, of course, continue to exist, but it was becoming a mere cover to disguise the extent to which Britain's economic destiny was controlled by the multinationals. Their power made a mockery of the claims of the revisionists in regard to the managerial revolution. To Holland, 'the rise of managerial capitalism has not diluted the power of capitalism as a mode of production, but has increased the power of managers in the dominant mesoeconomic sector'.[17]

The growth of the multinational company had a major impact on the international strength of the British economy. Since the war, the *inter*national system of trade and payment had been replaced by a *multi*national system in which trade was conducted between the *same* firms in different countries, intensifying the threat to national eco-nomic sovereignty. The normal incentives and constraints of the price system had been suspended by the multinationals because they were their own main market. Their global strength only served to reinforce their economic power in the British market, a power by which the effectiveness of traditional Keynesian policies had been totally undermined. For example, monetary policy had been nullified by the access of the multinationals to finance outside Britain, while fiscal policy was totally distorted by the need to offer tax concessions to attract and retain these giants in the home market.

To counteract this power, Holland argued that the Labour Party must realise that the present mix of the economy between the private and the public sectors had outlived its use. It was not the public sector which had failed. The state had merely concentrated its power in the social services and the infrastructure of the economy, a crucial but unprofitable sector of the economy which had been taken over to help the private sector. However, 'while such a public sector base is a *necessary* condition for the success of the remaining sectors, it is not a *sufficient* condition'. The public sector was a passive, growth-depen-dent sector which in itself was not capable of overturning a deficit in the trade balance or of promoting a more equitable regional sector.

It was the active growth-initiating sector of the economy, the private sector, which had really failed, according to Holland. It had failed to maintain a rate of growth high enough to maintain an adequate provision of social services; it had failed to sustain a level of invest-ment sufficient to guarantee price stability and full employment; it had failed to reduce the regional imbalance of wealth and jobs in the country; and it had failed to export sufficient goods to maintain Britain's strength in a competitive world. Through this failure the main source of revenue for the public sector, which inevitably derived from taxation of the wealth generated by the private sphere, had dried up, producing a fiscal crisis of increasing proportions. The private sector had thus become a deadweight on the British people.

It was in the context of a meso-economic private sector which was failing the public that Holland sought a socialist remedy of state intervention through planning and public ownership. The modern state had not fully realised the changes which had taken place in international capitalism, undermining traditional Keynesian solutions by undermining the national sovereignty on which those solutions were based. It was this inability to understand which had led to the failure of the Labour government's National Plan, according to Holland. As a capitalist plan it had aimed to alleviate rather than abolish poverty and had sought to maintain intact the class structure which was the principal cause of inequality. Summing up Labour's failure in 1964–70, Holland argued that, 'having failed to grasp that social redistribution depended on socialist transformation, it was forced to cut back on the very social expenditure supposed to alleviate injustice and inequality'.[18]

This was matched by a failure to learn the lessons of indicative planning in France after the war. As a result of the purges after the German occupation, France had enjoyed a timid Civil Service and a much greater control over private enterprise than that held by the Wilson government in Britain. In Labour's experience, the power of the Civil Service and the private sector over the interpretation of any policy had strangled national capitalist planning in its adolescence. The growing trend to monopoly and multinational domination had made nonsense of any plan which failed to challenge that domination.

Any government which seriously wished to counter the trend to meso-economic power must, according to Holland, harness the market power of leading manufacturing companies to its own purpose by an extension of state intervention. This intervention would take the two main forms of public ownership and a state agency which would directly guide private investment into socially useful sectors of the economy through planning agreements. The traditional socialist response of public ownership was necessary, of course, as a spearheading function which would give the government and the unions a leverage over the meso-economic sectors which had been hitherto unaccountable. It would enable a government to be more aware of the real structures of cost and price by providing comparative information in such subjects and by identifying areas in which the meso-economic sector would be able to transfer funds and profits. It would also place the government in a position to counter the blackmail employed by some of the multinationals on a hitherto passive public sector.

However, it was with the idea of a state planning agency that Holland hoped to show the new possibilities open to a more just economy. He looked to the Italian example of IRI (the Industrial Reconstruction Institute), set up by Mussolini and used by subsequent Italian governments to develop the economy. This had, of course, already been tried through the IRC (the Industrial Reorganization Corporation) set up as a part of the National Plan in 1966, but the IRC had been too small to have much effect on the British economy. A revamped IRC in the form of a National Enterprise Board would, however, have a major effect in stimulating the private sector through an active policy of state intervention and direction. To Holland, 'a British IRI type state holding company... could place an instrument of unprecedented flexibility and effectiveness at the disposition of the government'. Its own entrepreneurship in a multitude of sectors in the key manufacturing sectors which promoted economic growth would make a socialist plan a reality.

Holland was aware of traditional socialist objections that this was merely a new mix of the economy rather than an end to the private sector, but he rejected them as purist. The existing state could be used on behalf of the working class if that class was willing to learn from the new modes of state intervention used abroad to benefit the capitalist class. Holland argued that

to ignore the techniques of state capitalism because they *are* state capitalist is not only to allow the devil some of the best tunes, but also to risk siren seduction of some sections of the working class, who would readily change job insecurity for job security, whatever the prevailing mode of production.[19]

This did, of course assume that a British version of IRI in a 'mixed economy' would provide job security. It was not public ownership as much as increased state intervention which was required, according to Holland (though this did not rule out a later extension of the public sector).

He was, however, very much aware of the dangers of a renewed national corporation – IRI was, after all, founded as a key element of the corporate state in Italy – but he saw industrial democracy as the means by which this could be avoided. Through giving workers a *majority* control over decision-making at the plant level, a major step to a non-corporatist socialism would be taken. Thus,

> the question of social control is crucial.... Without a socialization of control, with new forms of industrial and economic democracy, and new negotiation of changed ends for the use of resources, the institutions of state ownership and planning would tend to mean corporatism or state capitalism rather than a transition to socialist planning and socialized development.[20]

In workers' control lay the escape from corporatism, but it was a long way from the direct democracy of the producer put forward in the syndicalist and Guild Socialist traditions.

Moreover, it was an industrial democracy restricted to the context of the nation-state. Holland's analysis was geared to the survival of the *British* economy in a competitive world market. As with Barratt Brown, the *British* capitalist was not the villain as much as the multi-national companies, floating around the world economy without any concern for national sovereignty. Holland therefore saw a Labour government as leading the nation by redirecting the *outward* flow of investment back into the British economy where it should be con-tributing to raising British industrial capacity. Indeed, Labour's 'hopes of acting on behalf of the nation *as a whole* have been under-mined by the erosion of national economic sovereignty by the new mesoeconomic power'[21] (my italics). The working class was seen by Holland as acting against the enemies of *the nation*, not against any class enemies it might itself have. The Marxist language used by Holland, as with so many of the New Left both inside and outside the Labour Party, disguised a very different type of politics.

GODLEY AND CRIPPS

Holland's analysis was not universally accepted by the Labour Left,[22] but its presuppositions of a corporatist economy dominated by supra-national companies, together with his prescriptions of a recapture by the state of national control, proved highly influential. The twin policies of Keynesian economics and corporatist management adopted by the Corporate Socialists were identified as defective for any socialist strategy, but the theorists of the Labour Left sought to remedy the defects by a process of updating the original model rather than rejecting it altogether.

Thus Wynne Godley and Francis Cripps, two leading members of the Cambridge Economic Policy Group and intellectual mentors of the new Tribune Left, accepted the *inadequacy* of Keynesian economics in the circumstances of the slumpflation of the 1970's (mainly because Keynes did not take money adequately into account), but this did not lead them to reject the Keynesian analysis. Instead, they worked 'to re-establish the quintessentially Keynesian principle of effective demand as the determinant of real output and employment'.[23] It was the absence of external controls over investment and imports which had negated the demand management policies used so successfully after the war. Fiscal policy was no longer sufficient to maintain a level of full employment and price stability in the face of a deteriorating performance of the country in international trade.

To offset this situation, Godley and Cripps called for import controls as a means of regaining control of the national economy. A policy of demand expansion and reflation could then take place without the increased expenditure being diverted to imports. This policy would both save British jobs and, if used against relatively successful countries with preferential treatment for non-industrialised countries, would lead to an expansion of world demand which would eventually benefit all nations. The dangers of setting off a protectionist war would be avoided if import controls were used correctly and discriminatively, as the relatively successful economies like West Germany and the United States would recognise the benefits of expanded trade for them from the increasing prosperity of the rest of the world.[24]

Godley and Cripps were able to maintain their faith in Keynesian economists only by transferring the causes of economic crisis to an unspecified source *outside* the nation-state in which demand management policies were supposed to work. Moreover, their hope that a trade war could be avoided was based on the belief that inflation could end the international crisis, and that other governments would sit idly by while it happened. However, the breakdown of the international system of regulated trade in the 1970s has increased the tendencies towards a trade war irrespective of different governments' economic policies, as pressure from domestic industries and unions to protect investment and jobs has intensified. The readiness of the United States to impose restrictions on steel imports from Europe is an indication that American economic policy is becoming governed by the fear of imports as much as the economic thinking of the Labour Left. As all other capitalist countries seem to characterise their failures by reference to everybody else as well, the real cause of economic crisis is probably concealed.

BENN

The hopes and aspirations of the Labour Left were savagely frustrated by the performance of the 1974–9 Labour government. Its radical potential was never fulfilled, and Wilson took advantage of the Left's defeat in the EEC referendum in June 1975 to shift Tony Benn from the sensitive Industry post to that of Energy. The economic crisis, culminating in the run on sterling in December 1976, led to a policy of subservience to the dictates of the International Monetary Fund, to wage restraint and to cuts in public expenditure. The Social Contract became a tactical measure to retain formal union support for the government, and was finally destroyed by the strikes which erupted in the 'winter of discontent' in 1978-9. The return of a government of the radical Right in May 1979, threw Labour into disarray as the social democratic wing of the party prepared to move out on its own. It was Stuart Holland who pointed out the ominous fact that

> the edge of Thatcher's axe was not only ground in the Treasury under a Labour administration, but fell and fell again in successive Labour budgets. The monetarism blue in tooth and claw which we now see . . . was adopted against Party opinion by Labour Ministers in the Treasury and Cabinet.[25]

In the face of this disappointment, the demands of the Left for democracy to be extended to the party as well as industry grew in intensity. Already in 1972 three Labour MPs, Frank Allaun, Ian Mikardo and Jim Sillars, had demanded the election of the party leader by the party as a whole in a Tribune pamphlet, *Labour – Party or Puppet?* Ken Coates had made a powerful plea for reform in his *Democracy in the Labour Party* (1977), where he compared the narrow circle of MPs who elected the Labour leader with the more democratic forms of election adopted by socialist and labour parties elsewhere. Coates specifically linked his call for the democratisation of the party with his own campaign for workers' control, as he pointed out that

> it becomes distinctly illogical for Labour activists to canvass vigorously for the widening of the industrial franchise, and yet to leave unquestioned all the rituals which have crystallised in the interaction between their own Party bureaucracy and the least desirable conventions of constitutional practice.[26]

The calls for increased democracy in the party and in society focused on the personality and politics of Tony Benn. Born in 1925 into a radical family (his father had been a minister in MacDonald's second Labour government), Benn achieved notoriety in the early 1960s, when he succeeded to his father's title as Viscount Stansgate and fought a long constitutional battle to renounce it. His eventual victory established his radical democratic credentials, but there was little else to mark him out as particularly left wing, and he became closely identified with the Wilsonian technocrats as Minister of Technology in 1966. However, as he himself said,

> it was then that my political position changed, because the more I saw of this process [i.e. state coaxing of the private sector] the more I became convinced (a) that it would not work, (b) that it was corporatist, and (c) that it was anti-trade union and undemocratic.[27]

He gradually moved to a much more militant position in the Labour Party, taking up the calls for workers' control, the radical redistribution of wealth, and unilateral nuclear disarmament. By the time of the 1979 election defeat, his standing as a cabinet minister with eleven years' experience gave him an authority which established him as a leader equivalent to Bevan in attracting the loyalty of the Labour Left and the obloquy of its opponents. In the speeches and articles collected together in his *Arguments for Socialism* (1979) and *Arguments for Democracy* (1981), he gave an authoritative exposition of the ideas of the new, 'Bennito' Left in the party.

He certainly rejected the Marxism of which he was often accused, basing himself instead on radical Christian doctrine. Like the Ethical Socialists, he placed himself in the long tradition of English radical-

ism, which had expressed itself in the language of religion in its call
for the establishment of a human brotherhood grounded in liberty
and equality. In reducing all emotions and moralities to the level of
economic forces, Marxism appeared to be unacceptable to Benn. His
libertarian sense of tolerance certainly led him to acknowledge the
debt owed by the Labour Party to Marx's teachings, and he accepted
a legitimate place in the party for Marxists. However, he himself
looked to Christian morality as the touchstone of his political motivation, describing himself as

> a Christian whose political commitment owes much more to the
> teachings of Jesus – without the mysteries within which they are
> presented – than to the writings of Marx, whose analysis seems to
> lack an understanding of the deeper needs of humanity.[28]

As a radical Christian, Benn pointed to the decline of democracy in
Britain as capitalism took on an increasingly corporatist form. The
powers which controlled the lives of the British people were becoming
more concentrated, international, secretive, and unaccountable, so
that parliamentary democracy itself was becoming a dangerous
facade behind which decisions were taken by an unrepresentative
group who were thinking only of their own interests. Its deliberations
concealed an impotence in the face of a systematic transfer of power
in Britain to the Common Market, the multinationals, the IMF, and
the Pentagon.

The establishment, according to Benn, had covered up this transfer
of power by means of its control over the media – part of its 'cultural
hegemony', in the language of the New Left. The media, which had a
tremendous power over public opinion, was owned by a few large
firms which used it to defend capitalist interests and policies. Over-
whelmingly pro-Conservative, it had split the Labour Party by a
sustained and long campaign to separate the Labour leaders from
what the press described as the 'extremists' of the constituencies. It
had constantly attacked the trade union movement, both openly and
in more subtle forms, as being opposed to the 'national interest', and
had conducted a skilful campaign to spread fear of the Soviet Union
in order to maintain the US military presence. The media had become
a major threat to the working of British democracy, and they were
virtually free from any accountability to the public.

In many ways, Benn's arguments were a continuation of the
Labour Marxist analysis of the British constitution by Harold Laski.

He pointed to the dangers of the Royal prerogative which could be used to unseat a constitutionally elected Prime Minister (as had happened to Gough Whitlam in Australia in 1975); the delaying power of the House of Lords; and the power of the media to mobilise popular opinion. Like Laski, he recognised the dangers of an unwritten Constitution created by the 'establishment'. He pointed out that

> unlike countries where the overthrow of elected governments by a non-elected military elite has to take place in open defiance of the constitutional safeguards enjoyed by the people, and is thus seen to be illegal, the British Constitution reserves all its ultimate safeguards for the non-elected elite. The democratic rights of the people can, in a crisis, be adjudicated to be illegal, thus legitimising the military in extinguishing them.[29]

His own experience as a Cabinet Minister had convinced him that sensitive information was kept a secret from the Cabinet itself.

However, Benn introduced the startling idea that Britain had now itself become a colony which faced a national liberation struggle to free itself from the United States, the IMF, and the unpatriotic establishment. He did admit to the paradox of the idea, as Britain had until recently been the centre of a great empire. However, as the colonies had won their freedom from the rule of the British imperial establishment, Britain was the last colony to be ruled by an establishment buttressed by the new colonisers of the Pentagon and the EEC. The sovereign right of any nation to make war or peace had itself been ceded in law to the United States, Benn believed, and in practice there was no limitation on the use of US nuclear weapons based in Britain. When British laws conflicted with the laws of the Common Market, the latter took precedence. In theory and in practice, Britain had become a colony of the international forces of capitalism. In declaring that she faced a struggle of national liberation, Benn was merely giving startling form to the ideas already elaborated since the late 1960s that Britain was no longer in control of her own destiny.

Like Laski, Benn did not reject the institutions of parliamentary democracy on which the Labor Party had been nurtured. He saw a constitutional Parliament with real power as a crucial element in the logjam of democracy which had arisen. The forces of capital and labour were mediated by the ballot box, which gave to the poor who have no financial resources the power to buy with their votes the hospitals and the schools which they need. The balance of forces between capital and labour was a very unequal one, though, since capital controlled the media through its wealth and was able to persuade the electorate that labour was responsible for the weakness of the economy. In this sense, a Labour government should realise that, 'until there is a new constitutional settlement between capital and labour and the electorate, what will happen is that capital when it is strong will be deadlocked by labour and the economy will fail'.[30] It was this new constitutional settlement, in which Labour had the part it deserved in running the country, which could alone recreate the consensus which would unleash the British economy from the vice in which it was caught.

However, these radical democratic and labourist ideas should not be confused with the type of socialism which sought the end of capitalism. Benn rejected full-blooded nationalisation, as he did the policy of no compensation for capitalists put forward by Marxists, in favour of the mixed economy. He sought to modify the behaviour of capitalism rather than to destroy it root and branch. He talked of a new constitutional settlement between capital and labour, and a continuing role for private investment, as did Holland and the Labour Keynesians.

It is in this light that Benn's radical proposals for workers' control should be seen. On the one hand, it was located in the New Left rejection of Corporate Socialism, as elaborated by Morrison and enacted by the post-war Labour government. As Benn argued

> we have waited too long for the transformation of the public corporation...We should be talking about the transfer of power within industry, and we should not accept existing forms of nationalization as a form for the future. We have had enough experience now to know that nationalization plus Lord Robens does not add up to socialism.[31]

As Industry Secretary, he encouraged the development of worker co-operatives on the model of the UCS work-in, and supported 'alternative' plans like that one drawn up by the Lucas Aerospace shop stewards, who called on their employers to plan production on the basis of social need rather than profit. He also wrote of the need to make consumer representation more effective and an increased integration of the planning mechanisms of nationalised industries to prevent unnecessary conflicts between them. Above all, he saw industrial democracy as a means of breaking down the secrecy in which decisions concerning the lives of millions were taken. It was essential if the existing public sector was not to develop into a corporatist nightmare.

It was a demand rooted in the radical democratic tradition, seeking to modify the relationship between capital and labour by establishing their partnership on a more genuine and equal footing. To Benn,

> Investors there will always be, but there is no valid reason why the investors' money should give them first claim to control, before those who invest their lives. Political democracy wrested the control of Parliament from those who owned the lands and the factories. Industrial democracy is a logical and necessary development of it.[32]

In his call for labour to control the capitalists in their own interest, Benn fell into the long labourist tradition which sought a better and more equal relationship with the capitalists, subjecting them to the democratic control of the unions. It was a better deal for labour in its relationship with capital, not the abolition of that relationship, which he sought. Thus, in spite of his analysis of the British Constitution as being designed against the working class, Benn and the Labour Left refused to jettison constitutional methods (just as Laski refused to fully accept the Leninist theory of the State in the 1930s). Democracy in Britain was only partial, and needed to be completed by major constitutional reform. Benn thus pressed for a whole series of measures, including a Freedom of Information Act which would confirm the statutory right of access to all public papers (with the exception of a clearly defined category of papers relating to defence and personal matters); a constitutional Civil Service, accountable and open to public inspection; abolition of the House of Lords; and a constitutional premiership under the control of the House of Commons. It was to be a completion of the work begun by English radicals in the late eighteenth and early nineteenth centuries. The Labour Party, as a democratic party born in the mass movement of the organised trade unions, was regarded by Benn as excellently placed to carry through these reforms, uniting the nation in a democratic Britain as it did so.

It was this conception of a national alliance, led by the labour movement against the forces of foreign capital, which was a major characteristic of the Bennite Left. Its nationalism was not chauvinism (as demonstrated by Benn's stand against the Falklands War of April–June 1982) and it enabled the Bennite Left to free themselves from the Cold War rhetoric of anti-Sovietism which began to rise in the late 1970s. Benn himself refused to go as far as advocating withdrawal from NATO, admitting that 'I'm an old collective security man because of my age, and I remember the pre-war years, and the idea that if nations are attacked they should defend one another is a sound principle'.[33] He did call for Britain to become a non-nuclear member of NATO, however, expressing the vague hope that NATO and the Warsaw Pact would be able to dismantle themselves through mutual trust and a recognition of the dangers that would otherwise confront the world. The fact that motives other than distrust might exist behind the two power blocs was not really investigated.

Nevertheless, the national alliance called for by Benn and the Labour Left fell into the long democratic traditions of the Labour Party's political thought. The assumption that the social forces which divided the nation should be healed as they are less important than the forces which united the nation fell into an established pattern of thought which had maintained the unity of the Labour Party in the Great War, and which had prevented the emergence of any Marxist politics outside the confines of that party.

The adequacy of 'Bennite' politics as a challenge to Corporate Socialism must be questioned. The two basic components of Corporate Socialism as it had developed by the 1930s were the Keynesian economic strategy of state guidance of the economy and the corporate form of public enterprises, run by experts free from daily interference by the State. It would be on this economic basis that the social services would grow into a true welfare state.

However, the Keynesian analysis was not rejected by the Bennite Left as much as modified. The Labour Left had always held to the underconsumptionist analysis of lack of 'effective demand' put forward by Hobson, and this had been merely reinforced by Keynes. The demand that wealth should be redistributed within the Keynesian framework was, indeed, a restatement of the Hobsonian ideas expressed by the ILP in *The Living Wage* in 1926. It was not too surprising, then, that the Left should fail to jettison Keynes altogether. Even Geoff Hodgson, one of the more radical economists of the Labour Left, wrote that 'there is no reason ... to abandon Keynesian policies; it is simply necessary to *supplement* them with radical intervention in the industrial sphere'.[34]

The problem was that Keynesian policies had manifestly failed as a means of offsetting crisis and regulating a capitalist economy. It had been formed in the specific conditions of the 1930s, at a time of high unemployment and falling prices, so that increased state expenditure ran little risk of the crippling inflation that bedevilled the mixed economy in the 1970s. The Left's call for a reflationary policy to expand demand was, therefore, based on a supplement to Keynes, which tries to explain a crisis as caused by *foreign* forces. The belief that foreign goods cause the crisis, and need to be controlled, may well make sense in looking at the world through national eyes, but from the viewpoint of capital as a whole it is a fallacy. Virtually every country regards the others as the cause of the crisis, and as a result there is a political *tendency* to protectionism and even trade wars. In this context, the Left's hopes that import controls could avoid a trade war appear increasingly forlorn. In retaining the essence of Keynesian policies, transferring the cause of the failure of Keynesianism out of sight by relegating it to other countries, the Bennite Left remained trapped within the confines of the Corporate Socialism which they sought to break.

There was a similar failure to break from the other tenet of Corporate Socialism by the advocacy of worker's control. In their underestimation of the political power of the State, and their over-estimation of the social power of the worker at the factory, the IWC failed to challenge the power of capitalist society effectively. It was the factory, rather than the State, which they hoped to influence, with the result that their own hopes of the educational value of the workers' co-operative were dashed by the hostile attitude of the government once Tony Benn had been shunted out of the Industry post. The workers' co-ops were finally destroyed by the harsh logic of the market, which they had never really challenged.

Indeed, the demand for workers' control had always been tied to the dynamics of the shop stewards movement. Just as the post-war depression of 1920–21 had destroyed the impetus behind the first shop stewards movement, so the increasing depression of the 1970s crippled the political power of the second. The fate of Hugh Scanlon, whose militancy declined along with the power of the shop stewards and who eventually went to the House of Lords, is an indication of the movement's failure. The demand for industrial democracy wavered, and then died, as the efficacy of workshop bargaining declined in the face of mass unemployment and the industrial nature of the working class itself withered.

Most crucially, in its emphasis on a change in relations between labour and capital to give the former more power, it failed to pose the abolition of wage-labour. It fell into the same trade union politics

which had predominated in the British labour movement since the
days of Hodgskin, in that its hostility to *capitalists* left the power of
capital intact. The destruction of the power of capital advocated by
Marx was shelved or cancelled altogether in favour of control by
capitalist enterprises, in the hope that employers would not conceal
vital information from their workforce. The call for a new constitutional settlement between capital and labour made by Tony Benn was
the logical result of this failure to make a fundamental challenge to
the power of capital. Without this challenge, however, the Bennite
demands for a constitutional premiership and a constitutional civil
service may well have run into the evasions and frustrations by elites
so brilliantly described by Robert Michels[35] when he formulated the
iron law of oligarchy. The hope that accountability through devices
like immediate recall and referendum might modify this law seems
forlorn if there are direct material and social interests at stake. Without the destruction of those interests, the Bennite Left may well find
themselves attacking the shadow rather than the substance of power.

The consequence of this failure to break from Corporate Socialism
adequately was the failure to resolve the dilemma of the Labour Party
analysed by Bevan in 1931 – whether Labour was to represent the
nation or the working class. The new Labour Left had hoped to
resolve the dilemma by demonstrating that Britain had become a
colony of the multinationals and the IMF. However, the basis of
their analysis of the strength of the multinationals in the British
economy was questionable statistically,[36] while figures on how far
the nature of domestic production was undercut by foreign competition are neither available nor easily computed.

Moreover, the undoubted presence of foreign competition and
multinational companies does not extract from the role played by
British capitalists both in their relation to British workers and in
relation to their own investment in the rest of the world. Benn's
description of Britain as a colony which must fight a national liberation struggle does not fit with the level of capital exports to Africa
and Latin America, nor with its imperial role in Malaya and Aden
since the last war. The role of the British Army in Northern Ireland,
and the refusal of British Labour to oppose that role, indicate a very
different part played by Britain in the post-war world than that of a
colony.

The Bennite Left, and Benn in particular, certainly opposed much
of the aggressive nationalism which came to the fore in the Falklands
War of 1982 and the Gulf War of 1991, on the basis of a humanitar-

ian radicalism which had much in common with the UDC and the ILP in the First World War. Their nationalism was liberal and humane, but the consequences in a world drifting towards potentially antagonistic trading blocs remained the same. Foreign goods were the cause of the crisis, and the solution was to keep foreign goods out of the country through import controls. It was exactly the same argument with which the Left supported non-racist immigration laws – it was foreign workers who threatened British jobs and foreign workers must therefore be kept out through immigration controls.

Behind the Bennite Left lay the assumption that the class divisions in British society were less important than the forces which united the nation against foreign capital. It was not a xenophobic assumption, but the Left should not have been surprised when the British labour movement saw foreign workers as well as foreign capitalists as the enemies. The same situation had occurred in August 1914, when socialists and workers of countries throughout Europe similarly lined up behind their rulers against the rulers and workers of other countries.

15 The Emergence of New Labour

The special Labour conference in January 1981, was the high-water mark of the Bennite Left. A fundamental change to the party constitution shifting the balance of power away from the parliamentary party to the unions and the party activists was accompanied by the adoption of a policy of unilateral disarmament, withdrawal from the Common Market and a radical programme of economic planning. Their victory in the Labour Party was not the same as a victory in the country as a whole, and the secession of the SDP in the spring of 1981 was a symptom as much as a cause of Labour's collapse in the 1983 election. The indecisive leadership of Michael Foot, faced as he was with the impossible task of keeping a warring party together, and the identification of Labour's radicalism with extremism and Trotskyist infiltration merely heightened the contrast with a decisive and increasingly successful government. The result was the lowest vote since the Great War (27.6 per cent, as against 25.4 per cent for the SDP–Liberal Alliance), with the failure to capture the vote of most trade unionists for the first time in decades.

It was a badly frightened party which elected the youthful Neil Kinnock as its leader in October 1983, and a party which would go to great lengths to avoid the extremist label which the majority believed to be responsible for bringing Labour to the brink of political dissolution. The defeat of the party in subsequent elections has reinforced this trend, if only because Kinnock's 'new realism' has effectively deflated the Alliance challenge to replace Labour as the main opposition to the government.

However, the period since the 1983 election has witnessed an evolution, rather than an end, to Labour's political thought, and it is an evolution which bears a strong mark of continuity with the British radical tradition. The rejection of Corporate Socialism, symbolised by the gradual acceptance of market forces and the eventual re-writing of Clause IV of the party constitution, is merely the culmination of the dissatisfaction with the Morrisonian model which had been building up since the revisionist controversy of the 1950s. The Left of the party has been split badly, and demoralised totally by the defeat of the long and violent miners' strike of 1984–5, followed as it was by the collapse of socialism as a credible force in the wake of the fall of the Soviet Union. They have been marginalised in the party, and have lost their hold on the constituency parties following an influx of new members after Tony Blair's election as party leader in July 1994.

MARKETS AND CLASS

The political thought of New Labour cannot be understood in isolation from the international context in which it has been formulated. There is a strong contrast to the 1930s, when the party gradually formulated a corporate socialist politics to meet the exigencies of a failed capitalism. Stalin's Five-Year Plans, Hitler's Four-Year Plans, and Roosevelt's New Deal buttressed the confidence of Labour's theorists that only a planned economy could halt Britain's economic malaise. In the new context of the 1980s and 1990s, the visible failure of corporatism has led to a revival of faith in the free market, underlined by abolition of exchange controls in November 1979, and by the shift of economic power from Westminster to Brussels which is making national planning an irrelevance. It is not merely the New Right which has advocated economic liberalisation and hostility to nationalisation, but the Left also has been forced to confront the vigorous market socialism of the Labour governments in New Zealand, the failure of Mitterand's expansionist strategy in France, and the collapse of the visibly inefficient and authoritarian command economy of the Soviet Union.

Advocates of a mixed economy in which the state has a viable role to play remain powerful. Alec Nove (1915–94), a long-time student of the Soviet economy, argued against a fully collectivised economy in *The Economics of Feasible Socialism* (1983), arguing convincingly that the inefficiency of authoritarian socialism there lay in the absence of an effective price mechanism to bring the forces of supply and demand together. The Stalinist rejection of the market had led to an absurdly incompetent system of a centralised bureaucracy charged with taking basic economic decisions on behalf of millions of consumers, fixing prices unrealistically from above. To Nove, 'the existing price system renders necessary the existence of the central apparatus',[1] and must be replaced by a market mechanism which combined state planning with autonomous enterprises owned by the workers. Moreover, Roy Hattersley, Labour's deputy leader under

Kinnock, continued to uphold the old Crosland revisionist ideas of a mixed economy run on Keynesian principles.[a] However, the collapse of the Soviet economy, long deemed by Labour as inherently superior to the anarchic market economy of capitalism, has led to an unprecedented collapse of ideological certainty on the socialist Left, creating a new context for political argument which has accepted the superiority of the market as an economically more efficient mechanism with a certainty once held only by the New Right.

The consequent collapse in faith in state planning has certainly not been universal within the party, as witnessed by the strong opposition to Blair's successful attempt to change Clause IV of the party constitution in 1994–5. Ken Coates strongly attacked the new party leadership's endorsement of the market as the dynamic force in the economy, and argued that 'competition invariably generates inequalities, but these are now less regulated than ever they were. Always, someone has lost. . . . But someone wins. The winners acquire monopoly powers over whole products and industries, and dominate all the people in them.'[3] Even so, Coates's faith in socialised planning was now presented as 'Euro-Keynesianism' in the form of large-scale spending by the EU to achieve full employment.[4]

However, for good or ill, the bulk of the party has accepted the market as a viable model for the production of wealth, with the concomitant that it is independent buyers and sellers, not dominant and subordinate classes, which meet in the market place to exchange their goods. The decline of the traditional working class – white, male and blue-collar – has undoubtedly contributed to a new approach which looks to political and social values rather than to that class power which shapes and is shaped by economic forces.

It was the Communist historian, Eric Hobsbawm (b. 1917), who has been particularly influential in analysing the dramatic change in social composition in Britain in the last thirty years. In his 1978 lecture to the Marx Memorial Library in London, subsequently printed as *The Forward March of Labour Halted?* (1981), Hobsbawm pointed to the major changes which had taken place in British capitalism in the past century, with increasing mechanisation and technological advances enabling the working class to enjoy a major rise in living standards. It was the political power of the labour movement rather than the laws of capital which mainly affected living standards in the post-war era, yet the working class itself had been fundamentally changed by the new capitalism. More women were employed in the workforce than ever before, with the number of married women employed rising from a fifth in 1951 to a half by the end of the 1970s. There was also an increased immigrant-descended section which had grown up, with no history of natural identification with the organised labour movement.

At the same time, the traditional working class had become less homogenous as manual occupations had declined, and a new white-collar working class was growing. Class consciousness had declined, as wage struggles had become directed at other workers, in their role as the consuming public, rather than the employers, and as militancy became economistic in the narrowest sense of the term. The decline in working-class politics could be measured by the decline in the Labour vote and by the extent of the membership crisis of the Labour Party, as it was by the failure of the trade union movement to make any significant advances in membership.

Hobsbawm believed that a party which catered to the small minority of left-wing activists rather than seeking to build a broad movement appealing to the mass of the population was a party doomed to electoral isolation and eventual disappearance. He argued that

> the future of Labour and the advance to socialism depends on mobilising people who remember the date of the Beatles' break-up, and not the date of the Saltley pickets; of people who have never read *Tribune* and who do not give a damn about the deputy leadership of the Labour Party.[5]

What was needed was a presentation of radical policies in a manner which would recapture the millions of voters who refused to vote Labour, and this could only be done by a modern version of the 1930s Popular Front of the middle and working class. The Popular Front tactic had formed Hobsbawm's own politics in his youth, and had generally served as the basis of the Communist Party's attempts to affiliate to the Labour Party since that time.

Hobsbawm's analysis, reinforced by an intensification of the changes to capitalism and the working class in subsequent years, had consequences which were perhaps unforeseen by its author. He had argued that principles need not be sacrificed to opportunism in order to win back the lost Labour voters of the South, yet a fundamental change in those principles from the radicalism of the 1970s was absolutely necessary if the votes of the 'upwardly mobile' working class were to be recaptured. Unilateralism had to be presented in terms of strengthening conventional defence, rather than in the

naively moralistic terms of *Keep Left*, if it was to appeal to a conservative electorate, and it was eventually dropped from the party
programme. A concern for the poor and homeless could not be
allowed to be associated with any major defiance of the law, whether
or not that law was just, if vital votes concerned about the 'Loony
Left' were not to be lost in the process. The fatal dilemma of a radical
party seeking the 'middle ground', especially when that ground was
being decisively shifted to the Right by a militant Conservative government, could not be avoided, unless that party was to remain in a
doomed principled opposition. The result was that Labour had to
adapt its political values to those of the non-socialist sections of the
population, hungering after an illusory security from the frightening
world outside.

COMMUNITY AND VALUES

The competitive values which triumphed under the Thatcher government, not the market economy which generated those values, were
seen as the ethical and political weak point of the New Right. The
illusion of great wealth which accompanied the house-price boom of
the 1980s, coinciding with a gross celebration of material wealth at
the expense of a large minority of unemployed and homeless people,
made the Labour leadership feel that it must present a moral as well
as a political lead to the nation by a stress on co-operative values as
well as the material success so long sought by working-class people,
and the result was the attempt to separate the market as a mechanism
for the production of wealth from the values of competition normally
associated with the market.

Neil Kinnock (b. 1942) sought to replace the quasi-Marxist politics
of the Bennite Left with the reversion to values – the values of community and political democracy – which had long been held by the
Ethical Socialists. He presented these ideas in a rhetorical style, repeating the same vague nostrums and moral platitudes which had once
allowed MacDonald to captivate the Labour conferences of the 1920s,
and shunned the charges of hypocrisy levelled at him by an outraged
Left.[6] His project, which was to provide a clear moral alternative to
Thatcher's divisive vision of a harsh enterprise culture without any
sense of community, allowed him to brush such objections aside.

To Kinnock, the community was not represented by the bureaucratic, Morrisonian state, ordering its subjects about, but by 'an

enabling state which is at the disposal of the people...a servant state',[7] which would provide for the poor while enabling the better-off to move up the social and economic ladder. In a lecture to the Fabian Society in October 1985, he sought to stress the importance of the values of liberty and equality to democratic socialists in order to convince a sceptical British electorate that Labour was the party which could prevent further unemployment. He argued that there was a need to educate that electorate 'in the truth that the great majority of people...have a direct vested interest in standards of care and opportunity which can only be provided with sufficient quantity and quality by collective, democratically administered services'.[8]

This concentration on values was the subject of a ferment of ideas on the Left, seeking to replace the traditional socialist attack on capitalist power with an attack on the selfish materialism which was coming to the fore in Thatcher's Britain. Bernard Crick (b. 1929), a retired academic already distinguished by his writings on the nature of politics, argued in *Socialist Values and Time* (1984) that 'when ordinary people have said that they no longer know what socialism stands for, it is unlikely that they are thinking either of details of policy in manifestos or striving for "the correct theoretical perspective"'.[9] Crick argued, against both the Marxists and the technocratic pragmatists, that it was values which bound a society together, and that socialists had to reassert the traditional values of liberty, equality and fraternity (within which he nervously included sisterhood), if they were to recapture their political appeal. To convince people that social reform was both possible and desirable, it would be a hopeless task to indulge in 'the refining and reiteration of abstract and sometimes incomprehensible socialist theories, but rather by reawakening traditions and...by argument appealing to existing common beliefs and common interest.'[10] This re-assertion of socialist values was not a cover for a political vacuum, but part and parcel of a strategy to win a crucial ideological battle against the acquisitive values of a pure market economy which cared nothing for the social failures of poverty and indignity.

Raymond Plant (b. 1945), an academic political philosopher who was prominent in the Socialist Philosophy group, was particularly influential in presenting this case. Like Crick, he argued that there was a need to dwell on the overall socialist vision rather than to get bogged down in detailed policies, in the belief that ideological clarity and conviction informs policies. Plant sought to express the precise relationship between the market and socialist values in the terms of political philosophy, a revival of which had been occurring in the Anglo-American academy since the publication of John Rawls's *A Theory of Justice* in 1971. Rawls's brilliant re-statement of liberal theories of equality had led to a major debate about the importance of the individual in the community, a debate which saw a powerful assertion of a communitarian philosophy by influential American writers such as Michael Walzer and Amitai Etzione (echoed by Britons such as Alasdair MacIntyre, once a prominent figure in the New Left, and Michael Sandel). This communitarian politics identified liberalism with a belief in the abstract, isolated individual whose natural *rights* were not balanced by any sense of the *duties*, which could only come from being an individual within a definite community of shared values.[11]

Plant himself was well aware of the indeterminate and dangerous senses in which the ideas of community and decentralisation were capable of being put. A concern for the community is notoriously difficult to define with any precision, since the notion of community is open to such widely differing interpretations. Plant had pointed out in 1974 that community involves many different meanings, referring to a particular view of human nature, Christian and football gatherings, and the need for some sort of spiritual wholeness as much as any political definition.[12] The organic community of the past had been extolled by conservatives such as T.S. Eliot and F.R. Leavis as well as by radicals like Charles Taylor. Plant also attacked decentralisation, whereby equality could be achieved in a small co-operative or firm, as failing to address relations between firms which are themselves dependent on fundamental differences between the skills and efficiency of labour and equipment. Decentralisation was incapable of redistributing the wealth between enterprises which is needed for equality; only the State could do this, and it had to be a state which was above the pressure of powerful sectoral lobbies. He recognised community as an important value, but 'there are difficulties with a grass-roots or communitarian socialism, and it is an illusion to think that criticisms of state power in a redistributive welfare society can be refuted by invoking the values of decentralisation and community'.[13]

COMMUNITY AND CITIZENSHIP

Nevertheless, his critique of the Thatcherite view of the market led him to a particular notion of community, linked to the idea of citizenship. In *Equality, Markets and the State* (1984), he countered the profoundly anti-egalitarian ideology of the 'neo-liberals' by connecting the values of liberty and equality. He argued that *unconstrained* markets were inherently unfair because individuals do not begin as equal actors; unlike a voter in the political market place, the wealthy individual in the economic market carries much more weight than the less wealthy. Moreover, individual actions within the market have unintended consequences which the individuals themselves did not foresee, and would not have chosen had they known – for example, a wealthy individual may choose private medicine while hoping that the National Health Service would look after the less wealthy, but if many individuals did so, then the prices of services in the NHS would rise. Unlike a government, which has the conscious task of looking after the whole community, the market cannot provide a framework in which strategic choices can be made – 'sometimes strategic decisions overriding market considerations taken by democratic governments may well reflect the strategic choice of individuals rather than the tyranny of small decisions in the market'.[14] It was the task of a democratic government, not the partially perceptive actors of the market, to take those decisions.

Plant sought a justification for a market economy in which the government took a directing role in the interests of equality. As such, he accepted that there was a need for incentives in a society which demanded production, and that these incentives involved a certain amount of inequality. However, he distinguished what he thought of as legitimate inequalities, which would encourage higher productivity and economic efficiency, from the vast range of illegitimate inequalities which had nothing to do with ability. Indeed, the extraneous material rewards which accrued to positions of power created social resentment, incompatible with economic efficiency, and should be heavily taxed as privileges unrelated to economic function. Thus, Plant called for a theory of legitimate inequality based upon considerations of rent of ability,[15] a theory which would 'require the marshalling of economic and social resources to enable individuals to live the kind of lives which they want to live,... trying to secure the distribution of resources which will mean that liberty is of roughly equal value to all persons'.[16]

This theory was provided by a particular conception of a democratic government as a representative of positive liberty, a conception which was rooted in the ideas of citizenship put forward by T.II. Green and the British Idealists at the turn of the century. In a study of the Idealist theory of the State, co-authored with Andrew Vincent, Plant discussed their contemporary relevance as a voice distinct from that of the New Right and the neo-Marxist Left. The 'liberal' underpinnings of a market economy leave the individual's relation to the State obscure – 'we lack a rich conception of political community, and with it a sense of membership and citizenship, and therefore of the way in which the state could embody the moral purpose of the community'.[17] A theory of active citizenship, rather than the negative citizenship espoused by the 'liberals,' gives politics a moral character in which important capacities and relations between persons can be realised. In this way, by which moral conceptions and values are developed until they become a part of ordinary, everyday consciousness, the old problem of how active citizenship can effectively operate in a large society rather than the small city republics extolled by Aristotle and Machiavelli, was resolved by the Idealists. Thus, 'to recognize that one is a member of the community, and to respond to the moral demands which this involves, is crucial to the moralistic as opposed to the more mechanistic, invisible hand procedures of mid-century social reformism'.[18] While Plant and Vincent expressed worries about the Idealist rejection of the facts of a class-divided society, and particularly about the consequences of seeing welfare as based upon altruism and charity rather than right, the Idealist view of the market as laying down forms of mutual interdependence, and its differentiation of social function, provides a new justification of the mixed economy.

It was Plant's conceptions of positive liberty and citizenship, serving as the basis for a whole raft of democratic reforms to the British Constitution, which had a profound effect on Labour politicians. Bryan Gould (b. 1939), at one time seen as the most articulate leader of a re-aligned Labour Left, explicitly used Plant's ideas to relate socialist values to the political realities of seeking support from an electorate profoundly suspicious of socialist ideas. Gould accepted that capitalism had reformed itself and performed better than predicted by its critics. Indeed, 'as more and more people have operated successfully in a capitalist or at best a mixed economy, they have become partisans of private property and of taking one's chances in the market'.[19] He argued that this was not wrong in itself if the question of freedom could be understood more carefully. With an explicit debt to Plant, Gould argued that individual freedom is inextricably bound up with equality, because unless freedom is distributed as widely as possible, some people would be free at the expense of others. This did mean that freedom could only be maximised if some wealthy individuals saw their power restricted, and that equality of opportunity would need to be replaced by an equal sharing of the benefits of social co-operation. It was a view of freedom, based on the communitarian idea of 'man in society – as a social creature',[20] the belief that individuals were not self-interested creatures, but exist and benefit from social relations with others, necessitating a surrender of some degree of control over one's own life in return for the social benefits which arise from co-operation.

Eschewing Plant's distrust of decentralisation, Gould sought to harness the new stress on republican citizenship and local devolution of power which was becoming popular among many Labour activists as a result of the Thatcher government's attack on local democracy which was then shaking Labour control of local government in the cities. In *A Future for Socialism* (1989), Gould noted the excessive centralisation of power by Thatcher's assault on local government, her opposition to devolution of power to Scotland and Wales, and her virtual abandonment of regional policy to allow economic power to concentrate in the south-east. While accepting that personal prosperity was the key to an increase in social prosperity, Gould rejected corporatism in favour of a diffusion of political power through regional and local decentralisation. Interestingly, he rejected the ideas of electoral reform as undemocratic, as they left the power to form a government in the hands of minority parties; and he also rejected ideas of a written Bill of Rights, because it would remove power from popularly elected representatives to unelected judges. Instead, he called for 'appropriate Government – the notion that Government functions should not be lumped together and carried out by one tier of Government, but should be consciously analysed and allocated to the institutions that are best placed to meet the needs of efficiency and democracy'.[21] However, his explicit rejection of corporatism in favour of participation and decentralisation left open the whole question of how accountability could be given substance in the light of a growing transfer of power to Brussels.

This communitarian republicanism was a common factor in much of the new thinking emerging within the Labour Party. Bernard Crick, producing an unofficial statement on Labour's aims and values with David Blunkett, argued that the egalitarian society desired by socialists had to be a democratic society in the fullest sense of the term, 'one in which popular participation is maximised and people are helped not just to help themselves but to interact with and to help each other'.[22] While the market has its place, the moral values of a co-operative community must take primacy, and these values could only be realised in the type of democratic society in which, once a national government had laid down national minimum standards and guidelines, localities and regions would cultivate participation through the maximum exercise of their freedom. Crick and Blunkett were not taking a particular side in the debate about centralisation as much as calling for a balance, but they did stress that 'community is also about participation. Democracy is best built up from local roots and activities'.[23]

The idea of citizenship was not confined to the newly realigned Left. Tony Benn, while retaining the socialist beliefs which had marked the more influential phases of his career, has continued to stress the radical politics of democracy which once made Bennism such a distinct phenomenon. In *Common Sense* (1993), he has advocated a Commonwealth of Britain Bill, demanding a republic based on democratic institutions, with a decentralisation of power to the English regions as well as to Scotland and Wales, together with the re-establishment of genuine power in local government. With its calls for an end to the Crown, the House of Lords and the Church Establishment, the Bill would have made any seventeenth-or eighteenth-century Commonwealthman feel at home, with the institutions of tyranny updated to include the golden triangle of the City, Whitehall and Westminster, which had combined to turn Britain into a province of a bureaucratic Europe.[24] Where Raymond Plant adopted a metaphysical set of values, in keeping with the neo-Hegelian philosophy of T. H. Green, Benn and his allies advocated a more institutional approach of a radical popular sovereignty manifested in a decentralised polity.

Peter Hain (b. 1950), a South African who had once organised demonstrations against his home country's sports teams when they visited Britain, sought to take the leadership of the re-aligned Left by laying claim to these ideas of republican citizenship. Joining the Labour Party from the Young Liberals in 1977, he has been elected MP for Neath and moved from a leading position in the Labour Co-ordinating Committee to chair the *Tribune* newspaper. Long an advocate of participatory democracy and libertarian socialism, Hain set out a mass of policy proposals to democratise British life, accompanying it with an attempt to divorce the politics of republican citizenship from communitarianism. He saw citizenship as a necessary extension of democracy from the state to the whole of civil society, arguing for a classical conception of politics in which 'it is only with interaction with others in political activity and civic action that individuals will fully realize their humanity'.[25] However, while he regarded community as central to the socialist ideal, he condemned the modern communitarian politics of fashionable writers such as Amitai Etzione, which he saw as basically reactionary, blurring as it did into the politics of the New Right by presenting fatherhood and family togetherness as an answer to the problems of single mothers and poverty-stricken households.

CITIZENSHIP AND MAASTRICHT

It was the problem posed by the shift of power from Westminster to Brussels which brought the whole question of active citizenship and democratic participation to the fore after the 1991 Treaty of Maastricht appeared to bring European union tangibly closer. Tony Wright (b. 1948), an authority on the writings of G.D.H. Cole and one of the most acute thinkers of the new intake of Labour MPs elected in 1992, sought to deal with the challenge which Maastricht posed to parliamentary sovereignty by moving to the argument that this raises the whole unresolved problem of democracy in Britain, a problem with its roots deep in British political history.

To Wright, democracy in Britain had been artificially grafted on to an elaborately hierarchical social structure and a rigid class system in a manner which had preserved rather than supplanted a profoundly authoritarian society. Democracy never became a living organic foundation of popular power and citizenship, merely a set of arrangements to which the old system adapted. Instead of a constitutional system of checks and balances, as existed in the United States, there was instead a continuation of the old doctrines of balance, continuity and adaptation. The result was to make the doctrines of representation and responsibility into fictions, concealing an increasing shift towards centralised executive power. Whether on the Westminster or Brussels model, the domination of the legislature by the executive through the party machine meant that the substance of sovereignty remained a fiction because of the nature of modern government, which is centralised – 'the growth of big government has outstripped the ability of representative institutions to keep up',[26] the result of which has been to turn assemblies into theatres of ritual confrontation rather than effective democratic bodies. The needs of strong government have come together with a deferential culture to make most Britons subjects, not citizens, ruled rather than rulers. The dangers of such a situation, first noted by Raymond Williams from the New Left, lie in delegitimising the whole political system – 'it is not necessary to believe that the whole responsibility for British economic decline may be laid at the door of the political system to think that a system which has not taken seriously the task of developing a participatory policy style might have difficulty in securing consent and legitimacy for its activities'.[27]

A common ideology of centralism lies behind the problem. A Tory ideology of the integrity of high politics and the territorial management of the Union had been matched by a Labour ideology of an exclusively class project which has sought to use and extend the resources of the central state. Thus, to Wright, 'a unitary dogma of sovereignty, traditionally buttressed by the ideological dispositions of the main twentieth century political traditions, has blocked the path to secure forms of shared and devolved power. Yet it is precisely this which is needed and demanded'.[28] It is needed in order to turn subjects into citizens, to turn members of a privatized domain into a participatory membership of the public realm (the *res publica*) as an active community founded upon civic responsibility.

Wright divorced Cole's radical anti-capitalism from his ideas of functional representation, based on a plural community of citizens who live in a dense network of interests and associations, and uses the pluralism to call for a written constitution and a Bill of Rights. This would establish Parliament as the ultimate register of the complex web of channels and devices of government in a modern society. It would be genuinely accountable because it would be based upon a civic community, having a social grounding for the rights and duties of citizens who would be both rulers and ruled at the same time. It would be a genuine democracy rather than the fiction existing today, because 'in the relationship that is governing, the citizen is a participant while the subject is a recipient. The difference matters';[29] it is the difference between a genuine democracy and the existing fiction of apparent sovereignty.

The difficulty, of course, lies in the attainment of a genuine citizenship within a modern international economy in which effective power over the economy cannot lie at the national level. David Miliband, the son of one of the leading neo-Marxists of the British New Left and lately one of Tony Blair's key members of political staff, has contributed to a series of publications exploring British political democracy in the light of Maastricht. Arguing that nations remain the keystones of cultural attachment within the European Union, Miliband and his co-author, Stephen Tindale, called for representative and accountable bodies to overcome the 'democratic deficit', the euphemism for the lack of democracy within the European Union. They agreed that a more democratic European Parliament would be too easy an answer, as it would merely give a democratic legitimacy to what would in practice be a tendency to centralise power. Instead, they called for a federalist constitution to reflect European diversity. with the rights of initiating legislation to be shared between the European Commission, Parliament and Council, while a troika of three Presidents nominated by governments would give the constitution a set of balancing and countervailing powers similar to the US Constitution. The lack of direct control of governing powers would thus be overcome by making the dual legitimacy of national and European representation clearly visible – 'if integration was to succeed, it must be accompanied by wider public understanding and support. Our proposals therefore seek transparency as well as practicality.'[30]

The problem of how to attain political sovereignty when economic power is outside the grasp of government remains one to answer, however. In a period of intensified economic interdependence, the goal of any European social democratic strategy – to 'develop a political counterpoint to the laissez-faire anchor established by the economic right'[31] – still remains faced with the problem of how to direct effectively a macro-economic policy largely outside the scope of national governments. Once a European central bank is established, the idea of a national exchange rate policy or a foreign trade policy – the means by which post-war governments sought some control over the hostile movements of international capital markets and competition from cheap labour markets – becomes redundant.

POLITICS AND THE ECONOMY

Given the unsuitability of Keynesian economic nostrums during the Wilson and Callaghan governments, and the success of the Thatcher government once these nostrums had been discarded, the economic thought of New Labour is obviously crucial. The actual economic policies, like the constitutional and political policies, have significance in their being informed by a general understanding, or theory, of how the economy works, and New Labour has gradually shifted from the ๑๑๐n๐mi๐ ๑xpansionism of the Keynesian Left to take on a form consonant with its politics.

In doing so, they have been forced to stretch the republican idea of citizenship from the polity, in which it was originally grounded, to a market economy driven by social forces distinct from any political order. The economy has been seen in narrowly political terms, understood as a form of active participation rather than as a mechanism for satisfying material needs. The need to understand the forces which drive the economy, a need shared in their different ways by Marx, the neo-Classical economists and Keynes, has reverted to the original paradigm of political economy of the eighteenth century. Then, at the dawn of the new financial capitalism, the political categories in which the state's relations with its subjects were interpreted were transferred uncritically to the market.[32]

The need to move from Keynes, the cause of the crisis in Labour's economic thinking, was registered by John Eatwell (b. 1945), an academic at Trinity College, Cambridge, who became Neil Kinnock's economic adviser. Eatwell argued that Keynes's critique of the neo-Classical orthodoxy that the market was a self-adjusting mechanism with a tendency to economic equilibrium was flawed, because Keynes remained within the general thinking of that orthodoxy, unable to conclusively refute the argument that the level of effective demand was essentially a function of the price mechanism, and unable to offer any alternative mechanism for changing the structure and behaviour of the economy outside government action. The change in the political climate had therefore allowed the old orthodoxy to return with a vengeance.

To move the Left's thinking about the economy forward from Keynes's failure, Eatwell sought a theoretical alternative on which to base economic policies, and for this he turned to the revival of the classical political economy of David Ricardo begun by the Italian theorist, Piero Sraffa, in *Production of Commodities by Means of Commodities* (1960), and popularised at Cambridge by theorists such as Joan Robinson and the Communist, Maurice Dobb. In this short but tightly argued book, Sraffa had argued that prices were an expression of the rate of profit (understood in the Ricardian sense of the relationship between profit and wages, of course, not the Marxist sense of the relation between profit and capital as a whole) rather than the price mechanism. This apparently esoteric conclusion had the dramatic effect of demolishing the proposition that prices are connected with the movement of supply and demand, the foundation of all orthodox thinking about output and employment.

The result of the theoretical transformation wrought by Sraffa was decisive, according to Eatwell, as it demanded 'a new approach to industrial structure and performance, which explains the role of prices in a market economy and the process of accumulation'.[33] The cause of 'structural unemployment' was the micro-economic behaviour of decisions by individual enterprises, constituting as it did the overall level of output and employment, and it was this behaviour which had to be influenced if unemployment was to be reduced. This was why the Sraffian revival of political economy was so important, as it argued that prices were determined by the conditions of the production of commodities and by the distribution of income between wages and profits, themselves determined by institutional and historical contexts. If the different rates of investment in Britain were compared with Germany, then specific historical factors need to be studied, such as the role of the state and financial system, the structure of trade, the state of technological development and industrial relations. As there was no automatic market mechanism for changing this, then economic policy would involve a process of continual structural transformation in which the state and its citizens would need to be involved. Eatwell himself looked to the partnership between Labour and the TUC to be the active subject in changing the economy, but the connections with the enabling state propagated by the political philosophers of New Labour are clear.

In practice, Eatwell's own brand of economics did not fundamentally differ from the policy conclusions of Keynes – he wrote that 'the classical theory of value may be regarded as being congruent with Keynes's principle of effective demand'.[34] However, it was the political economy which underlay these policy conclusions which manifested Labour's new economic thinking so clearly. Eatwell believed that 'both classical and Keynesian theories are necessarily "political" theories of the market economy, which portray the market mechanism as operating within an explicit "political" context'.[35] Labour's economic thinking was to be political economy in the old sense of the term. The socio-economic understanding of the forces driving a market economy towards the continued accumulation of capital was now being replaced by a narrow political understanding of the economy in terms of the old republican categories of virtue as active participation by citizens, and corruption as the private decisions of interest groups and individuals taken without reference to the public good.

CITIZENSHIP, COMMUNITY AND POLITICAL ECONOMY

David Marquand (b. 1934), a Labour MP for Ashfield from 1966 to 1977 and a prominent supporter of Roy Jenkins who had joined the SDP to become their leading theorist (and was to rejoin Tony Blair's New Labour) presented a particularly influential exposition of this in *The Unprincipled Society* (1985), in which he argued that 'Britain's adjustment problems have as much to do with politics as with economics, and with tacit political understandings as with political institutions'.[36] This political culture was one in which society was seen as a collection of separate, atomistic individuals pursuing their private interests without regard for any more general purpose. This had been the cause of Britain's economic rise, but also of her economic decline. The notion of a *public* purpose was alien to Britain's political class, with the result that there was 'an intellectual and moral vacuum at the heart of the political economy'.[37] A fragmented society of possessive individuals (in the sense used by the Canadian political theorist C. B. Macpherson) was the fundamental illness which had to be overcome if Britain was to find its public purpose, and the individualist philosophies of liberals such as Rawls are as unsuited to this task as the New Right's selfish commitment to market economics. Instead, an older notion of politics as concerned with the common wealth, the *res publica* of classical political theory, had to be re-discovered if the political arena was to become a living arena. It was the political domain as a public realm, the classical republic of active and equal citizens,[38] which belonged to political economy as much as the polity with which it had begun.

The market as a mechanism for the production of wealth was not questioned; merely the competitive values which appear to have accompanied that mechanism. This was the philosophy underlying Raymond Plant's view of a market economy as governed by the moral principles of citizenship. In a series of pamphlets and articles on citizenship and rights from the late 1980s, he stressed the opposition between the virtue of active participation and the corruption of private interests as a crucial determinant of the economy, in total opposition to the free market doctrines of Thatcherism. He held that 'the market itself needs a framework of civic responsibility within which to operate just as interest groups like unions do. Unless such a civic vision is articulated and defended, not just as a matter of altruism but as something which is in all our interests, then the political community will fall victim to strong special interests whether in politics or in markets.'[39]

It was in this sense that David Miller (b. 1946), another academic political philosopher, this time a Reader at Nuffield College, Oxford, and a leading advocate of market socialism, could connect the values of the community with those of the market, arguing that 'communitarian ideals find their practical expression in the shaping of markets to meet social objectives and in social policies which aim to satisfy a range of needs. The sense of community would be fostered through participation at work, and through non-market forms of association, especially political assemblies.'[40]

It was the crisis of Labour thinking on the economy, the cause of this revival in political economy, which explains the phenomenal popularity and influence of Will Hutton's *The State We're In* (1995). Unlike many Labour thinkers such as Eatwell, Hutton (b. 1950) regarded Keynes as the figure who could lead Labour and the country out of the problems in which they found themselves, trumpeting 'a remarkable resurgence of Keynesian ideas'.[41] However, while Hutton's Keynes may have offered an alternative theory of capitalism as rooted in the real world of production rather than the world of self-regulating equilibriums portrayed in mathematical models, it was not the expansionist figure who had become accepted as an essential element of Corporate Socialism. From early in his career, Hutton had felt that neo-Keynesianism had over-stressed the role of fiscal policy in managing the economy at the expense of the political role which the state must play. He argued that Keynesianism was not really about demand management, or even about government spending, but was a demand that the state change the behaviour of financiers and businessmen in the interests of the public good,[42] correcting a market which could not balance itself by looking to the much larger framework of financial and monetary leverage.

Indeed, this political approach to Keynesianism dovetailed with the stress on the supply side of the economy presented by the Labour economists of the 1980s, and with the republican stress on citizenship of Labour's political philosophers. In an economist's version of Plant's approach to moral rules and markets, Hutton revived in a particularly sharp form the old categories of political economy characteristic of its birth, when economics was seen as an expression of republican virtue as opposed to private corruption.[43] Hutton saw Keynes's economics as a solution to a moral rather than an economic problem – the need for commitment and trust which was lacking in monetarist Britain. These virtues had been the hallmark of successful capitalist economies such as the United States, which selflessly held up the world economy, and East Asia, where the family firm predominated, but they were absent in Britain, where the private realm was celebrated. The cause of this sad state of affairs was the predominance of a centralised banking structure which had gone hand-in-glove with the centralisation of political power in London. Hutton argues that this system lay behind the social injustice and economic inefficiency which has become such a hallmark of British society – 'the disintegration of family life and the decline in the public realm that disfigure contemporary Britain may seem far removed from London's financial markets, but they are as linked to them as remote shocks are to the epicentre of an earthquake'.[44]

Co-operation and commitment could only result from the building of an interdependent institutional structure, and this requires a very new type of British state – 'Britain needs what might be called a republican attitude to its culture and institutions'.[45] This did not involve the abolition of the monarchy necessarily – although it would necessitate a stripping of prerogative powers and the hereditary principle – but it did involve a civic culture based on citizens rather than subjects. Benn and Wright also talked of this, but Hutton gave it an economic expression by writing of stakeholder capitalism (possibly a variant of the popular capitalism called for by Thatcher), with a republican central bank which would serve as the servant, not the master, of business, with a federal structure to match the republican structure of the new state. Thus, regional bankers would report to a central bank, whose chief executives would be appointed by the elected parliaments of the appropriate region. The commitment of the shareholders would be to the community, rather than to short-term gain at any cost, because stakeholder capitalism involved a genuine stake in the common good as much as in any firm (a moral rather than a selfish form of capitalism, as advocated by the American communitarian, Amitai Etzione[46]). It could only have been in the context of the collapse of faith in any form of real planning that Hutton's argument that 'these feasible and achievable reforms must be accomplished if the dynamism of capitalism is to be harnessed to the public good'[47] could have appealed to the Left.

BROWN AND BLAIR

The success of Hutton's work may well be tied to the success of
Blair's Labour Party in capturing a mood that morality and efficiency
were intimately connected by a balance between duty and rights. Both
Tony Blair and Gordon Brown, the dynamic leaders of New Labour,
were elected to Parliament in 1983 (Brown for Dunfermline East and
Blair for Sedgefield), and were raised to political maturity under the
auspices of Neil Kinnock, who sought to bring a new generation into
politics unaffected by the anti-capitalist radicalism which had characterised the New Left.

Gordon Brown (b. 1951), who eventually emerged as Blair's shadow chancellor, had long been linking constitutional and political
reform to economic reform. In a lecture to the radical pressure group,
Charter 88, in March 1992, he had used his native Scotland as a
model of the need for a sense of national identity and purpose,
linking a strong community to an active and accountable government. He explicitly relied on Etzione to argue for a community of
neighbours rather than a land of competing strangers – 'People do
not live in isolation. People do not live in markets. People live in
communities. I think of Britain as a community of citizens with
common needs, mutual interests, shared objectives, related goals and
most of all linked destinies.'[48] The similarity of adjectives, with their
common language of sharing, is a measure of the emphasis on values
rather than detailed policies which was to prove a means of identity
for New Labour.

Brown gave this an economic expression by arguing for the need
to educate Britain's citizens in the new skills needed in a modern
global economy where capital, raw materials and technology can
be mobilised internationally. Brown followed the ideas of Robert
Reich, the new US Labour Secretary appointed by Bill Clinton, in
arguing that skills and education were the determinants of future
economic growth – 'Education is the foundation, the well-spring
of a successful economy.'[49] A new economic egalitarianism
was needed to create an opportunity-based economics which
looked to develop skills to equip people to fulfil their new roles in
the community. This required an enabling state to end poverty by
fostering personal responsibility – the virtuous citizen of classical
republican political theory – and a commitment to attack all
entrenched private interests and privileges, whether based on sex, race
or class. This was the basis for a 'New Settlement' – a new constitu-

tional understanding between the individual, the community and
the state.

It was Tony Blair (b. 1953) who emerged as the most important
spokesman of this new ideology when he was propelled into the
leadership of the party after John Smith's untimely death in May
1994. A close associate of Gordon Brown, Blair's interest in communitarian ideas had been manifested early, according to one biographer,[50] and were clearly presented in the terms made popular by
Labour's political philosophers, with an emphasis on citizenship and
the importance of seeing social problems in the political terms of
citizenship and the constitution. In a Charter 88 discussion immediately after the 1992 election, he talked of the need to 'integrate the
notion of constitutional changes and a more democratic structure for
our society into our politics so that our constitution is not actually a
fringe issue any more but is central to the whole process of political
life'.[51] The commitment to a more democratic polity could have made
this a speech given by any respectable Bennite once the economic
commitments to nationalisation and economic planning were not
taken into account.

Blair presented a sharp contrast to his predecessor. John Smith had
been a strong consensus leader of the party, refusing to raise the
revision of Clause IV of the party constitution while modifying union
power in the conference through his advocacy of one-person-one-
vote. Blair was as conscious as Kinnock of the necessity of tailoring
ideas to win elections, and was in a far better position to actually do
so given the deep-seated desire for a political change after more than
fifteen years of Conservative government. This led him to successfully
pose a challenge to Clause IV, committing the party to common
ownership, replacing it with a vague and strongly communitarian
statement. In a lecture in July 1995, on the fiftieth anniversary of the
1945 Attlee government, the apogee of Labour's history, he pointed
out that that government had not suddenly emerged from a vacuum;
its programmes had been slowly shaped and moulded to a point
where its greatness could emerge. The reality was that 'it cut decisively with, not against the grain of political thinking, and that its
progress at the election was strongest in the new direction it offered,
not the minutiae of policy detail'.[52]

The moral to be drawn was clear. Labour had to act with and not
against the political direction of the times. The fact was, according to
Blair, that Labour in 1945 had never resolved certain fundamental
questions of ideology and organisation which had since re-asserted

themselves in a very different society. Labour had continued to be tied to an obsolete definition of socialism as nationalisation and to an increasingly undemocratic power structure at a time when the British economy had become interlocked with a global economy, making economic isolation from the nations's main trading partners both undesirable and unfeasible. At the same time, service industries were replacing manufacturing, leading to a consumer culture rather then the producer culture with which Labour had been traditionally associated, while the revolution at work had massively expanded the part-time, often female work-force at the expense of the old male, cloth-cap worker with the expectation of a full-time job for life. An information economy was emerging in which skill and talent had become critical as knowledge and education played a greater role, and the result was the emergence of new elites and new class divisions, between those with technical skills and a higher education and the unskilled and under-valued sections of society who would be in need of the skills and education which were being called for by Gordon Brown.

In these circumstances, a new socialism, or what Blair called socialism, was needed. It had to be distant from the centralised state control of industry and production associated with Marx (although such a conception was in fact more closely associated with Stalin and Morrison), a philosophy which had failed to recognise that the state could become as fierce an oppressor as any capitalist, and which had finally died with the fall of the Soviet Union. Instead, there had to be a revival of the Ethical Socialism which had inspired the Labour pioneers, based on a society of communitarian citizens. The Labour attack on social injustice and economic power would then be connected to the liberal values of free thought and the awareness of the political abuse of power as well as the economic. The rights of social citizenship adumbrated by T. H. Marshall were cited by Blair as an offshoot of more fundamental political and civic rights.

To Blair, the objectives were the same as those of the Labour pioneers – economic strength in a new world; jobs and security for all; the use of the welfare state and labour market to attack poverty; a sense of civic pride and responsibility; and the leadership of a community of nations. It was the means that had changed, and the change to Clause IV was a symbol of Labour's recognition of that fact. Now, there was to be a partnership between government and industry to achieve high economic growth; financial independence for citizens instead of keeping subjects on demeaning benefits; education which

had a higher quality and a higher degree of parental choice; an attack
on the symptoms and the causes of high crime; a National Health
Service more responsive to consumers; major constitutional changes
to the House of Lords and the secrecy traditionally cocooning British
government from its citizens; and international co-operation on Europe. The specific policies on these issues could await the realities of
government – it was the basic values which counted. It was this new
approach to socialism which was extolled by Blair – 'It is, if you will,
social-ism. It contains an ethical and subjective judgement that individuals owe a duty to one another and to a broader society – the left
view of citizenship'.[53]

The publication of the manifesto *New Labour, New Life for Britain*,
in July 1996, brings together this new thinking to supersede the mass
of detailed policy proposals and reviews which had evolved during
Labour's long years in the political wilderness. The section on the
economy, with its stress on investment in education and training to be
paid for from a windfall tax on the privatised utilities, was written by
Gordon Brown. However, the rest of the document was apparently
written by Tony Blair himself from individual submissions by sha-
dow-cabinet members.

The economic expansionism promised by the Labour Keynesians
of the 1930s, such as Durbin, Gaitskell and Jay, has been replaced by
a commitment to reduce state intervention in the economy, the omis-
sion of any redistributive taxation, and a restriction of government
spending and borrowing in order to control inflation and lower
interest rates. The social philosophy which led the Labour leaders
of a now-distant past to call for social security against poverty and
unemployment is still echoed by demands for a national minimum
wage and the signature of the Social Chapter of the Maastricht treaty.
However, the precise level of the minimum wage is to be set with the
advice of employers (unlikely to be anything but low), while Labour
stresses that any genuinely radical changes to company law could be
vetoed by a British government. The party created by the trade
unions to protect their rights against the greater power of the employers now accepts the changes in law on ballots, picketing and solidarity
strikes wrought by the radical Conservative governments of the
1980s.

Instead, the emphasis has shifted from the social to the narrowly
political, with Labour's demands for constitutional reform standing
out as the most ambitious of its proposals. Even so, devolution to
Scotland and Wales (together with any willing English regions),

reform of the House of Lords, and a Freedom of Information Act are mere echoes of the radical democratic demands of the Bennite Left (and the Young Liberals) which once threatened to shake British society to its roots.

Accusations have been levelled (from a wider circle than the hard Left) that Blair has betrayed the traditions of the Labour Party, and the once-powerful left-wing miners' leader, Arthur Scargill, has even sought to create a new socialist labour party, but the accusation hardly stands up to close examination. If the ideas of Corporate Socialism or the Marxist politics of Scargill had triumphed, they would have been as much in line with Labour tradition as those of New Labour. The Labour Party as a 'broad church' has always contained a great diversity of ideas, and Blair's emphasis on community and citizenship is certainly in line with the Labour pioneers. The socialist tradition has a strong communitarian trend, with prominent Bennites like Geoff Hodgson accepting the division between competitive values and the market as a mechanism for the production of wealth. The civic virtue of the community was central to the political thought of Ramsay MacDonald, who argued that 'the community idea must be the dominant note; the thought must be of the co-operation of citizens, not of workmen nor of consumers'.[54] This communitarian philosophy was common to William Morris and the Ethical Socialists, while R. H. Tawney's attack on the acquisitive values of capitalist society was also built on communitarian foundations.

A greater doubt exists about the efficacy of New Labour's ideology in a society marked by heavy under-employment, increased poverty and homelessness, and fierce competition from cheap-labour economies. There is arguably room for economic growth to take place without inflation, given the recent structural changes in the economy, but the problem is that the values which have occupied Labour thinking in the last decade are neutral on this crucial issue. Indeed, the elastic nature of the values of community and citizenship mean that they can be made to fit any type of policy or situation. The need to serve the public good and work together can lead to a redistributionist policy, an expansionist policy based on deficit spending, or an economy marked by a slowly declining growth in which every citizen can smile at one another. Values in themselves don't bite, unlike the corporate socialist ideology of the 1930s where specific policies with specific aims were tied to a definite analysis of a failed market economy. The type of abstractions beloved of Oxbridge political philosophers can be helpful in limited circumstances, but they do not generate particular policies *in themselves*, much less resolve the problems of low wages and under-investment for which the labour movement seeks an answer. In a world becoming divided into different currency zones – the dollar, the yen and the D-Mark – where trade wars and their concomitants are a constant source of danger, and where there is the ever-present threat that the violence inflicted on the Third World will return to the anxious populations of the First, the Labour Party will need a much stronger analysis of the world economy and its dynamics if it is not to be swept away by the powerful economic and political tides of a 'post-Communist' age.

There remains the question of the contemporary role of labourism in the party, but this is really a question of power rather than ideology. Labourism was never a coherently worked out ideology, but a living practice of trade union activity containing within it a theoretical structure which can be discerned in the early writings of Hodgskin. Labourism has been central to the Labour Party because the unions from which labourism derives are central to the party, not because of any theoretical superiority. That central position – in terms of voting power and finance – remains, but the different context gives it a different function. Where in the 1930s or the 1970s, the strength of the unions was self-evident, in the 1990s the unpopularity and structural weakness of the unions in the economy make them vulnerable and aware of themselves as a possible political embarrassment to Labour's electoral chances. As a result, they are open to a great deal of pressure from the political wing of the movement, ready to give ground in the hope that a Labour victory may be able to relieve them of at least some of the restraints placed upon them by seventeen years of government by the radical Right.

If the unions should ever recover their strength, then Labour's ideology will need to position itself once more to their labourism. If not, or if the threat of returned Conservative rule keeps them in line with a Labour government, then labourism may cease to have a central position in the party, and it will become just one element among several competing views (as is the case in the US Democratic party). If that happens, the Labour Party will be such in name only.

Notes

Chapter 1: Introduction

1. The two main accounts, apart from some useful anthologies, have been G. D. H. Cole, *A History of Socialist Thought*, 5 vols (Macmillan, 1953–60) and, before him, Max Beer, *History of British Socialism* (G. Bell & Sons, 1929). A recent interesting work has been Nicolas Ellison, *Egalitarian Thought and Labour Politics: Retreating Visions* (Routledge, 1994).
2. The difficulties of conceiving this has led to misunderstandings of the nature of this work – see, for example, Ellison, ibid., p. x.
3. J. M. Keynes, *The General Theory of Employment, Interest and Money* (Macmillan, 1974 edn) p. 383.
4. H. M. Drucker, *Doctrine and Ethos in the Labour Party* (George Allen & Unwin, 1979).
5. Leo Panitch, *Social Democracy and Industrial Militancy: The Labour Party, the Trade Unions and Incomes Policy, 1945–74* (Cambridge University Press, 1976).
6. *The Labour Party Foundation Conference and Annual Conference Reports, 1900–1905* (London, 1967) p. 12.
7. Noel Thompson has written about Hodgskin in *The Market and its Critics: Socialist Political Economy in Nineteenth-Century Britain* (Routledge, 1988), but he virtually ignores Hodgskin's writings on trade unionism at the expense of the pro-market enthusiasm of the years when Hodgskin was editor of *The Economist*. In contrast, Edward Thompson has pointed to the contemporary importance of Hodgskin's labourism in *The Making of the English Working Class* (Penguin Books, 1968 edn) pp. 569, 887.
8. Thomas Hodgskin, *Labour Defended Against the Claims of Capital* (Labour Publishing Co., 1922 edn) p. 89.
9. Karl Marx, *Theories of Surplus Value*, Part III (Lawrence & Wishart, 1972 edn) p. 296.
10. Hodgskin, *Labour Defended*, pp. 89–90.
11. Ibid., p. 106.
12. Ibid., p. 26.
13. See, for example, R. Samuel and G. Stedman Jones, 'The Labour Party and Social Democracy', in R. Samuel and G. Stedman Jones (eds), *Culture, Ideology and Politics: Essays for Eric Hobsbawm* (Routledge & Kegan Paul, 1983). The labourism thesis has been put forward by a number of New Left writers, notably Perry Anderson and Tom Nairn in 'The Nature of the Labour Party', *New Left Review*, no. 27, September–October 1964, and no. 28, November–December, 1964. However, it was never stated with precision as a set of political *ideas*, its radical aspects were ignored by a concentration on its conservative aspects, and its relationship with socialism was never adequately defined.

Introduction to Part Two: The Formation of British Socialism

1. E. Durbin (ed.), *Socialism: The British Way* (Essential Books, 1948) p. 1.

Chapter 2: Marxists, Fabians and Ethical Socialists: The Traditions of British Socialism

1. Stanley Pierson presents an interesting account of the British nature of Marxism *in Marxism and the Origins of British Socialism* (Cornell University Press, 1973), though he overestimates Hyndman's radicalism and does not relate the ideology to labourism.
2. Karl Marx, *Capital*, vol. 1 (Lawrence & Wishart, 1974) p. 558.
3. Marx defined the rate of profit as the ratio of surplus value to the total capital in society, differentiating it from the rate of surplus value of labour power. Hodgskin confused the rate of profit with the rate of surplus value and did not recognise the importance of the falling rate of profit. To Marx, this fall was 'in every respect the most important law of modern political economy, and the most essential for understanding the most difficult of relations' (*Grundrisse*, trans. M. Nicolaus, Penguin, 1973, p. 748).
4. Marx, *Theories of Surplus Value*, Part III (Lawrence & Wishart, 1972) especially p. 296.
5. See, for example, Marx's letters on Ireland in Marx, *The First International and After*, ed. D. Fernbach (Penguin, 1974).
6. Quoted in Marx, ibid., p. 270.
7. Marx and Engels, *On Britain* (Lawrence & Wishart, 1968) p. 574.
8. See, for example, H. M. Hyndman, *The Historical Base of Socialism in England* (Kegan Paul, 1883) p. 287.
9. Engels to Sorge, 4 May 1887, in Marx and Engels, *Selected Correspondence* (Progress, 1975).
10. Tom Mann, *What is the ILP Driving At?* (Labour Press Society, 1894) p. 11.
11. G.B. Shaw, *Bernard Shaw and Karl Marx: A Symposium* (Random House, 1930) pp. 170–1. This contains the early debates on Marx's theory of values in the Fabian Society.
12. Quoted in N. and J. McKenzie, *The First Fabians* (Weidenfeld & Nicolson, 1977) p. 153.
13. Ibid., p. 8.
14. Shaw, *The Impossibilities of Anarchism* (Fabian Tract 45, London, 1893) p. 27.
15. Labour Party, *Annual Conference Report* (1923) p. 178.
16. *Fabian News*, November 1896, p. 35.
17. *Fabian News*, January 1897, p. 43.
18. *New Statesman*, 2 August 1913, p. 525.
19. Beatrice Webb, *Our Partnership* (Longmans, Green, 1948) p. 195. See also Shaw, 'Illusions of Socialism,' in Edward Carpenter (ed.), *Forecasts of the Coming Century* (Clarion Press, 1896).
20. Ibid., p. 539.
21. Stephen Yeo, in 'Notes on Three Socialisms – Collectivism, Statism and Associationism', in C. Levy (ed.), *Socialism and the Intelligentsia, 1880–*

1914 (Routledge & Kegan Paul, 1987) brings out the ambiguous nature, conservative and radical, of the vague term 'community'.
22. Quoted in C. Tsuzuki, *Edward Carpenter, 1844–1929* (Cambridge University Press, 1980) p. 117.
23. J. B. Glasier and K. St John Conway, *The Religion of Socialism* (Labour Press Society, 1890) p. 16.
24. Robert Blatchford, *Merrie England* (Clarion Office, n.d.) p. 119.
25. Ibid., pp. 47–8.
26. R. Blatchford, *Britain for the British* (Clarion, 1902), p. 151.

Chapter 3: The Emergence of British Socialism

1. Duncan Tanner gives an account of the ideas in Labour politics in this period in *Political Change and the Labour Party* (Cambridge University Press, 1990), but, as with so many otherwise excellent historians, it is couched in terms of political strategies. See Stanley Pierson, *British Socialists: The Journey from Fantasy to Reality* (Harvard University Press, 1979) for a different approach to ideas as *Weltanshauungen*.
2. *Labour Leader*, 19 September 1904.
3. *Labour Leader*, April 1893.
4. Keir Hardie, *From Serfdom to Socialism* (George Allen, 1907) p. 35.
5. Ibid., p. 44.
6. Ibid., p. 24.
7. Ibid., p. 79.
8. Ibid., pp. 77–8.
9. *Labour Leader*, January 1894.
10. Keir Hardie, *Labour Politics* (Independent Labour Party, 1903) p. 8.
11. Keir Hardie, *My Confession of Faith in the Labour Alliance* (Independent Labour Party, 1909) p. 5.
12. Ibid., p. 6.
13. Ibid., p. 12.
14. Quoted in Frank Johnson, *Keir Hardie's Socialism* (Independent Labour Party, 1922) p. 9.
15. Quoted in ibid., p. 11.
16. Keir Hardie, *My Confession*, p. 3.
17. Isabella Ford, *Women and Socialism* (Independent Labour Party, 1904) p. 8.
18. Keir Hardie, *From Serfdom to Socialism*, p. 63.
19. Ibid., pp. 68–9.
20. *Labour Leader*, 26 January 1901.
21. *Labour Leader*, 27 January 1900.
22. Keir Hardie, *India: Impressions and Suggestions* (Independent Labour Party, 1909) pp. 78–9.
23. Winston Churchill, *Great Contemporaries* (Thornton Butterworth, 1937) p. 293.
24. Philip Snowden, *The Christ That Is To Be* (Independent Labour Party, 1903) p. 10.
25. Philip Snowden, *The Economic Case for Socialism* (Independent Labour Party, 1921) p. 11.

26. Philip Snowden, *Labour and the New World* (Cassell, 1921) p. 10.
27. Ibid., p. 112.
28. *Hansard* (1924) vol. 172, col. 1610.
29. Philip Snowden, *The Way to Industrial Peace* (The Brotherhood Movement, 1927) p. 13.
30. *Hansard* (1930–1) vol. 248, col. 448.
31. MacDonald to Crisp, 16 July 1894, quoted in David Marquand, *Ramsay MacDonald* (Jonathan Cape, 1977) p. 36.
32. James Ramsay MacDonald, *Socialism and Society* (Independent Labour Party, 1905) p. 29.
33. Ibid., p. 31.
34. Ibid., p. 2.
35. Ibid., p. 61.
36. Ibid., p. 70.
37. Ibid., p. xx.
38. James Ramsay MacDonald, *Parliament and Democracy* (National Labour Press, 1920) pp. 35, 71.
39. MacDonald, *Socialism and Society*, p. 127
40. James Ramsay MacDonald, *Socialism* (T. C. & E. C. Jack, 1907) p. 12.
41. Ibid., p. 55.
42. James Ramsay MacDonald, *Socialism, Critical and Constructive* (Cassell, 1921) p. 175.
43. James Ramsay MacDonald, *The Social Unrest: its Cause and Solution* (T. N. Foulis, 1913) p. 104.
44. Quoted in Marquand, *Ramsay MacDonald*, pp. 83–4.
45. MacDonald, *Socialism and Society*, pp. 159, 164.
46. *Hansard* (1929–30) vol. 229, col. 65.
47. Marquand, *Ramsay MacDonald*, p. 641.
48. Quoted in Carl F. Brand, *British Labour's Rise to Power* (Stanford University Press, 1941) p. 69.
49. ILP, *Annual Conference Report* (1915) pp. 109–10.
50. Labour Party, *Annual Conference Report* (1917) p. 82.
51. H. N. Brailsford, *The War of Steel and Gold* (G. Bell & Sons, 1915 edn) p. 62.
52. Ibid., p. 63.
53. Ibid., p. 80.
54. Ibid., p. 231.
55. Ibid., p. 80.
56. Ralph Miliband, *Parliamentary Socialism* (Merlin, 1972 edn) p. 62.

Chapter 4: R. H. Tawney and the Philosophy of British Socialism

1. For the varied nature of interpretations of Tawney, see Ross Terrill, *R. H. Tawney and His Times* (André Deutsch, 1974), who sees him as a Fabian and Ethical Socialist; and J. M. Winter, *Socialism and the Challenge of War* (Routledge and Kegan Paul, 1974), who points to the influence of Christianity and Guild Socialism on Tawney.
2. For his revisionism, see his article 'British Socialism Today', in Rita Hinden (ed.), *The Radical Tradition* (George Allen & Unwin, 1964).

3. For Laski and Cripps, see Chapter 8 below.
4. R. H. Tawney, *The British Labour Movement* (Yale, 1925) pp. 144–5.
5. Published as *The Attack and Other Papers* (George Allen & Unwin, 1953).
6. R. H. Tawney, *Religion and the Rise of Capitalism* (Pelican Books, 1938 edn) p. 253.
7. See J. M. Winter and D. M. Joslin (eds), *R.H. Tawney's Common Place Book* (Cambridge University Press, 1972).
8. Diary entry for 6 March 1913, ibid., p. 54.
9. R. H. Tawney, *The Acquisitive Society* (G. Bell & Sons, 1921) p. 13.
10. Ibid., p. 32.
11. Ibid., p. 34.
12. Ibid., pp. 93–4.
13. R. H. Tawney, *Equality* (George Allen & Unwin, 1952 edn) p. 38.
14. Ibid., pp. 86–7.
15. Ibid., pp. 198–9.
16. Ibid., p. 158.
17. Ibid., p. 185.

Chapter 5: The Syndicalist Challenge

1. See R. J. Holton, *British Syndicalism, 1900–1914: Myths and Realities* (Pluto Press, 1976).
2. Ridley, *Revolutionary Syndicalism*; see also G. D. H. Cole, *History of Socialist Thought*, vol. III, Chapter 8; George Woodcock, *Anarchism* (Penguin, 1970) pp. 298–304.
3. See Patrick Renshaw, *The Wobblies: The Story of Syndicalism in the United States* (Doubleday, 1967).
4. *The Socialist*, January 1906, p. 1.
5. *The Industrial Syndicalist*, vol. 1, no. 10, April 1911 (Spokesman Books edn, 1974) pp. 327–28.
6. Ibid., vol. 1, no. 7, January 1911, p. 221.
7. Ibid., vol. 1, no. 3, September 1910, p. 80.
8. Ibid., vol. 1, no. 1, July 1910, p. 45.
9. The Unofficial Reform Committee, *The Miners' Next Step – Being a Suggested Scheme for the Reorganisation of the Federation* (Pluto Press edn, 1973) p 15.
10. Ibid., p. 19.
11. *The Socialist*, August 1905, p. 4.
12. *The Industrial Syndicalist*, vol. 1, no. 5, November 1910, p. 145.
13. Owen Dudley Edwards and Bernard Ransom (eds), *James Connolly, Selected Political Writings* (Jonathan Cape, 1973) p. 322.
14. Connolly never ceased to hold to the ideas of Industrial Unionism, collaborating with Irish Nationalists such as Padraig Pearse in an armed rising in 1916 only on the grounds that it was an exceptional situation.
15. *James Connolly, Selected Political Writings*, p. 273.
16. Ibid., p. 281.
17. Quoted in R. Page Arnot, *South Wales Miners: A History of the South Wales Miners Federation, 1898–1914* (George Allen & Unwin, 1967) p. 244.

18. *The Miners' Next Step*, p. 29.
19. *The Industrial Syndicalist*, vol. 1, no. 1, July 1910, p. 47.
20. Ibid., pp. 49–50.
21. *Hansard* (1912) vol. 38, col. 520.
22. Quoted in Renshaw, *The Wobblies*, p. 277.
23. J. T. Murphy, *New Horizons* (John Lane, 1941) p. 44.
24. James Hinton, *The First Shop Stewards Movement* (Routledge & Kegan Paul, 1973) p. 131.
25. *New Statesman*, 7 June 1913.
26. Ibid., 24 May 1913, p. 204.
27. Ibid., 21 June 1913, p. 334.
28. In this book, the Webbs argued for a social parliament, separate from a political parliament, although it would have equal powers. The foreign, military and coercive powers would lie with the political parliament; the social parliament would oversee industrial administration. Rodney Barker sees this as the fullest attempt to deal with a social democratic state in 'The Fabian State', in Ben Pimlott (ed.), *Fabian Essays in Socialism*, p. 29, criticising its lack of concern for civil liberties; however, it is a specific model proposed in a period when the Webb's main political influence was passing.

Chapter 6: G.D.H. Cole and the Guild Socialist Response

1. See J. Klugmann, *History of the Communist Party of Great Britain*, vol. 1, Ch. 1 (Lawrence & Wishart, 1968).
2. See *The Second Congress of the Third International*, vol. II (New York, 1977 edn) pp. 178–88.
3. Quoted in Roberts, *The Syndicalist Tradition and Italian Fascism*, p. 255.
4. Quoted in ibid., p. 233.
5. G. D. H. Cole, 'The Genesis of French Syndicalism – and Some Unspoken Morals', in *New Age*, vol. XIV, 12 February 1914, p. 458.
6. Arthur Penty, *Restoration of the Gild System* (Swan Sonnerschein, 1906) p. 57.
7. S. G. Hobson, *National Guilds: An Inquiry into the Wage System and the Way Out*, ed. A. R. Orage (G. Bell & Sons, 1914), p. 3.
8. Ibid., p. 16.
9. Frank Matthews, 'The Ladder of Becoming: A. R. Orage, A. J. Penty, and the Origins of Guild Socialism in England', in David E. Martin and David Rubinstein (eds), *Ideology and the Labour Movement: Essays Presented to John Saville* (Croom Helm, 1979) p. 147.
10. See W. Golant, 'The Early Political Thought of C. R. Attlee', *Political Quarterly*, July–September, 1969.
11. G. D. H. Cole, *Self-Government in Industry* (G. Bell & Sons, 1917) p. 110.
12. G. D. H. Cole, *The World of Labour – A Discussion of the Present and Future of Trade Unionism* (G. Bell & Sons, 1928 edn) p. 319.
13. Ibid., p. 21.
14. Cole, *Self-Government*, p. 30.
15. Cole, *World of Labour*, p. 126.

16. Ibid., p. 25.
17. Ibid., p. 17.
18. G. D. H. Cole, *Guild Socialism Restated* (Leonard Parsons, 1920) p. 14.
19. Ibid., p. 33.
20. Cole, *World of Labour*, p. 9.
21. G. D. H. Cole, *The Next Ten Years in British Social and Economic Policy* (Macmillan, 1930 edn) p. 17.
22. Cole, *Guild Socialism Restated*, p. 58.
23. See, for example, Cole, *World of Labour*, p. 259.
24. G. D. H. Cole, 'Recent Developments in the British Labour Movement', *American Economic Review*, vol. VIII, no. 3, September 1918, p. 490.
25. Cole, *World of Labour*, p. 11.
26. See, for example, G. D. H. Cole and William Mellor, *The Greater Unionism* (National Labour Press, 1913).
27. Cole, *World of Labour*, p. 213.
28. Ibid., p. 363; also see p. 369.
29. Ibid., p. 26.
30. Ibid., p. 352.
31. Ibid., p. 27.
32. Ibid., p. 196.
33. Ibid., p. 45.
34. G. D. H. Cole, 'Conflicting Obligations', *Proceedings of the Aristotelian Society 1914–15*, vol. XV (London, 1915) p. 157.
35. G. D. H. Cole, *Labour in Wartime* (G. Bell & Sons, 1915) p. 18.
36. G. D. H. Cole, *Labour in the Commonwealth* (Headley Brothers, 1919) p. 50.
37. See G. D. H. Cole, with Bertrand Russell and C. DeLisle Burns, 'Symposium: The Nature of the State', *Proceedings of the Aristotelian Society, 1915–16*, vol. XVI (London, 1916).
38. Cole, *Labour in Wartime*, p. 19.
39. Cole, *World of Labour*, pp. 242–3.
40. Cole, *Self-Government*, p. 76.
41. Cole, *World of Labour*, pp. 405–6.
42. See Cole, *Self-Government*, Appendix B.
43. Ibid., p. 326.
44. Here, I must disagree with J. M. Winter, who overestimates the impact of war on Cole's political thought; see Winter, *Socialism and the Challenge of War: Ideas and Politics in Britain, 1912–18* (Routledge & Kegan Paul, 1974) Chapter 5.
45. Cole, *Labour in the Commonwealth*, pp. 104–5; see also Cole, *Guild Socialism Restated*, p. 180.
46. Cole, *Guild Socialism Restated*, p. 358.
47. Ibid.
48. Cole, *Self-Government*, p. 104.
49. Ibid., p. 16.
50. Cole, *World of Labour*, p. 392.
51. Ibid., p. 25.
52. William Mellor, 'A Critique of Guild Socialism', *Labour Monthly*, vol. 1, no. 5, November 1921, p. 402.

53. See Allen's memo on his visit to Soviet Russia in Arthur Marwick, *Clifford Allen. The Open Conspirator* (Oliver & Boyd, 1964) pp. 62–4; see also H. N. Brailsford, *Parliament or Soviets?* (London, 1919).
54. See *Report*, ILP Conference 1922, pp. 92–3.
55. Cole, *Self-Government*, p. 163.
56. Letter from John Parker M. P, quoted in A. W. Wright, *G. D. H. Cole and Socialist Democracy* (Clarendon Press, 1979) p. 109, n. 13.

Chapter 7: The ILP and the Keynesian Challenge

1. See, for example, J. Ramsay MacDonald, *Why Socialism Must Come* (Independent Labour Party, 1924).
2. The Labour Party, *Labour and the Nation* (The Labour Party, 1928) p. 6.
3. H. N. Brailstord, *The Life and Work of J. A. Hobson* (Oxford University Press, 1948), p. 13.
4. J. A. Hobson, 'Neo-Classical Economics in Britain', *Political Science Quarterly*, vol. XL, no. 3, September 1925, p. 352.
5. Ibid., p. 142.
6. J. A. Hobson, *Industrial System*, p. 79; also see p. 210.
7. See J. A. Hobson, *Imperialism: A Study* (James Nisbet, 1902). Such thinking became a hallmark of the Labour Left.
8. 'The "overflow" stream of savings is of course fed not exclusively from the surplus income of the "rich"; the professional and industrial middle classes and to some slight extent the workers contribute. But the "Hoarding" is distinctly due to the automatic saving of the surplus income of rich men' (Hobson, *Imperialism*, p. 90).
9. J. A. Hobson, *Confessions of an Economic Heretic*, p. 126.
10. Hobson was not a member of the ILP. See note 4.
11. See Adrian Oldfield, 'The Independent Labour Party and Planning, 1920–6', *International Review of Social History*, vol. XXI (1976), for the immediate context of this document.
12. See, for example, Philip Snowden, *The Living Wage* (Hodder & Stoughton, 1912).
13. H. N. Brailsford, J. A. Hobson, E. F. Wise, and A. Creech Jones, *The Living Wage* (Independent Labour Party, 1926) p. 2.
14. Ibid., p. 8.
15. Ibid., p. 37.
16. Ibid., p. 7.
17. Alan Bullock, *The Life and Times of Ernest Bevin*, vol. I: *Trade Union Leader, 1881–1940* (Heinemann, 1960) p. 390.
18. ILP, *Annual Conference Report* (1926) p. 83.
19. Ibid., p. 78.
20. Brailsford *et al.*, *The Living Wage*, p. 53.
21. A. Fenner Brockway, *Make the Workers Free: The Industrial Policy of the ILP* (Independent Labour Party, 1925) p. 13.
22. J. A. Hobson to Ramsay MacDonald, 7 October 1926, quoted in David Marquand, *Ramsay MacDonald*, p. 455.
23. See, for example, his *Tract on Monetary Reform* (1923), *Collected Works*, vol. IV, p. 85.

24. John Maynard Keynes, *The Economic Consequences of Mr Churchill* (1925), *Collected Writings*, vol. IX, p. 224.
25. John Maynard Keynes, *Essays in Persuasion* (1931), *Collected Writings*, vol. IX, p. 258.
26. Ibid., p. 297.
27. Ibid., p. 309.
28. John Maynard Keynes, 'Liberalism and Industry', in H. L. Nathan and H. H. Williams (eds), *Liberal Points of View* (Ernest Benn, 1927) p. 208.
29. Keynes, *Essays in Persuasion*, p. 311.
30. Keynes, *General Theory*, p. 376.
31. Keynes, *Tract on Monetary Reform*, p. 56.
32. John Maynard Keynes, 'A Drastic Remedy for Unemployment – A Reply to Critics', *The Nation*, vol. XXXV, no. 10, 7 June 1924, p. 312.
33. 'On grounds of social justice no case can be made out for reducing the wages of the miners. They are the victims of the economic juggernaut. They represent in the flesh the "fundamental adjustments" engineered by the Treasury and the Bank of England to satisfy the impatience of the City Fathers' (Keynes, *The Economic Consequences of Mr Churchill*, p. 223).
34. Keynes, *Essays in Persuasion*, p. 113.
35. Liberal Industrial Enquiry, *Britain's Industrial Future* (Ernest Benn, 1928) p. 81.
36. Ibid., p. 77.
37. Ibid., p. 222.
38. See Hobson–Keynes correspondence in Keynes, *Collected Writings*, vol. XIII, pp. 330–6; see Peter Clarke, who has noted the ambiguity of Keynes's relationship with Hobson, *Liberals and Social Democrats* (Cambridge University Press, 1978) and 'Hobson and Keynes as Economic Heretics', in Michael Freeden (ed.), *Reappraising J. A. Hobson: Humanism and Welfare* (Unwin Hyman, 1990).
39. Keynes, *Essays in Persuasion*, p. 138.
40. Keynes, *General Theory*, p. 27.
41. See, for example, ibid., Chapter 19.
42. Ibid., p. 374.
43. Ibid., p. 104.
44. Keynes sat on the Liberal benches when he entered the House of Lords in 1942 and expressed great alarm at the prospect of a Labour victory in 1945 – see R. F. Harrod, *The Life of John Maynard Keynes* (Macmillan, 1951) p. 331.

Chapter 8: The Emergence of Corporate Socialism

1. See, for example, C. Cooke and J. Stephenson, *The Slump: Society and Politics During the Depression* (Jonathan Cape, 1977).
2. See D. H. Aldcroft, *The Inter-War Economy: Britain, 1919–39* (Batsford, 1970) p. 34.
3. A. Fenner Brockway, *The Coming Revolution* (Independent Labour Party 1932) p. 13.
4. R. H. Tawney, *The Choice Before the Labour Party* (London, 1932) p. 7.

5. Ibid., p. 9.
6. Stafford Cripps to William Graham, 1 September 1931, quoted C. Cooke, *The Life of Richard Stafford Cripps* (Hodder & Stoughton, 1957) p. 130.
7. Stafford Cripps, *Can Socialism Come by Constitutional Methods?* (Socialist League, 1933) p. 2.
8. 'More and more the National Government is tending toward the ideology of the Fascist State – the Totalitarian Society which is compelled by force to adopt a united policy for the preservation of private property at all costs', Stafford Cripps, *The Choice for Britain* (Socialist League, 1934) p. 4.
9. Harold Laski, *Grammar of Politics* (G. Allen & Unwin, 1941 edn) p. xii. Commentators see Laski's Marxism as a fashionable veneer rather than a real change. See H. Magill, *English Political Pluralism* (Columbia University, 1941), and Bernard Zylstra, *From Pluralism to Collectivism: The Development of Harold Laski's Political Thought* (Van Gorcum, 1968). In fact, such commentators underestimate the radical nature of Laski's change in thinking in the 1930s.
10. Harold Laski, *The State in Theory and Practice* (G. Allen & Unwin, 1935) p. 331.
11. Harold Laski, *Parliamentary Government in England* (G. Allen & and Unwin, 1938) p. 219.
12. Ibid., p. 20.
13. Ibid., p. 37.
14. Ibid., p. 38.
15. Ibid., p. 52.
16. Ibid., though Laski attempted to be ambiguous on this issue, which was very touchy for a constitutional party like Labour.
17. See Harold Laski, 'Lenin and Mussolini', in *Foreign Affairs*, vol. ii, no. 1, September 1923; and *Communism* (Williams & Norgate, 1927).
18. Harold Laski, *The State*, p. 213.
19. Harold Laski, *Democracy at the Crossroads* (NCLC Publishing, not dated) p. 24. See also Laski, *Parliamentary Government*, p. 62.
20. Isaac Kramnick and Barry Sheerman in *Harold Laski: A Life on the Left* (Allen Lane, Penguin Books, 1993) pp. 260–2, give a different view, a result of a loose interpretation of Marx in my opinion.
21. Harold Laski, *The State*, p. 160.
22. Clement Attlee, *The Labour Party in Perspective* (Victor Gollancz, 1937) p. 114.
23. Ibid., p. 117.
24. Labour Party, *Annual Conference Report* (1935), p. 176.
25. Ibid., p. 156.
26. Stafford Cripps, *The Struggle for Peace* (Victor Gollancz, 1936) pp. 57–8.
27. See, for example, ibid., p. 114.
28. See, for example, G. D. H. Cole, *The People's Front* (Victor Gollancz, 1937) and John Strachey, *What Are We to Do?* (Victor Gollancz, 1938) part iii.
29. Clement Attlee, *The Labour Party in Perspective*, p. 219.
30. See Leon Trotsky, *The Spanish Revolution* (Pathfinder Press, 1973); George Orwell, *Homage to Catalonia* (Penguin Books, 1972), especially Chapter 5.

31. Labour Party, *Annual Conference Report* 1929, pp. 227–8.
32. See Oswald Mosley, *My Life* (Nelson, 1968) p. 178.
33. Oswald Mosley, *Revolution by Reason* (Birmingham Borough Labour Party, 1925) p. 12.
34. Elizabeth Durbin has written an excellent book on the Labour Keynesians, including her father – *New Jerusalems: The Labour Party and the Economics of Democratic Socialism* (Routledge & Kegan Paul, 1985) – although I found that her discussion of the technical aspects of economic theory often concealed the political implications of this group; the critique of orthodox economics by Michal Kalecki has led some to write of the Kaleckian rather than the Keynesian Revolution, but his writings (in Polish) had a highly formal and mathematical presentation, based on the realisation of surplus value, derived from Rosa Luxemburg, and his main influence on discussion came only at the end of the decade – see Maurice Dobb, *Theories of Value and Distribution since Adam Smith* (Cambridge University Press, 1973) pp. 221–5.
35. E. F. M. Durbin, *Purchasing Power and Trade Depressions: A Critique of Underconsumptionist Theories* (Jonathan Cape, 1933) p. 107.
36. Ibid., p. 74.
37. E. F. M. Durbin, *Socialist Credit Policy* (Victor Gollancz, 1934) p 30.
38. Hugh Dalton, *Practical Socialism for Britain* (George Routledge & Sons, 1935) p. 182.
39. Labour Party, *Annual Conference Report* (1932) p. 183.
40. Hugh Dalton (ed.), *Unbalanced Budgets* (George Routledge & Sons, 1934) p. 458.
41. See Hugh Dalton, *Practical Socialism*, p. 213.
42. Quoted in Alan Bullock, *Ernest Bevin*, vol. I, p. 430.
43. Ernest Bevin, *The Britain I Want to See* (The Labour Party, 1934) p. 7.
44. Ernest Bevin and G. D. H. Cole, *The Crisis* (New Statesman, 1931) p. 38.
45. Trades Union Congress, *Annual Report* (1930) p. 286.
46. See, for example, G. D. H. Cole, 'Obituary – J. A. Hobson 1858–1940', in *Economic Journal*, June–September 1940.
47. G. D. H. Cole, *The Next Ten Years*, p. 177.
48. Ibid., p. 108.
49. G. D. H. Cole, 'What is Money', in Cole (ed.), *What Everybody Wants to Know About Money* (Victor Gollancz, 1933) p. 62.
50. See, for example, G. D. H. Cole, *Socialist Economics* (Victor Gollancz, 1950) p. 50.
51. G. D. H. Cole, 'J. A. Hobson', *New Statesman*, 5 July 1958, p. 12.
52. G. D. H. Cole 'Mr Keynes Beats the Band', *New Statesman*, 15 February 1936, p. 222.
53. See the speech by Aneurin Bevan at the 1944 Labour Party Conference.
54. Oswald Mosley, *The Greater Britain* (British Union of Fascists, 1932) p. 26.
55. Ibid., p. 29.
56. See Keith Middlemas, *Politics in Industrial Society: The Experience of the British System Since 1911* (André Deutsch, 1979) Chapter 13.
57. Trades Union Congress, *Annual Report*, (1928) p. 451.

360   *The Labour Party's Political Thought*

58. See, for example, G. D. H. Cole, 'Planning and Socialism', *New States-man*, 9 May 1936.
59. G. D. H. Cole, *The Next Ten Years*, p. 21.
60. Ibid., pp. 154 and 84.
61. G. D. H. Cole, *Socialist Economics*, p. 53.
62. Herbert Morrison, *Socialisation and Transport* (Constable, 1933) p. 281.
63. Labour Party, *Annual Conference Report*, (1932), p. 212.
64. Barbara Wootton, *Plan or No Plan* (Victor Gollancz, 1934) p. 312.
65. See Moshe Lewin, *Political Undercurrents in Soviet Economic Debates* (Pluto Press, 1975); H. H. Ticktin, 'Towards a Political Economy of the USSR', *Critique*, no. 1 (Spring, 1973). See also Nikolai Preobrazhenski, *The New Economics*, trans. Brian Pearce (Clarendon Press, 1965).
66. Barbara Wootton, *Plan or No Plan*, p. 345.
67. Hugh Dalton (ed.), *Unbalanced Budgets*, p. 455.
68. Hugh Dalton, *Practical Socialism*, p. 99.
69. Harold Clay, 'Workers' Control', in Christopher Addison (ed.), *Problems of a Socialist Government* (Victor Gollancz, 1933) p. 217.
70. See Labour Party, *Annual Conference Report* (1932) p. 215.
71. G. R. Mitchison, 'Corporate State or Socialist Plan', in *Socialist Leaguer*, November–December, 1934, quoted in Ben Pimlott, *Labour and the Left in the 1930s* (Cambridge University Press, 1977).
72. G. D. H. Cole and William Mellor, *Workers' Control and Self-Government in Industry* (Victor Gollancz, 1933) p. 8.
73. See, for example, G. D. H. Cole, *The Essentials of Socialisation* (New Fabian Research Bureau, 1932).
74. Ben Pimlott, *Labour and the Left*, p. 59.
75. Keith Middlemas, *Politics in Industrial Society* (André Deutsch, 1978) Chapter 13; Leo Panitch, 'The Development of Corporatism in Liberal Democracies', *Comparative Political Studies* (1977) pp. 61–90.

Chapter 9: The Revisionist Forerunners

1. See Paul Addison, *The Road to 1945* (Quartet, 1976).
2. Labour Party, *Annual Conference Report* (1946) p. 167.
3. Labour Party, *Annual Conference Report* (1948) p. 122.
4. On the non-socialist nature of Labour's record in power, see D. N. Pritt, *The Labour Government, 1945–51* (Lawrence & Wishart, 1976); David Coates, *The Labour Party and the Struggle for Socialism* (Cambridge University Press, 1975) Chapter 3; David Howell, *British Social Democracy* (Croom Helm, 1976).
5. For the importance of Durbin in Labour's adaptation of Keynesian ideas, see Chapter 6.
6. Evan Durbin, *The Politics of Democratic Socialism* (G. Routledge & Sons, 1940) p. 50.
7. Ibid., p. 190.
8. Ibid., p. 241.
9. Ibid., p. 271.
10. Ibid., p. 276.
11. Ibid., p. 126.

12. Ibid., p. 263.
13. See, for example, Evan Durbin, *What Have We to Defend?* (G. Routledge & Sons, 1942).
14. Durbin, *Politics of Democratic Socialism*, p. 111.
15. Durbin, *Socialist Credit Policy*, p. 5.
16. Evan Durbin, *Problems of Economic Planning: Papers on Planning and Economics* (Routledge & Kegan Paul, 1949), p. 45.
17. Douglas Jay, *The Socialist Case* (Faber & Faber, 1937), p. 3.
18. Ibid., p. 111.
19. Ibid.
20. Ibid., p. 237.
21. Ibid., p. 326.
22. See, for example, the editorial in *Socialist Commentary*, October 1947.
23. *Socialist Commentary*, August 1950, p. 111.
24. Quoted in Partha Sarathi Gupta, *Imperialism and the British Labour Movement 1914–64* (Macmillan, 1975) p. 326.
25. *Socialist Commentary*, April 1949, p. 85.
26. *Socialist Commentary*, April 1950, p. 85.

Chapter 10: The Revisionist Heyday

1. See Michael Kidron, *Western Capitalism since the War* (Penguin Books, 1970 edn), p. 267.
2. See, for example, F. Zweig, J. H. Goldthorpe *et al.*, *The Affluent Worker* (Cambridge University Press, 1968).
3. See Stephen Taylor, 'Democratic Socialism: A Restatement', Research Department 356, May 1950.
4. See T. H. Marshall, *Citizenship and Social Class* (Cambridge University Press, 1950) pp. 10–11, for the definitions of these concepts of citizenship.
5. C. A. R. Crosland, 'The Transition from Capitalism', in R. H. S. Crossman, *New Fabian Essays* (Turnstile Press, 1952), p. 35.
6. Roy Jenkins, 'Equality', in *New Fabian Essays*, p. 83.
7. See Roy Jenkins, *Pursuit of Progress* (Heinemann, 1953), pp. 104–5.
8. Ibid., p. 161.
9. John Strachey, *Contemporary Capitalism* (Victor Gollancz, 1956) p. 95.
10. Ibid., p. 27.
11. C. A. R. Crosland, *The Conservative Enemy* (Jonathan Cape, 1962) pp. 91–2.
12. C. A. R. Crosland, *The Future of Socialism* (Jonathan Cape, 1956) p. 35.
13. Ibid., p. 286.
14. Ibid., p. 96.
15. Ibid., p. 496–7.
16. C. A. R. Crosland, *The Conservative Enemy*, p. 12.
17. C. A. R. Crosland, *The Future of Socialism*, p. 113.
18. Ibid., pp. 185–6.
19. Ibid., p. 235.
20. Ibid., p. 322.
21. Norman MacKenzie, 'After the Stalemate State', in Norman MacKenzie (ed.), *Conviction* (Macgibbon & Kee, 1958).

22. See, for example, his preface to Richard Titmuss, *Essays on the Welfare State* (Allen & Unwin, 1958).
23. See Richard Titmuss, *Income Distribution and Social Change* (Allen & Unwin, 1962).
24. See the Introduction by Brian Abel-Smith to the 1976 edition of *Essays on the Welfare State* for this.
25. Richard Titmuss, *Essays on the Welfare State*, p. 52.
26. Ibid., p. 27.
27. Richard Titmuss, *The Irresponsible Society* (Fabian Tract 323, 1960) p. 17.
28. Richard Titmuss, 'Goals of the Welfare State', in Perry Anderson (ed.), *Towards Socialism* (Fontana, 1965) p. 365.
29. Richard Titmuss, *The Gift Relationship: From Human Blood to Social Policy* (Allen & Unwin, 1970) p. 224.
30. James Griffiths, quoted in Philip Williams, *Hugh Gaitskell: A Political Biography* (Jonathan Cape, 1979) p. 547.
31. Labour Party, *Annual Conference Report* (1959) p. 112.
32. Hansard, *Parliamentary Debates 1955–56*, vol. 558, col. 1861.
33. For the different Labour attitudes to race and immigration in this period, see Paul Foot, *Immigration and Race in British Politics* (Penguin Books, 1965).
34. Hansard, *Parliamentary Debates 1961–62*, vol. 649, col. 803, 799.
35. Ibid., col. 800.
36. Labour Party, *Annual Conference Report* (1962) p. 159.
37. Hugh Gaitskell, *In Defence of Politics* (Birkbeck College, 1954) p. 8.
38. Labour Party, *Annual Conference Report* (1960) p. 199.
39. Denis Healey, 'Power Politics and the Labour Party', in *New Fabian Essays*, p. 166.
40. Denis Healey, *Neutralism* (Ampersand, 1955).
41. Denis Healey and John Freeman, *Disarmament – How Far?* (Fabian Tract 288, 1951) p. 25.
42. C. A. R. Crosland, *The Conservative Enemy*, pp. 150–1.
43. Philip Williams, *Hugh Gaitskell*, p. 539.
44. Labour Party, *Annual Conference Report* (1959) p. 109.
45. C. A. R. Crosland, *The Future of Socialism* (Jonathan Cape, 1964 edn) p. xi.

Chapter 11: Revisionism in Crisis

1. See Roy Jenkins and Douglas Jay, *The Common Market Debate* (Fabian Tract 341, 1962).
2. Quoted in Paul Foot, *The Politics of Harold Wilson* (Penguin Books, 1968) p. 127.
3. Harold Wilson, *The New Britain: Labour's Plan for Progress* (Penguin Books, 1964) p. 9.
4. Labour Party, *Annual Conference Report* (1963) p. 140.
5. Harold Wilson, *Purpose in Politics: Selected Speeches* (Weidenfeld & Nicolson, 1964) p. ix.
6. Thomas Balogh, 'The Drift Towards Planning,' in Perry Anderson (ed.), *Towards Socialism*, p. 76.

7. Ibid., pp. 64–5.
8. Thomas Balogh, *Unequal Partners*, vol. I: *The Theoretical Framework* (Basil Blackwell, 1963) pp. xi–xii.
9. Thomas Balogh, *Planning for Progress* (Fabian Tract 346, 1963) p. 15.
10. Ibid., p. 5.
11. For estimations of the failure of the government, see Wilfred Beckerman (ed.), *Labour's Economic Record, 1964–70* (Duckworth, 1972); David Howell, *British Social Democracy*, Chapter 9; David Coates, *The Labour Party and the Struggle for Socialism*, Chapter 5
12. For the horror felt by Jenkins at Callaghan's illiberalism at the Home Office, see John Campbell, *Roy Jenkins: A Biography* (Weidenfeld & Nicolson, 1983) p. 127.
13. Hansard, *Parliamentary Debates, 1967–68*, vol. 759, col. 1591.
14. On this point, see the conflicting claims in Peter Townsend and Nicolas Bosanquet, *Labour and Inequality* (Fabian Society, 1972).
15. Labour Party, *Annual Conference Report* (1968) p. 138.
16. See Harold Wilson, *The Labour Government, 1964–70: A Personal Record* (Weidenfeld & Nicolson, 1971) especially pp. 34–8, 236.
17. Tony Crosland, *Socialism Now, and Other Essays* (Jonathan Cape, 1974) p. 24.
18. Ibid., p. 34.
19. Ibid., p. 44.
20. Roy Jenkins, *What Matters Now* (Fontana, 1972) p. 14.
21. Dick Taverne, *The Future of Labour* (Jonathan Cape, 1974) p. 147.
22. John Mackintosh, 'Britain's Malaise: Political or Economic?', May 1978, in David Marquand (ed.), *John P. Mackintosh on Parliament and Social Democracy* (Longman, 1982) p. 203.
23. John Mackintosh, 'Taming the Barons', December 1974, in Marquand, *John P. Mackintosh*, p. 115.
24. John Mackintosh, 'Anybody Still for Democracy?', November 1972, in Marquand, *John P. Mackintosh*, p. 112.
25 John Mackintosh, 'Socialism or Social Democracy?', October–December 1972, in Marquand, *John P. Mackintosh*, p. 167.
26. Roy Jenkins, 'Home Thoughts from Abroad: The 1979 Dimbleby Lecture', in Wayland Kennett (ed.), *The Rebirth of Britain* (Weidenfeld & Nicolson, 1982) p. 14.
27. Ibid., p. 21.
28. Ibid., p. 23.
29. Shirley Williams, *Politics is for People* (Allen Lane, 1981) pp. 33–4.
30. Ibid., p. 45.
31. Ibid., p. 23.
32. Ibid., pp. 150–1
33. Ibid., p. 118.
34. David Owen, *Face the Future* (Jonathan Cape, 1981) p. 55.
35. Ibid., p. 5.
36. Ibid., p. 295.
37. Ibid., p. 44.
38. Ibid., p. 147.
39. Tony Crosland, *Socialism Now*, p. 78.

Chapter 12: The Bevanite Left

1. Harold Laski, *Reflections on the Revolution of Our Time* (George Allen & Unwin, 1943) p. 143.
2. Aneurin Bevan, *Why Not Trust the Tories?* (Victor Gollancz, 1944) p. 25.
3. Hugh Dalton, *The Fateful Years* (Muller, 1957) p. 481.
4. *Keep Left* (New Statesman, 1947) p. 15.
5. Ibid., p. 35.
6. Ibid., p. 43 .
7. Ibid., p. 44.
8. Ibid., p. 24; see also Ian Mikardo, 'The Problem of Nationalization', in *Current Affairs*, no. 60 (7 August 1948) and Ian Mikardo, *Consultation or Joint Management?* (Fabian Tract 277, 1949).
9. Harold Laski, *Trade Unions in the New Society* (George Allen & Unwin, 1950) p. 156.
10. Quoted in Ken Coates and Anthony Topham, *Industrial Democracy in Great Britain: A Book of Readings and Witnesses for Workers' Control* (MacGibbon & Kee, 1968).
11. Michael Foot, *Tribune*, 20 May 1949. See also Ian Mikardo's contribution in the same issue for a counter-argument.
12. Aneurin Bevan, *In Place of Fear* (Heinemann, 1952) p. 169.
13. Ibid., p. 1.
14. Aneurin Bevan, *Why Not Trust the Tories?*, p. 83.
15. Aneurin Bevan, *Socialist Values in a Changing Civilisation* (Fabian Tract 282, 1951) p. 7.
16. Aneurin Bevan, *In Place of Fear*, p. 5.
17. Ibid., p. 3.
18. Ibid., p. 118.
19. Labour Party, *Annual Conference Report* (1959) p. 153.
20. Hansard, *Parliamentary Debates, 1943–44*, vol. 401, col. 527.
21. See, for example, Aneurin Bevan, *Why Not Trust the Tories?*, p. 61.
22. Aneurin Bevan, *In Place of Fear*, p. 103.
23. See Mark Jenkins, *Bevanism: Labour's High Tide* (Spokesman Books, 1979).
24. Hansard, *Parliamentary Debates, 1943–44*, vol. 395, col. 1617.
25. Michael Foot, *Aneurin Bevan 1897–1945*, p. 197.
26. Aneurin Bevan, *In Place of Fear*, p. 135.
27. Aneurin Bevan, Harold Wilson and John Freeman, Foreword to *One Way Only* (Tribune, 1951) p. 9.
28. See Hansard, *Parliamentary Debates, 1950–51*, vol. 487, col. 37.
29. Aneurin Bevan, *In Place of Fear*, p. 143.
30. Labour Party, *Annual Conference Report* (1957) p. 181.
31. For the betrayal thesis, see Leslie Hunter, *The Road to Brighton Pier* (Arthur Barker, 1959); for the argument that Bevan was too partial towards Stalinism, see Mark Jenkins, *Bevanism*, p. 248; Michael Foot, *Aneurin Bevan 1945–1960* (Granada edn, 1975) pp. 425–6 points out Bevan's consistency.
32. See John Campbell, *Nye Bevan and the Crisis of British Socialism* (Weidenfeld & Nicolson, 1987) for an elaboration of this view, albeit from a different standpoint.

33. Quoted in Michael Foot, *Aneurin Bevan, 1945–1960*, p. 647.
34. Richard Crossman, 'Towards a Philosophy of Socialism', in *New Fabian Essays*, p. 27.
35. Labour Party, *Annual Conference Report* (1959) p. 131.
36. Ibid., p. 85.
37. Richard Crossman, 'Planning for Freedom', in Richard Crossman (ed.), *Planning for Freedom* (Hamish Hamiton, 1965) pp. 62–3.
38. Ibid., p. 73.
39. See Richard Crossman, 'The Affluent Society' (1959), in his *Planning for Freedom*, where he develops the argument that 'the prime function of the Labour Party, like the Liberal Party before it, is to provide an ideology for nonconformist critics of the Establishment' (p. 91) even at the cost of semi-permanent opposition.

Chapter 13: The Challenge of the New Left

1. See Andy Anderson, *Hungary 56* (Solidarity, 1964).
2. See Duncan Hallas, 'Building the Leadership', *International Socialism*, no. 40 (October–November, 1969).
3. E. P. Thompson, 'The New Left', *New Reasoner*, no. 9 (Summer 1959) p. 7.
4. Stuart Hall, 'The Supply of Demand', in E. P. Thompson (ed.), *Out of Apathy* (Stevens & Sons, 1960) p. 63.
5. E. P. Thompson, 'Outside the Whale', in Thompson (ed.), *Out of Apathy*, p. 181.
6. Editorial, *New Left Review*, no. 1 (January–February 1960) p. 1.
7. Raymond Williams, *Culture and Society, 1780–1950* (Chatto & Windus, 1958) p. 269.
8. Ibid., p. 303.
9. Raymond Williams, *Modern Tragedy* (Chatto & Windus, 1966) p. 13.
10. See Frank Parkin, *Middle Class Radicalism: The Social Bases of the Campaign for Nuclear Disarmament* (Manchester University Press, 1968).
11. Stuart Hall, *NATO and the Alliance* (London: CND, 1961) p. 4.
12. Stuart Hall, *Breakthrough* (Combined Universities CND, 1958) p. 22.
13. Quoted in Richard Taylor and Colin Pritchard, *The Protest Makers: The British Nuclear Disarmament Movement of 1958–65, Twenty Years On* (Pergamon Press, 1980) p. 53.
14. Quoted in ibid., p. 59.
15. Stuart Hall, 'The Supply of Demand', pp. 95–6.
16. Raymond Williams, *The Long Revolution* (Chatto & Windus, 1961) p. 303.
17. Editorial, 'Scarborough and Beyond', *New Left Review*, no. 6 (November–December 1960) p. 6.
18. Ralph Miliband, *Parliamentary Socialism* (Merlin Press, 1972 edn) p. 13.
19. Ralph Miliband, 'The Politics of Contemporary Capitalism', *New Reasoner*, no. 5 (Summer, 1958) p. 46.
20. For contrasting reasons for the failure of CND, see Peggy Duff, *Left, Left, Left: A Personal Account of Six Protest Campaigns, 1945–65* (Alison & Busby, 1971), who argues that there was insufficient political clarity (p. 200), and Taylor and Pritchard, *The Protest Makers*, who argue that there was too much politics for a moral campaign (p. 13).

21. E. P. Thompson, 'Peculiarities of the English', in Ralph Miliband and John Saville (eds), *Socialist Register 1965* (Merlin Press, 1966).
22. See Perry Anderson, 'Components of the National Culture', *New Left Review*, no. 50 (July–August, 1968).
23. See Pamela M. Graves, *Labour Women: Women in British Working-Class Politics, 1918–1939* (Cambridge University Press, 1994) for an interesting exploration of this topic.
24. Shirley Williams, *Women in Politics* (Bedford College, University of London, 1980) p. 7.
25. Juliet Mitchell, 'Women: The Longest Revolution', *New Left Review*, no. 40 (November–December 1966) p. 15.
26. The most important of these attempts was Michele Barrett, *Women's Oppression Today* (Verso Books, 1980); see also Sheila Rowbotham, Lynne Segal and Hilary Wainwright, *Beyond the Fragments: Feminism and the Making of Socialism* (Merlin Press, 1979).
27. See, for example, some of the essays in Lydia Sargent (ed.), *Women and Revolution: A Discussion of the Unhappy Marriage of Marxism and Feminism* (Pluto Press, 1981).
28. Lin Chun, *The British New Left* (Edinburgh University Press, 1993), is an excellent recent history; Michael Kenny, *The First New Left* (Lawrence & Wishart, 1995) assesses their influence on subsequent British cultural life.
29. Frank Parkin, *Middle Class Radicalism*, p. 41.
30. Witness the excited reception given to Ian Steedman, *Marx After Sraffa* (New Left Books, 1977), on its publication.

Chapter 14: The Bennite Left

1. The critique of the workings of the mixed economy by Paul Mattick, *Marx and Keynes: The Limits of the Mixed Economy* (Merlin Press, 1971), remains interesting and cogent.
2. Michael Foot, 'Credo of the Labour Left', *New Left Review*, no. 49 (May–June 1968), p. 25.
3. Michael Foot, 'Can We Save the Government?', *Tribune* (29 March 1968) p. 12.
4. See, for example, the savage attacks on the Labour Left in Paul Foot, *The Politics of Harold Wilson* (Penguin, 1968).
5. Report, Plenary Session of the Workers' Control Conference, 1968, in Ken Coates and W. Williams, *How and Why Industry Must Be Democratised* (IWC, 1969) p. 25.
6. Ernie Roberts, 'Workers' Control and the Trade Unions', in Ken Coates (ed.), *Can the Workers Run Industry?* (Sphere Books, 1968) p. 97.
7. For this process, see Keith Middlemas, *Politics in Industrial Society* (André Deutsch, 1979).
8. See, for example, Colin Barker, 'The British Labour Movement: Aspects of Current Experience', *International Socialism*, no. 28 (Spring 1967).
9. Hugh Scanlon, 'Interview', *New Left Review*, no. 46 (November–December 1967), p. 4.
10. Michael Barratt Brown, 'Limits of the Welfare State', in Ken Coates (ed.), *Can the Workers Run Industry?*, p. 31; see also Andrew Glyn and

Bob Sutcliffe, *British Capitalism, Workers and the Profits Squeeze* (Penguin, 1972) for a development of this Ricardian argument.

11. Michael Barratt Brown, *From Labourism to Socialism: The Political Economy of Labour in the 1970s* (Spokesman, 1972) p. 224.
12. Ibid., p. 12.
13. Ibid., p. 62.
14. Ken Coates, 'Socialists and the Labour Party', *Socialist Register 1973* p. 177.
15. Arthur Scargill, 'The New Unionism', *New Left Review*, no. 92 (July – August 1975) p. 4.
16. Stuart Holland, *The Socialist Challenge* (Quartet, 1975) p. 51.
17. Ibid., p. 70.
18. Ibid., p. 34.
19. Stuart Holland, *Socialist Challenge*, p. 154.
20. Stuart Holland, 'Introduction', in Stuart Holland (ed.), *Beyond Capitalist Planning* (Basil Blackwell, 1978), p. 3.
21. Ibid., p. 155.
22. See, for example, Geoff Hodgson, *Labour at the Crossroads: The Political and Economic Challenge of Labour in the 1980s* (Martin Robertson, 1981), who points out that transfers of capital are due to the lack of profitability rather than the nationality of any particular owner of capital.
23. Wynne Godley and Francis Cripps, *Macroeconomics* (Oxford University Press, 1983) p. 305.
24. For the classic case for import controls, see Wynne Godley and Francis Cripps, 'Control of Imports as a Means to Full Employment and the Expansion of World Trade: The UK Case', *Cambridge Journal of Economics*, vol. 2, no. 3 (September 1978). The authors saw deflation and devaluation as the only alternative to import controls.
25. Stuart Holland, 'Capital, Labour and the State', in Ken Coates (ed.), *What Went Wrong?* (Spokesman, 1979) pp. 208–9.
26. Ken Coates, *Democracy in the Labour Party* (Spokesman, 1977) p. 15.
27. Tony Benn, *Parliament, People and Power* (Verso, 1982) p. 10.
28. Tony Benn, *Arguments for Democracy* (Jonathan Cape, 1981) p. 130. See particularly his lecture to the Marx Memorial Library printed in *Marxism Today* (May 1982).
29. Tony Benn, *Arguments for Democracy* p. 9.
30. Interview with author, *Capital and Class*, no. 17 (Summer 1982) p. 27.
31. Tony Benn, *Arguments for Socialism* (Penguin, 1980) p. 60.
32. Ibid., p. 43.
33. Interview with author, ibid., p. 26. He later advocated withdrawal from NATO – see *Marxism Today* (January 1986) p. 14.
34. Geoff Hodgson, *Labour at the Crossroads* (Martin Robertson, 1981) p. 210.
35. Robert Michels, *Political Parties: A Sociological Study of the Oligarchical Tendencies of Modern Democracy* (London, 1915).
36. See the discussion in Jim Tomlinson, *The Unequal Struggle: British Socialism and the Capitalist Enterprise* (Methuen, 1982) Chapter 6.

Chapter 15: The Emergence of New Labour

1. Alec Nove, *The Economics of Feasible Socialism* (Allen & Unwin, 1983) p. 101.
2. See especially Roy Hattersley, *Choose Freedom: The Future for Democratic Socialism* (Michael Joseph, 1987).
3. Ken Coates, *Common Ownership and the Labour Party* (Spokesman, 1995) p. 16.
4. See Ken Coates, 'The Loss of Our First Freedom', in Ken Coates (ed.), *The Right to Work* (Spokesman, 1995) p. 4.
5. Eric Hobsbawm, *The Forward March of Labour Halted?* (Verso, 1981) p. 181.
6. See Richard Heffernan and Mike Marqusee, *Defeat from the Jaws of Victory: Inside Neil Kinnock's Labour Party* (Verso, 1992), for the extraordinary bitterness of the Left's reaction to Kinnock's authoritarian rule of the party.
7. Neil Kinnock, 'It can be done, it must be done', speech to Labour Party Conference, Bournemouth, 1985 (Labour Party, not dated) p. 4.
8. Neil Kinnock, *The Future of Socialism* (Fabian Tract 509, 1986) p. 2.
9. Bernard Crick, *Socialist Values and Time* (Fabian Tract 495, 1984) p. 12.
10. Ibid., pp. 8–9.
11. There is an excellent summary of communitarian arguments in Will Kymlicka, *Contemporary Political Philosophy* (Clarendon Press, 1990).
12. See Raymond Plant, *Community and Ideology* (Routledge & Kegan Paul, 1974) pp. 19–22.
13. Raymond Plant, *Equality, Markets and the State* (Fabian Tract 494, January 1984) p. 15.
14. Ibid., p. 12.
15. Ibid., p. 23.
16. Ibid., p. 6.
17. Andrew Vincent and Raymond Plant, *Philosophy, Politics and Citizenship* (Blackwell, 1984) p. 165.
18. Ibid., p. 181; also see Raymond Plant, *Citizenship, Rights and Socialism* (Fabian Tract 531, October 1988) p. 19.
19. Bryan Gould, *Socialism and Freedom* (Macmillan, 1985) p. 2.
20. Ibid., p. 54.
21. Bryan Gould, *A Future for Socialism* (Jonathan Cape, 1989) p. 51.
22. David Blunkett MP and Bernard Crick, *The Labour Party's Aims and Values: An Unofficial Statement* (Spokesman Pamphlet No. 87, 1988) p. 12.
23. Ibid., pp. 23.
24. Tony Benn and Andrew Hood, *Common Sense: A New Constitution for Britain* (Hutchinson, 1993).
25. Peter Hain, *Ayes to the Left: A Future for Socialism* (Lawrence & Wishart, 1995) p. 31.
26. Tony Wright, *Citizens and Subjects: An Essay on British Politics* (Routledge, 1994) p. 4.
27. Ibid., p. 52.
28. Ibid., pp. 83–4.

29. Ibid., p. 127.
30. Stephen Tindale and David Miliband, *Beyond Economics: European Government After Maastricht* (Fabian Society Discussion paper, 1991) p. 24.
31. David Miliband, 'Introduction: Expansion and Integration,' in David Miliband (ed.), *A More Perfect Union? Britain and the New Europe* (Institute for Public Policy Research, 1992) p. 6.
32. See J. G. A. Pocock, *The Machiavellian Moment: Florentine Political Thought and the Atlantic Republican Tradition* (Princeton University Press, 1975) Ch. XIII; this is a seminal work in the development of interest in republican theory.
33. John Eatwell and Roy Green, 'Economic Theory and Political Power', in Ben Pimlott (ed.), *Fabian Essays in Socialist Thought* (Heinemann, 1984) p. 201.
34. John Eatwell and Murray Milgate, 'Introduction', in John Eatwell and Murray Milgate (eds), *Keynes's Economics and the Theory of Value and Distribution* (Duckworth, 1983) p. 16.
35. Eatwell and Green, 'Economic Theory and Political Power', p. 202.
36. David Marquand, *The Unprincipled Society: New Demands and Old Politics* (Jonathan Cape, 1988) p. 10.
37. Ibid., p. 11.
38. See ibid., pp. 231–2.
39. Raymond Plant, *Citizenship, Rights and Socialism* (Fabian Tract 531, October 1988) p. 19.
40. David Miller and Saul Estrin, 'Market Socialism: a Policy for Socialists' in Ian Forbes (ed.), *Market Socialism; Whose Choice?* (Fabian tract 516, November 1986); also see David Miller, *Market, State and Community: Theoretical Foundations of Socialism* (Clarendon Press, 1990).
41. Will Hutton, *The State We're In* (Jonathan Cape, 1995) p. 247.
42. Will Hutton, *The Revolution That Never Was: An Assessment of Keynesian Economics* (Longman, 1986) p. 118.
43. See J. G. A. Pocock, *Virtue, Commerce and History* (Cambridge University Press, 1982), as well as *The Machiavellian Moment* cited above.
44. Will Hutton, *The State We're In*, p. 168.
45. Ibid., p. 256.
46. See Amitai Etzione, *The Moral Dimension: Towards a New Economics*, especially Chapter 12 and p. 199.
47. Hutton, *The State We're In*, p. 326.
48. Gordon Brown, *Constitutional Change and the Future of Britain* (Charter 88 Trust, 1992) pp. 6–7.
49. Gordon Brown, *Fair is Efficient – A Socialist Agenda for Fairness* (Fabian pamphlet 563, 1994) p. 21.
50. See Jon Sopel, *Tony Blair: The Moderniser* (Michael Joseph, 1995) p. 32, for a brief and unsatisfactory discussion of the importance of the Scottish communitarian philosopher John MacMurray.
51. Tony Blair, with Shirley Williams, Graham Mather and Carole Tongue, *Is There Democratic Life after Maastricht?* (Charter 88 Trust, the Third Sovereignty Lecture, 15 June, 1992) p. 15
52. Tony Blair, *Let Us Face the Future – The 1945 Anniversary Lecture* (Fabian pamphlet 571, 1995) p. 3.

53. Tony Blair, *Socialism* (Fabian pamphlet 565, July 1994) p. 4.
54. James Ramsay MacDonald, *Parliament and Democracy*, p. 71; also see his *Socialism and Society*, p. 61.

Chronology

(Relating the principal writing to major events.)

1791–2	Tom Paine, *The Rights of Man*.
1813–14	Robert Owen, *A New View of Society*.
1825	Thomas Hodgskin, *Labour Defended Against the Claims of Capital*, coincides with the beginning of the modern trade unions movement.
1834	Defeat of the Grand National Consolidated Trades Union.
1848	Karl Marx, *The Communist Manifesto*. Defeat of Chartism, followed by a period of moderate trade unionism.
1862	John Ruskin, *Unto This Last*.
1867	Karl Marx, *Capital*, vol. I.
1881	(Social) Democratic Federation; H. M. Hyndman, *England For All*.
1882	Edward Carpenter, *Towards Democracy*.
1884	Fabian Society; William Morris's Socialist League.
1888	Scottish Labour Party.
1889	*Fabian Essays in Socialism*; Dock strike heralds the New Unionism.
1890	J. B. Glasier and K. St. John Conway, *The Religion of Socialism*.
1893	Independent Labour Party (ILP).
1894	Robert Blatchford, *Merrie England*.
1899–1902	Boer War.
1900	*Fabianism and Empire*; Labour Representation Committee (LRC).
1903	Philip Snowden, *The Christ That Is To Be*; Gladstone–MacDonald pact; Socialist Labour Party.
1904	Isabella Ford, *Women and Socialism*.
1905	J. Ramsay MacDonald, *Socialism and Society*.
1906	Twenty-nine Labour MPs elected; LRC becomes Labour Party.
1907	J. Keir Hardie, *From Serfdom to Socialism*.
1910	Industrial Syndicalist Education League (ISEL).
1911	J. Ramsay MacDonald Labour leader; mass strike-wave erupts, involving, among others, miners, dockers, railwaymen.
1912	*The Miner's Next Step*.
1913	G. D. H. Cole, *The World of Labour*.
1914	Labour supports World War I; ILP opposes; MacDonald resigns as leader.
1915	Labour under Arthur Henderson enters coalition; Clyde Workers Committee; National Guilds League (NGL).
1917	Leeds Convention; G. D. H. Cole, *Self-Government in Industry*.

1918   New Labour Party Constitution; Labour gains 3 million votes in the election, but only 57 MPs.
1919   Post-war unrest, including strikes and riots.
1920   J. Ramsay MacDonald, *Parliament and Democracy*; Communist Party of Great Britain.
1921   Black Friday sees the defeat of the miners; G. D. H. Cole, *Guild Socialism Restated;* R. H. Tawney, *The Acquisitive Society.*
1922   Failure of Builders' Guild, as ILP adopts Guild Socialist ideas in its constitution; Labour, with 142 MPs, becomes the official Opposition, under MacDonald.
1924   First Labour government under MacDonald.
1925   Harold Laski, *A Grammar of Politics;* Oswald Mosley, *Revolution by Reason.*
1926   *The Living Wage*; General Strike.
1928   *Labour and the Nation*; the Cook–Maxton manifesto denounces 'Mondism', or class collaboration; The Liberal Yellow Book, *We Can Conquer Unemployment,*
1929   G. D. H. Cole, *The Next Ten Years*; Second Labour government, under MacDonald.
1930   Mosley Memorandum.
1931   R. H. Tawney, *Equality*; collapse of Labour government; MacDonald forms a National Government, and is expelled, along with Snowden; only 46 Labour MPs returned in election.
1932   John Strachey, *The Coming Struggle for Power*; ILP disaffiliates; Socialist League forms.
1933   Herbert Morrison, *Socialisation and Transport*; Evan Durbin, *Purchasing Power and Trade Depressions.*
1935   Hugh Dalton, *Practical Socialism for Britain*; Harold Laski, *The State in Theory and Practice*; R. G. Bassett, *The Essentials of Parliamentary Government.*
1936   John Maynard Keynes, *The General Theory of Employment, Interest and Money.*
1937   Clement Attlee, *The Labour Party in Perspective*; Douglas Jay, *The Socialist Case*; Socialist League dissolved.
1938   Harold Laski, *Parliamentary Government in England.*
1939   Cripps and Bevan (temporarily) expelled for their support of a Popular Front.
1940   Evan Durbin, *The Politics of Democratic Socialism*; Labour enters Churchill coalition.
1942   The Beveridge Report advocates a system of social security from 'the cradle to the grave'.
1943   Harold Laski, *Reflections on the Revolution of Our Time.*
1944   Employment White Paper.
1945   Attlee forms first majority Labour government, after landslide election victory, and sets about a programme of state intervention in industry and welfare.
1947   *Keep Left.*
1950   T. H. Marshall, *Citizenship and Social Class.*

1951	Bevan and Wilson resign over attacks on the National Health Service; Labour election defeat begins a 13-year period of opposition.
1952	Aneurin Bevan, *In Place of Fear; New Fabian Essays.*
1955	Gaitskell party leader.
1956	C. A. R. Crosland, *The Future of Socialism*; John Strachey, *Contemporary Capitalism*; Suez crisis; Soviet invasion of Hungary. A New Left emerges.
1957	*Industry and Society*; Bevan attacks unilateralism at the Brighton Conference.
1958	Campaign for Nuclear Disarmament.
1959	Richard Crossman, *The Affluent Society*; Gaitskell unsuccessfully seeks a change to Clause IV of the party constitution after Labour's third election defeat.
1960	*New Left Review*; Richard Titmuss, *The Irresponsible* Society. Unilateralist victory at the Scarborough conference, reversed a year later.
1963	Richard Titmuss, *Essays on the Welfare State*; Harold Wilson, party leader on Gaitskell's death, gives 'Science and Socialism' speech at Scarborough conference.
1964	Labour government under Wilson; Institute of Workers Control.
1965	George Brown presents his National Plan, aiming at a 25 per cent increase in output by 1970 through corporatist planning.
1966	Juliet Mitchell, *The Longest Revolution*; wage freeze effectively ends Labour's National Plan.
1967	Devaluation, followed by cuts in defence and welfare.
1969	*In Place of Strife*; British troops sent to Northern Ireland.
1970	Labour defeated at election; Conservative government under Heath.
1971	Industrial Relations Act (virtually nullified by industrial action on the docks and railways the following year).
1972	Anthony Crosland, *Socialism Now*; Roy Jenkins, *What Matters Now*; Michael Barratt Brown, *From Labourism to Socialism*; John Mackintosh, *Socialism or Social Democracy*; Roy Jenkins resigns as deputy leader.
1973	*Labour's Programme 1973.*
1974	A miners' strike leads to an election, and a Labour government under Wilson.
1975	Stuart Holland, *The Socialist Challenge*; EEC referendum defeat for Labour Left.
1976	James Callaghan Prime Minister; sterling crisis.
1978	Eric Hobsbawm, *The Forward March of Labour Halted?*
1979	Roy Jenkins, *Home Thoughts from Abroad: The 1979 Dimbleby Lecture*; Tony Benn, *Arguments for Socialism*; Conservative government under Thatcher.
1980	Michael Foot party leader.
1981	Shirley Williams, *Politics is for People*; David Owen, *Face the Future*; Tony Benn, *Arguments for Democracy*; Constitu-

	tional changes in the Labour Party; Social Democratic Party formed.
1982	The Falklands War.
1983	Neil Kinnock party leader after disastrous election defeat for Labour.
1984	Raymond Plant, *Equality, Markets and the State*; Bernard Crick, *Socialist Values and Time*.
1984–5	Miners' strike.
1985	David Marquand, *The Unprincipled Society*; Bryan Gould, *Socialism and Freedom*; Kinnock's attack on the Militant Tendency begins the isolation of the Left.
1987	Policy Review Groups established after Labour's third election defeat.
1988	Charter 88 is established to campaign for constitutional reform and civil liberties.
1989	*Meet the Challenge, Make the Change.*
1990	John Major succeeds Thatcher as Prime Minister.
1992	John Smith party leader after Labour's fourth election defeat.
1994	Tony Wright, *Citizens and Subjects*; Tony Blair party leader after Smith's death.
1995	Will Hutton, *The State We're In*; Clause IV is changed at special party conference; Tony Blair, *Let Us Face the Future*.
1996	*New Labour, New Life for Britain* manifesto.

Index